An Anthropology of Indirect Communication

Sometimes we convey what we mean not by what we say but by what we do, wear or eat; sometimes it is by a gesture of the hand, a curl of the lip or a raising of an eyebrow. The authors of this new volume ask what kind of communication occurs when we employ these indirect means of conveying our intentions. Anthropologists soon learn that understanding the codes of conventional behaviour in a foreign setting requires paying special attention to what is *not* said as much as to what *is*.

From patent miscommunication, through potent ambiguity to pregnant silence, this incisive collection examines the many possibilities of indirect communication. A complex and important aspect of social life, indirection itself has rarely been the focus of ethnographic study. In this volume, for the first time, different modes of indirect communication are brought together and examined in the light of anthropological ideas and concepts.

Drawing on their experiences in the field, from a Mormon theme park in Hawaii, through carnival time on Montserrat, to the exclusive domain of the Market, the case studies examine the many ways in which we can communicate indirectly, both verbally and non-verbally. The authors discuss how indirect communication can be deliberate and how the most expressive form of communication is often the most indirect. By illustrating how food, silence, sunglasses, martial arts and rudeness can all constitute powerful ways of conveying meaning, *An Anthropology of Indirect Communication* is a fascinating and engaging text which provides a challenging introduction to this growing area of thought and study.

Joy Hendry is Professor of Social Anthropology at Oxford Brookes University. Her main area of interest is Japan and her publications include *An Anthropologist in Japan* (1999). **C. W. Watson** is Senior Lecturer in Anthropology at the University of Kent at Canterbury. He is a specialist on Indonesia and Malaysia and his publications include *Multiculturalism* (2000).

ASA Monographs 37

Titles available:

An Anthropology of Indirect Communication

Edited by Joy Hendry and C. W. Watson

London and New York

First published 2001
by Routledge
11 New Fetter Lane, London EC4P 4EE

Simultaneously published in the USA and Canada
by Routledge
29 West 35th Street, New York, NY 10001

Routledge is an imprint of the Taylor & Francis Group

Typeset in Bembo by Taylor & Francis Books Ltd
Printed and bound in Great Britain by Biddles Ltd,
Guildford and King's Lynn

British Library Cataloguing in Publication Data
A catalogue record for this book is available from the British
Library

Library of Congress Cataloging in Publication Data
An anthropology of indirect communication / edited by Joy
Hendry and C. W. Watson.
        p. cm. – (A.S.A. monographs; 37)
        Papers presented at the ASA Conference held 1998,
        Canterbury, Eng.
        Includes bibliographical references and index.
        1. Nonverbal communication–Congresses. 2. Communication
        and culture–Congresses.
        I. Hendry, Joy. II. Watson, C. W. III. Association of Social
        Anthropologists. Conference (1998: Canterbury, England.)
        IV. Series.
        P99.5 .A58 2001
        302.2'22–dc21   00-051705

ISBN 0–415–24744–6 (hbk)
ISBN 0–415–24745–4 (pbk)

Contents

Contributors

Annabel Black did research on the topic discussed in this book as a Research Associate at Oxford Brookes University. She has lectured in European Community Studies at the Université Libre de Bruxelles and has worked as Spouse Employment Adviser in the British Foreign Office. She is currently training to become a furniture restorer.

Nicole Bourque is a Senior Lecturer in the Department of Sociology and Anthropology at the University of Glasgow. Her research interests include popular religion and syncretism in the Andes, and conversion to Islam in Britain.

James G. Carrier teaches Social Anthropology at the University of Edinburgh. His recent publications include the edited collections *Meanings of the Market* (Berg 1997) and *Virtualism* (with D. Miller; Berg 1998). He has begun research on political economy and environmental protection in the Caribbean.

Pia Christensen is a Lecturer in Social Anthropology at the University of Hull. Her main interests and publications are in the anthropological study of children's everyday lives and of children's health, with a particular focus on the individual and collective actions of children. Her most recent research (with A. James and C. Jenks) is a study of the perception, understanding and social organisation of children's time, a project funded by the ESRC under the Children: 5–16 research programme.

Joy Hendry is Professor of Social Anthropology at Oxford Brookes University. She has worked in various parts of Japan over the last twenty-five years, and her recent publications include *Wrapping Culture: Politeness, Presentation and Power in Japan and Other Societies* (Clarendon Press 1993), *An Anthropologist in Japan* (Routledge 1999), and *The Orient Strikes Back: A Global View of Cultural Display* (Berg 2000).

Jenny Hockey is a social anthropologist and Senior Lecturer at the University of Hull. She has published widely on ageing, death and bereavement, including *Beyond the Body: Death and Social Identity* (co-authored with E. Hallam and G. Howarth; Routledge 1999).

Felicia Hughes-Freeland is a Senior Lecturer in Anthropology at the University of Wales, Swansea. She has edited *Ritual, Performance, Media* (ASA Monograph 35), and *Recasting Ritual* (EASA series, with Mary Crain), and the film *Taybuan: Dancing the Spirit in Java*. A monograph on Javanese dance is forthcoming.

Allison James is Reader in Applied Anthropology at the University of Hull. Her main research interests are in childhood, ageing and the life course. Her most recent publication is *Theorising Childhood* (with C. Jenks and A. Prout; Polity Press 1998). She has just completed a study of children's perception and understandings of time (with P. Christensen and C. Jenks) on a project funded under the ESRC Children 5–16 research programme.

Lisette Josephides teaches anthropology at Queen's University, Belfast. Her most recent publication, 'Disengagement and desire: the tactics of everyday life', appeared in the *American Ethnologist*. Her continuing interest in politics and the deployment of social knowledge now includes research interests in issues of morality and human rights.

Roger Just is a Senior Lecturer in Social Anthropology at the University of Melbourne. His recent publications include *A Greek Island Cosmos: Kinship and Identity on Meganisi* (James Currey Publishers 2000).

Tamara Kohn is a Lecturer in Anthropology at the University of Durham and teaches Human Sciences at the University's Stockton campus (UDSC). She has conducted fieldwork in the Scottish Hebrides, East Nepal, the north of England and California. She is currently working on a monograph based on her recent research with martial artists in California.

Helen Lambert is a Senior Lecturer in Medical Anthropology at Bristol University. Her research interests include popular Hinduism, medical pluralism and kinship in India, and medical anthropology in relation to public health issues. Recent publications include 'Illness, auspiciousness and modes of healing in rural Rajasthan', *Contributions to Indian Sociology* (n.s.) 31(2) 1997; 'Caring for the well: perspectives on disease prevention', in T. Kohn and R. McKechnie (eds) *Extending the Boundaries of Care: Medical Ethics and Caring Practices* (Berg 1998); 'Methods and meanings in anthropological, epidemiological and clinical encounters: the case of sexually transmitted disease and HIV control and prevention in India', *Tropical Medicine and International Health* 3(12) 1998; and 'Sentiment and substance in north Indian forms of relatedness', in J. Carsten (ed.) *Cultures of Relatedness: New Approaches to the Study of Kinship* (Cambridge University Press 2000).

Peter Parkes lectures in the Department of Anthropology at the University of Kent at Canterbury, and has previously taught at Goldsmiths College, London and at the Queen's University, Belfast. He is the author of several articles on the Kalasha of northern Pakistan, and of the forthcoming *Kalasha Community: Configurations of Enclavement in the Hindu Kush.*

Sarah Pink has recently been appointed to the University of Loughborough. She previously taught at the University of Derby. Her recent publications include her book *Women and Bullfighting: Gender, Sex and the Consumption of Tradition* (Berg 1997).

Nigel Rapport is Professor of Anthropological and Philosophical Studies at the University of St Andrews. His recent publications include *Transcendent Individual: Towards a Literary and Liberal Anthropology* (Routledge 1997); *Migrants of Identity: Perceptions of Home in a World of Movement* (co-edited with Andrew Dawson; Berg 1998), and *Social and Cultural Anthropology: Key Concepts* (co-written with Joanna Overing; Routledge 2000).

Ursula Sharma is Professor of Comparative Sociology at the University of Derby. She has conducted extensive fieldwork on gender and the household in north India. More recently she has researched the growth and usage of complementary therapies in Britain. Her publications include *Women, Work and Property in North West India* (Tavistock 1980); and (with Sarah Cant) *A New Medical Pluralism? Alternative Medicine, Doctors, Patients and the State* (UCL Press 1999).

Jonathan Skinner is a Social Anthropologist lecturing in the Division of Sociology at the University of Abertay, Dundee. He was the Sociological Review Fellow 1998–9 at Keele University, where he finished working on a book about diverse representations of Montserrat, a British Dependent Territory in the eastern Caribbean. His interests are in narrative and biography, performance, postmodernism and ethnographic representation. A recent publication pertinent to his chapter in this book is 'Of elephants and men: the freak as Victorian and the contemporary spectacle', in Gary Day (ed.) *Culture and Society: Varieties of Victorianism* (Routledge 1998).

Neil Thin is a Senior Lecturer in the Department of Social Anthropology at the University of Edinburgh. His postgraduate field research (1986–8) was on festivity among Irula forest people in southern India. His current research specialisms are environmental management, civil society, and social dimensions of development. Since 1988 he has spent most of his time providing social development advice and training to international development agencies. From 1992 to 1999 he convened the DFID Social Development Resource Centre at the University of Edinburgh.

Andrew Turton is Reader in Anthropology at the School of Oriental and African Studies, University of London, Chair of Anthropology, and former Chair of the Centre of South East Asian Studies at SOAS. He has spent several years living and researching in Thailand, especially the northern region, since 1962 when he spent two years as British Council Assistant

Representative based in Bangkok. His publications since 1972 have challenged existing paradigms on such issues as matriliny and gender, class and
ideology, state and local powers, discourse and knowledge. He is currently
working on the ethnography of diplomatic mission in relation to Thai
states, and editing the journals of early soldier-diplomats in the region.

C. W. Watson lectures at the University of Kent at Canterbury. His research
interests range from Islam and politics in Southeast Asia to the study of
non-Western autobiography. He has recently published *Of Self and Nation:
Autobiography and the Representation of Modern Indonesia* (University of Hawaii
Press 2000).

Terry D. Webb spent fifteen years in Hawaii at the University of Hawaii and
Brigham Young University, Hawaii Campus, prior to becoming Dean of
the Guggenhiem Library of Monmouth University in West Long Branch,
New Jersey. During that time he conducted research on the Polynesian
Cultural Center, which led to publications in various journals. He has also
published a number of articles and books on information technology and
library administration.

Acknowledgements

The present volume represents only some of the papers which were presented at the ASA conference held in Canterbury in 1998. In putting together our selection we were spoilt for choice, and we did briefly consider trying to convince Routledge that we should do two volumes, but careful examination of the contributions suggested that it would be best to avoid confusing readers by bringing together papers which, though they all treated indirection in one way or another, did not sit thematically well with each other. In particular we regret having to omit the papers by linguists which provided some fine illustrations of indirection in language usage.

Those whose papers do not appear here but whose contributions were much appreciated and whose comments enlivened our discussions include: Seth Kumin, Dina Dahbany-Miraglia, Lanita Jacobs-Huey, Eva Reimers, Yoshimi Miyake, Timothy Fitzgerald, Fiona Kerlogue, Mario Aguilar, David Zeitlyn, Peter Skalnik, Britt-Marie Öberg, Vieda Skultans, Paul Stirling and Kenneth Maddock.

We also wish to express our gratitude to those who chaired the sessions of the conference and added their wisdom to our proceedings: Roy Ellen, Glenn Bowman, Peter Parkes, Nadia Lovell, Nigel Rapport, Felicia Hughes-Freeland, Iain Edgar, John Corbin, Wendy James, Pat Caplan, John Davis, Penny Vera-Sanso and Christian McDonaugh. We also owe a special word of thanks to our keynote speaker Esther Goody, whose book on issues of politeness (*Questions and Politeness: Strategies in Social Interaction*) published in 1978 was one of our principal inspirations in preparing for the conference.

Finally as regards the conference we want to express our warm appreciation of the excellent job done by Alan Bicker, who was responsible for the administration of the proceedings from start to finish. That the conference ran so smoothly and efficiently is fully attributable to him.

A special words of thanks is due to Nicola Kerry-Yoxall in the Department of Anthropology at Canterbury for so patiently responding to our endless requests to type and retype sections of papers, translate them back and forth into different word-processing programs and deal with tricky questions of formatting and compatibility, and helping to contact contributors.

Thanks are given for permission to reprint lyrics from 'Let's Talk About Sex', words and music by Herbie Azor. © 1988 Sons of K-oss Music Inc, USA. Warner/Chappell Music Ltd, London W6 8BS. Reproduced by permission of International Music Publications Ltd.

Introduction

Joy Hendry and C. W. Watson

Why even I myself I often think know little or nothing of my real life;
Only a few hints, a few diffused clews and indirections ...
Walt Whitman, 'When I read the book', in *Leaves of Grass*

Anthropology is a lot like espionage, a shifty business carried out by individuals regarded by the general community with suspicion, and who are in their own eyes nothing so much as persons *manqués*, ever on the margins, desperately seeking acceptance but knowing deep in their souls that they belong nowhere: agents with language skills thoroughly trained and prepared by special tutors, dropped into a foreign environment and given the task of finding out important, often secret, information. To achieve their aims they employ a variety of techniques and methods, the primary one being to work themselves into the confidence of significant individuals who have the required information and elicit it from them. At the same time, very much aware that that what they are told may not correspond to the reality of the situation, not to put too fine a point on it, may be downright lies, deliberate ploys to mislead, bluffs and counter-bluffs, they must constantly observe and monitor the fit between what they hear and the events which they witness. Often the work requires learning how to decipher obscure messages, recognising code-names and painstakingly assembling disparate and discrete pieces of data into a unified whole in order to make sense of the wider picture. Understanding is never easy.

We could continue drawing out further parallels, alluding, for example, to the problematic nature of fieldwork, dubious research methods, the agent's own coding of information and the reports of the assignment ultimately delivered to the paymasters, but for our purposes we simply wish to use the comparison to highlight how much the pursuit of anthropology, like the art of spying, involves delving into a world of unsureness and uncertainty, subterfuge and deceit, puzzles and plots. For both the anthropologist and agent, the only way to rise above the intellectual and moral chaos which constantly threatens them is through the deployment of stratagems of interrogation to test their immediate observations, what they hear and what they see, since above all they hold firm to the belief that not all in life is at it seems. And it is precisely the examination of the anthropological encounter between *seems* and *is* which lies at the heart of this book.

In our invitation calling for papers for the conference from which the book derives, we chose to use the words 'indirection' and 'indirect communication' to convey a sense of this role of uncertainty in anthropology. To those who enquired what precisely we had in mind we explained that what we meant by indirection was the communication of thoughts not directly, straightforwardly or unambiguously, but in a manner which to some degree or another deliberately obscures, hides or 'wraps' the message. More positively, we pointed out that such indirectness can be creative, enhancing the message and increasing the possibilities of what may be communicated, and we referred in this context both to some anthropological texts and to Empson's well known work in literary criticism (1953). For anthropologists in their specific researches, as for literary critics, the obscuring and the ambiguous can and often does occur in texts and in narrative discourse through, for example, metaphor, symbolism, allusion and of course irony; but it can also take non-verbal forms, and indeed does so very commonly: actions and performances, the use of conventional symbols – consider the so-called language of flowers – dress, food, gift-giving. All these apparently different modes of behaviour can in fact be ways of covertly conveying specific ideas and sentiments to a recipient. In all these cases, however, the initial puzzle for the reader, listener or observer is the same: are we all, like it or not, as Whitman implies, condemned by the nature of things to communicate in this way? Yet if this is so, why on some occasions, knowing the problems of meaning, do we deliberately choose an opaque means of expression? Why do the parties to the exchange of information not come straight out with it? What is to be gained by indirection?

There are several possible answers that we might give: to avoid giving offence or, on the contrary, to give offence but with relative impunity; to mitigate embarrassment and save face; to entertain through the manipulation of disguise; for aesthetic pleasure; to maintain harmonious and social relations; to establish relative social status; to exclude from a discourse those not familiar with the conventions of its usage and thereby to strengthen the solidarity of those who are. Clearly the pursuit of what precisely is occurring in each case, and what the motivations underlying the indirection might be in any social context, are of interest not only to anthropologists but to all scholars who are concerned with semiotic demonstrations of motivation and intention. The works of philosophers of language such as Grice, Austin and Wittgenstein, socio-linguists such as Levinson and Brown, and sociologists such as Mead, Simmel and Goffman, bear testimony to this, and, as references to their work indicate, they have proved an inspiration to the contributors to our volume. In terms, however, of which elements within the general topic of indirection lend themselves to anthropological scrutiny in particular, both with respect to its subject matter and to its methodological approach to social phenomena, we can distinguish three areas (allowing for some degree of overlap with other disciplines).

First of all the anthropologist is concerned with the relationship of indirection to other modes of social intercourse within the society. As we know, rather than try to isolate a social phenomenon anthropology takes the broad view, and tries to contextualise it within the general dynamics of social organisation, arguing that such contextualisation works to illuminate the culture of a society. Furthermore, once that act of contextualisation has been effectively carried out and the appropriate connections made, then the shifting of focus back again to the individual phenomenon, or 'social fact' in Durkheim's usage, allows for a more sophisticated and informed analysis of the original observation. As this might apply to examples of indirection, what we are concerned with, then, are questions such as: under what circumstances do individuals resort to indirection; in what domains; among whom and on what occasions; what is its general incidence within the society?

The second set of issues comprises the specific forms which indirection takes, and how one might distinguish the characteristics of each form and identify the connections among them. As we have seen, indirection is not limited to oral or written discourse, and can occur in action, performance and display. Here the questions which the anthropologist addresses concern the relative weight being attached to the form, that is, the significance attributed to it by members of the society: is verbal indirection the principal mode of rhetorical persuasion; is the form valued for its own sake as an aesthetic frill or a medium for entertainment; is it formalised with specific conventions; does it have a formulaic character; are there individual specialists in its use?

A third broad area for investigation links the anthropological with other disciplinary perspectives, namely the matter of intention to which we have already referred. Assuming that we possess the ability to perceive that within a specific communication forum performers are employing indirection and their audience understand this, we want to know what in fact the implicit message is, what the connotations are of what we are witnessing, and what we need to know in order to decipher the code. Now although in some contexts, say a public theatrical performance, allusions can be readily picked up, there is for the observer a difficult problem of interpretation when it comes to the analysis of the dynamics of domestic discourse. The reason for this is clear. Allusions, critical comments, satirical remarks, signficant gestures, all refer to a past history and if one is not privy to that history then one simply misses the import of the indirection. But this surely is where anthropology comes into its own, since we pride ourselves on having exactly that knowledge of the history thanks to our relatively long acquaintance with a society and its individuals. Ideally this gives us that inwardness which allows us to recognise at least partially the allusions as they arise. We demonstrate this in our ethnographic practice when in our descriptions of occurrences and incidents, the case study method, we provide the reader with information on the antecedents of a situation and its later consequences.

The word 'ideally' above was used advisedly, since anthropologists know that they never achieve the degree of intimacy they would like. Indeed the ideal is beyond our reach. Again as Whitman suggests, we can never know ourselves fully, never know what reflects the real me and what is disguise and performance in the presentation of ourselves in everyday life, so *a fortiori* we will encounter acute methodological problems in accounting for the intentions of others. However, one of the great strengths of anthropology, it seems to us, is the recognition of the problem. The standard injunction which is given to all anthropologists about to embark on fieldwork, whether for the purposes of an undergraduate exercise or for a sustained period of research, is always the same: take care to distinguish between what people say they do, what they say they ought to do and what in fact they do do. This advice is predicated on what some might regard as a rather cynical assumption that in all human communication there is an element of subterfuge, prevarication, obfuscation, sometimes designed deliberately to mislead (misdirection?), sometimes in good faith believing one is responding as required (indirection?). Being aware, then, of the likely employment of indirect communication by informants, anthropologists are, one could argue, predisposed to look out for it. However, methodological awareness does not always translate immediately into practice, and there would be few anthroplogists who would deny that it is only through long familiarity with members of a society that one acquires the confidence to distinguish between the transparent and the opaque, the straightforward and the devious, the direct and the indirect. The longer one resides within a society, however, the more accustomed one becomes to picking up the cues, the hints and suggestions, and the less dependent one is on having to rely on the observation of only explicit action or direct statement.

All anthropologists away in the field – or indeed at home or in any of the environments where they carry out their research – absorb and acquire an understanding of modes of communication within their new social surroundings, often after initial, embarrassing mistakes. Very rarely, however, are they explicit about the tactics of communication with which they learn to engage, since their research interests lie in the substance of the communication and not in the tactics themselves nor in their own growing familiarity with strategies of indirection. Their perceptions become part of the everyday taken-for-granted reality which requires no special attention. In fact, of course, the elucidation of these styles of indirection, precisely because they are a feature common to all human intercourse – though whether unique to humankind, as is sometimes argued, is a moot point (see Byrne and Whitten 1988) which was raised in the conference – but differ in form from one society to another, should be the very stuff of anthropology. And this was an additional rationale for our conference: to make colleagues more self-conscious of the way in which they had assimilated indirect forms of communication, and to ask them for that comparative ethnography which would allow us to identify similarities and differences both in a society's emphasis on indirection as a strategy for communication, and in the forms of the disguise – verbal and non-verbal – which indirection takes. Before discussing how the contributors to this volume responded to our invitation, however, it is worth recalling some of the existing anthropological literature on forms of indirection which has provided the intellectual context for much of the theoretical reflection of ourselves and our colleagues.

Background to the choice of topic

The specific background on which we drew, as editors of this volume, comprises Hendry's linguistically based research on speech levels in Japanese society, and Watson's (unpublished) work on *sindiran*, a form of indirect communication in Malay. Hendry's work led to a much wider area, which she came to call 'wrapping' (Hendry 1993; 1999) where she argued that the use of gift packaging to communicate degrees of formality and respect could in Japan be applied conceptually to other forms of indirect communication, such as through the choice of clothes, arrangements of a room, serving of food, and the organisation of time, as well as in the selection of polite forms of speech. All these forms of communication can be understood as ways of wrapping the message involved in a way which is quite recognisable elsewhere.

Sindiran is a form of allusive communication found commonly in everyday communication in Malay and Indonesian society which contains elements of satire and criticism, and can sometimes be quite humorous but is often quite biting, particularly in the more refined language of Malay political intrigue, where open criticism is carefully packaged in apparently courteous and innocuous phrases. Watson's work identifies examples of the layers of meaning which may be incorporated into the speech of the most skilful, who coincidentally gain status through their ability to use it. In Java, social distance can be plotted through the choice of degrees of allusive language. Allusive behaviour may also be witnessed in close family relationships, and oblique speech has considerable power in courtship. In matrilocal Minangkabau society, a mother-in-law shouting at an allegedly lazy cat to indicate disapproval of her daughter's lazy husband might be enough to trigger a divorce.

The notion of *sanza* discussed long ago by Evans-Pritchard (1962) was an example of the use of allusive language of this sort, found in political discourse among the Azande, and again containing levels understood to varying degrees by different members of a group. Collections on political language (Bloch 1975; Brenneis and Myers 1984) have already indicated a breadth in the use of indirect communication in various parts of the world, particularly strong amongst communities in the Pacific, where it can be positively dangerous to make too clear an element of anger. Weiner (1983), for example, described poignantly the severe warning she received on complaining too vociferously about her broken bicycle in the Trobriand Islands.

In Malay, indirection is closely associated with etiquette, and as such serves as a mechanism to make critical remarks while at the same time avoiding embarrassment and maintaining harmonious social relations. As Moertono points out (1981: 19), in Javanese society, where indirect forms of communication are known as *pralambang* or *pasemon*, the directness of communication is in direct proportion to the degree of social distance between interlocutors, so that whereas a slave might be kicked and an insinuation serve for a lower official, a smile, a look or a slight gesture should be sufficient for equals adept at recognising the cues of indirect communication, and indeed may carry even greater power. There is a close overlap here with Japanese, a language which refined the notion of etiquette in pre-modern times to the extent that a man could be killed, or forever shamed, for a breach of its use. Today, the importance of etiquette in Japan is perhaps more associated with the language of women (see for example Hendry 1992; Ide 1986; Shibamoto 1987), but it is carefully passed on to children as a way of demonstrating superior social status.

Expressions which reflect the idea of wrapping are by no means confined to Japan. The veiled speech of Mount Hagen is well known for Papua New Guinea (Strathern 1975), and Gell's (1993) historical study of the Marquesan Islands, *Wrapping in Images*, contains much in the way of indirect communication beyond the main focus of tattooing. In Sulawesi, too, the phrase 'wrapped words' has been chosen by Atkinson (1984) to describe the skilful use of poetical language in political intrigue. A classic study on the subject of greeting etiquette and its indirect implications is that of Irvine (1974) on the way that relative status may be manipulated in the negotiation of a series of different possibilities for a greeting sequence among the Wolof.

Another form of indirect communication already documented in the works of several anthropologists is to be found in strategic forms of deception used in Greece, the Caribbean, and Middle Eastern countries. Du Boulay's careful analysis (1976) of lying in a Greek community is one well known example; another is John Campbell's (1964) description of the protective use of deception in the competitive social world of the Sarakatsani shepherds, also in Greece. Hirschon (1992) has examined the way that children in Greece are taught to recognise lying as a legitimate form of communication of which they should be cautious from an early age, and she introduces the notion of verbal play into her analysis of this phenomenon.

Joking relationships provide another example of the existence of communication which is far from direct, and these were documented in the earliest anthropological studies (Radcliffe-Brown 1940; 1949; cf. Watson 1992: 49–57). Howe and Sherzer (1986) provided a poignant example of the misunderstanding of the anthropologists in this context, in their description of the way a Panamanian informant of one of them reported the death of the other, as a joke, a joke which was the cause of much anxiety and took some time to be revealed. Sherzer (1990) went on to publish a detailed description of the verbal art of the San Blas Kuna Indians with whom he worked, emphasising the importance of the performance and artistry of the various forms of oral language he presents. This kind of skill is another important area open to analysis in terms of indirection.

Gilsenan's (1976) discussion of the relationship between lying and honour in the Lebanon also described the verbal play in which children engage in acquiring the skills of appropriate levels of deception in social life, but he noted too that games are deadly serious. His analysis is essentially a transactional one, dealing with the practicalities of the constitution and maintenance of selves in the complex politics of daily life, but a footnote which expresses the hope that his work will complement the more classificatory and structural theoretical perspective of Douglas, Turner and Lévi-Strauss (*ibid.*: 214) could be cited as an agenda for the present volume. Another footnote also anticipates some of our work here by making clear that silence may be used to even greater effect than lies (*ibid.*: 202, 216).

Beyond spoken language, there is a range of works on the communicative properties of cloth and clothes. On the former, the works of Annette Weiner (1976; 1992) and Gillian Feeley-Harnick (1989) are probably amongst the best known. Weiner's work on the inalienable possessions of the women of the Trobriand Islands, has opened up a whole new theoretical approach to the understanding of systems of exchange, unrecognised by years of exclusive attention to the activities of men. Feeley-Harnick has likewise made readers aware of a new understanding of the treatment of ancestors in Madagascar.

On the subject of clothing, there has been a proliferation of recent publication (see for example Brydon and Niessen 1998; Griggs 1998; Haynes 1998; Warwick 1998), but the works of Baizerman on the Jewish headgear, the Kippa Suruga, used by women to communicate to each other the care they take of their menfolk, and of Cort on the kimono sleeve, a charming expression of many subtle messages (Barnes and Eicher 1992), are particularly interesting on the subject of indirect communication. Likewise, a number of studies discussing the meaning and possibility for manipulation of the veil (e.g. Casajus 1985; Murphy 1964; Rasmussen 1991; Parkin 1995) may be cited as related former studies. On the communicative properties of the kimono, Dalby (1988) and Goldstein (1997) have presented respectively historical and highly modern accounts.

Using the body indirectly to communicate messages of power and status is not confined to the use of clothes, of course, and the work of O'Hanlon (1989) on the political implications of bodily decorations of the Wahgi of the Highlands of New Guinea is a particularly insightful analysis, as is Gell's documentary study (1993) of the tattoos of the native inhabitants of the Marquesan Islands. Tattoos in Japan are also extremely elaborate, and although covering much of the body, they may be entirely concealed by clothes. This situation, along with a strong association of tattoos with the gang world, allows for a very powerful shock if they are suddenly revealed (Richie and Buruma 1980), and illustrates physically the degree to which outside communication can be distinguished from an inside view.

With work such as the above in mind, the subject of indirection was proposed for the 1998 ASA conference. We described the theme as concerned with language and its interpretation but also with extra-linguistic modes of communication, such as through gifts, clothes, buildings, ceremonies and so forth (described as wrapping in Hendry's terminology). Subjects on which we suggested papers might be appropriate included codes of politeness, dissimulation, joking behaviour, non-verbal communication, formal and informal political discourse, negotiating style, and cross-cultural analysis of euphemistic speech.

We felt that a conference on this general subject would provide the opportunity to make comparisons between languages, and between different cultural and linguistic groups within any one language. Devices used to communicate indirectly are undoubtedly used in all languages, but we suggested that their different manifestations would be very much open to anthropological interpretation, and that some of them might raise ideas which had to date seldom been addressed by anthropologists.

The present collection

An idea that impressed Hendry rather forcibly when thinking through the content and discussion of the papers presented at the conference is that, in English, people are very often indirect without really thinking consciously about it. It is almost as though some users of the language have been socialised subtly to use indirection, which may or may not communicate itself to others, but which may explain why people appear to get on with or hit it off with others from a similar background. Hendry's own Yorkshire matrilineal relatives had used the forms of silence discussed by Christensen *et al.* in her childhood, but she had not until that opportunity noticed it at all.

A corollary of this idea of socialisation into the use and understanding of indirect communication within a sub-culture is that this private knowledge within the community can be exploited to exclude others or, more sinisterly, exercise power over them. This would certainly seem to be the case in some English sub-cultures. Diplomacy is one good example, and the papers of Turton and Black illustrate some of the actual forms used. James G. Carrier's discussion of management discourse illustrates a similar principle, forever separating and privileging those trained in management-speak over the managed, whoever they are.

Indirection, then, as well as being a form of communication among peers, can frequently become an instrument of domination and social exclusion, in some contexts transparently so, in others almost indetectably. It is, then, issues of authority as much as issues of communication that the papers in this volume address.

Part I of the book moves straight into a consideration of the subject of indirection in the English language, by addressing head-on a selection of diverse ideas about its use. In the opening paper, Nigel Rapport proposes, somewhat pessimistically, that indirection – which he defines as intentional or unintentional miscommunication – is an irrevocable part of everyday life related to the physical boundaries of the human body. The location of his study is a Yorkshire village, but the principle of perpetuating a miscommunicated idea is taken up in the second paper at a very different level. Here Roger Just draws the reader into a series of situations of indirection he encountered while doing fieldwork on a Greek island, but which he suggests signal a long-term miscommunication (or as he terms it mismatching) at the level of English language analysis of the well known concept of honour. The implication here is that translation, especially in relation to those words which are considered key terms for the interpretation of a cultural ethos, can often lead to slippage and thus to a form of indirection in the ideas conveyed by the anthropologist as self-styled interpreter. Although the social contexts may seem very different, both papers are ultimately concerned with inter-cultural as well as intra-cultural communication.

This same theme is continued in the third paper in Part I, but by the consideration of a very practical issue in Helen Lambert's analysis of the problems encountered by health workers attempting to introduce knowledge about the HIV virus in the Indian subcontinent. She argues that trouble was caused by a general tendency to prioritise verbal communication over forms of indirect communication, and on the subject of sex this was entirely inappropriate. She lays the blame partly at the feet of the anthropologists employed to help because she felt that they reinforced this bias and missed important non-verbal semantic possibilities, of which, again, silence was not the least important. Her paper is thus a beautiful illustration of the centrality of indirection within a culture and how effective communication there depends on the skill and ability to employ its various forms in the appropriate context, something which social workers ignore at their peril.

The final paper in Part I brings us back to Yorkshire, where the experience of anthropologists working in an agricultural community begins to offer us a clue to unravelling the problems apparent in discussing the use of indirection in the English language. This is the paper by Christensen et al., which addresses the way that certain aspects of the social life of the community are never discussed, or as they put it, better left unsaid. We see again how critical silences may be as a form of indirection (cf. Basso 1990) and how in such contexts at least they can be almost sacred.

The chapters in Part II move on from considerations of language and silence to examples of indirect communication through the medium of material goods. First, Nicole Bourque discusses the offering and presentation of food in the Andes, where she finds it is used in different ways to express and manipulate social and economic relations, to voice grievances between wives and husbands, and to make statements about ethnic identity and differences of wealth, in an area where Indians and *mestizos* live side by side. The next paper, by Sarah Pink, considers similar forms of communication in North Eastern Guinea Bissau, where valuable outside relations with Europe are expressed particularly through the use of clothes and other accessories, specifically the sunglasses and suitcases of her title. But, as she points out, in this case the symbolic use of the paraphernalia is so evidently and blatantly part of communicative tactics as are the *indirecta* or transparent hints by which information is disseminated in the society, that one is hard-pressed at times, especially as an outsider anthropologist, to distinguish between direct and indirect.

As something of a contrast, the third paper in Part II, by Ursula Sharma, examines the reason why money and expensive gifts brought from the outside to a community in North India should be handed over under conditions of strict secrecy. She thereby raises another interesting question about a more subtle form of indirection found in the perceived value of careful and measured deceit in maintaining the quality of personal relations. Here some resonance may be found with the case of silence in the Yorkshire farming community, and, for different reasons, with the power of silence in the village in Lebanon discussed in 1976 by Michael Gilsenan.

The fourth paper in Part II, by Terry Webb, introduces an even more embedded form of indirection, probably known only to a limited number of members at the top of a spiritual hierarchy. He examines the architectural form, and the design of performance, in the Polynesian Cultural Centre in Hawaii, a theme park for tourists, and finds clear parallels with, if sometimes reversals of the structure and rites, the neighbouring holy Temple, open only to members of the Mormon Church. The theme park is owned by the Mormons and employs Polynesian students so that they may pay their way at Brigham Young University. Webb argues that they also indirectly communicate to tourists their Mormon view of the world.

In Part III we turn our focus to the body, and the papers given here should enable the reader to think again about Rapport's assertion that the constraints of the body prevent clear lines of communication. Instead we have two cases where it is precisely the body – carefully trained – which provides the means of communication. In the first case, Felicia Hughes-Freeland looks at dance as a representation of, and indeed training for, indirect communication in a Javanese context, noting in particular its value as a code for dissimulation and the expression of identity, and reminding us of the power conferred by skill in these arts. In the second, Tamara Kohn wrestles with local interpretations in Durham of Japanese qualities expected in the practice of the martial art aikido. Besides mentioning that in this context too silence is an element of indirect communication, she lays an important stress on corporeal forms of expressing thought and emotion (cf. Strauss 2000)

Armed with all these examples of non-verbal communication, it is hoped that the reader will now be better equipped to understand further possibilities for indirection in *verbal* forms, and Part IV introduces examples from four different parts of the world. The first paper in fact serves as a bridge from non-verbal to verbal modes, as Jonathan Skinner examines the singing and stylised bodily postures of calypso music, which he argues provides a necessarily ritual means to express legitimately resentment and criticism on the island of Montserrat. He thus makes clear the role of carnival in allowing the expression of otherwise silenced opinions, providing a good example of the association between indirection and the unmentionable.

The second paper in Part IV also examines the role of ritual in allowing the expression of matters which it would be inappropriate to discuss directly in daily life, but points out that even or perhaps especially in a ritual context, it is important to remain at least to some extent indirect. Neil Thin's paper is an account of the language associated with séances which take place at forest festivals among the Irula people of Southern India, and he raises the important issues of the entertainment value of indirection, its face-saving quality for individuals, groups and deities, and the political implications of this mechanism of indirect communication.

In the next paper in Part IV Lisette Josephides introduces recent developments in the languages used in the Highlands of Papua New Guinea, one of the areas from which work has for long been available on indirect communication (e.g. Strathern 1975; O'Hanlon 1989; Weiner 1992). Her subject matter is neither the traditional veiled speech, nor the communicative properties of adorning the body, however. Instead, aware of this context, she examines the intentions behind and implications of the way in which young people, notably young women, reject formerly accepted communicative devices.

The last paper in Part IV, by Peter Parkes, opens up an interesting area of further complexity by contrasting the communicative possibilities drawn upon by the Kalasha community, an egalitarian enclave in the Chitral district of Pakistan, dominated by the more overtly hierarchical Khó. First laying out the type of politeness used traditionally in the Persian court, and its influence on the ostensibly higher-class people of the Chitral district, he then examines various forms of rudeness employed by the Kalasha and emphasised by them as characteristic of their wildness. This state is of course preferred by the Kalasha themselves, who characterise the more civilised Khó as untrustworthy and manipulative. The double-bind – shades of Bateson's schismogenesis – illustrated here is also placed within a robust theoretical framework.

In Part V, the final part of the book, and in the context of the rich fund of examples we have drawn from the ethnography of our previous contributors, we turn to present again the indirect use of the English language. Here we are reassured that we have certainly always had the possibility of being skilful in the intentional use of indirection, even though we may have been less than open about this skill. Annabel Black presents the case of ambiguity as a form of indirection not only in the setting of diplomacy, but in internal communication within the British diplomatic community itself where, as among the Javanese, it would seem that hierarchy is a critical issue. Andrew Turton demonstrates our former skills and some of the problems encountered in intercultural indirection in an historical account of British relations with the Thai Court.

Finally, we come right back to home territory and the continuing present, where James G. Carrier's paper nicely illustrates our underlying thesis when he warns us of the dangers of remaining unaware of the powerful possibilities of indirect communication for those who are able to use and manipulate an esoteric version of the English language. He has chosen to analyse the language of the Market, and demonstrates clearly the full strength that command of an indirect mode of communication can bestow. Like some other forms of indirection, it effectively protects an elite, and as outsiders pick it up, the language must change to exclude them.

The book thus brings the reader full circle from the experiences of the editors of the skilful manipulation of indirect communication in Japan and Indonesia, through a series of more specific examples of the missed and bungled possibilities of indirectional languages – as well as their successes – back to show that the English language is capable of the same subtlety.

The range of the contributions, both in terms of the geographical and temporal span of the ethnographies and in the description of the forms which indirection can take, has provided strong confirmation of our suspicion that here was a topic calling out for anthropological research which had not yet received the attention it deserved. At the same time the variety of contributions also helps us to understand why the subject has been so relatively understudied. Who at first sight would have thought that there were theoretical links to be made between serving guinea pigs to guests in the Andes and discussions of landscape in the Yorkshire dales? Where anthropology has created categories for cross-cultural comparison, these have usually been demonstrably self-evident – kinship, politics, economics, religion (though these too have been unravelling fast for some time) – and indirection does not seem to sit easily within such a taxonomic system. Yet paradoxically it is precisely because of the lack of easy assimilation into a ready-made category that, as anthropologists, we should have appreciated that these forms of behaviour, which seemed strange but oddly familiar, might be accessible to a comparative anthropology. After all, this style of comparison is exactly what earlier generations of French anthropologists had alerted us to. What is Mauss' book, *Le Don*, if not an exercise in bringing together apparently curious and disparate examples of social exchange under the rubric of an institution labelled gift-giving, and demonstrating the common principles which underlie the different forms that institution can take? We would not be so pretentious as to claim that, by drawing attention to the significance of indirect communication as a universal institution, our tentative speculations are in any way comparable to that great work. We would, however, like to associate ourselves with the same enthusiasm for broad cross-cultural comparisons. What contributors to this volume have convincingly argued is that modes of indirect communication, whether easily discernible or not, are characteristic of social intercourse, and as anthropologists we should give them our serious consideration. We look forward to further examples and a greater theoretical elaboration of the issues in the future work of our colleagues.

References

Abu-Lughod, L. (1986) *Veiled Sentiments*, Berkeley and London: University of California Press.

Atkinson, J. M. (1984) 'Wrapped Words: poetry and politics among the Wana of Central Sulawesi, Indonesia', in D. Brenneis and F. R. Myers (eds) *Dangerous Words: Language and Politics in the Pacific*, New York: New York University Press.

Baizerman, S. (1992) 'The Kippa Sruga and the social construction of gender', in R. Barnes and J. Eicher (eds) *Dress and Gender: Making and Meaning in Cultural Contexts*, Oxford: Berg.

Barnes, R. and Eicher, J. (eds) (1992) *Dress and Gender: Making and Meaning in Cultural Contexts*, Oxford, New York: Berg.

Basso, K. H. (1990) 'To give up on words: silence in Western Apache culture', in Keith H. Basso, *Western Apache Language and Culture*, Tuscon and London: University of Arizona Press, pp. 80–98.

Bloch, M. (1975) *Political Language and Oratory in Traditional Society*, London, New York and San Francisco: Academic Press.

Brenneis, D. and Myers, F. R. (1984) *Dangerous Words: Language and Politics in the Pacific*, New York: New York University Press.

Brydon, A. and Niessen, S. (1998) *Consuming Fashion: Adorning the Transnational Body*, Oxford: Berg.

Byrne, Richard and Whitten, Andrew (eds) (1988) *Machiavellian Intelligence: Social Expertise and the Evolution of Intellect in Monkeys, Apes, and Humans*, Oxford: Clarendon Press.

Campbell, J. (1964) *Honour, Family and Patronage*, Oxford: Clarendon Press.

Casajus, D. (1985) 'Why do the Tuareg veil their faces?', in R. H. Barnes, Daniel de Coppet and R. J. Parkin, 'Contexts and levels', *Journal of the Anthropological Society of Oxford*, Occasional Papers no. 4, Oxford, pp. 68–77.

Cort, L. (1992) 'Whose sleeves? Gender, class and meaning in Japanese costume of the 17th century', in R. Barnes and J. Eicher (eds) *Dress and Gender: Making and Meaning in Cultural Contexts*, Oxford: Berg.

Dalby, L. (1988) 'The cultured nature of Heian colors', *Transactions of the Asiatic Society of Japan*, 4(3):1–19.

du Boulay, J. (1976) 'Lies, mockery and family integrity', in J. Peristiany (ed.) *Mediterranean Family Structures*, Cambridge: Cambridge University Press.

Empson, William (1953) [1930] *Seven Types of Ambiguity*, 3rd edn, London: Chatto and Windus.

Evans-Pritchard, E. E. (1962) 'Sanza, a characteristic feature of Zande language and thought', in *Essays in Social Anthropology*, London: Faber and Faber.

Feeley-Harnik, G. (1989) 'Cloth and the creation of ancestors in Madagascar', in J. Schneider and A. B. Weiner (eds) *Cloth and Human Experience*, Washington DC: Smithsonian Institution Press.

Gell, A. (1993) *Wrapping in Images: Tattooing in Polynesia*, Oxford: Clarendon Press.

Gilsenan, M. (1976) 'Lying, honor and contradiction', in B. Kapferer (ed.) *Transaction and Meaning: Directions in the Anthropology of Exchange and Symbolic Behavior*, Philadelphia: Institute for the Study of Human Issues, pp. 191–219.

Goldstein, O. (1997) *Packaged Japaneseness: Weddings, Business and Brides*, Richmond: Curzon.

Griggs, C. (1998) *S/he: Changing Sex and Changing Clothes*, Oxford: Berg.

Hannerz, U. (1996) *Transnational Connections: Culture, People, Places*, London: Routledge.

Haynes, M. T. (1998) *Dressing Up Debutantes: Pageantry and Glitz in Texas*, Oxford: Berg.

Hendry, J. (1992) 'Honorifics as dialect: the expression and manipulation of boundaries in Japanese', *Multilingua*, 11(4): 341–54.

——(1993) *Wrapping Culture: Politeness, Presentation and Power in Japan and Other Societies*, Oxford: Clarendon Press.

——(1999) *An Anthropologist in Japan: Glimpses of Life in the Field*, London: Routledge.

Hirschon, R. (1992) 'Greek adults' verbal play, or, how to train for caution', *Journal of Modern Greek Studies*, vol. 10: 35–56.

Howe, J. and Sherzer, J. (1986) 'Friend Hairyfish and friend Rattlesnake; or keeping anthropologists in their place', *Man* (n.s.) 21(4): 680–96.

Ide, S. (1986) 'Sex difference and politeness in Japanese', *International Journal of the Sociology of Language*, vol. 58: 25–36.

Irvine, J. (1974) 'Strategies of status manipulation in the Wolof greeting', in R. Bauman and J. Sherzer (eds) *Explorations in the Ethnography of Speaking*, Cambridge: Cambridge University Press.

Kochman, T. (ed.) (1972) *Rappin and Stylinout: Communication in Urban Black America*, Urbana: University of Illinois Press.

Moertono, Soemarsaid (1981) *State and Statecraft in Old Java: A study of the Later Mataram Period, 16th to 19th Century*, Monograph Series (publication no. 43) revised edn, Modern Indonesia Project, Southeast Asia Program, Ithaca NY: Cornell University.

Murphy, R. F. (1964) 'Social distance and the veil', *American Anthropologist*, vol. 66: 1257.

O'Hanlon, M. (1989) *Reading the Skin: Adornment, Display and Society among the Wahgi*, London: British Museum Publications.

Parkin, D. (1995) 'Blank banners and Islamic consciousness in Zanzibar', in Anthony P. Cohen and Nigel Rapport (eds) *Questions of Consciousness*, London: Routledge, pp. 198–216.

Radcliffe-Brown, A. R. (1940) 'On joking relationships', *Africa*, 13(3): 195–210.

——(1949) 'A further note on joking relationships', *Africa*, 19(2): 133–140.

Rasmussen, S. J. (1991) 'Veiled self, transparent meanings: Tuareg headdress as social expression', *Ethnology* 30(2): 101–17.

Richie, D. and Buruma, I. (1980) *The Japanese Tattoo*, New York and Tokyo: Weatherhill.

Segal, D. A. and Handler, R. (1989) 'Serious play: creative dance and dramatic sensibility in Jane Austen, ethnographer', *Man* (n.s.) vol. 24: 322–38.

Sherzer, J. (1990) *Verbal Arts in San Blas: Kuna Culture through its Discourse*, Cambridge: Cambridge University Press.

Shibamoto, J. (1987) 'The womanly woman: manipulation of stereotypical and nonstereotypical features of Japanese female speech', in S. Philips, S. Steele and C. Tanz (eds) *Language, Gender and Sex in Comparative Perspective*, Cambridge: Cambridge University Press.

Strathern, A. (1975) 'Veiled speech in Mount Hagen', in M. Bloch (ed.) *Political Language and Oratory in Traditional Society*, London, New York and San Francisco: Academic Press.

Strauss, Sarah (2000) 'Locating yoga: ethnography and transnational practice', in Vered Amit (ed.) *Constructing the Field: Ethnographic Fieldwork in the Contemporary World*, London: Routledge.

Warwick, A. (1998) *Fashioning the Frame: Boundaries, Dress and Body*, Oxford: Berg.

Watson, C. W. (1992) *Kinship, Property and Inheritance in Kerinci, Central Sumatra*, Canterbury: Centre for Social Anthropology and Computing and the Centre of South-East Asian Studies, University of Kent at Canterbury.

Weiner, A. B. (1976) *Women of Value, Men of Renown*, Austin and London: University of Texas Press.

——(1983) 'From words to objects to magic: hard words and the boundaries of social interaction', *Man* (n.s.) vol. 18: 690–709.

——(1992) *Inalienable Possessions: The Paradox of Keeping-While-Giving*, Berkeley, Los Angeles and Oxford: University of California Press.

Part I

Intercultural communication and the anthropologist

Chapter 1

Communicational distortion and the constitution of society

Indirection as a form of life

Nigel Rapport

> People agree in the language they use: this is agreement in form of life not opinions.
>
> (Ludwig Wittgenstein, *Philosophical Investigations*)

This paper is concerned with interactional systemics and language in personal usage, also with the extent to which indirection – understood as intentional and unintentional miscommunication – serves as a root metaphor for social interaction *per se*. In elaborating how it is possible for two individuals, Doris and Sid, regularly and habitually to talk past each other in the English village of Wanet, this chapter enters into a discussion on interiority, and the indirection which inevitably occurs when language is 'refracted' by the boundary of the body: when the privacy of an individual's internal conversation meets the publicity of external exchange. A view of society is posited as an indirect coming-together (unintentional and intentional) of a diversity of individual worlds of meaning.

The common forms of local behaviour

> You'll have to look like a farmer, Nigel, if you're gonna be round here or people will start talking: 'Who's that on Cedar High?' And you don't see farmers with beards, Nigel, either. ... You'll have to say 'tup' not 'tuhp' when you mean Barney, the ram, or no-one from round here'll understand you. ... And then when you're wanting to be fed you say: 'I'm so hungry my belly's touching my backbone'. Or else Fred's favourite: 'I'm so hungry my stomach thinks my throat's been cut'. You'll have to learn our words if you're gonna be local and live here! ... Don't you ever stroke my sheepdog, Jet, like that again. It spoils them. She's a working dog, not one of your lazy, petted, city dogs. Jet's a farm dog, aren't you Jet? Y-e-s. And she doesn't like these stupid offcomer dogs you see around. ... You know, you and me are gonna have a real barney if you drive that tractor by the shippon again when I'm milking. I'd just put on the

suckers and now you've aggravated the cows and they've kicked them off and shit them all up again. I tell you, we'll have a right set-to, my lad, 'cause then *I'll* be the one who's getting aggravated, and we'll just see who cracks first. ... And what are you carrying two bales of hay at a time for? Do you think you're strong? That's not strong. You're not strong. Fred's strong. He can carry on all day and not stop. That's real manly strength. You haven't got that. ... Now Nigel. When the National Park Inspector comes today, say nowt. Fred and me'll see what he wants and soon sort him out here in the kitchen. Snooping busybodies. But you just say nowt. Look like you had a hard night on the pop or something! Okay?

It was through these sorts of cues that I learnt to play my part in the routine life of Cedar High Farm in the rural Cumbrian dale of Wanet in the early 1980s, working as an apprentice farmhand for Doris Harvey and her husband, Fred. Here are some of what I would call the regularities of behavioural form, from the verbal to the non-verbal, in which Doris instructed me so that we could engage in habitual relations. In this way, over the months, Doris moulded me into her social universe and I learnt how, as a farmhand and as a surrogate child of the farm, I should fit in with her daily routines.

Similarly, there were habits of interaction which I learnt for my routine personal relations with Fred (as farmer with farm boy), and then again with Sid, Fred and Doris' brother-in-law and handyman (as builder with builder's mate) when he came to put up a new shed and self-feed silo for Fred and Doris' dairy cows. 'Learning to play my part in the everyday life of Cedar High Farm' meant learning an assemblage of behavioural routines which I played out with each of them. Here were versions of 'good form' which each regarded as normal and normative, to which each felt their behaviour closely approximated, and which each expected to find replicated by others.

A 'culture', I suggest, might be described as a fund of behavioural forms. In use, moreover, this fund has a distributional aspect. Hence, Doris would see certain behaviours as proper for herself or her family, other behaviours as appropriate for immediate neighbours, for Wanet locals, for fellow-dalesmen, for visiting tourists, for Britons, for foreigners, and some behaviours as legitimate for none. Not only should locals of Wanet speak as she instructed me, then, but tourists should not be allowed to bring big cars like Jaguars on to Wanet's narrow and winding roads, while Pakistani immigrants in the cities should not be allowed to live in indecent numbers in single rented rooms at all.

There are two overlapping variables in this distribution: like-me-and-mine/unlike; and proper/improper. Doris and Fred and Sid were alike in thinking in these spectral terms: some behaviours, all knew, were both more local and more proper than others. Indeed, the notion of properly local behaviours was well nigh universal in Wanet. Moreover, these local behaviours aroused far more concern than nation-wide and 'British' proprieties, somehow more distant. On my arrival in the dale I had thought that I might begin to belong and negotiate personal relations on the basis of what I regarded as society-wide interests, or at least gender-inclusive ones. After all, I was 'British', 'middle class', and I knew how to roll up my sleeves and 'get serious' about my darts down the pub, over a tankard of beer, the same as the next 'man'. I came to realise, however, that all that these forms initiated, with Doug the pub landlord, say, or Arthur, one of his regulars, were the polite but distant and superficial reciprocations which Doug and Arthur variously introduced into interactions which they defined as taking place with visitors. So they would play me at darts, jokingly have bets with me (as a Welshman) on the outcome of the annual Triple Crown rugby competition, and voice opinions about machinations at Whitehall, but soon get bored and turn to their more regular talking-partners for more interesting exchanges. The universalistic forms did not lead me to any greater closeness, but, on the contrary, kept me in Doug and Arthur's distanced category of outsider. These were the appropriate ways of dealing with 'offcomers' (those who came to Wanet from off-aways), and the ways which offcomers probably used when dealing with one another. When faced by strangers, interaction was certainly safer within this set of limited forms (the code which they seemed to prefer) because you were really never to know what they might do beyond it. Hence, a non-local, non-familiar form helped control the unfamiliar interactant: a universal code for hopefully universal protection against all manner of potential randomness in offcomer behaviour.

Whenever possible, however, the local forms of behaviour were far more comfortable: they had long been under what felt like personal and community control. So Doug and Arthur soon returned to their more regular, local and private interactions. Indeed, it was a dale-wide talking point when someone eschewed local proprieties and preferred the strange, offcomer form – when a neighbour decided, for example, that Arthur's sheep being loose on the road yet again was the last straw, something that had gone beyond the bounds of decent local behaviour and informal arbitration or self-help, and so informed the Leyton police that Arthur had been driving his tractor with bald tyres. In short, outside forms of behaviour were for outsiders, and their use by locals inside the dale insinuated the same. Talking international rugby or national politics with Arthur and Doug down the pub was them labelling me as an offcomer, rather than a step towards my overcoming this divide. To be a local, as Doris advised me, was to interact in local ways. Why talk and act as just anyone might when in Wanet local behavioural forms were a recognisable emblem of a more special belonging? In the exchange of local forms (from which the outsider was debarred) was a place to feel comfortable, secure, and at home.

The polythetic usage of local behaviours in Wanet

It would be wrong, however, to think of these local behavioural forms in terms of standardised essentials: in terms of standard, dale-wide exchanges that held every time a local was polite to an offcomer, or interacted with an offcomer, or indeed with a fellow-local, a farmer or a publican or child. Hence, while there were common mentions of the meanness of a particularly reclusive farmer, of the rudeness of a new shopkeeper, of the hardships of a glorious Wanet past, of the weirdness of folk in neighbouring dales, these always took place within the context of a particular habitual 'talking-relation-ship' (cf. Rapport 1987). And between these particular relationships, I would argue, there were less uniform correspondences than 'families of resemblance'.

That is, rather than anything more unitary, the forms of behaviour in common use in the dale amounted to polythetic categories (ABC, BCD, CDE, DEF, etc.; 1234, 2234, 2567, 3234, 3567, 38910, etc.). Elements might overlap but there was nothing essentially the same linking the different usages of common behavioural forms. For example, I have said that Doug and Arthur treated me as an offcomer when I arrived in Wanet and we exchanged pleasantries on a number of suitably distant and limited topics. 'Talking to an offcomer' would be something that many people in Wanet would have notions about, even offcomers themselves: notions concerning the proprieties and improprieties of good form. And yet these interactions were still distinc-tive; being treated as an offcomer by Doug, the landlord (an ex-offcomer himself) – eager for my custom and yet anxious to run a 'locals' ' pub rather than one seen as geared to visitors – was not the same or even especially similar to being treated as an offcomer by Arthur, the farmer – keen to recall army days outside Wanet as a foil to present economic difficulties and disagreements with parochial neighbours.

The particularity and 'polytheticality' of common Wanet forms in use became clearer to me still as I slowly gained acceptance in local relationships and began to slough off the offcomer taint. For I never became a 'local' *per se* so much as someone with whom Doris and Fred, and Sid and Arthur and Doug came habitually to meet in what they regarded as the proprieties of local behavioural forms. I became a local, that is, as Doris's farm lad, as Arthur's domino partner, and as Sid's builder's mate. They were alike in seeming legitimate, even typical, ways for locals in Wanet to behave – Doris and Arthur and Doug *et al.* might all regard their relations with me as prop-erly 'local' – but there were no more shared or even similar facets to these different relations than this. To be 'a good local' was for me to engage in habitual interaction with others who regarded me and my behaviour as such. True, to be a local and not an offcomer was often linked to one of a set of *other* apt behavioural forms – throwing a straight 'arrow' at the darts board, bringing up respectful children, working farmers' hours – but these, similarly, would never be expressed in an abstract sense. One would always be talking *about* somebody being a good local *to* somebody, and as the context changed (the same interactant, perhaps, but a different subject of discussion; or the same subject but a different interactant; or the same interactant and subject but a different mood or place or time) so the same common behavioural form or set of interlinked forms could mean something else. Hence while there were many forms of behaviour which Wanet people agreed in regarding as special to them – being polite to offcomers, being a good local (which in turn included being a good farmer, or helpful to fellow-dalesmen) – I found no standard definitions of what these entailed. Rather, every usage was connected to and expressed within a particular interactional context; and a juxtaposition of these usages would reveal not one way of being polite as such, or helpful, or a good farmer, but a wide range of ways of behaving, with polythetic not common-denominational connections: 'proper' behaviours could be poles apart with nothing in common at all.

For individuals in Wanet would *personalise* the behavioural forms which they heard and saw legitimated by others around them, and construct their own versions within the conditions and contexts of their own lives. Hence, the way Sid behaved towards me as an offcomer, an apprentice, a neighbour, was not the same as the way Doris did. Each would see the other behaving, would remember how they had seen offcomers and apprentices and neighbours being treated in Wanet in the past, would take their cues from a variety of sources, and then place their own signatures on the behavioural forms, coming upon them with different motives, different world-views, and a variety of different meanings to express and fulfil. In use, the forms which many would agree upon as common and proper to Wanet came to be mediated by a diversity of individual ends, and were the means for achieving satisfaction of a variety of individual kinds and amounts.

Hence, when Doris and Sid, for instance, would engage in their everyday exchanges, conversing together in the farmyard or the farmhouse kitchen about the state of the world and the farm and their families and neighbours and enemies, their interaction was such that meanings were not necessarily shared. Doris and Sid may have both been born in Wanet, may have grown up together, may have continued their regular conversational intercourse into adult life, but still, I felt there was a fundamental sense in which, *personalising (verbal) forms within the contexts of distinct world-views*, they talked past each other:

'You know, Doris', Sid says, 'Wanet locals are just the salt of the earth. But, with all due respect, I think they worry too much about these offcomers and their committees. Nowt better to do all day than turn down your farm plans. ... These buggers just need burning; they want to do a bit of work themselves for a change!'

'We need someone local to represent us', Doris replies. 'But I can't think of anyone still living here who's knowledgeable or strong enough. I can't think of anyone who's moved off either: who knows all the local stuff about Wanet but who has the right temperament and manner and who is experienced in all the channels you gotta use. ... But village folks can't abide being told what to do'.

[*Sid means:* Don't you remember the worry-free times when, as children, we used to run around Wanet together and have the place to ourselves. Local folks knew who their friends were then. And who their enemies were. And friends who stuck together, worked and played together and put their heads together could outwit their enemies, so that they and their plans came unstuck. ... Well the same could be true still today: offcomers and their committees are no tougher than enemy gangs from our youth. If only locals today – like you, Doris – would recognise who their true friends were – like me – confide in them and seek their help.]

[*Doris means:* Traditionally, folks respected hard work, and those who wanted to get on in the world and be a bit better and bigger than they were. I've built up this farm from nothing. I've spent fourteen years of my life working here, I've brought up four local children – I've worked hard for the village too, and I've brought business and capital to it – and now I'm really determined that no-one is going to keep me and my family down. Folks prefer to pity you than envy you nowadays, but no-one is going to keep us pitiable. Together, me and my children and husband will show all those outsiders – from offcomer bureaucrats to fickle neighbours, like Sid – that we need the help of no-one off the farm to survive.]

What I have adumbrated here are those particular, detailed ways in which Doris and Sid associate together and employ the common behavioural (here, verbal) forms which they exchange – as interpreted by me, based upon the lengthy tutoring I received from each, respectively, on the matter of our individual relationships. Meaning, we have appreciated since Saussure, is a matter of symbolic association and differentiation. Privy to the detailed associations which Doris and Sid intend through their use of such symbolic forms, I would contend that they construct different worlds of meaning to each other. Their full cognitive associations of the forms which pass between them in abbreviated fashion in everyday interaction, amount to them living in different cognitive contexts, in different worlds (cf. Rapport 1986; 1992).

A particular apprehension of context is becoming apparent here. Context comes to be understood as something cognitive and contingent, in origin private to the individual, rather than something publicly shared and intrinsic to an interactional setting (cf. Rapport 1999). Concerning the ways in which individuals connect and associate symbolic forms and so accord them meaning, context is something which individuals bring to their interactions with others and deploy in their actions and interpretations. Here are Doris and Sid exchanging common forms of behaviour which their local cultural milieu has afforded them, agreeing on their appropriateness and legitimacy, and yet, it is argued, remaining cognitively distant from each other (unaware, moreover, of the continuing gulfs between them), because of their individual and diverse contextualisations.

Ultimately, in short, the polytheticality of symbolic forms in use (such as English words) translates into miscommunication and misunderstanding. Cognitively connecting up common verbal forms in different ways, contextualising them in different associative sets, individual speakers may understand very different things through the interactions they routinely share.

An anthropological review

Communicational distortion, miscommunication of the sort I would describe for Doris and Sid *et al.* in Wanet, has been variously treated in social-scientific commentary. A number of factors and variables have been mooted for a hypothesising of the likelihood and capability of 'successful communication', understood as one interactant comprehending another in the manner each intends.

For example, communicability has been linked with the regularity and repetitiveness of exchange: the more frequent, the more successful (e.g. Berger and Luckmann 1966: 140–1); especially if the community is simple and small (Goodenough 1963: 264). Also, communicability has been linked with the status and exercise of power, the 'patron', then (Paine 1971: 8), being he who is capable of having values of his choosing affirmed by his client – as opposed to mere go-betweens and brokers, and not to mention the poor, whose structural disadvantage makes it almost impossible for them to control the frame of interpretation imposed on their actions by others (Wikan 1980: 42). In similar vein, communicability has been tied to the inequalities of class, the lower class being deprived of speech which uniquely fits their personal intentions and experiences or allows them to elaborate upon these (Bernstein 1972: 476); the ideological dictatorship of the ruling class resulting in them only having the symbols and pre-definitions of a public language, so that all their private meanings are distorted and repressed (Zaslavsky 1982: 83–4). Then again, communicability has been linked with the prevalence of conventionalised forms of stylised speech: the more interactants share a tacit agreement about the normative definition of a situation and a working consensus about each others' statuses and role-obligations within it, the more immediate and heart-felt feelings and wants may be suppressed and concealed (Goffman 1978: 20–1). For still others, communicability is a feature of national character or cultural identity: the English, for example then, being a taciturn people whose actions must hopefully speak for themselves (Berger 1967: 93). Finally, communicability is seen as an aspect of cultural vitality, with consciousness and intellectuality being impaired the more imprecise, abstract and stale language becomes (Steiner 1967: 45–6).

While these hypotheses may offer hints towards an elaboration of the situation in Wanet – interaction through an exchange of conventionalised and routine (even clichéd) verbal and non-verbal forms limiting, through their very sharedness and publicness, the amount and quality of personal and uncommon information that can be communicated – there is a further important element which has thus far not been broached, the question of intention: successful communication as an aspect of the wish to communicate. And here we find more, interesting commentaries in the literature. For these recognise the social truths that in the sphere of daily social exchange, what Bateson (1951: 179) distinguishes as information-seeking behaviour on the one hand (learning about the world) and value-seeking behaviour (judging the world) on the other is collapsed, such that no information is constructed value-free. Furthermore, communicability is not something objectively measurable in terms of approximations to an ideal linguistic or other standard but is, rather, situation-bound and tied to individual purpose and situation.

Hence, desirability of communication becomes a variable, for example, where the basic work of interaction is the penetration of one individual's personal space by the words and actions of another: the domination of someone else's persona and the protection of one's own. Here, then, social interaction proceeds through formalised speech and ritualised exchange only in order that personal thoughts and events may remain disguised (Weiner 1983: 692–4); or so that one's strategy, friendliness and power must at least be guessed at, and interlocutors' decisions about ripostes – to fight or truce – are always made more difficult (Favret-Saada 1980: 10–11). Desirability of communication also becomes a variable where interaction is a means of matching behaviour against a prescriptive social order, expressed in a clear public code. Here, the institutionalisation of secretness creates those ambiguities and flexibilities by which the stasis and clarity of the code and the flux and blurredness of everyday life can coexist; through deception and invention one preserves honour and dignity (Gilsenan 1976: 211). Then again, the desire to communicate may be variable where the social environment is a highly segmented or factionalised one, the 'true state of one's heart' being revealed only to co-members and hidden from rivals (Pitt-Rivers 1974: xvi–xvii). Or again, desirability of communication is a variable where people live in such close proximity that there is the threat they will find out too much about one another, thus making social relationships impossible. It may not only be the relationship which disappears with such a total exchange of information, indeed, but its components too: if individuals as social persons communicated everything they would cease to exist as such (Pocock 1961: 101). This applies not only both to dyadic relations – hence characterised by 'beliefs and blindnesses' (Compton-Burnett 1969: 30) – but also to relations of wider array;

mendacity may be of great service in all instances in turning a surplus stock of mutual knowledge into 'ample doubts and few convictions' (Murphy 1972: 227–8). Non-communication and a keeping secret of information become means of maintaining not only those distinctions between people which are necessary for their relationship, but also a propensity (at least a potential) for personal integrity. As Chesterton pithily phrased it: 'I should think very little of [an Englishman] who did not keep something in the background of his life that was more serious than all this talking' (1975: 18).

Returning to Wanet then, on this English note, what further might be made of the distortion in communication between Doris and Sid (and others too) who interact so habitually and so superficially? How is it that Doris and Sid can continue to contextualise the words of their routine exchanges in such diverse cognitive associations that they mean something very different by them and yet do not recognise these differences when they meet, and so talk past each other? It cannot be a question of frequency or foreignness, for they are neighbours in a small village community who meet almost every day. Moreover, it is not that they conceal their feelings out of duty to their inter-related roles: their feelings are often openly admitted and, they intend, on display. Nor do they suffer from 'structural impoverishment': they are accomplished and highly skilled, and own their own means of production; in local terms they are not lacking in resources. Certainly they are not intellectually retarded or verbally restricted! On the contrary: they are talkative and highly articulate, despite being English.

What I would say, first, is that Doris and Sid's miscommunication is a question of the proprieties of styles of exchange in Wanet. That is, in habitual interaction with each other, as fellow-adults, Doris and Sid both feel they know what the other has to say and should or will say, and also what they mean. It might be legitimate to lecture children at length – to brook no interruption as one elucidates the ways of the world – and it is apposite for children to listen in silence. Hence, I could learn of Doris or Sid with little need for verbal prompting or reciprocation (and also, I have contended, learn of gross differences in their contexts of interpretation). When talking to fellow-adults, however, there will be less lecturing and more interrupting, while the interruptions are less searching and the narrative of exchange more guarded (more 'muted' in Skinner's sense [this volume, Chapter 11]). Because adults can be expected to know already: to know of people, to know of events, and to know of the normative ways in which these are to be evaluated. Talking with fellow-adults is more of an exercise in comparison than of exposition. One compares one's information to check on one's rectitude, and to confirm the parameters and coordinates and boundaries of one's social landscapes; and this, as we have seen, is generally accomplished.

Second, as adults, Doris and Sid entered into interaction with each other ironically spurred by contradictory intents; and, in conjunction with the above, this amounted to interaction of great complication and duplicity. They wanted to talk in order to realise their expectations and see their world-views fulfilled in each other's actions and reactions; from public exchange they gained proof of their social existence and its nature. And yet, they did not want to talk for fear of playing into the hands of the inferior and immoral, and having what they said misconstrued. Doris and Sid talked in order to gain sympathy and support from their moral fellows: to share their fears and to rouse indignation and receive emotional compensation for troubles suffered and wrongs incurred. And again, they talked to gain superordination over their worthless fellows: to assure themselves of the latters' continuing immorality; without laying themselves open to similar aspersions. So they were prepared to talk in order to bolster their fellows and unite with them against common opposition; and yet they did not want to talk in case what they revealed about themselves was misused, taken as a sign of weakness or ignorance, or otherwise fitted into their enemies' machinations. They enjoyed to talk because this was how people in Wanet displayed and experienced their belonging; and yet they were frightened to talk in case it was overheard by those who variously did not belong, appropriated and adulterated.

In short, Doris and Sid were almost certain that they could continue to maintain order in their worlds, even amid a crowd of 'outsiders', but they were also afraid that they might one day find out they were wrong. By engaging in routine interactions as fellow-adults, exchanging words and actions which were indeed so familiar that they could be taken *in brevito*, even interrupted with ease, Doris and Sid assisted one another in keeping this day well distant. And by regularly coming together and helping fulfil one another's expectations, they succeeded in keeping their worlds – even as 'fellow-locals' – very much apart.

Local Wanet behaviours and ego-syntonism

There is a fund of behavioural forms common to Wanet, I have argued. In use in individuals' different habitual talking-relationships, however, as these are individually interpreted, the forms come to imply, to refer to, different things; such that the connection between different uses is at best partial, and the aggregation of these uses amounts to a commonality which is polythetic. Individuals like Doris and Sid personalise behaviours so that far from being representative of community-wide norms of exchange, they represent them alone. Commonality is hence transformed into diversity.

Nevertheless, the forms can be seen to assist in important synthesising processes by which the threads of different individuals' lives are interwoven. If Sid's usage was idiosyncratic, if my relations with Sid and with Doris were special to us, if I became member of 'a local Wanet community' in a number of inherently different ways – then all of these practices were still undertaken in terms of the same fund of behaviours. Devereux has suggested the term 'ego-syntonism' to refer to the cultural provision of behavioural forms which individuals of different motivations can at the same time perceive as suitable for the expression and gratification of a variety of subjective meanings and emotions (1978: 126; also cf. Rapport 1994).

Behavioural forms are able to provide for this diversity because of a basic ambiguity and abbreviation: 'friendly ambiguities', as Sapir put it (1956: 153), conspiring to reinterpret for one individual the behaviour observed in others only in terms of 'those meanings which are relevant to his own life'. A language of common forms thus comes to mediate between the actions of one individual and the interpretations of another (cf. Josephides, Chapter 13 in this volume, on perlocutionary as distinct from illocutionary acts).

The ambiguity of common forms also affords them a certain inertia. Vague and simplistic outside a particular context of interpretation, they can be handed down between generations, adapted to a variety of settings; they are ready-made formulae always capable of animation by new motivations and moods. This point is crucial. The forms of behaviour common to a community such as Wanet are necessary for individuals to come together in interaction and for meaning to be constructed, but they do not represent a sufficient precondition. Most of the forms of the English language which Sid and Doris use, for example, existed long prior to their usage and will, in all probability, outlive them – and they could not express themselves without them – but they do not tell Doris or Sid what they can or should or must mean. The vocabulary of English and its grammatical construction are limited, the phrasal expressions of behavioural forms common to Wanet even more so ('Village people can't abide being told what to do', 'He's a right twined, narrow-backed bastard', 'Offcomers' plans always get through the Park Committee'), but what Doris and Sid can and do say through them is not limited. Indeed, the forms live and carry meaning only in the individual contexts of their use: English lives on in Wanet because Doris and Sid and others continually employ it in certain specific ways as their medium of expression.

In short, the relationship between form and meaning is one of interdependence and multifactoriality. Individuals depend upon these common attributes of their culture for the capacity to express meaning. Moreover, since the conditions of their use remain essentially public, it is in coordination with significant others and in certain routine and limited ways that these expressions come to be made. And yet, the vitality of the forms depends on individuals with meanings they endemically want to express through them.

Commonality and difference, in short, must needs be seen as two sides of the same coin. Personalised in usage and realised in possibly idiosyncratic fashions, behavioural commonalities become instruments of diversity and difference, the 'wrappings' of individuality (cf. Hendry 1993).

Meaning and interiority

I have argued that distortion in communication (intentional and unintentional) marks the interaction between two individuals in a small English village. But I would also wish to claim an ambiguity of exchange and a diversity of perception as characterising social interaction as such. Meanings are matters of interiority, of internal conversation, I would contend, before becoming an aspect of external exchange, and miscommunication is the inexorable result of meanings being channelled through, and refracted by, the boundary of the individual body.

At one point in the novel *Orlando* (1980: 192–6), Virginia Woolf suggests that in the body there are a multitude of different people, of personae, residing. Each has different attachments, sympathies, contributions; each makes different terms regulating its appearance. Perhaps, Woolf goes on, when people talk aloud it is because their different personae are conscious of disseverment and are trying to communicate; when the attempt has been made, they fall silent again. Besides a hypothesis concerning the multiple self to which I would also subscribe (cf. Rapport 1993), Woolf introduces an interpretation of speech-acts which posits a vital link between what is said and what goes on inside the head and body of the speaker. Speech is a continuation of thinking through (and living in) personae by other means; speech is a translation of cognitive activity, of the flow of consciousness, which otherwise operates internally and in silence. What breaks through the surface of the body are fragments, the pinnacles of individual mind, while the extensive connecting landscape of significant space remains hidden, and mute, below.

What Woolf has mooted novelistically, George Steiner posits more technically. Communication of information between different people is perhaps only a secondary part of discourse, Steiner suggests (1975: 473). Internal conversation within and between selves is primary, and prior to any (short-lived) externalisation; and much linguistic expression is focused inward. Not only does this lead to a proliferation of languages, often mutually incomprehensible, but also an ironical playing with incomprehension as a means of realising and expressing individuation.

More precisely: 'the totality of human linguistic production, the sum of all significant lexical and syntactical units generated by human beings, can be divided into two portions: audible and inaudible, voiced and unvoiced' (Steiner 1978: 91). The unvoiced component spans a wide arc: from the subliminal flotsam of word or sentence-fragments which are a presumable current or currency of every phenomenology of consciousness, to the highly defined and focused articulacy of the silent recitation of a learned text. Quantitatively, there is every reason to believe that human beings speak inwardly and to themselves more than outwardly to others; qualitatively, this may enact primary and essential functions of identity, testing and verifying an individual's 'being there'. Even if sounds break through the surface of the body, quantitatively and qualitatively it is better to treat these as partial and short-lived effusions, and continuations, of what are matters of internal expression and communication. As Steiner concludes: 'the major portion of all "locutionary motions", this is to say of all intentionalities of verbalization, whether audible or not, is *internalized*' (1978: 62). Analytically, at the least, this means rejecting any empirical inevitability of meaning, any objectivity, any coercive historicity or moral authority, in a language of institutional and habituated forms.

Indirection in Wanet and beyond

Far from mouthpieces of universal social structures and members of a singular community, I have described individual interactants in Wanet as aggregations of idiosyncrasies whose most vibrant and significant communities were ultimately, perhaps, private to themselves; it was within the boundaries of self that their most significant conversations perhaps took place and their most important truths resided. It was not that individuals did not attempt to communicate, rather that they both wanted to be understood (to share and compare, to boast and reaffirm experiences) and not to be understood (to protect and preserve, to maintain and celebrate individuality) at the same time. This the exchange of common Wanet behavioural forms enabled them to do, since they always mediated between the actions of the one and the interpretations of the other. Individual interactants could be described as becoming complete social entities and complete personal entities through the same process of exchange; 'society' in Wanet existed through an ongoing exchange of cultural forms and the construction of individual worlds of meaning in the same interactions at the same time (cf. Simmel 1964: 351).

If miscommunications in the village of Wanet can point up something beyond itself (and further field research in the Canadian city of St John's and the Israeli development-town of Mitzpe Ramon has suggested to me that they do), then here is an image of routine social interaction as far from neat: a picture of formal regularity, of sameness in ways of behaving, being facilitated and maintained by individual differences in ways of interpreting.

Ambiguity and irony are the keywords here (cf. Watson 1995: 94–5). Interaction is best appreciated as a muddling-through, based on possibly discordant variety; something not singular, but the aggregation of a multiplicity of private orders which collide, abut, overlap, and need not consistently coordinate or coincide; something not final, but dependent on the continual meeting of individuals through common forms; and something not direct, but representative of individual behaviours influencing one another in all manner of possibly unintentional ways. In Wilhelm von Humboldt's aphoristic summation:

> All understanding is at the same time a misunderstanding, all agreement in thought and feeling is also a parting of the ways.

References

Bateson, G. (1951) *Communication*, New York: Norton.

Berger, J. (1967) *A Fortunate Man*, London: Penguin.

Berger, P. and Luckmann, T. (1966) *The Social Construction of Reality*, New York: Doubleday.

Bernstein, B. (1972) 'A sociolinguistic approach to socialisation: with some reference to educability', in J. Gumperz and D. Hymes (eds) *Directions in Sociolinguistics*, New York: Holt Rinehart Winston.

Chesterton, G. K. (1975) *The Man Who Was Thursday*, Harmondsworth: Penguin.

Compton-Burnett, I. (1969) *Mother and Son*, London: Panther.

Devereux, G. (1978) *Ethnopsychoanalysis*, Berkeley: University of California Press.

Favret-Saada, J. (1980) *Deadly Words*, Cambridge: Cambridge University Press.

Gilsenan, M. (1976) 'Lying, honour and contradiction', in B. Kapferer (ed.) *Transaction and Meaning*, Philadelphia: ISHI.

Goffman, E. (1978) *The Presentation of Self in Everyday Life*, Harmondsworth: Penguin.

Goodenough, W. (1963) *Cooperation in Change*, New York: Sage.

Hendry, J. (1993) *Wrapping Culture: Politeness, Presentation and Power in Japan and Other Societies*, Oxford: Clarendon Press.

Murphy, R. (1972) *The Dialectics of Social Life*, London: Allen and Unwin.

Paine, R. (1971) 'A theory of patronage and brokerage', in R. Paine (ed.) *Patrons and Brokers in the East Arctic*, St John's: ISER.

Pitt-Rivers, J. (1974) *The People of the Sierra*, Chicago: University of Chicago Press.

Pocock, D. (1961) *Social Anthropology*, London: Sheed-Ward.

Rapport, N. J. (1986) 'Cedar High Farm: ambiguous symbolic boundary: an essay in anthropological intuition', in A. Cohen (ed.) *Symbolising Boundaries*, Manchester: Manchester University Press.

——(1987) *Talking Violence: An Anthropological Interpretation of Conversation in the City*, St John's: ISER.

——(1992) 'From affect to analysis: the biography of an interaction in an English village', in J. Okely and H. Callaway (eds) *Anthropology and Autobiography*, London: Routledge.

——(1993) *Diverse World-Views in an English Village*, Edinburgh: Edinburgh University Press.

——(1994) 'Trauma and ego-syntonic response: the Holocaust and the "Newfoundland Young Yids", 1985', in S. Heald and A. Duluz (eds) *Anthropology and Psychoanalysis*, London: Routledge.

——(1999), 'Context as an act of personal externalization: Gregory Bateson and the Harvey family in the English village of Wanet', in R. Dilley (ed.) *The Problem of Context*, Oxford: Berghahn.

Sapir, E. (1956) *Culture, Language and Personality*, Berkeley: University of California Press.

Simmel, G. (1964) 'How is society possible?', in *Georg Simmel*, New York: Free Press.

Steiner, G. (1967) *Language and Silence*, London: Faber.

——(1975) *After Babel*, London: Oxford University Press.

——(1978) *On Difficulty and Other Essays*, Oxford: Oxford University Press.

Watson, C. W. (1995) 'The novelist's consciousness', in A. Cohen and N. Rapport (eds) *Questions of Consciousness*, London: Routledge.

Weiner, A. (1983) 'From words to objects to magic: hard words and the boundaries of social interaction', *Man*, 18(4).
Wikan, U. (1980) *Life Among the Poor in Cairo*, London: Tavistock.
Woolf, V. (1980) *Orlando*, London: Granada.
Zaslavsky, V. (1982) *The Neo-Stalinist State*, New York: Sharpe.

Chapter 2

On the ontological status of honour

Roger Just

> In working in the Kiriwinian language, I found still some difficulty in
> writing down the statement directly in translation which at first I used to
> do in the act of taking notes. The translation often robbed the text of all its
> significant characteristics – rubbed off all its points – so that gradually I
> was led to note down certain important phrases just as they were spoken,
> in the native tongue.
>
> (Malinowski 1992 [1922]: 23)

In 'Belief and the problem of women', Edwin Ardener drew attention to
what he described as 'an interesting failing in the functionalist observational
model', namely that 'statements about observation were always added to the
ethnographer's own observations.' For Ardener this was less a criticism of
ethnographic method than its inevitable condition, but as he went on to
comment, 'The confusion had many serious consequences; in particular the
difficulty of dealing with statements that were not about "observation" at all
(relegated to "belief" and the like)' (1989: 75). In this paper I want to explore
some of the consequences of that confusion in the context of anthropological
accounts of 'honour', once the mainstay of 'Mediterranean anthropology' and
now its virtual bogey-man.[1] Like some other contributors to this volume
(particularly Rapport, Hughes-Freeland, and Sharma) I shall thus be as much
concerned with how we as anthropologists come to divine the intentions of
others as I shall be to show how, in another culture, others communicate
amongst themselves. In either case, however, we are confronting the same
question of human intersubjectivity, and it is perhaps as well to state from the
start that the two aspects of my enquiry are not far apart. As Ardener suggests,
much of what we state about others we have not derived from their statements, but from their behaviour. Similarly, much of what is communicated
between the members of any society is communicated between them not
through words but through context and action. As anthropologists, however,
as professional sense-makers of other people's sense-making (Strathern 1992),
we are accustomed to making explicit what is in reality implicit, to expressing
in language much more than is ever linguistically expressed. That in itself is

no bad thing. That, indeed, is part of our job. The trouble is that in so doing we run the risk – and I think it is a grave risk – of sometimes representing all that is implicit in action and context as if it were the explicit content of the linguistic terms that social actors habitually employ. We thus commit a twin error. On the one hand we mistranslate those terms – build into their meanings more than (and other than) their users themselves would consider them to contain; on the other hand we deny social actors the very ambiguity and indirection which, in context, their enunciation of those terms so often entails. In fact we arrive at a paradox: it is anthropologists' common human ability to pick up on what is not said that tempts them to portray those whom they study as much more baldly forthright than they are.

Let me commence my account in the time-honoured tradition of an anecdote (consider it the 'reflexive' part of my paper).

Mismatch 1: an anthropologist's honour

In 1980 I was working on the tiny Ionian Island of Meganisi for a fisherman called Alkis. We were fishing for *palamidhia*, horse-mackerel, a shoal fish that arrives somewhat irregularly to spawn in the coastal waters around Meganisi and the adjacent islands in summer, and thereafter disappears to parts unknown. When (and if) the *palamidhia* are plentiful, a ten-metre caïque such as Alkis owned requires a crew of at least three: one man to steer, one to guide the nets over the pulley on the bow and to extract the fish, and one at the aft to steer and to stack the nets as they come off the winch. Alkis and I, however, were fishing alone. I had volunteered because as a (then) young anthropologist I was delighted at the opportunity genuinely to participate in the work of a Greek villager. It was only later that I realised that I was also the only person stupid enough to accompany Alkis, for we were fishing late into the season when local weather conditions are highly changeable. Alkis had been told by other villagers not to go out, but he had pressing financial needs, and when my friends counselled me not to accompany him, I took this to be simply over-solicitousness. Besides, the opportunity to gain 'anthropological experience' was too good to miss.

One night, about midnight, after we had laid out our nets (some 1,500 metres of them, twenty-six fathoms deep, which Alkis had spent the winters of several years knitting) we were hit by a storm. Rain and fog closed in. Visibility was virtually nil. The swell in the usually placid waters off Meganisi built up to a couple of metres. The caïque which, like all caïques, had no keel, wallowed like a camel, standing on its end one minute, plunging nose-first into the sea the next, and viciously twisting between-times. I should add that caïques are decked, but have no sides to speak of, and I lost my footing several times. I first began really to worry, however, when Alkis shot off distress flares, for he was an experienced sailor, and certainly not the sort of man to ask for help if he could possibly avoid it. I was even more worried when Alkis asked

me if I could swim. In fact I am a reasonable swimmer, but I doubt if I would
have lasted long in that sea fully clothed. I confess, however, that I was utterly
petrified when Alkis cut his nets so that we could run for home, for I knew
their cost (at least in terms of a labour theory of value). But to cut a long
story short, we did make it home, with Alkis standing at the tiller as if his feet
were nailed to the deck, and the anthropologist lying flat on his belly with his
feet wrapped round the mast, vomiting profusely over the side.

The next day (of course) dawned clear and still. About mid-morning, feeling
still very ill and not a little sheepish, I went down to the quay where Alkis
was mending what was left of his nets. I set about helping. After about half an
hour a bunch of *ta pedhia*, 'the boys' (ranging in age from about eighteen to
seventy-five), wandered down.
      'Bit of a storm last night?' said one.
      Alkis said nothing. He had made a fool of himself. He had suffered as a
consequence, and he knew when to keep his mouth shut.
      Getting no response from Alkis, they turned to me.
      'Bit of a storm last night?'
      'Yes,' I said.
      '*Fovithikes*? [Were you scared?]' asked one.
      'Was I scared?' I said. 'Was I scared [standard complex Greek expletive
deleted]? I have never been so [expletive deleted] scared in my [expletive
deleted] life.'
      There was absolute silence. You could have heard a fish-hook drop. Then
one of the younger men, a friend of mine, stood forward from the group and
said, 'No, Rogeri, you were not scared.'
      'Oh?' I said.
      At which point the group turned and shuffled off, visibly embarrassed.

I have thought about this episode long and hard on both personal and anthropological grounds. In point of fact I am not much inclined publicly to declare
myself a coward. I too have been socialised in what is probably a pretty
common form of male dissimulation. Clearly, however, I had adopted a rather
particular cultural idiom for my dissimulation, call it 'British', call it
'Australian', call it some combination of both – national names are, after all,
only labels for cultural habits that come from somewhere. What was significant was that in this instance they did not work, and I was seriously
misunderstood. On reflection (and I had not previously much reflected on the
matter), I guess that my willingness verbally to admit to fear, in fact verbally to
emphasise my fearfulness, rested on an unstated logic to the effect that if you
get in first, then no one can follow; that if you accuse yourself of cowardice,
then no one else can call you a coward – because, by some peculiar imputation of modesty, the admission of cowardice *amounts to* an assertion of
fearlessness. And if this all sounds like so much sloppy introspection, the fact

remains that in a Greek village what I said did not work. It took a friend of mine to stand forward from the group and to say on my behalf more or less what I should have said for myself: 'Scared? I have *never* been scared in my life.' Unfortunately I had thought 'Scared? I've never been *so* scared in my life' amounted (under the circumstances) to the same thing.

What I experienced, then, was a mismatch: not of mismatch of 'language' in the sense of lexical items ('*Fovithikes?*' can be unproblematically rendered as 'Were you scared?'), nor even a mismatch of intentions (both I and my friend had wanted to assert, in our different ways, that I had *not* been afraid, despite the fact that I *knew* I had been afraid, and that he would have been a idiot if he had not guessed that I had been afraid), but a mismatch between the socially appropriate idioms of denial – though the term 'idiom' should not be taken to imply that the mismatch was superficial, inconsequential, something that could be 'got around' in a few minutes' further discussion. The idioms were worlds apart – or at least, they were 'cultures' apart. What I experienced was, I think, an example of what Ardener referred to as the 'critical lack of fit' between one world-view and another, from which, he claimed, 'The anthropological "experience" derives' (1989: 7) – and it was an experience by which I was seriously discomfited. It was also one that made me reflect on some further matters.

It seemed to me at the time that what I had been involved in was a minor but good example of what had been referred to in the ethnography of Greece (and generally of the Mediterranean) as 'honour'. Indeed, I think it would easy to make the case – though here I shall have to be brief. 'Honour,' wrote Pitt-Rivers, who offered its most succinct formulation,

> is the value of a person in his own eyes, but also in the eyes of his society. It his estimation of his own worth, his *claim* to pride, but it is also the acknowledgment of that claim, his excellence recognised by society, his *right* to pride.
>
> (1966: 21, original emphases)

In practice it also amounts to the continual assertion of personal worth before a court of popular opinion that is always potentially hostile, since it is made up of people equally anxious to assert their own worth in a currency whose value is strictly comparative. It entails a public competition for the recognition of virtue that leaves little room for the admission of failure (cf. Peristiany 1966: 11). My performance that day on the quay was a disaster. Indeed, it was a public embarrassment – and if it speaks well of the Meganisiots that they were prepared to defend someone who did not know how to defend himself, that also rather proves my point. For them, my response had been literally disarming.

Cultural translation and the idiom of honour

If, however, the little episode on the quay that I have just described was the sort of stuff that prompted anthropologists in the 1950s, 1960s and 1970s to talk about honour (and I assert that it was), two further points should be noted. First, at no time were any of the Greek words that are standardly translated or glossed as 'honour', or which have been related to the concept of 'honour', uttered. No one spoke of honour, no one called me dishonourable, no one cried 'shame'. For all I know, my actions and character *might* have been dissected in those terms after the event, but the event itself, though largely verbal, did not employ any particular vocabulary. My recognition of it (even perhaps my misrecognition of it – for we must keep that possibility open) as being to do with 'honour' did not rely on the enunciation of any particular word or words. 'Honour' simply seemed the appropriate English-language description for a form of behaviour that struck me because it was not what I was used to within my own society, and because it coincided with other examples of behaviour proffered as illustrations of 'honour' that I had read about in the ethnographic literature.[2] Second, as I have already suggested, inasmuch as the whole episode on the quay (as I understood it) was concerned with the social necessity (though in my case, failure) of individuals to assert their possession of personal virtue (in this case bravery or fearless-ness), I too, as an Australian or an Englishman or whatever, was in the grip of that necessity. There was nothing particularly 'foreign' to me about wanting to be thought well of, or even about wanting to be credited with bravery or fearlessness. The 'foreignness' lay in the idiom, or perhaps 'style', through which that could be achieved.

Idioms and styles might sound, however, like rather flimsy sorts of differ-ence for an anthropologist to hone in on. They might seem to refer, indeed, only to superficialities of form and not to matters of substance. I would disagree, as I think would other contributors to this volume (see again Rapport, Chapter 1, and particularly Hughes-Freeland, Chapter 9); neverthe-less it is the case that Mediterranean ethnographers of the 1950s to the 1970s (ethnographers nowadays rather blithely labelled 'functionalist') had been trained to search for kinds of difference that were rather more robust. For a previous generation of British social anthropologists (their teachers) even 'culture' was wishy-washy, and the preferred object of comparative analysis had been 'social structure'.[3] But 'social structure', at least as it was understood in African contexts, seemed disappointingly lacking in the Mediterranean.[4] Fortunately there was another candidate for consideration. Evans-Pritchard's *The Nuer* might have been the paradigm study of social structure, but his earlier *Witchcraft, Oracles and Magic among the Azande* provided a brilliant model for something else: the investigation, the 'translation', of alien concepts – in Evans-Pritchard's case, *mangu* or 'witchcraft'.[5] Such translation was, of course, anything but mere verbal translation. It was not a search for appro-priate English-language terms for alien words (indeed, one could argue that 'witchcraft' was a rather bad verbal translation of *mangu* – a point of no real consequence). Rather, what was aimed at was 'cultural translation' – the slow and comprehensive description and explanation of the total social and ideational context within which such terms as *mangu* operated, so that their meaning could gradually be grasped as part of what Wittgenstein would have referred to as a 'form of life'.[6] It was the translation not of indigenous words, but of indigenous ideas and concepts, that was sought, *such ideas and concepts being evidenced as much in daily actions and in institutions as in language.* Nevertheless words remained a guide. Evans-Pritchard was clear on the point: 'the most difficult task in social anthropological fieldwork is to determine the meaning of a few key words, upon an understanding of which the success of the whole investigation depends' (1951: 80).

The phrase 'cultural translation' is nowadays somewhat passé. Nevertheless I would suggest that the aim of cultural translation served, and continues to serve, anthropology well. The exploration of the meaning of *named* alien concepts as they operate within particular interlocking matrices of institutions, ideas and practices (perhaps I should nowadays say 'as they are formed within particular discursive fields') has become a standard anthropological enterprise – think of Ilongot *liget* (Rosaldo 1980), or Dinka *jok* (Lienhardt 1961), or indeed, see Hughes-Freeland's account of Javanese *alus* in Chapter 9 of this volume. I stress 'named', however, because the existence of particular indigenous terms not only provided a pointer towards what might be worthy of investigation, but, very importantly, also seemed to provide some guarantee that what was being investigated did genuinely form part of another culture or society's apprehension of the world rather than being (like 'class' or 'religion' or even 'culture') an analytic (or ethnocentric) concept imposed on it.[7] Indeed, the existence in another culture of a number of verbally difficult-to-translate 'key words' that pointed towards the existence of a number of conceptually difficult-to-convey 'key ideas' provided anthropologists of the period with exactly the sort of robust differences between societies they sought to investigate. For the Azande who talked about *mangu*, explained events in terms of *mangu*, pointed to instances of *mangu*, it seems clear that there existed a named something out there which, whether 'real' or not, formed part of another conceptual universe.

There was nothing particularly surprising, therefore, about anthropologists fixing on 'honour' as a prime candidate for investigation when attention turned to the Mediterranean in the 1950s. The cultural translation of 'indigenous concepts' had become orthodox practice; there was a rich vocabulary of honour terms to be found throughout the Mediterranean; and honour seemed to be implicated in a variety of institutions and practices, from sheep-stealing and vendetta through to marriage negotiations and domestic hospitality, in a way that was not the case in, say, Britain or the United States. But it is at this stage that the confusion (perhaps it would be better to say 'fusion') that Ardener refers to between what anthropologists (notably foreign anthropologists) could *observe*, and what native social actors were *talking about*, starts to become troublesome, for in what might seem a quite innocent move, the tendency was for anthropologists to build into their own understanding of honour the observation of just the sort of behaviour (or just the sort of episode) of which I have given an example at the beginning of this paper, and then to present such behaviour (cumulatively, so to speak) as if it were the referent of the indigenous term (or terms) standardly translated as 'honour'. In short, the words and language of another culture appeared to provide the anthropological objects of translation *qua* 'signifiers' (in the Saussurian sense), but their 'signifieds', the 'concepts' to which they were deemed to refer (and with which 'cultural translation' was ultimately concerned), were largely constructed, or reconstructed, from the observation of behaviour.

On the face of it, this does not sound like such a bad way to proceed, and the move may have been not only innocent, but almost inevitable. After all, as Josephides states in Chapter 13 of this volume,

> In attributing intention to actors I rely on … [a] mixture of description, contextualisation, and the empathy of long-term association – with the further understanding that an interactive event should be contextualised within its antecedents and sequels as well as within the local community's cultural usages.

And since we do not have direct access to the inside of people's heads, how else could we know, or how else could we learn, what people are on about? Admittedly, in the example of 'honour behaviour' I have offered, 'honour' was not spoken of (and I deliberately chose such an example to make a point); but as I suggested, it well could have been, and generally language and behaviour come as part of the same package. A great deal of honour behaviour actually incorporates the enunciation of words for honour, so that events, and the indigenous description of events, interpenetrate. In fussing about the anthropological fusion of what can be observed, and native statements (or silences) about what it is that is being observed, am I not perhaps trying to pull apart what human activity routinely conjoins?

Mismatch 2: values and concepts

The point is that a considerable fuss has been made about anthropologists' 'translations' of the concept of honour, which now seem to please no-one, least of all those anthropologists who share in those cultures said to be characterised by honour (de Pina-Cabral 1989). Something does seem to have gone genuinely amiss, and I would contend that it relates (in part, at least) to a mismatch between what has been observed, and the 'meaning' of indigenous terms in the sense of the sort of ideas that are conjured up in the heads of social actors when they reflect on them. In fact I would go so far as to say that the problem stems from the assumption that 'honour' can be treated as a 'concept' at all – or at least, that it can be treated as anything analogous to, say, Azande witchcraft.[8] Unlike *mangu*, honour is not a named 'something out there', real or imagined. It is not an entity. Linguistic forms notwithstanding, it is an evaluation, a social judgement.[9] People may be described as having honour, or being honourable. Actions may be said to be honourable or dishonourable. But (and here I am merely restating in a different context Socrates' classical dilemma) it is only instances of behaviour judged to be honourable, or of people considered to display honour, that can be pointed to, not honour itself. For a start, this makes the 'native concept' of honour a little difficult to pin down, for it always manifests itself as a matter of opinion. Consider the following instance. One evening my host, a coffee-shop proprietor, politely suggested to Kostas, a reasonably wealthy Meganisiot sailor, that he had forgotten to pay for the round of drinks he had bought his friends – a matter of a few dollars. Furious, Kostas pulled from his wallet a 1,000 drachma note (about fifteen dollars at the time), screwed it up, flung it on the floor, and marched out. The coffee-shop proprietor was upset. 'Ah, well,' said one of Kostas' friends, 'You know Kostas, he is so *filotimos* [honourable/fond of honour].'

'Bah!' said one of Kostas' enemies, 'That wasn't *filotimo* [honour/love of honour], that was *eghoismos* [egotism].'

Who was right? Did Kostas' action instantiate the indigenous concept of *filotimo* or not? How could an ethnographer tell? Take a poll?

In a sense, however, taking a poll is exactly what we do. In the course of participant observation, and equipped with 'the empathy of long-term association' (Josephides), conventional wisdom enjoins the ethnographer to note how such words as *filotimos*, etc. are routinely used, to whom they are generally applied, in what contexts they most occur, what standard events they are invoked to explain. That is how we come to discover the meanings of alien (or simply new) concepts – and, by the way, it is presumably how native speakers themselves come to understand the terms of their own language, and how and when to use them. And we might find, for example, that in some parts of the Mediterranean to be judged honourable a man might have to murder his own daughter if she were discovered to have been seduced. Or we might find that out of family solidarity an honourable man is expected to avenge the murder of his brother (Campbell 1964). Or we might simply find that men and women are called honourable if they pay their debts, do not cheat, and don't try to leave the coffee-shop without paying for their round of drinks. As a matter of fact honour was talked about on Meganisi in just such a variety of contexts, and just such a variety of contexts are reproduced by ethnographers in their explanations and descriptions of honour. But if the meaning of honour is constructed in this way, not only does honour become simply tantamount to the list of whatever is judged in a particular society to be morally appropriate,[10] but the resultant formulation is also liable to be quite dangerous, or at least open to sincere denial. State, for example, that on Meganisi an honourable man is someone who, when accused of not paying his bill, throws down on the floor ten times the claimed amount and storms out, and in some ways, or for some people, one must have got it wrong. Worse, attempt to specify what honour is across the Mediterranean by reference to the variety of contexts in which it is invoked, and inevitably it will turn out to be a rag-bag, so that no wonder critics of honour can complain that anthropologists (or other anthropologists) have got it wrong, because where they come from (or where they have done their fieldwork) honour has got nothing to do with the chastity of women, or the sexual prowess of men, or with sheep-stealing or with vendettas – because where they come from it probably hasn't. Moreover, no wonder that critics of honour should also scratch their heads about why the Mediterranean has been written about in terms of honour when Mediterraneans are scarcely the only people on ethnographic record to worry about the chastity of women or to avenge their kinsfolk or, for that matter, to dislike being accused of not paying their bills. Build into the concept of honour the variety of things that might be judged honourable, and honour is going to end up as diverse and as uncertain as those judgements. At best one arrives, cross-culturally, at a set of normative values which does not tell us anything about honour itself and renders the 'concept' of honour virtually redundant (cf. Herzfeld 1980: 340); at worst one ends up, in the study of a single community, unifying judgements that by their very nature are the subject of social dispute.

Can we then admit that the observation of instances of what might (or might not) be judged honourable is not going to get us far, and instead try to specify what social actors themselves think honour is, what their own concept of honour is? Unfortunately this doesn't get us very far either, for a vicious circularity soon sets in. Ask a Meganisiot what it is to be *filotimos* (honourable/fond of honour) – what the word *filotimos* 'means' – and with varying degrees eloquence one will be told that it means to possess honour (*timi*), that it means to have worth (*aksia*), that it means to be honest (*endimios*), that it means to be generous and hospitable (*filoksenos*), that it means to be upright (*orthios*), that, indeed, it means to be good (*kalos*). Ask what it means to be good, or to have worth, or to be upright, and one will be told that it means to be generous, to be honest, that indeed it means to be honourable (*filotimos*) ... and so it goes. Alternatively, an example or examples of being honourable will be proffered: an honourable person, someone who is *filotimos* (or for that matter, someone who is good, *kalos*, or has worth, *aksia*), is the sort of person who, when hungry, will still give you the food from his plate if you ask for it. Nothing, by the way, is particularly surprising about this, and in a sense such questions place the native informant in much the same predicament as the foreign anthropologist. People everywhere are really not very good at defining the nature of abstract virtues (and again I refer back to Socrates' dilemma) – but on the assumption that we don't want to rocket off into the superlunary world in search of a set of Ideal Forms, we still, of course, have to assume that people know what they are saying when they call someone *filotimos*, etc. After all, if they don't, who does? Besides which, they give every appearance of understanding each other. They know how to play Wittgenstein's language game, how and when to use such terms appropriately. I, too, quite quickly learned how to use them appropriately. The problem is only that such terms don't seem to amount to much more than marks of approval or moral ticks.[11] And if such terms as *filotimos* (honourable) are not much more than moral ticks, then the investigation of the indigenous 'concept' of *filotimos* (or *timi*, or *aksia*) to which the terms presumably refer is liable to be uninteresting. Certainly it will not yield, and does not account for, all the anthropological concern that has been shown in Mediterranean honour. I would suggest, however, that there is something else that does account for it, but that its congruence with indigenous 'concepts' of honour is at best partial, while at times it is seriously out of kilter with them. Let me proceed by way of another anecdote.

Mismatch 3: values and styles

One afternoon I was sitting in the coffee-shop with an older man called Iannis. Iannis was being hospitable. He had bought me a drink, and was letting me know that if ever I had need of anything in the village, then I should turn to him for whatever it was: oil, cheese, fruit, vegetables. All I had to do was ask – he had produce in abundance. Moreover, the assistance he was offering was not just material. Should I ever find myself in any trouble, I should come to him. '*Ime edho* [I am here]', he said. In short, Iannis was offering to be my provider and protector, and to tell the truth I had become fairly used to such protestations of assistance, for I had found myself at the centre of a minor competition amongst the older men that took the form of generosity. The generosity was real enough. At one stage (in a process that remarkably resembled Sharma's account, in Chapter 7 of this volume, of gift-giving in a north Indian village), I had accumulated over a gallon of olive oil in my room (well beyond my modest needs) as a result of the continual visits of old men who clandestinely pressed a bottle on me. Nor was any notion of material recompense or the return of the gift involved. It was decidedly not a case of *do ut des*. Their reward was in the demonstration of their ability to give, and in my acknowledgment of that ability and dependence on it (cf. Herzfeld 1997: 83; 1987). But it had to be an exclusive acknowledgment and an exclusive dependence that raised them above their fellows, and I had painfully come to learn just how sensitive an issue this was, for any admission to one old man of the generosity of another was liable both to give offence and to provoke a series of dark remarks about the morally dubious nature of the Meganisiots in general, and of unnamed individuals in particular. Iannis that afternoon was thus staking out his exclusive rights to demonstrate his superior virtue, and the conversation (or rather his monologue) came to a quite dramatic head when he leant towards me across the table, slammed it resoundingly with his knuckles, and pronounced, '*Egho, Rogeri, egho ime kalos anthropos* [I, Roger, I am a good man].'

'Honour', it should be noted, was once again not mentioned, though it could have been. Iannis could have said, '*Egho, Rogeri, egho ime filotimos* [I, Roger, I am honourable]' – and plenty of other people said just that to me, along with pointing out that they were generous and hospitable (*filoksenos*), honest (*endimios*), gentlemanly (*kirios*), or a good fellow (*chiftis*). As it happened, Iannis just slammed the table, pointed to his chest, stuck out his chin, looked me straight in the eye, and firmly pronounced with every sign of conviction that he was a good man. And no amount of semantic analysis of the meaning of 'good' (or, if we want to be exact, of *kalos*) explains what was interesting, or what was (at least for some sort of an Anglo-Australian such as myself) notable about Iannis' statement. But what was notable about the state-ment (I for one found it startling) was the ability of someone actually to make it, for I have little doubt that were any one of my Melbourne anthropological colleagues, members of polite, academic, middle-class, anglophone society after all, to sit down with a comparative stranger, smash his or her knuckles on the table, and flatly assert 'I am a good person,' the result would be rather the same sort of social embarrassment that I caused when on Meganisi I said that I had never been so scared in my life – and this despite the fact that most polite, middle-class, anglophone academics are notoriously convinced of their moral virtue. In short, the ethnographic interest of Iannis' statement 'I am a good man' lay not in its 'meaning' (nor even in the self-estimation it provided), but in its utterance; not in what was said, but in that it *could* be (was even required to be) said. And I would suggest that it is the 'observation' of this sort of 'speech act', of this sort of 'performative' in Austin's terms (1962), that is tied up with what has generally been recognised and labelled by anthropologists as 'honour', and not the 'meaning' of such terms as *filotimos* etc. at all. Similarly, I would suggest that Kostas' behaviour in the coffee-shop – rather typical behaviour on Meganisi (a quickness to take offence, a dramatic gesture of disdain, a public denial of any interest in material concerns coupled with a public humiliation of an offender through the impu-tation of *his* material concern: 'I've *thrown* it away; now you *grovel* for it') – is the sort of thing that has entered into the anthropological understanding of what 'honour' is about. So, I think, does the behaviour of my old friends slip-ping around to press bottles of olive oil on me while disparaging anyone else they discovered to have done the same. Or so, finally, does the behaviour of Petros, an old man who offered me a drink one winter's evening as we sat watching television in the coffee-shop. I politely declined. That was accepted. But then, an hour later, having become engrossed in the television show, I decided that I would like a drink, and absent-mindedly called for one from the proprietor. The next second Petros picked up his glass and hurled it across the room to smash at my feet and marched out of the shop. I had slighted his hospitality. I had offended his honour – except that the proprietor, who apologised for Petros' behaviour, didn't think (or didn't *say*) that it had been honourable. He said that it had been barbarous.

As Herzfeld has recently argued in his commentary on a somewhat similar incident, whether or not behaviour such as Petros' is going to be called 'barbarism' (as opposed to a manifestation of honour) by social actors remains always a matter of context.[12] As he pithily puts it, 'Such terms [as barbarism] do not make sense in the abstract; indeed, to attempt a decontextualized definition of them violates their semantics' (1997: 48). But the indeterminacy – indeed, the very nature – of indigenous semantics aside, for the outsider, for the (foreign) anthropologist, such incidents still exemplify a quite observable propensity to behave in a particular way – a quite particular attitude towards events, a quite particular style of existence. And at least on Meganisi that style came through consistently and characteristically as a sort of elbows-out approach to life – but an elbows-out approach in which the struggle to be first and best was also the struggle to be morally first and best, and to ensure that that moral primacy was recognised by all and sundry. And it is, I think, just such behaviour, just such an attitude, just such a style, that struck ethnographers of the Mediterranean (particularly British, American and French ethnographers, whose own idioms of competition, self-assertion and moral rectitude tend, on the whole, to be more restrained).[13] We are, indeed, back to Pitt-Rivers' definition of honour:

> the value of a person in his own eyes, but also in the eyes of his society ... his estimation of his own worth, his *claim* to pride, but ... also the acknowledgment of that claim, his excellence recognised by society, his *right* to pride.
>
> (1965: 21)

But if this is a quite legitimate definition of honour, quite an accurate summation of what appears to motivate a good deal of behaviour in at least some Mediterranean societies, it must be recognised that it is not the same thing as, nor even congruent with, the actors' 'concept' of honour. It is an outsider's concept of (Mediterranean) honour, constructed from the observation of behaviour and events, not the 'translation' of an indigenous 'concept', nor even the glossing of an indigenous term. To be sure, that behaviour may in part be verbal (someone's straightforward assertion that they are a good person). Some part of that verbal behaviour may also involve the use of an indigenous vocabulary of honour ('I am an honourable man!'). But in these instances it is the performative aspect of the utterance, not the bland nature of the all-purpose virtue invoked, that really fits the anthropologist's construct – and those performative aspects are notably left out of indigenous concepts, for no one on Meganisi would be inclined to say that an honourable man was somebody who went around saying 'I am an honourable [*filotomos*] man', even though it is the Meganisiots' propensity to do just that which strikes the foreigner. In the end the indigenous concept of honour (that of an ideal value) accounts for only a small part of what has been built into the anthropological construction of honour. If I were to report that the Meganisiots thought that an honourable person was someone who always paid a debt, did not cheat, never stole, and was unstintingly generous, I am certain that the Meganisiots would say that I had got it right; but if I also said that the Meganisiots thought that an honourable person was someone who continually tried to assert his or her moral superiority at the expense of a neighbour, they would certainly say that I had got it wrong – for that is not what they hold honour to be.

Herein, then, the misrepresentation, the bastard formation, to which Ardener alludes, for we have assumed that the way people behave instantiates ideas they hold (an intellectualist fallacy), and have thus attempted to tease out from observable behaviour the 'cognitive values', the 'concepts' (Pitt-Rivers 1971: xviii) that give rise to that behaviour. Then, in a well intentioned attempt to stay true to the classifications and categories of those whom we have studied, we have presented those concepts and values – in fact largely *our* concepts for what we have observed, largely *our* evaluations of that behaviour – and placed them under *their* labels: our signifieds, their signifiers. To put the matter in a slightly different way, it is as if we had translated the observable manifestations of what Bourdieu refers to as a *habitus* (1977; 1990) into the fully conscious referents of indigenous terms. That, I should like to stress, does not invalidate our observations, nor even (with all the caveats of relativism) our evaluations of what we have observed – but it does misplace them. My own remedy would be simply to admit that in the case of honour, anthropologists are often talking a different language from the people they are studying. One advantage might be that 'honour' as an etic classification for a socially determined style of behaviour, or attitude, or predisposition, might be both freed from the Mediterranean and extended to other parts of the world, for example Melanesia.[14] Whether it would prove a useful tool remains to be seen. It would be a difficult tool, for the risk of creating stereotypes and of reduplicating many of the errors of the 'culture and personality' school would be high.[15] More modestly and perhaps more realistically, the frank recognition (in what is inescapably a relativistic discipline) that what 'we' observe as interesting about the behaviour of 'others' may be only partially accounted for by ideas that others have about themselves, would at least mean that Mediterranean peoples would not be saddled with 'values' they do not hold.

Notes

1 The study of 'honour' is now a deeply unfashionable topic, trenchantly criticised on a variety of grounds ranging from its conflation of regionally various terms and concepts in the interests of creating a false Mediterranean 'culture area', to its

concentration on the study of small-scale rural communities, its promotions of ethnocentric stereotypes, its neglect of divisions of class, gender and age, and its failure to offer any sociological or historical explanation for the occurence of ideological values it describes (e.g. Herzfeld 1980; 1984; 1987; de Pina-Cabral 1989; Goddard et al. 1994; Lever 1986; Goddard 1994).

2 In an important article written in 1980, to which this paper owes much, Michael Herzfeld reminds us that 'honour' is only a crude English-language gloss for a variety of regionally various terms whose meanings are far from identical. As the honour industry grew, however, it conflated these terms into a false unity. Herzfeld's recommendation is that anthropologists return to the careful ethnographic particularism that marked the first writings on honour, and pay more attention to linguistic differences throughout the Mediterranean. I agree. Ethnographic particularism and the close study of linguistic usages are essential, and one strays from them at one's peril. But I think that such recommendations still leave some issues untouched, for, as I shall argue, whatever 'honour' is in the Mediterranean, it is not always unpacked into language, and certainly what anthropologists have written about under the rubric of 'honour' does not necessarily relate to the meanings of indigenous terms.

3 Meyer Fortes (1970 [1951]), in a brief but pertinent account of developments in British anthropology up to 1950, summarises British structural-functionalists' dissatisfaction with the Malinowskian concept of 'culture', and the advantages of following Radcliffe-Brown in taking 'social structure' (by which was meant primarily kinship, political and legal institutions) as the basis of comparative analysis. He gives two main grounds. First, a 'global concept of culture' makes it impossible to establish a priority of importance amongst interdependent institutions. Second, and I think more importantly, '[A] culture ... has no clear-cut boundaries. But a group of people bound together within a single social structure have a boundary' (1970: 74). For the structural-functionalists, it was this boundedness that allowed for 'scientific' comparison.

4 Mediterraneanists still talked of 'social structure', but it is interesting to note just how stretched the notion became when transferred to the Mediterranean. Thus in the preface to The People of the Sierra, Pitt-Rivers defines 'social structure' as the relationship not only between interdependent institutions and groups, but between 'activities', and then slides quickly into talking about 'values' and 'beliefs' (1971 [1954]: xxv–xxvi). This is not, as he admits in the preface to the second edition, quite what Africanists had been talking about – or at least not under the rubric of 'social structure' (1971: xv–xix). Cf. Goddard et al. (1994: 8).

5 Fortes (1970 [1951]) respectfully criticizes this work precisely for its failure sufficiently to relate witchcraft to social structure, i.e. political organisation. Cf. Goddard et al., who note the 'interesting parallels between [American] cultural and [British] social anthropology' during the formative years of Mediterranean anthropology (1994: 4).

6 The phrase 'cultural translation' may have been coined by Evans-Pritchard, or it may simply have been in general currency in the 1960s and 1970s. Note, however, the title of the collection of essays edited by Beidelman and presented to Evans-Pritchard: The Translation of Culture (1973).

7 Most readers will be familiar with the situation where, in a seminar, someone elaborates a particular concept in connection with the people that he or she has worked with, only to be pointedly asked from the audinece, 'Ah, yes, but do they have a word for it?' – the implication being that if they don't, then the concept is probably not relevant. The injunction to concentrate on the meaning of indigenous words (and concepts) is perhaps most forcefully and consistently made throughout the works of Rodney Needham and Mary Douglas.

8 Pitt-Rivers' comments are again interesting, for although he (and other British Mediterraneanists) talked of 'values', he states that 'they are not in my usage purely ethical but in the first place *cognitive* values, *concepts* whose ethical content is built into them and becomes apparent only according to context, as part of the ethnography ...' (1971: xviii, my emphases). As Pitt-Rivers makes clear, such values are not explicitly stated, but rather revealed in action; nevertheless, the anthropological aim remained one of arriving at something explicit ('cognitive values', 'concepts'). Indeed, Pitt-Rivers goes on to explain that he was led to investigate 'values' in Andalusia precisely because the Andalusians, unlike 'Africans', did not readily state their customs, belief and norms.

9 Greek speakers do routinely use substantives for honour, and will argue whether or not someone does, or does not 'have honour', but nothing in this makes me think that Greek-speakers conceive of honour as any sort of entity (substantial or insubstantial).

10 In the introduction to the edited volume that launched 'honour' as the dominant theme of Mediterranean anthropology, Peristiany himself raises this problem:

> A study of the value judgements concerning honour and shame involves the study of the supreme temporal ideals of a society and of their embodiment in the ideal type of man ... This way of reasoning can only lead to the conclusion that as all societies evaluate conduct by comparing it to ideal standards of action, all societies have their own forms of honour and shame. Indeed they have.
>
> (1966: 10)

Peristiany goes on to say that honour and shame are nevertheless 'the preoccupation of individuals in small scale, exclusive societies where face to face personal, as opposed to anonymous, relations are of paramount importance and where the social personality of the actor is as significant as his office' (1966: 11). Even with this qualification, however, Peristiany's definition of honour and shame could not be seen as particular to the Mediterranean – and indeed, perhaps he did not intend it to be so. For discussion and criticism of the subsequent tendency to see honour and shame as intrinsic to the construction of a Mediterranean 'culture area', see Herzfeld (1980; 1984), de Pina-Cabral (1989), Goddard *et al.* (1994), Goddard (1994); cf. Cole (1977), Boissevain *et al.* (1979).

11 I am not here committing myself to any philosophical position on a second-order ethical question (Mackie 1977: 9); nor am I claiming that the 'meanings' of the Greek terms mentioned above are identical. They are not – as simple substitution test will show. I am, however, suggesting that in practice, in common *social* usage, the attribution of the term *filotimos* carries with it a very generalised sense of commendation. That, indeed, is why Peristiany can state that a study of honour and shame 'involves the study of the supreme temporal ideals of a society and of their embodiment in the ideal type of man' (see note 10 above).

12 The choice of classification relates to what Herzfeld terms 'disemia' – 'the formal or coded tension between official self-presentation and what goes on in the privacy of collective introspection' (1997: 14) – whose manipulation constitutes part of what Herzfeld calls 'social poetics'. For a fuller account of these concepts (and their development in Herzfeld's work), see particularly Herzfeld 1985; 1987; 1992; 1997.

13 de Pina-Cabral astutely comments,

> One is ... tempted to think that one of the reasons middle-class and upper-middle-class young Anglo-American scholars are so deeply impressed with

the agonistic display of malehood among southern European peasants is that they are so ignorant of working-class behaviour in their own countries of origin.

(1989: 402)

Quite so – but this does not deny the existence of such display.

14 Which may well have been the original intention of the Mediterraneanists who launched 'honour and shame' – see Peristiany's comment cited in note 10 above, and the suggestive observation by Pitt-Rivers that 'the early anthropologists might well have translated the word *mana* as *honour*' (Pitt-Rivers 1977: 13, cited Herzfeld 1980).

15 It would, historically, be interesting to know just how much (if at all) early Mediterraneanists' notions of honour and shame were influenced by Benedict's *The Chrysanthemum and the Sword*. To the best of my knowledge, however, acknowledgements were not made.

References

Ardener, E. (1989) 'Belief and the problem of women', in M. Chapman (ed.) *Edwin Ardener: The Voice of Prophecy and Other Essays*, Oxford: Blackwell, pp. 72–85.

Austin, J. L. (1962) *How To Do Things With Words*, Cambridge MA: Harvard University Presss.

Beidelman, T. (ed.) (1973) *The Translation of Culture: Essays to E. E. Evans-Pritchard*, London: Tavistock.

Benedict, R. (1947) *The Chrysanthemum and the Sword: Patterns of Japanese Culture*, London: Secker and Warburg.

Boissevain, J. (1979) 'Towards a social anthropology of the Mediterranean' (published together with 'Comments' by Aceves, Beckett, Brandes, Crump, Davis, Gilmore, Griffin, Padiglione, Pitt-Rivers, Schonegger, Wade, and a 'Reply' by Boissevain) *Current Anthropology*, 20(1): 81–93.

Bourdieu, P. (1977) *Outline of a Theory of Practice*, trans. R. Nice, Cambridge: Cambridge University Press.

——(1990) *In Other Words: Essays towards a Reflexive Sociology*, Stanford: Stanford University Press.

Campbell, J. K. (1964) *Honour, Family, and Patronage: A Study of Institutions and Moral Values in a Greek Mountain Community*, Oxford: Oxford University Press.

Cole, J. W. (1977) 'Anthropology comes part-way home: community studies in Europe', *Annual Review of Anthropology*, 6: 349–78.

Coombe, R. J. (1990) 'Barren ground: re-conceiving honour and shame in the field of Mediterranean ethnography', *Anthropologica* 32: 221–38.

Evans-Pritchard, E. E. (1937) *Witchcraft, Oracles and Magic Among the Azande*, Oxford: Clarendon Press.

——(1940) *The Nuer: A Description of the Modes of Livelihood and Political Institutions of a Nilotic People*, Oxford: Clarendon Press.

——(1951) *Social Anthropology*, London: Cohen & West.

Fortes, M. (1970) [1951] 'The structure of unilineal descent groups', in *Time and Social Structure and Other Essays*, London: Athlone Press.

Goddard, V. (1994) 'From the Mediterranean to Europe: honour, kinship and gender', in V. Goddard, J. R. Llobera and C. Shore (eds) *The Anthropology of Europe: Identities and Boundaries in Conflict*, Oxford: Berg.

Goddard, V., Llobera, J. R. and Shore, C. (eds) (1994) 'Introduction: the anthropology of Europe', in V. Goddard, J. R. Llobera and C. Shore (eds) *The Anthropology of Europe: Identities and Boundaries in Conflict*, Oxford: Berg.

Herzfeld, M. (1980) 'Honour and shame: problems in the comparative analysis of moral systems', *Man* (n.s.) 15: 339–51.

——(1984) 'The horns of the Mediterraneanist dilemma', *American Ethnologist*, 11: 439–54.

——(1985) *The Poetics of Manhood: Contest and Identity in a Greek Mountain Village*, Princeton: Princeton University Press.

——(1987a) *Anthropology Through the Looking-Glass: Critical Ethnography on the Margins of Europe*, Cambridge: Cambridge University Press.

——(1987b) ' "As in your own house": hospitality, ethnography, and the stereotypes of Mediterranean society', in D. Gilmore (ed.) *Honour and Shame and the Unity of the Mediterranean*, special publication of the American Anthropological Association, no. 22: 75–88, Washington.

——(1997) *Cultural Intimacy: Social Poetics in the Nation-State*, London: Routledge.

Lever, A. (1986) 'Honour as a red herring', *Critique of Anthropology*, 6(3): 83–106.

Lienhardt, G. R. (1961) *Divinity and Experience: The Religion of the Dinka*, Oxford: Clarendon Press.

Mackie, J. L. (1977) *Ethics: Inventing Right and Wrong*, Harmondsworth: Penguin.

Peristiany, J. G. (ed.) (1966) *Honour and Shame: The Values of Mediterranean Society*, Chicago: University of Chicago Press.

Pina-Cabral, J. de (1989) 'The Mediterranean as a category of regional comparison', *Current Anthropology*, 30(3): 399–406.

Pitt-Rivers, J. (1966) 'Honour and social status', in J. G. Persitiany (ed.) *Honour and Shame: The Values of Mediterranean Society*, Chicago: University of Chicago Press.

——(1971) [1954] *The People of the Sierra*, Chicago: University of Chicago Press.

——(1977) *The Fate of Schechem or the Politics of Sex: Essays in the Anthropology of the Mediterranean*, Cambridge: Cambridge University Press.

Rosaldo, M. Z. (1980) *Knowledge and Passion: Ilongot Notions of Self and Social Life*, Cambridge: Cambridge University Press.

Strathern, Marilyn (1992) unpublished conference paper.

Chapter 3

Not talking about sex in India

Indirection and the communication of bodily intention

Helen Lambert

Let's talk about sex, baby
Let's talk about you and me
Let's talk about all the good things and the bad things that may be –
Let's talk about sex

(Salt 'n' Pepa)

Talking about sex is a taboo in India.

(Solomon *et al.* 1998: 102)

The title of this chapter plays on the words of a successful rap song, excerpted above, which sprang unbidden to mind as I reflected on some recent experiences supervising a pair of rapid studies of sexual relations and sexual health in two Indian cities;[1] the second quotation is from a paper on the epidemiology of HIV in southern India, found long after the chapter was first drafted. My starting point for the following reflections is an observed tension between the drive to develop culturally appropriate and locally effective strategies for the control of HIV in South Asia, and the employment of discourses about sexuality and sexual behaviour that are new to the contexts within which these strategies are being implemented. In this chapter a gendered analysis of the place of 'talk' in sexual relations will attempt to elucidate the ways in which our dependence as anthropologists on language may not only obscure, but actually transform local conceptions of sexuality and sexual relationships.

Probably the most frequently identified obstacle to the control of HIV transmission and promotion of sexual health in India is that public acknowledgement or discussion of sex and sexuality is strongly disfavoured. Commentators on these matters agree – with remarkable unanimity and without qualification – that sex cannot be spoken about; the quotation at the beginning of the chapter from a paper on prevalence and risk factors for HIV infection in Tamil Nadu (Solomon *et al.* 1998: 102) and a comment such as, 'open discussions about sex and sexual matters remain taboo' in a recent article on the effects of HIV testing and counselling on behaviour (Bentley *et al.* 1998: 1870) are typical examples. While in no way seeking to refute the indisputable evidence that public discussion of matters sexual is indeed highly problematic, this chapter investigates the grounds for these broad assertions from several directions – not least because silence or refusal to talk may be just as illuminating as what is said. A brief introduction to some essential background on the situation with regard to HIV and other sexually transmitted diseases in India, and on governmental and societal responses to HIV over the past decade, prefaces a consideration of dominant contemporary discourses about sex and sexuality in India. Here, public affirmation of the phenomenon of 'not talking about sex' is analysed as a politically and historically situated meta-commentary on the rectitude of Indian society. Language about sexual relations in a variety of specific social contexts is then considered, with indirection and allusion emerging as dominant modes of linguistic communication in everyday speech, while those verbal references to sex and sexual relations that are more direct are shown to be framed temporally, spatially and linguistically by the use of particular oral genres which are deployed in particular settings on specific types of occasion. Third, the extent to which speech tends – in both anthropology and public health – to be conflated with and taken to encompass communicative forms in general is discussed, via a consideration of different forms of non-linguistic communication. Finally, some observations on the possible transformational consequences of the use of 'scientific' and other languages, and on the interpretation of discourses relating sexuality to health, draw out methodological and theoretical issues that may be of more general importance with respect to studies of, and talk about, sex, health and bodily practices in the subcontinent and elsewhere.

Context-setting: HIV in India

The HIV epidemic in South Asia is projected as the fastest rising in the world (Bollinger *et al.* 1995) and with a population of almost one billion people, India was expected to have more infected people by the year 2000 than any other single country, the numbers being currently estimated at more than 1.5 million. There are major apparent variations in the degree to which HIV is established in different populations and parts of the country, ranging from 40–50 per cent in female commercial sex workers in cities such as Bombay and Pune, and up to 36 per cent among patients at sexually transmitted disease clinics, to less than 0.1 per cent among pregnant women in many states. The epidemic focus in Manipur and the north-eastern states is largely related to intravenous drug use in heroin addicts, but elsewhere the majority of cases of HIV are acquired by heterosexual contact. Although a wide range of sexualities and types of sexual relationship are in fact to be found in India (as in most other places) they have as yet been little documented, and while this chapter seeks to consider issues pertaining generally to sexual discourses and practices, to the extent that it considers particular forms of sexual relation, my focus is essentially confined to consideration of the normative – that is, to heterosexual sex and gender relations.

The first AIDS case in India was reported in May 1986 (NACO 1994), and several female sex workers were diagnosed as HIV positive shortly thereafter. An HIV quarantine law was passed and there were calls to screen foreigners and to repatriate African students found to be HIV positive. The initial government response was to deny the possibility of the epidemic taking hold within India, due to its 'traditional' values, by which was meant the strong emphasis on chastity and on sex as being contained exclusively within marriage. With growing evidence of the rapid increases in prevalence of HIV and increasing concern among international donor agencies, however, the Indian Government was eventually forced to make some response. The International Monetary Fund attached to its economic rescue package the condition that India institute an active AIDS control programme, and the National AIDS Control Organization (NACO) was established in 1992 with assistance from the World Bank. At this stage AIDS Cells were set up in each state of the country (NACO 1994), but despite active efforts from the centre, functioning surveillance systems have only been maintained in a few sites. This means that it is extremely difficult to monitor the epidemic, and only around 70,000 HIV infections had been reported officially by 1997, though it is accepted that the real figure is much higher than this.

Although there are now active AIDS prevention efforts in many parts of the country, disputes over projections as to the likely scale of the HIV epidemic in India, continuing failures to spend the generous budgets allocated to AIDS prevention activities, and inaction in many places around developing such activities, illustrate a continuing ambivalence about such efforts and point to an ongoing tension between recognition of the potential seriousness of the HIV problem and dominant discourses about both the nature of Indian society and its relations with the West. The complexities of national and international relations in shaping the debate about the impact of AIDS in India can be alluded to only briefly here, but it is clear that strongly nationalistic views which were developed through the experience, and rejection, of colonialism, have continued to inform both independent India's economic policies and the state's attitude to Western influence in all its forms. Despite – or perhaps in reaction to – the recent (partially externally imposed) transition towards free market capitalism, growing liberalisation and the lowering of bureaucratic controls, there is ambivalence in many quarters about the influence of international agencies in setting health policy and other agendas. A dispute between NACO and UNAIDS which occurred relatively recently over the likely numbers of HIV-affected people in India (leading to a newspaper headline, 'The AIDS scare in India could be aid-induced' [Mohan 1996]) could be analysed in Foucauldian terms as bearing hallmarks of resistance to the imposition of monitoring and surveillance from the centre, a characterisation of international relations which could also be applied to federal relations within India between central and state governments in the health sector.

Beyond the political economic shaping of health policies, however, another set of dominant discourses profoundly influences responses to the HIV epidemic. Appeals to 'traditional' values which greeted the advent of AIDS in India a decade ago have been mentioned; the public image of Indian society revolves around the alleged moral quality of indigenous culture. The representation of Indian culture as 'moral' is also posed as an explicit counterpoint to popular perceptions of Western society as immoral and degenerate, particularly with respect to a putatively rampant and indiscriminate sexual promiscuity. This contrast provides a neat inversion of the situation described by Parkes in Chapter 14 of this volume for the Kalasha, who (as a cultural minority) represent themselves as engaged in a 'rude reversal' of the social norms of their Khó neighbours. In India, the spread of HIV is frequently and explicitly associated not just with western influences but with the presence of Western foreigners. For example, popular perceptions in southern Kerala hold that commercial sex and the threat of HIV are both prevalent in the popular beach resort of Kovalam due to the presence of European tourists – despite clear evidence that the limited amount of prostitution which does exist is almost exclusively directed at, and confined to, Indian male tourists visiting the area. Again, a furore greeted the revelation in Rajasthan that a male camel driver working in the tourist industry around Jaisalmer had tested HIV positive, the presumption being that such men expose themselves to risk by having sexual contact with European women. (This is not, of course, to suggest that such risks do not exist, but rather that their public prominence in this case was out of all proportion to their scale relative to the risks of sexual contact with non-foreigners.) There is no space here to detail the colonial history which has shaped these representations within India, but it is certainly plausible to consider whether the often explicitly made contemporary contrast between the putatively promiscuous and individualistic West and the moral integrity of Indian society is not itself a response to earlier orientalist representations of native society – and particularly Hinduism – as morally degenerate, heathen and degraded.

The moral integrity of Indian society is popularly held to reside largely in the sexual virtue (read chastity) of women. Despite the breadth of evidence for an enormous range of variation in local cultures and social formations across the subcontinent, sociological and anthropological studies have in their turn largely replicated Indian – and particularly Hindu – self-representations of India as possessed of a profoundly sexually chaste culture in which the honour of women and the institution of the family are generally pre-eminent. Attention has also been given, particularly by historians, to 'subalterneity', and among feminist scholars to the negative aspects of the Brahmanic emphasis on women as the repositories of caste integrity and family honour in contributing to female subordination. The organisation of gender hierarchy has been linked to the cultural definition of female sexuality as all-devouring and destructive, and early universal marriage of women and continuous control by men over women within patriarchal family structures are seen as institutionalised solutions to the 'problem' of female sexuality (Ramasubban 1992). Most anthropological studies of sexuality and sexual relations in India have, accordingly, been subsumed into broader social structural considerations of kinship and marriage, or subordinated to cultural analyses of the caste and religious ideologies which are held to determine gender relations. This subordination of matters sexual to normative systems and ideologies may not be particular to India; Tuzin (1991) provides a historical reading of anthropology's engagement with matters sexual to argue that this indirection towards the topic is characteristic of the discipline's approach over the past sixty years.

Nevertheless, contemporary social mores concerning (hetero)sexual relations as a form of gender relations certainly have their own materiality. The frequent characterisations of Indian women as repressed and submissive have been contested as only partial truths by feminist scholars anxious to recover the 'voices' of the oppressed and to demonstrate the existence of alternative modes of expression indicative of resistance to patriarchal norms. AIDS campaigners, however, have been quick to point to the difficulties of, for example, promoting condom use for HIV prevention. In a social context in which condoms have been heavily – but largely unsuccessfully – promoted as family planning tools, strict marital monogamy is a normative standard largely applied in practice only to women, and women's generally subordinate status means that there is little potential for them to assert control over their sexual and reproductive health. In such an environment, the associations of HIV and other sexually transmitted diseases with moral pollution and societal degeneration render acknowledgement of the presence of this epidemic in India, and engagement with it as a *health* problem, particularly fraught.

The insertion of anthropology into public health

One reason for the relatively slow pace at which HIV prevention activities have been initiated (though as indicated in the previous section, by no means the only one) is a lack of knowledge concerning the extent to which local populations are vulnerable to the spread of HIV, since so little is known about either sexual behaviour and networks, or about the prevalence of sexually transmitted infections.[2] In consequence, initiatives (such as, for instance, health education or promotion of condom use among sex workers) tend to be set up either on the basis of pre-existing assumptions or by using what are often inappropriate models imported from elsewhere, rather than on accurate knowledge of the local situation. There is a growing demand within international health generally for anthropologically informed studies to help develop locally appropriate prevention and control programmes, and this applies to the case of sexually transmitted diseases and HIV in India as elsewhere. This sensitivity to 'local culture' and the associated development of a range of increasingly systematised methods for gathering sociocultural data, has come about after decades of failure to successfully implement potentially useful 'biomedical' solutions to public health problems. Anthropologists were first enlisted when it was realised that imported technical 'fixes' could not successfully be introduced into new contexts without taking into account existing local understandings of and cultural resources for dealing with the health problem in question. In response, various approaches to the rapid collection of qualitative data – some formally dignified by acronyms such as RAP ('Rapid Anthropological Procedures'), FES ('Focused Ethnographic Studies') or REA ('Rapid Ethnographic Assessment') – have been developed for use in the limited time frames usually available for conducting research before a health intervention is initiated, with guidelines provided in the form of handbooks or manuals (see Herman and Bentley [1992] and Manderson and Aaby [1992] for discussions of this trend). In such approaches, investigation usually focuses on the local terminologies (vocabularies) used to refer to the symptoms, diseases and behaviours of interest and on people's treatment-seeking patterns. A further additional stimulus to the use of both qualitative research and anthropological involvement in international health has been the advent of AIDS, due to its inherent links with the unarguably sensitive subjects of sex and sexuality, together with the absence of any obvious possibilities for control of the epidemic other than through behavioural change.

My exposure to applied anthropology of this sort has entailed working over the past two years with a multidisciplinary India- and UK-based team of researchers on the development of a methodology for carrying out what has come to be known as 'SASHI' ('Situational Analysis of Sexual Health in India'), a strategy for collecting information that can be used to prioritise and design locally appropriate HIV and STD prevention and sexual health promotion projects. This methodology has been piloted by local research teams in two sites in Gujarat and Kerala, since part of the intention is that local researchers can undertake the necessary research themselves. Our methodology differs from some of the rapid assessment procedures mentioned above, in that it includes not only elements which might be called anthropological but also clinical and epidemiological components to assess the prevalence of sexually transmitted infections, as well as other sociological work on treatment providers and their services. My reflections here, though, concern only those components which seek to investigate sexuality and sexual behaviour.

Although neither our methodology nor indeed many other examples of rapid assessment are dignified by an acronym specifically denoting a form of rapid anthropological research, all such procedures share certain features by dint of the fact that they are necessarily all forms of applied social research directed at producing usable information in a relatively short time frame.

These characteristics largely result from methodological and practical constraints. In the case of work on sexual health, the almost universally private character of sexual acts in particular means that they cannot be directly observed, and participant observation is generally impossible (cf. Friedl 1994; Tuzin 1991: 870) or ethically dubious; while the need to produce information relatively rapidly for use in the design of AIDS prevention initiatives means that the traditional strategy of long-term ethnographic fieldwork is arguably too slow to utilise for applied purposes (cf. Manderson *et al.* 1996: 5). As a result, the information collected in rapid assessments, particularly on these topics but also more generally on other health problems, is almost exclusively derived from people's *accounts* of what goes on, rather than also from knowledge of what actually does go on. The consequent separation from the everyday situations within and through which more traditional ethnographic material is conventionally collected, tends to privilege the production of cognitive models which are divorced from the selective and particular utilisation of local understandings in practice, yet are taken to be predictive of actual behaviour. More critically for the present argument, these anthropological procedures also come to endorse implicitly a model of culture and human behaviour as being represented directly in language.[3]

Talking about sex indirectly

What then if verbal accounts are not readily elicited or expressed? Most verbal references to sex and sexuality in India are, indeed, highly allusive. In northern India, sexual intercourse is referred to euphemistically, through terms such as 'meeting' (*milna*), 'sitting' (*baithna*) or 'conversing' (*bacit*). Women are decidedly more reluctant than men to describe these and other sexual encounters in directly referential terms. Nirmala Murthy's (1998) study of sexuality and sexual behaviour among youth in three Indian cities offers some interesting observations about the research process in this respect. Many of the female respondents initially approached were deeply suspicious of the intentions of the researchers and the purpose of the investigation, either refusing explicitly to participate or failing to turn up to appointments. Finally girls had to be recruited through the college authorities via a sympathetic psychology professor, and those prepared to be involved asked for their parents not to be approached directly for permission. The boys, on the other hand, were recruited directly through peer networks, and the main problem was to retain their interest in the study. The issue of verbalisation is particularly pertinent: in a 'free listing' exercise of terms to describe 'what is sexual behaviour', the boys tended to report words verbally while the girls wrote them down because they felt uncomfortable in verbalising them. Similarly, the boys tended to compete in trying to produce as long a list as possible, whereas the girls had to be prompted, and many said that they knew the behaviours but could not express them in words. In later work, which involved developing scenarios to illustrate particular forms of sexual behaviour, the boys talked about their own patterns of behaviour as well as those of friends and neighbours, asserting that they often talked about such things amongst themselves anyway. The girls, on the other hand, unanimously described scenarios concerning friends, neighbours or other girls in their college, never using themselves as examples.

What this appears to suggest is either that girls and women seem to lack a language with which to talk about sex and sexuality directly; or, that the implications of verbalisation so unequivocally associate the speaker with the activities being referred to, that women are socially constrained not to speak of them explicitly. Some support is lent to the former hypothesis by Murthy's observation that girls 'knew' the relevant behaviours but did not have words for them, and also by Das's account of the socialisation of Punjabi girls, in which she describes how taboos regarding menstruation are communicated entirely without speech, and how 'one of the most important ways in which women must learn to communicate is by non-verbal gestures, intonation of speech, and reading meta-messages in ordinary languages' (1988: 198). Das notes that menstruation is the first event which reveals to girls that 'women must never use words which make emotions explicit ... or subvert the authority of the ordering principles of language and law, especially in domains that include relations between men and women'. Conversely, support is lent to the alternative hypothesis that women are socially constrained not to speak of sexual relations and sexuality explicitly by Annie George's (1997) study of a slum community in Bombay, which reported that the topic of sexual needs, preferences and pleasures was the one which women felt most uncomfortable talking about. She notes that women felt it was not appropriate — that it would jeopardise their honour — to admit to having sexual feelings. It was considered 'improper' to talk about sexual needs or to express sexual feelings to husbands, in some cases because such behaviour may give rise to suspicions about the woman's general conduct. This is remarkably reminiscent of Susan Gal's analysis of women in the French Revolution, who supported the revolutionary cause but could not actively participate in discussion at political meetings due to fear of offending social propriety, as being offered 'either speech or respect, but not both' (1991: 180–1).

It is certainly suggestive that sexual intercourse between a husband and wife is frequently referred to among women in northern India by the terms *bacit* (converse) or *bat karna*, to speak. Here, we find a direct inversion of the kinds of data that are sought in interrogating subjects about their sexual lives; the metaphor of verbal communication is used in order to express physical intimacy. The symbolic association between verbal communication and intimacy between speakers is consistent with the prohibition which is part of the social institution of *parda* (purdah) in this region, against women not only being seen by, but also speaking to, men in certain categories of relatedness. In situations where communication with prohibited categories of kin is unavoidable, women always respond to such a man's request or enquiry indirectly by conveying a reply via any other suitable person who happens to be present, where necessary (as for example when the only person available is a young child) in a stage whisper. If talk implies intimacy, then not talking clearly communicates a lack of it, and this is consistent with the strong constraints on explicit discussion of sex by women as an element of maintaining social propriety.

As illustrated by this example, silence can be expressive, and generalisations regarding interactions between men and women in terms of women's 'silence' or 'inarticulacy' allow little space for the existence of a variety of non-verbal forms of communication and understanding, or for highly context-specific variations in language use. Hence Das, in the same article cited earlier, goes on to suggest that the 'rules' that place women outside the realm of formal communication may be broken among women themselves, albeit in highly indirect forms, such as the situation in which a woman failing to conceive was advised by her sister-in-law to 'exchange her quilt'. In situations in which women's status depends greatly upon the preservation of honour and the appearance of respectability, the verbalisation of sexual disposition and intent in direct ways may be highly inappropriate and even risky communicative strategies for women. Intentionality with respect to sexual desire – or lack of it – is largely expressed indirectly, not only through the use of verbal euphemism, allusion, substitution (whispers ostensibly directed to others) and avoidance (silence) but through a range of bodily communications, discussed in the next section.

Further support is lent to the hypothesis that women at least do not so much lack a language for verbalising matters relating to sex but rather do not usually express such things publicly in ordinary speech, by work on women's oral genres. Ann Gold's (1994) analysis of Rajasthani folk songs, for example, demonstrates that within particular genres of song, explicit sexual references both to body parts and to sexual acts are entirely acceptable – these songs are most often performed at the time of marriage and are directed as insults at affinal relatives. As Susan Gal has observed, however, the intention to discover women's 'voices' too often becomes synonymous with women's 'conscious-ness' so that silences or lack of literal voice get identified with subordination and 'mutedness'. The identification of particular oral traditions in which women verbally express sentiments apparently counter to prevailing social norms tends to take on undue prominence as evidence, while the role of silence and non-verbal communication is ignored. As Lutzen comments in relation to historical research, 'the study of sexuality is not only a study of "La mise en discours" – but also of silence' (1995: 27), in which refusal to talk about certain areas can be just as interesting as what is said. The political 'silence' around the AIDS epidemic which for a long time characterised the Indian governmental response, further exemplifies this point.

Not talking about sex: non-linguistic communication

The existence and expression, within Rajasthani folk songs or other strands of popular culture, of linguistic terms to denote sexual parts and activities, only demonstrates with surety that within certain socially prescribed contexts – within which, notably, men and women are physically distanced from one another in single-sex groups – it is permissable to describe sexual relations and acts explicitly. These communicative acts, while comprising verbal forms, are also marked off from everyday language through the use of particular registers which are evoked in certain socially specified contexts, such as the song genres previously mentioned, wedding jokes, or the bawdy dramas that are enacted in domestic settings prior to marriage and in public at certain times of year in association with religious performances. In other situations, however, these registers would be inappropriate and ordinary verbal commu-nication about sexual activity may be entirely impermissible. More evocative, to me, of local resonances regarding sexuality than the explicit terms used in bawdy songs is Gold's discussion (1994: 47–52) of Rajasthani song variants which describe the erotic uses and implications of the wrap or veil (*orhni*), a characteristic item of clothing generally taken by outsiders to express women's subordination. As a village ethnographer in Rajasthan, the multiple meanings of veiling were gradually revealed to me as, having initially seen only the uniform facelessness of in-married women with their covered faces, I slowly acquired the ability to 'read' visually the multiple messages indicating demeanour, age, caste affiliation, relative status and kin relation to others in the immediate vicinity and affect, in the positioning and constant subtle manipulation of the *orhni*. Although one element which I did not experience directly was that of erotic sensibility, I have no doubt whatsoever as to the enormous communicative possibilities of 'veiling' in this respect. Recollecting this socialised visual apprehension led me in turn to reflect on the apparently banal assertions of male informants in one of our recent pilot studies of the SASHI methodology, that prostitutes are instantly recognisable by their dress – the colour of their saris and blouses, the style of their hair and jewellery. Initially the local researchers who carried out fieldwork could not 'see' these women at all, but once identified, the visual notification of their working identities became entirely self-evident. These observations strengthen a growing conviction that the difficulties which the local research teams in both of our studies experienced in attempting to gather information about sexual behaviour may not have been due so much to the relative youth and lack of ethnographic experience of the fieldworkers, as to the inherent inaccessibility of this domain of social experience through the sort of language that the applied purposes of our research required. Other non-verbal modes for communicating about sex are common, from the palm-slapping employed by hijras ('transsexuals' or those of the 'third sex' who are predominantly male in origin but may undergo castration, dress as women and live together in segregated groups) specifically to denote sexual intercourse, to the subtle arrangements of eye contact, posture and clothing which can be employed to signal slight but intensely significant departures from the normative expression of non-erotic social relations between men and women (cf. Osella and Osella [1998] on flirting among boys and girls in Kerala).

These observations suggest not that the relative 'mutedness' of sexual behaviour and sexuality relates to something that is not generally known or recognised, but rather that it may not be expressed directly in speech. Certainly my experiences in a Rajasthani village hardly support a presumption that states of sexual intimacy are fully concealed. The closest I ever came to an explicit account of sexual infidelity was from a group of women whom I encountered gossiping in a courtyard one day when I came by to visit; the barely suppressed hilarity with which a reported sighting of illicit sex was being discussed suggested a rather different attitude from that given in most anthropological accounts regarding the moral weight placed on marital monogamy. This, however, was a rare experience; generally, matters pertaining to sex were not spoken of directly, although as suggested above, allusive references and deliberately suggestive comments in the context of conversations about children, for example, made it very clear that there was general appreciation amongst women at least of both the pleasures and the illicit quality of sexual activity. As noted by Sharma (Chapter 7 in this volume), in contexts where complete privacy is hard to accomplish, conventions maintain a façade of ignorance; in Friedl's words, 'Symbolic seclusion through civil inattention reigns when actual privacy cannot be managed' (1994: 834).

Talking about sex through talking about health

To argue that individuals are constrained not to discuss sexuality openly, rather than that they lack a language in which to do so, does not mean that there is a ready-made set of verbal constructs ready for use which are simply avoided. The injunctions on qualitative researchers in 'rapid assessment' manuals to ascertain 'local terms and vocabularies' for use in appropriate health education messages, assumes that the relevant terms are actually readily available in local language. In our own recent work, this often proved not to be the case. While various slang words could be found, these are no more likely to be appropriate for the purpose of sexual health promotion than the terms 'pussy' or 'cunt' would be in English. Moreover, even among the researchers undertaking the data collection for our studies, many of these words were simply not known, at least to the younger women, while the more esoteric, formal terms in Gujarati or Malayalam were just not used in everyday speech. Male as well as female informants were reluctant to describe events and phenomena relating to sex explicitly, and an elaborate vocabulary appeared to be absent. Among both the researchers and many of their male informants, the use of English words to describe both sexual behaviour and those engaging in it was striking. Reciprocally, very similar difficulties with finding appropriate vernacular terms were reported in a study that attempted to determine appropriate methodologies for studying sexual behaviour in India (Basu 1994).

These observations contribute to the contention that avoidance or indirection are the usual speech forms for communicating about sex, such that the use of a foreign vocabulary is easier than using one's own language, particularly where verbalisation of matters concerning sex tend to attribute to the speaker personal experience of these matters (as described previously with respect to women's reticence). This resonates intriguingly with the case described by Josephides (Chapter 13 in this volume) of code-switching between different languages in which the use of non-indigenous vocabulary provides a powerful alternative; English in India has comparable associations with accomplishment and prestige, such that familiarity with relevant technical terms (as discussed below) undoubtedly has status value, but the reluctance to use local language to articulate activities or situations relating to sexual practices or relationships, together with the style that we encountered of interspersing specific English words within what is otherwise entirely vernacular discourse, indicates that here the critical feature may be the disassociation which the use of 'other' terms provides from connotations of personal (experiential) knowledge. These observations regarding the use of language also support my speculation that interventions for sexual health and accompanying studies may involve not simply eliciting but actually creating a new language for verbal expression on matters pertaining to sex and sexuality. The use of 'scientific' categories in sex research may risk both ignoring indigenous understandings of what sex means, and misrepresenting what in fact (as indicated by Salt 'n' Pepa's words) is always and universally an aspect not of individual behaviour but of relationships between individuals if, as Bloch (1991) has argued, cognitive categories are not necessarily 'language like' and are likely to be transformed by expression in language.

In the arena of sexual health research and intervention, participants – from anthropologists to local activists working in non-governmental organisations to government officials formulating health policy – are rapidly socialised into the use of a range of terms and acronyms used to denote the areas of interest, such as 'high risk behaviour' or 'HRB', CSW (commercial sex worker), STD (sexually transmitted disease) and MSM (men who have sex with men). These terms can be seen as part of a strongly normalising scientific discourse, and they have the effect of stripping the moral loading from what is signified by these terms – such as the replacement of 'prostitutes' by CSWs, of 'promiscuous' by 'high risk behaviour', of 'homosexual' by MSM. There is some evidence – for example in the case of the latter acronym – for the creation of new social categories and identities associated with other sexualities – men working for a NGO in Calcutta promoting sexual health and AIDS awareness among men who have sex with men have now co-opted this acronym as a reference to their own sexual identity, as in 'I am MSM' (P. Boyce, personal communication). This seems rather resonant of Foucault's (1990: 53 ff.) discussion of the production and proliferation of 'scientific' discourses about sex in modern, Western society, in and through which new categories of 'other' are identified and created.

Up to this point my focus has been on talk about sex *per se* and the possible effects of using methodologies which presume that accurate information about sexual behaviour can be collected in words which describe their referents in literal terms. The discussion of language developed and employed in the field of sexual health internationally brings us to a consideration, in turn, of health-related discourse within India. Here I can sketch only briefly the background of ethnographic, Indological and psychiatric research which has documented various indigenous discourses tracing relationships between sex and bodily well-being; however, it seems clear that the ways in which biomedicine envisages medical conditions and social behaviours relevant to the HIV epidemic may be missing an indigenous language which already makes the connection.

Over several decades, from the work of the anthropologist and psychiatrist Morris Carstairs onwards, a growing body of research has documented among Indian men a particular preoccupation with 'semen loss' (also referred to as the '*dath* syndrome', '*jiryan*' or 'semen anxiety') which is associated in Hinduism with indigenous moral physiology (Bottero 1991; Carstairs 1956, 1957; Edwards 1983). More recently, work on women's health deriving from the upsurge of international interest in this field has documented a very common female preoccupation with 'white discharge' which, together with the general perception that females as well as males are considered to have sexual fluids, seems to indicate that this concern is not confined to men alone. Anthropologists and Indologists have tended to view these preoccupations as 'culture-bound syndromes', and have traced the relations between 'semen loss' and indigenous understandings of the body and the social, ecological and moral environment. Ayurveda and popular therapeutic traditions alike place strong emphasis on the maintenance of humoral balance, which is achieved through moderations of diet and lifestyle appropriate not only to seasonal conditions but to the particular humoral constitution of the individual. These behaviourally based forms of regulation encompass not only appropriate times and amounts of sleeping and eating, but also of sexual activity. Associated, but not consonant with, these ethnomedical concerns are a set of well documented ideas, related to the religious values placed upon asceticism in Hinduism, concerning the spiritual and physical benefits accruing to men from sexual continence. Running counter to these ideas are representations of women as inherently lustful and lacking in sexual discernment which, as noted earlier, are often used to justify male control over women. Illustrations of these ideas were plentiful in my earlier fieldwork in Rajasthan, for example in references to the wasting physical effects of excessive sexual intercourse on men (women were said to have 'eaten' men who appeared to be less than hearty following marriage) together, according to local Ayurvedic practitioners, with a common male preoccupation with the condition of 'semen loss' and, conversely, the circulation by men of apocryphal stories such as the unwitting adultery committed by a woman who, in the dark, could not tell that the man who approached her for sex was not her own husband.

Rather than surmising that there is an absence of specific and appropriate language through which to discuss sex at all, we might thus conclude that there is a sophisticated language of sexual health. It is not the biomedical language invented to describe this domain, most recently for the purpose of controlling infections associated with 'sexual mixing'. The language of sexual health in India is one which speaks of appetite and the regulation of desire. It is bound up with considerations of the place of sexuality in promoting or depleting bodily strength, vigour and fertility and which – more problematically – inherently poses male virility as opposed to the proper satisfaction of female desire, since the retention of virility requires sexual abstinence.

This is not to suggest that in India at least, talking about sex itself is as invariant a 'taboo' as many commentators tend to assume. The various examples considered here indicate some of the many situational, temporal and gender-specific particularities concerning talk about sex, while there are clearly other social structural dimensions of relevance in shaping both values concerning and practices related to, as well as communication about, sexual relationships and practices. Hence, among women explicit discussion of issues concerning sexual relations tends to occur mainly among married women, and particularly mothers, while being generally curtailed in the presence of unmarried (and presumptively virginal) girls. Again there are likely to be strong social class (as well as regional and ethnic) differences; although the instances I have considered scarcely provide adequate evidence for generalisation across such a vast country, they do coincide with both personal impressions and some observations about the social class distribution of sexual values, behaviour and discussion which suggest that the educated middle class is most affected by 'social taboos about the subject' (Basu 1994: 575), by contrast with both lower (less educated and poor) and the uppermost (Westernised, liberal) social classes.

While both the indigenous discourse of sexual health and the social patterning of sexual communication described above may be specific to the context of India, sexual discourse also includes fundamentally and universally a 'language' of bodily interaction which extends the boundaries of communication well beyond the limits of what is or perhaps can be spoken. There may be a complementarity between those realms of human experience where the body is most eloquent and those where spoken language has least to add. The lack of attention to other forms of (non-verbal) communication including embodied action in anthropology is paradoxical given the important place of participant observation, with its ability to examine the relation between normative statements and phenomenal actions and events (Friedl 1994: 834;

Tuzin 1991: 867), as an essential component of ethnographic fieldwork. Anthropological studies of specific forms of bodily performance such as dance, sport, or possession ritual (see Hughes-Freeland, Kohn, and Thin, Chapters 9, 10 and 12 respectively in this volume, for examples) demonstrate that only where bodily action is deliberately elaborated or consciously symbolic is it usually taken as a worthy object of investigation. Within medical anthropology too, a dominant focus of studies dealing (for example) with illness 'experience' has been the 'illness narratives' thus produced. It may be that the dominant emphasis in anthropology on verbal expression and linguistic data (see Hughes-Freeland, Chapter 9 in this volume) relates to an assumption that focusing on action or bodily practice, in so far as it concerns 'behaviour', implies a privileging of the biological and points towards a Desmond Morris-style etiolated (but popular) ethology. An overemphasis on language, however, misses not the superficiality of behaviourist analysis but the purposive semantics of non-linguistic communication.

Edwin Ardener's reflections on translation apply well to the transformations of bodily and other non-linguistic, as well as verbal, communication that can occur when they are re-presented in other languages as well, potentially, as in anthropology; 'What lies at the end of the road of translation ... is a kind of entropy of the translated system – a total remapping of the other social space in the entities of the translating one' (1989: 178). In practical terms, applying my reading of the language of sex and health at least provides a starting point which is both familiar to the intended 'targets' of such strategies and which does not do violence to the terms within which sexuality is locally conceptualised. By contrast, the 'scientific discourse' about sex of the international and national health agencies is a set of specifically linguistic practices that impose their own definitions of events and actions in a form of symbolic domination (cf. Gal 1991: 177). The entirely understandable efforts within public health to come to grips with 'what is going on' actually transform what is going on in the act of translating it.

Notes

1 These studies (described in more detail later in the chapter) were designed to gather information for use in the development of projects for preventing HIV infection and promoting sexual health in India, and were funded by and undertaken on behalf of the UK government's Department for International Development, although the views expressed here are entirely my own. My discussion draws on this work as well as on more conventional ethnographic research undertaken previously in Rajasthan, which was supported by the Economic and Social Research Council as part of a D.Phil.

2 Rendering 'the problem' as a lack of information is the reading of many donor agencies and others concerned with AIDS prevention, but this may not be the only plausible explanation. While there are now large numbers of voluntary organisations eager for financial support to promote 'public awareness' of HIV and AIDS, attempts to initiate more 'targeted' strategies focused on particularly vulnerable populations (once these are identified) have often been greeted with

ambivalence. It is conceivable that for implementing agencies, 'lack of information' is not so much of a problem as the difficulties of confronting the social inequality, poverty and marginality that tend to characterise communities at particular risk of HIV and other sexually transmitted infections, and the social stigma that being associated with such communities is perceived to bring.

3 See Lambert (1998) for a more detailed description and critique of rapid anthropological assessments.

References

Ardener, E. (1989) 'Comprehending others', in M. Chapman (ed.) *The Voice of Prophecy and Other Essays*, Oxford: Blackwell.

Basu, D. P. (1994) 'Appropriate methodologies for studying sexual behaviour in India', *Indian Journal of Social Work*, LV(4): 573–88.

Bentley, M., Pelto, G. H., Straus, W. L., Schumann, D. A., Adegbola, C., de la Pana, E., Oni, G. A., Brown, K. H. and Huffman, S. L. (1988) 'Rapid Ethnographic Assessment: applications in a Diarrhea management programme', *Social Science and Medicine*, 27(1): 107–16.

Bentley, M. E., Spratt, K., Shepherd, M. E., Gangakhedkar, R. R., Thilikavathi, S., Bollinger, R. C. and Mehendale, S. M. (1998) 'HIV testing and counseling among men attending sexually transmitted disease clinics in Pune, India: changes in condom use and sexual behavior over time', *AIDS*, 12: 1869–77.

Bloch, M. (1991) 'Anthropology and cognitive science', *Man*, (n.s.) 26(2): 183–98.

Bollinger, R. C., Tripathy, S. P. and Quinn, T.C. (1995) 'The human immunodeficiency virus epidemic in India: current magnitude and future projections', *Medicine*, 71(2): 97–106.

Bottero, A. (1991) 'Consumption by semen loss in India and elsewhere', *Culture, Medicine and Psychiatry*, 15: 303–20.

Carstairs, G. M. (1956) 'Hinjra and jiryan: two derivatives of Hindu attitudes to sexuality', *British Journal of Medical Psychology*, 29(2): 128–38.

——(1957) *The Twice-born: A Study of a Community of High-caste Hindus*, London: Hogarth Press.

Das, V. (1988) 'Feminity and the orientation to the body', in Karuna Chanana (ed.) *Socialisation, Education and Women: Explorations in Gender Identity*, New Delhi: Sangam.

Edwards, J. (1983) 'Semen anxiety in South Asian cultures: cultural and transcultural significance', *Medical Anthropology*, 7(3): 51–67.

Foucault, M. (1990) [1976] *The History of Sexuality Volume 1: An Introduction*, Harmondsworth: Penguin.

Friedl, E. (1994) 'Sex the invisible', *American Anthropologist*, 96(4): 833–44.

Gal, S. (1991) 'Between speech and silence: the problematics of research on language and gender', in Micaela di Leonardo (ed.) *Gender at the Crossroads of Knowledge: Feminist Anthropology in the Postmodern Era*, Berkeley: University of California Press, pp. 175–203.

George, A. (1997) *Sexual Behaviour and Sexual Negotiation among Poor Women and Men in Mumbai: An Exploratory Study*, Baroda: SAHAJ Society for Health Alternatives.

Gold, A. G. (1994) 'Sexuality, fertility, and erotic imagination in Rajasthani women's songs', in Gloria Goodwin Raheja and Ann Grodzins Gold, *Listen to the Heron's Words: Reimagining Gender and Kinship in North India*, Berkeley: University of California Press, pp. 30–72.

Herman, E. and Bentley, M. (1992) 'Manuals for ethnographic data collection: experience and issues', *Social Science and Medicine*, 35: 1369–78.

Lambert, H. (1998) 'Methods and meanings in anthropological, epidemiological and clinical encounters: the case of sexually transmitted disease and human immunodeficiency virus control and prevention in India', *Tropical Medicine and International Health*, 3(12): 1002–10.

Lutzen, K. (1995) '*La mise en discours* and silences in research on the history of sexuality', in R. Parker and J. Gagnon (eds) *Conceiving Sexuality: Approaches to Sex Research in a Postmodern World*, New York and London: Routledge, pp. 24–32.

Manderson, L. and Aaby, P. (1992) 'An epidemic in the field? Rapid assessment procedures and health research', *Social Science and Medicine*, 35: 839–50.

Manderson, L., Almedom, A. M., Gittelsohn, J., Helitzer-Allen, D. and Pelto, P. (1996) 'Transferring anthropological techniques in applied research', *Practising Anthropology*, 18(3): 3–5.

Mohan, S. (1996) 'The AIDS scare in India could be aid-induced', *The Times of India*, Mumbai, 20 September.

Murthy, N. (1998) 'Sexuality and sexual behaviour in the context of HIV/AIDS and STDs: a study of youth in India', paper presented at Third Meeting of the Working Group on Sexuality and Sexual Behaviour Research, Mahaballipuram.

NACO (National AIDS Control Organization) (1994) *Country Scenario: An Update*, New Delhi: Government of India.

Osella, C. and Osella, F. (1998) 'Friendship and flirting: micro-politics in Kerala, South India', *Journal of the Royal Anthropological Institute*, 4(2): 189–206.

Ramasubban, R. (1992) 'Sexual behaviour and conditions of health care: potential risks for HIV transmission in India', in Tim Dyson (ed.) *Sexual Behaviour and Networking: Anthropological and Socio-cultural Studies on the Transmission of HIV*, Liège: Editions Deronaux-Ordine, pp. 175–202.

Salt 'n' Pepa, 'Let's Talk About Sex'. Words and music by Herbie Azor (1988), copyright Sons of K-oss Music Inc., USA. Warner/Chappell Music Ltd, London W6 8BS. Reproduced by permission of International Music Publications Ltd.

Solomon, S., Kumarasamy, N., Ganesh, A. K. and Amalraj, R. E. (1998) 'Prevalence and risk factors of HIV-1 and HIV-2 infection in urban and rural areas in Tamil Nadu, India', *International Journal of STD and AIDS*, 9: 98–103.

Tuzin, D. (1991) 'Sex, culture and the anthropologist', *Social Science and Medicine*, 33: 867–74.

Chapter 4

Talk, silence and the material world

Patterns of indirect communication among agricultural families in northern England

Pia Christensen, Jenny Hockey and Allison James

Introduction: a legible landscape

It is midway through the project and the anthropologist is alone, writing up some notes about an incident earlier the same day. She has just shared the men's midmorning coffee break in the farmhouse kitchen and now, in search of privacy, is lying in a field. It is hot, the middle of harvest time. Her privacy proves to be precarious. The farm workers are driving their machines back to the fields and Neil and Gary wave to her as they pass by. The view over the fields is of ripening corn and the anthropologist closes her eyes, picturing where the family members are and what they are doing. Gary will soon take over the combining from Ian, who was left on one of the fields so that the work wouldn't stop during the coffee break. It is usually Gary, however, who does most of the combining as he is the most skilled. Neil will be driving the tractor which will carry away the corn to Peter, working in the dryer in one of the farm buildings. Each of these men's tasks is interconnected and yet, over the years, has been distributed in such a way that, although they can all substitute for one another, the tasks match their separate interests and skills. Some distance away, on her own in the farmhouse, Bridget will be washing up the coffee cups and beginning to prepare the men's midday meal. She is always on her own in the farmhouse, the only woman, apart from the female anthropologist who has recently been a source of company. There will be many days, however, when she sees no other women.

The landscape thus offers a silent testimony to the loneliness of farming. The combine moves with a stubborn, dozy rhythm, mechanically combing the field; the tractor driver, alone in his cab, listens to music; one man stands on watch as the temperature rises within the dryer. And, embraced in the segregated landscape, the anthropologist finds herself visibly estranged, becoming the object of the gaze of the woman who daily observes the routine comings and goings of her menfolk from the farmhouse windows. The anthropologist visualises the long drive up to the farm, which lies some distance from the main road. This drive makes it possible to track the visible progress of visitors to the farm through the landscape – the inhabitants of the farmhouse are therefore always well prepared for any visit – and, while watching, they can draw on an intimate knowledge of the everyday life of neighbours, of friends and of acquaintances and be keenly alert to the arrival of the stranger in that landscape.

It is in ways such as these that the landscape can be read, in silence, by those who live in it and live off it. As a central feature within the lives of members of the farming community, the material environment is both a resource and a constraint whose significance often, quite literally, goes without saying. It acts as both a source of, as well as focus for, the many forms of indirect communication which, as this paper will show, help to sustain the interdependent character of everyday life in an agricultural community.

Cultural connectedness

To communicate implies connection: talk passes between persons, engaging, informing, reassuring, sympathising, encouraging, discussing, criticising; links are made between one person and another; between peoples and places; between objects and subjects. But forging those links need not necessarily privilege spoken language nor be confined to speaking subjects. As Wilden comments, 'all behaviour is communication, with message value, whether intended or conscious or not' (1987: 69). Persons are connected through the simple raising of an eyebrow, the empathetic sharing of emotions, the conjoining of physical labour or the joint remembering of a mutual history. This chapter addresses such forms of cultural connectedness in a context where indirect forms of communication predominate and where silence, rather than talk, represents the apogee. As Wilden notes:

> Language is one type of communication and one type of semiotic. ... Communication is goal seeking activity. ... There are no intransitive systems of communication and no intransitive messages ... every act, every pause, every movement in living and social systems is also a message; silence is communication; short of death it is impossible for an organism or a person not to communicate.
>
> (Wilden 1987: 124)

Our context – an agricultural community in the north of England – offers a challenge to the authority of language to inscribe experience, for among the agricultural families, whose lives we depict below, the importance of the spoken word is minimised. Thus, following Howes (1991) and Stoller (1989), we explore their 'cultural communications' as embodied sensory, as well as rational, experiences which are, in part, mediated by the materiality of a rural landscape. Devoid of the urban paraphernalia of streets, shopping precincts and housing estates, its inhabitants live apart from one another and yet their lives are intimately intertwined, bound together by the very land which divides them – and indeed by the silences through which they communicate. These speak loudly about the routinisation of shared lives and joint histories tied to the land. In these ways 'the farming way of life' – a trope which reverberates through our field data – becomes both enacted and embedded. Central to its production, we argue, is the land's role as a mediator between people, a materiality which shapes the structures of communication that dominate in this community. Our paper sets out to reveal the complexity of its compass as, day by day, year in, year out, families will follow, with little discussion, 'the farming way of life'.

The early recognition of the multi-valency of symbols (Turner 1967) and of the potency of implicit knowledge (Douglas 1966, 1975) indicates a long established understanding of the sensory, less direct ways in which cultural meanings may be both invoked and shared. However, in this chapter, we focus not simply on the power of objects or contexts to signify, but on their role as mediating devices. We show how such mediations are central to the relationships of interdependency through which 'the farming way of life' is constituted (Christensen 1999) and, in particular we focus here on one – the practice of silence. Here we pay particular attention to its various forms as a channel of indirect communication, distinguishing between silence

1   about that of which there is no need to speak, the taken-for-granted;
2   about that which is known but should not be spoken of; and
3   finally, the silence of that which it is barely conceivable to articulate in language.

Mary Douglas (1966) has shown that the sacred is to be found in that which is set apart, constituted through purity or danger. Both these aspects are to be found in the silences which shape that which is sacred to farming. As our material indicates, it is the relations of connectedness and interdependency through which the community is constructed which are not, or cannot, be put into words. Silence or non-speech provides continuity for a way of life vulnerable to the capriciousness of the land, weather and the animal world; it also provides connection between and across sets of potential contradictions and tensions in a network of social relations which could threaten the community's well-being were they ever to be voiced.

For example, silence allows people to work successfully as autonomous units in their individual farm businesses – without publicly accentuating that their personal ascendancy, as farmers, depends not only on their skill in relation to the management of land and livestock but also, crucially, upon their social and economic network of local and regional connections, including most importantly those of the family. As noted elsewhere (Christensen *et al.* 1996) farming families are bound to one another in a web of dependencies – on one another as kin, on the quality of the land or on the vagaries of the weather.

Thus some things rarely find form in talk since they constitute the essence of what farming means and how the farming way of life is lived. Other matters, in contrast, are set apart from everyday conversations through silence because they would be too dangerous to discuss openly. They would threaten the forms of livelihood and patterns of family life which sustain the community. Finally, however, as our chapter will show, some things are perhaps more literally muted: they are beyond words, if not also outside the realm of conceptualisation itself. And such silencing of thought is itself a sacred, potentially dangerous act. Thus, as people would explain, 'we just get on with it', 'the farming way of life'. They do not, dare not, talk of it, we suggest, lest its inherent fragility becomes apparent. It is towards an explanation of how people do this – and not just that they do – that this chapter is directed through its revelation of the ways in which particular kinds of indirect and silent communication take place between people, and between people and the material world upon which they are so materially and socially dependent.

Finding our feet indirectly in the field

Mapplethorpe and Needlemoore are neighbouring villages, both of them embedded in the folds and curves of the Wolds. Though these villages have seen an influx of newcomers, they are still quite evidently farming communities, encircled and conjoined by farmland with sheds for livestock – pigs, sheep and cattle – dotted about the streets. Joint local activities between the villages take place regularly in Needlemoore village hall and church while the village cricket field at Mapplethorpe sees a sometimes fierce rivalry played out between the two village teams.

In Mapplethorpe, the shrinking centre of the old village is surrounded by enclaves of new housing which has doubled the population in the last 10–15 years, so that the village now numbers some 800 people. The local villagers live mainly in the heart of the village, with the newer estates at the fringe housing the incomers. Mapplethorpe's population is able to sustain a couple of local shops and pubs, as well as a village primary school. Older inhabitants describe the interrelationships between local 'villagers' and the newcomers as ambiguous and tense. Sharp divisions of opinions and contesting views sometimes reach flashpoint over local planning initiatives, such as the occasion when complaints were raised about the siting of a pig unit in the village. Newcomers feared that countryside smells would drift from the old heart of the village to contaminate their more urban-style houses.

In Needlemoore, by contrast, small enclaves of new residential areas are distributed evenly within the village. With about 225 inhabitants, its village streets contain old cottages squeezed between the few remaining farms and the bungalows, newly built in cul-de-sacs running off the main roads of the village. Needlemoore has seen a decline in local businesses and services over the years and, although a popular local pub remains, every attempt to keep the village school, shops and post offices have so far proved fruitless. Here, in contrast to Mapplethorpe, people see their co-habiting as generally harmonious although, in conversation, they might refer to instances of conflict between farming families and newcomers over the years.

The lives of the agricultural families who live in these communities present a radical contrast to those of city dwellers. The latter live in close proximity to one another in the legacy of nineteenth-century terraced streets, high-rise blocks and Barratt-style dolls-houses. Yet despite such spatial proximity, urban family and working lives are typically closed off from one another. They take place in different spaces within the city and routes of communication between them are relatively inaccessible. By contrast, family and working life are synonymous in an agricultural community. The land is both a space to live in as well as a resource to live off. Urban-style anonymity is rare. Knitted together via ties of kinship and business, the only obstacle to communication might seem, therefore, to be the physical miles which divide farms and villages, but it is something easily overcome in this relatively affluent community where private transport and mobile phones are plentiful. In practice, however, as we shall show, strong constraints upon particular kinds of communication persist, even when these physical separations have been overcome.

The material which we present in this chapter therefore concerns itself as much with absences as presences. Although, like much fieldwork, the study used talk as one of its investigative strategies, it was in talk that, ironically, that which is not talked about was constituted. If fieldwork consists primarily of an assault on the senses, which the ethnographer later constructs as anthropological knowledge, then it was precisely the absence of some kinds of talk which provided an initial clue as to the nature of 'the farming way of life' and the motivation to 'just get on with it' when times are difficult in farming. Thus, for example, although one of the original aims of the study had been to explore how families coped at times of ill health, as we explore below, explicit talk about serious mental and physical illness surfaced only rarely and then obliquely. Similarly, knowledge of business troubles and family conflicts was routinely silenced in general conversation so that we often came to know about them more indirectly.

In response to these practices, fieldwork communication took full advantage of more indirect forms of engagement. Farming men, for example, characteristically establish their connections with one another through physical labour. Work is often conducted in silence. Male informants were therefore best accessed via a companionable participation in their work routines: sitting in the driver's cab while combining or helping in the darkness of the lambing shed.

In contrast to the sense of tradition and comforting familiarity which this kind of silence produces, however, the study also revealed a darker aspect: a reflexive awareness by some members of this community of the power of silence to mute others and thus its potential as problem or a threat. From the outset, for example, there was an almost overwhelming demand made on the ethnographer that time be found to 'talk' by certain people – women at home with young families and older people. For these groups, the silencing of their lives and voices by tradition was experienced as problematic and the chance to talk with someone new was welcomed. Modes of talking and patterns of silence in and around Mapplethorpe and Needlemore were therefore diverse and cannot be reduced to a single account.

It goes without saying ...

Urban divisions between work and home, colleagues and family are absent within farming communities. Instead friendship and paid work are often coterminous with family. The family is not only a site where land is held, work is organised and friends are found, but is also an imperative which can override other kinds of social networks. Family networks are not, however, sustained purely by ties of blood or marriage. They are a set of connections which are made rather than simply given – but made from and within a repertoire of social possibilities which is recognised locally as 'family'. Furthermore, it is the fixity of the relationship between local families and local land which characterises communities of this kind. The occupation of local housing and the husbandry of local land continues in the hands of a relatively small nexus of extended families, who, despite occupational and leisure-based mobility, always return to a highly localised set of family and business interests. 'Getting on' with family and 'getting on' in business are coterminous within this densely patterned community, but it is an interdependency which remains unvoiced. Both activities have to be managed, therefore, to avoid dispute, and it is through strategies of silence and indirection that any potential for rupture is controlled.

For example, among farming families, it is on marriage that women gain entry into kinship systems which are tightly intermeshed with the business of farming. Here farming is not seen as an occupational category but as 'a way of life', a specifically rural intermeshing of domains which has both benefits and costs. Kinship links are sustained as a social and economic necessity since the kin group is the source of livelihood both in the present and the future, through children and later grandchildren. Thus any severance of family ties is potentially highly costly in terms of the loss of both inheritance and the fruition of labour and capital in the hands of sons and grandsons.

What we are describing, therefore, is a way of life which is characterised by positively perceived, shifting sets of connections, something which finds not only temporal and spatial, but also social and material form. It is the core through which the 'farming way of life' is constituted and need not, and indeed should not, be spoken of. It is simply taken on, in silence, for to speak explicitly about such interconnectedness – about the capricious links between the material environment of the land, weather and animal and the families who farm – would be to risk temporalising or fragmenting that which is, and must be, experienced as continuous and enduring. Actions speak louder than words, and women and men proceed with each individual task, whether it be child care, combining or cricket. In this way momentum is maintained and breaks in continuity are resisted, and the orderliness and purity of the farming way of life is sustained.

Thus farming has a temporal and spatial dimension, one which extends from a shared past into a known future and, in this, the land is central. It provides both the context as well as the focus for men's work and relationships and it is valued for its enduring timelessness, something which usually goes without saying. As Harry put it:

> People don't know how attractive the country is … it's rolling … everything has its own beauty … I'm not sentimental but I appreciate it, I must admit. I'm lucky to be here – but usually it's just there – I just accept it for what it is.

It is the land which also silently mediates women's lives within this community. Rosemary and Joan, two of its older inhabitants, give voice to the ties which bind farming families to the land, a land which daily they gaze upon. Although it is largely the men who work the land, for women, too, through their sons and grandsons, the land also provides a welcome sense of security and continuity:

> From outside they do this every year and do that every year. But its continuity to us that is the comforting part … that it's carrying on, that they do the same things.

This pattern of silent and indirect communication provides the continuity in farming through privileging watching and doing. This can be seen in the ways in which men begin their working lives. Rather than a compartmentalised urban sequencing of schoolwork, play, occupational training and, finally, employment, boys 'evolve' gradually over time as farmers. Ian, for example, is in his early fifties. He works the family farm, together with his brother and his sons. His mother and aunt live in a cottage on the family's land and, in the adjacent farmhouse, his wife takes care of every aspect of their shared domestic life. Recalling his early days on the farm, Ian said:

To learn farming means to be watching and looking and learning and reading. Mostly I believe, in farming, it's by watching – like a driving test – start with a dual control car. The sons have learned through practice: There's no answer to that you have to ask questions 'what's that switch for daddy' etc. etc. – that's how we all start – and you finish up doing the job – it all goes back to evolvement.

Ian's recollections, phrased here in terms of an organic and natural process of learning and growth are echoed by another farm worker, Fred. Although he grew up outside the farming community, it is precisely through the seamless process of 'evolvement' that he finally gained membership:

My father being a frustrated farmer wasn't so very far away from a farm and so, because I used to run along at his heels and he just used to go and talk to farmers and he knew them and I used to go with him and I mean, I just soaked it all up, I just drank it all, it was absolutely the breath of life to me. I mean to go and look at the cart horse was, well, it was better than going on week's holiday, if he could take me to a farm for half a day, I just didn't want anything else. It was absolute heaven to me, just to go to a farm, stand in a stable and look at a row of cart horses was … and just the smell the muck and all the … and everything else with it was absolute heaven (laughs) … it was really.

As in Ian's case, Fred is recruited to farming, not through the direct verbal communication of an itemised tool-kit of knowledge and skills, but rather through an indirect, multisensory experience. It is a continuous process within which 'you finish up doing the job' as tasks and relationships unfold in a continuous, temporal sequence that requires neither comment nor commentary. As described in this chapter's introduction, men who farm carry out their tasks instead through unspoken, physical coordination. Their bodies become paired in shared activities.

And indeed, since so little emphasis is given to verbal instruction or reflection, talk is not a predominant characteristic of men's social relationships, with the art of conversation often supplanted by teasing. Citing practical advice from a radio doctor, Fred stressed the positive value of laughter with a male friend:

he comes round nearly every day … and we have a good laugh … if we haven't anything to talk about we tell jokes and all the rest of it.

This silent engagement with different kinds of communication, translation and understanding is, we suggest, a crucial aspect of the art and practice of farming. For example, men learn the importance of communicating with animals by imitating the tone and sound of the sheep. This was most impressively demonstrated during lambing time where the men's directions to the sheep served to keep a labouring sheep calm or reassure the newly born. Likewise the shouts and monotonous rhythms of the voice were crucial for gaining the attention and keeping control of the cattle during the process of moving a herd in and out of the field. Similarly, we suggest, the silence of the landscape gives preference to using senses and ways of communicating other than language in order to understand the changes and the differences in the farming milieu. It was, for example, common sense amongst farmers that worrying about the weather is a wasteful occupation, because its unpredictability meant that they had to respond flexibly. There was therefore a sense of the unavoidable necessity of working with the weather (as well as other aspects of a changing environment) and not against it. Neither a man nor a woman were seen as being able to achieve anything if they tried to work against what the weather communicates. Successful farmers understand implicitly the flexible, interconnected and manifold environmental processes that have to be reflected in a farmer's work, and know that by listening to and understanding the complex and diverse information from a field that they, as farmers, can, in turn, shape the natural world.

In this sense, then, the material world mediates in the forging of bonds between men, between husbands and wives, between parents, grandparents and grandchildren, bearing silent but visible witness to the webs of interconnections which necessarily tie each to another and about which little needs to be said.

Better left unsaid ...

For farming families the land is, of course, not only the space within which they live and socialise. It is their most fundamental resource, that from which, as noted above, their past, present and future are inseparable. And it is precisely through the highly visible nature of the material layout of farms, cottages and village streets that those who can read it can gain much knowledge about the history of the community. Where a person lives is a continual reminder to others of their ancestry. Those who are from local farming families know how to locate each village house through reference to both its present occupant or previous incumbent. And the relationship of past to present is usually that of kinship; houses are occupied by mothers then sons, grandchildren, nieces or nephews. While the temporal and spatial continuity of local husbandry of the land therefore provides a reassuring visual environment for villagers such as Rosemary and Joan, less welcome evidence of social divisions and occupational diversity is also to be found inscribed in the village landscape. Such evidence throws light on more troubled and problematic aspects of the community's past, or indeed its present.

For example, the amount and quality of land held by the members of a particular family can work to create a problematic social stratification in the form of an implicit local hierarchy of 'big' farmers and 'little' farmers. Paradoxically, the interdependent nature of family labour on the farm, combined with hard work and auspicious material circumstances, can produce social divisions which single out particular local families as 'big farmers'. Benjamin, for example, grew up as his father's farm business expanded, and he recognises that the people he once knew are now small farmers compared with them. This concerns him. He sees it as a creating distance between his family and the other farmers, as signalling a breakdown of connections which are locally valorised over and above the independence ascribed to farming:

> When I was younger I would often think, I don't want to get too big otherwise people will think – big farmer, he won't want to know us. I didn't want to get so big that I lost touch with some of my friends … people might think – big farmers, big head.

And indeed an interview with two 'small' farmers reveals that Benjamin's concerns are well founded. In conversation, Harry and Bill compare 'big farmers' or gentleman farmers unfavourably with small farmers who make 'a life' as well as a 'living' on the farm by working alongside their wives and receiving help from others only at busy times such as harvest. This image of the interdependent running of the farm, in their view, is an ideal model of 'the farming way of life'. When men get big farms, however, they get 'big implements, big heads … and they say bugger the little man'. They are critical of the way that, rather than being prepared to rent land from small farmers, big farmers buy the land up and put them out of business, a strategy which they as small farmers regard as 'just greed'. Thus, for those in the know, the acres of land owned by a big farmer signal a disregard for local social relations and the local community itself. Such an approach to farming breaks up the interdependencies through which that community is constituted. Big farmers improve their lot to the detriment of others.

But to talk explicitly about such imbalances of power or wealth would threaten the unarticulated and unacknowledged sets of interdependencies which ideally and practically constitute the local community (Newby 1975; Christensen et al. 1999). In such circumstances, therefore, a communal silence is carefully sustained through adherence to a certain social and moral code, and although Benjamin, Harry and Bill are willing to engage in direct verbal communication about such matters with outsiders such as ourselves, within the context of their local social networks they remain silent. Such communications touch on the sacred and must, therefore, remain secret. Thus, while the extensive acreage of Benjamin's father's farm is an open secret, visible to all, few comment directly upon his wealth, and Benjamin's father, we learnt later, had for many years kept his BMW hidden in his garage lest this additional material evidence of his wealth should estrange him further from the local community.

Divisions based on land holdings and wealth therefore constitute sacred, unspeakable rifts in the seamless fabric of the farming way of life. Splits within farming families transcend the economic and social disruption which occurs within the urban family, for they manifest themselves upon the very landscape within which the family lives and works. They are highly visible in terms of fractured land holdings and business interests. The costs of family rifts in terms of lost income, land and property are known and feared and, in these circumstances, divorce constitutes that which cannot be spoken of. Thus, as noted elsewhere (Christensen *et al.* 1997), it is a farmer's daughter or a woman who comes from a farming family who is the preferred spouse for a farmer's son. Such a woman need not to be told about or instructed in the farming way of life; she will know how to 'get on with it'; she will know how to be a farmer's wife, rather than the wife of a farmer. Thus the threat to land, property and the future which divorce would entail is lessened.

Such examples of social division are matched and indeed closely interconnected with other kinds of differences, such as those wrought by ill health or mental illness. All of them are highly visible, and, similarly, none of them are made a focus for direct communication. Thus we learnt, only over time and then obliquely, about those farmers who had neglected to 'just get on with it' and had sought, instead, to gain ultimate control over their material environment. These were individuals who failed to acknowledge the dependency of every farmer upon the land and weather: soil fertility, the condition of animals, rainfall and temperature at times generate and sustain a family's livelihood, but at other times can wreck an entire season's labour. Though little is put into words, this refusal of an ultimate environmental dependency inevitably produces highly visible and indirect signs of madness. Thus the farmer who relentlessly harrowed his field in a desperate attempt to improve a poor yield, clearly laid out the fruits of his madness upon the landscape in a way which few failed to take note of but about which little comment was made.

It is in circumstances of this kind that silence plays its crucial role: it acts as a sanction against personal criticism, the exposure of ill health, mental illness or financial failure in an inappropriate context, and forbids interference in someone else's affairs. Such communicative practices would bring an uncomfortable, indeed unmanageable, closeness in this context characterised by a stoical adherence to a culture of balanced interdependency which, while sustaining the competent, can also therefore undermine the less able.

Thus that which this community treats as 'sacred', that which cannot be spoken about, is nonetheless highly visible. Social divisions, whether between big and little farmer or between sick and healthy individuals, are often literally written in the landscape and always, therefore, potentially fracture the prevailing cultural ethos. In a material environment of this kind they cannot be contained or confined. Made known indirectly as a result of their visibility, wealth, ruin and madness are therefore made manageable only through silence. It is within this context that one tumbled-down farmhouse stands silent witness to an irrevocable rift which took place many years ago between two brothers; a tie of interdependency broken, rarely articulated but constantly visible in the broken down walls of an abandoned farmhouse.

Beyond silence

The continuity of the farming way of life, an endeavour which, as we have been arguing, depends heavily upon the connectedness and interdependency of the members of families and the local community with one another and with their material environment, is therefore put at risk by internal divisions, hierarchies or separations. And it is the unwelcome, and yet inevitable, emergence of difference which is managed through silence. But silence also shrouds, or indeed eliminates, other more dangerous threats to the continuity of farming which might undermine the core of what constitutes 'the farming way of life'. Here, then, silence embraces a range of exclusions which, collectively, constitute the unspeakable if not the unthinkable. Central to this kind of silence is the muting of alternatives to farming as an occupational category, a lifestyle and a way of being.

First there is the conceptual exclusion of other forms of work which might fragment the social and work community of farming families. Despite the growing presence of newcomers within villages such as Needlethorpe and Mapplethorpe, and with them the visibility of an alternative to a farming way of life in the occupational diversity which they represent, the notion of work outside farming rarely forms the substance of direct communication between parents and children or families and incomer wives. Rather, what we find is a consistent set of silences or exclusions about occupational diversity, for it is assumed that it is to farming that their children will turn. Though the children of rich farmers may be sent away to be educated, ostensibly to make them 'independent' within the confines of local boarding schools, children are unlikely to be exposed to alternative ways of life. While parents emphasised that they would not discourage or indeed prevent their children from pursuing a career of their own choice, the exclusion of any direct communication about other avenues of employment indirectly shapes their futures.

While growing up, the farming way of life becomes the focus of children's, and in particular boys', daily work tasks and also their leisure time. Once recruited, men therefore find that their knowledge of the world has become highly focused. Thus Benjamin describes himself as 'a one track man' – someone who can only talk about farming. Farm work and farming forms of communication thus become dominant in a way which excludes other avenues and interests, such as music and the arts, or even taking holidays. As Benjamin says, 'If I go out with a few farmer friends there is plenty of conversation but I would probably find it hard to make conversation about anything else'. His sister, Jane, also says of Paul her husband, 'if he goes out he likes to talk about farming and nearly all our friends are farming people'. Through a series of exclusions and silences, therefore, occupational diversity is side-stepped, and with it the fragmentation of the farming community.

Men's leisure time, while highly focused around meetings with other men, and particularly in playing cricket, does not entirely exclude women. However, although physically present in the pub or at meals out, women described how they gave up trying to introduce other topics of conversation or other modes of communication. The difficulty which women experience when their husbands refuse a social life among the friends which their wives may have made before they married, may be further compounded by the silences which predominate within their private marital relationship. Not only does the land demand men's time in a way which transcends any temporal boundaries, it also distances them from women spatially as they work on remote fields. In the time which is spent together, however, many women find their menfolk to be unwilling confidants, not easily drawn into conversation which concerns their personal and emotional life. Resistant to any form of dependency, men adhere to the stoic independence necessary to retain their position within a wider network of interdependent social relations. Emotional vulnerability is therefore a potentially dangerous direction from which women are discouraged, both by men's silences and other women's admonitions to just 'get on with it'. Jane's view, for example, is that farmers keep their worries to themselves and do not show anyone their feelings because 'they have an image that they have to be quite hard ... and ready and rough'. And, since Paul, her husband, chooses not to communicate directly and intimately, she goes to her mother, Anne, if she has a problem. As a way of being and a style of interaction, vulnerability, particularly for men, is therefore beyond the bounds of possibility. Although women may retain scope for some power within the social and emotional field, that scope can be limited by the more powerful silences of men, whose all-consuming work and leisure commitments – their power within the physical or occupational field – augment their capacity for conversational withdrawal. Men's communicative forms, including silence, and their strong farming orientation thus privilege men at the cost of suppressing women and their modes of expression.

Much previous research has already raised these and similar points, arguing for the recognition of farming as a strong, male-biased environment (Shorthall 1992; Whatmore 1991; Wallace *et al.* 1996) and for women in farming to be seen as a muted group (Ardener 1975). This body of work has, however, left unexplained the paradoxical observation that the women themselves express strength and contentment in their everyday life, at the very same time as they expose their experiences of hardship and inferiority in relation to particular situations or certain periods of their life. In a previous paper (Christensen *et al.* 1997) we have suggested that by looking at women's life course over different farming periods it can be shown that women strategically balance constraint with opportunity at different points in their lives, seeing the future as very much part of the present.

Here, however, we wish to make a different and larger point. We suggest that what in fact gets 'muted' in farming is human discourse itself – that is the expressive modes of both women *and* men. Farming people join together in silence to pay heed to a legible landscape. Information derived from a view of the land must be translated, understood and communicated if a farm is to be successful and a family to survive. We have shown how 'silence', in the particular forms we have described, plays a crucial part in the indirect communication which takes place in a farming community. Through particular attention to the different forms of non-verbal communication we have been able to show that, not only do people not talk about some things or others depending on a specific context, but also that this is necessary to protect the 'sacred' of this particular community. The interconnectedness of social relationships and the landscape make for a way of life where social divisions and occupational and economic diversity threaten both the coherence as well as the continuity of this ultimately fragile set of interdependencies. Constituted as the sacred by virtue of their unutterably risky nature, the social divisions produced through economic success or failure, good health or madness, whilst highly visible upon this shared landscape, are nonetheless managed through sets of strategic silences.

In brief, this is an understanding and enactment of the interrelated and interdependent nature of the social *and* the material world. We have further argued that, in an agricultural community, there is an intention, or even a necessity to set apart different forms of knowledge because, in some circumstances, they may hinder or cause a breakdown of present relationships, or may even eventually harm those future connections which are waiting to be made. It would thus, inevitably, affect the livelihood of the whole. For the members of a community which lives and works within so legible a landscape, silence persists as the preferred medium of communication.

References

Ardener, E. (1975) 'Belief and the problem of women', in S. Ardener (ed.) *Perceiving Women*, London: Dent/Malaby Press.

Christensen, P., Hockey, J. and James, A. (1996) ' "You just get on with it": questioning welfare dependency in a rural community', in I. Edgar and A. Russell (eds) *Anthropology and Welfare*, London: Routledge.

——(1997) 'You have neither neighbours nor privacy: ambiguties in the experience of emotional well-being of women in farming communities,' *The Sociological Review*, 45(4): 621–45.

——(1999) ' "That's farming Rosie … ": power and familial relations in an agricultural community', in J. Seymour and P. Baggaley (eds) *Relating Intimacies: Power and Resistance*, London: Macmillan.

Douglas, M. (1966) *Purity and Danger*, London: Routledge and Kegan Paul.

——(1975) *Implicit Meanings*, London: Routledge and Kegan Paul.

Howes, D. (1991) *The Varieties of Sensory Experience*, Toronto: University of Toronto Press.

Newby, H. (1975) 'The deferential dialectic,' *Comparative Studies in Society and History*, 17: 139–64.

Shortall, S. (1992) 'Power analysis and farm wives', *Sociologia Ruralis*, 32: 431–51.

Stoller, P. (1989) *The Taste of Ethnographic Things*, Philadelphia: University of Pennsylvania Press.

Turner, Victor W. (1967) *The Forest of Symbols*, Ithaca NY: Cornell University Press.

Wallace, C., Abbot, P. and Lankshear, G. (1996) 'Women farmers in south-west England', *Journal of Gender Studies*, 5(1): 49–62.

Whatmore, S. (1991) *Farming Women: Gender, Work and Family Enterprise*, London: Macmillan.

Wilden, Anthony (1987) *The Rules Are No Game: The Strategy of Communication*, London: Routledge and Kegan Paul.

Part II

Indirection beyond language

Chapter 5

Eating your words
Communicating with food in the Ecuadorian Andes

Nicole Bourque

Introduction

In Sucre, a peasant community in the Central Ecuadorian Andes,[1] the actions of preparing, distributing, accepting and eating food in particular social and spatial contexts are used to communicate, confirm, reject and transform notions of relatedness and difference; tradition and modernity; age; gender and ethnic identities; and economic, political and social status. This communication takes place in a context of, and is shaped by, changing economic circumstances at the micro and macro level, the introduction of new cooking techniques, and variations in the availability of foodstuffs. Most of the messages that are intentionally or unintentionally sent and received using food are non-verbal. This is possible because the meanings of particular foods and actions are, to a large extent, understood by all of the people (men, women, Indians, *mestizos*,[2] adults and children) in the region. The non-verbal language of food is taught, learned and shaped as people openly discuss the messages that they have received and sent. When looking at non-verbal communication with food, it is important to consider not only the relationship between the sender and receiver of messages, the intentions of the sender, and the understanding of the receiver, but also the context and consequences of conversations about food.

Most studies of food[3] and communication have their roots in structuralism. Lévi-Strauss (1965; 1968; 1970) urged researchers to look beyond the social functions of food, and claimed that the cultural rules which govern the classification and preparation of food reflect unconscious mental structures. In a now famous analogy, Lévi-Strauss compared cuisine to language. A particular item of food could only take on meaning according to its position with respect to other food items, just as a syllable or a word can only take on meaning when juxtaposed to other syllables or words according to certain structural rules (i.e. grammar). Similarly, Barthes (1975) saw all foods as signs in a system of communication. Certain foods could be used to signify concepts such as tradition, modernity, masculinity or femininity. Mary Douglas (1966; 1975) also treated food as a code. For Douglas, however, encoded messages were about social events and relations, such as social inclusion or exclusion, hierarchy, boundaries and movement across these boundaries.

By the 1980s, studies of food as a language declined as the criticism of structuralism grew. Goody (1982) and Mennell (1985) claimed that structuralism failed to consider the history of food use; the impact of external social and cultural influences; internal differentiation; the social process of food production and consumption; the social relations of power in food transactions; and micro- and macro-economic processes. In response to these criticisms, studies of food focused on historical change (Mintz 1985) and class differentiation (Bourdieu 1986). As anthropologists began to take more of an interest in gender and ethnic identity, studies of food were turned to the examination of the role of food in the creation and maintenance of individual and group identity. Nevertheless, some of these studies, such as Weismantel (1988), still relied on a modified form of structuralism. As bodies and embodiment became the vogue, attention also turned to the relationship between food and the body. For example, Fischler (1988), Willets (1997) and Harbottle (1997) look at how identity is created through the process of eating as the meanings attached to food are literally internalised.

In my analysis of food in Sucre, I return to the issue of communication. However, instead of using a structuralist approach to disclose the non-verbal grammar of food, I want to focus on how this language is learnt and used by social actors. The limitations of the structuralist approach aside, I feel that the non-verbal language of food, like a spoken language, is easier to learn if one first considers the context of its use rather than its grammar. Accordingly, instead of listing the various meanings of particular foods and the different ways that food is used (the vocabulary and grammar of food), I aim to build up an understanding of the language of food in the Andes by narrating a number of incidents and events where food was used as a form of non-verbal communication (most of these events will also include verbal discussions about food). From these episodes, we will gain not only an understanding of the grammar and vocabulary of food, but also (and more importantly) an idea of how individuals use and manipulate this language in different circumstances. My description of each episode will be followed by an explanation of how this incident helped me to learn the language of food and how to use it.

Episode 1: feeding workers and the spatial dynamics of eating

One of my most vivid memories of fieldwork comes from my first week in Sucre (late July 1989). In an effort to meet people, I had volunteered to help a family plant maize. At the end of the day, I was invited to the family's house and instructed to sit on a stool on the front porch. Everyone disappeared inside of the house. A girl stuck her head outside of the door and smiled at me encouragingly. I told her, in far from fluent Spanish, that I did not mind going inside of the house (thinking that I had been left outside on the stool because they thought that a white woman might not want to enter an Indian house). This provoked a loud round of laughter. I sat on my stool in the increasing darkness wondering what I was expected to do. The girl came out and gave me a bowl of soup. I accepted the bowl, saying 'Dios le pague' (God will pay you).[4] She stood in the doorway and announced to the people inside that I was eating the soup. I could hear the sound of spoons clinking on enamelled bowls as the family consumed their soup inside of the house. The girl reappeared and took my empty bowl. I repeated my thanks and began to rise from the chair. She indicated that I was to sit down. I was given another bowl of soup, which I thankfully accepted and consumed. I was full, it was dark and I was concerned about finding my way back to my rented house. However, I was given a third bowl of soup. In spite of my protests that I was full, I was also given a fourth bowl before I was allowed to make my way home.

Commentary

This incident alerted me to the importance of food and reciprocity in the Andes. It also made me aware of the household as a spatial, social and economic group (Bourque 1997). In the Andes, household membership is not defined by common kinship but by eating together (Brush 1977: 13). Joint work is also an important part of household membership. In Sucre, land is owned by individuals, but joint work in agricultural production gives all members of the household ownership of the harvest and of the food that is produced from the harvest. To some extent, this notion extends to include temporary workers from other households.[5] At the end of a working day, it is an obligation to feed everyone who worked in the fields. Nevertheless, during this meal, a physical boundary is maintained between household and non-household members.[6] Household members eat inside of the house whereas all others eat outside. Non-household members are only invited inside the house during certain festivals or once they form ties of friendship or kinship with household members.

Relationships of land and labour exchange are seen as being between households rather than individuals. So, any member of one household may be sent to repay a labour debt to another household. Similarly, the meal that is given to an outside worker can be seen as an offering to their entire house-hold.[7] A month after my arrival in Sucre, I was sitting outside a house along with other workers and struggling with my third bowl of soup, when I spotted that my neighbour drank the broth of his soup and put the potatoes in a carrying cloth. He said that he would take them home for his family's soup and handed the plate back to his hostess. This was accepted by everyone present. I discovered that there is a special term, *la huanga*, for food that is treated in this way. This incident revealed, first, that it was important to accept food but that it was not necessary to consume it oneself; and second, that, in Sucre, the act of incorporating food does not only involve food entering the body (as described by Fischler 1998) but also the household.

A final issue revealed by this episode is over-consumption. This has been discussed in other parts of the Andes, notably by Allen (1988). The generosity of my hosts in continuing to offer me food, even though I had declared myself full, is itself a meaningful act. Over-consumption demonstrates the generosity of the hosts, and it also acknowledges their ability to provide. Over-consumption of food and drink is the norm during festivals as it is deemed, by the Indians, to be an appropriate way of pleasing supernatural beings.

Episode 2: feeding friends and relatives on the day of the dead

The first major festival I attended in Sucre in 1989 was *Finados* (the Day of the Dead) which is held on All Souls Day, 2 November (Bourque 1995a). Weeks before the festival, I helped one household and their share-croppers harvest, thresh, winnow and grind their wheat. For my efforts, I was given a small bag of flour. Sofia, the Indian woman who owned the field, asked me where I was going to bake my bread. Not understanding the significance of the question, I said that I did not know how to bake bread and that I would use the flour to thicken soup (which I hoped was a suitable response). Ignoring my comments, she insisted that I should ask my *mestiza* landlady, Maria, when she was going to bake her bread. Maria could then teach me how to make my bread and let me use her oven to bake it. Upon arriving home, one of my neighbours, Ortensia, spotted and enquired about my bag of flour. When I told her how I had obtained it, she informed me that I should visit Sofia's house during *Finados*. She would feed me because I was one of her workers. This was my first clue that there was a connection between the wheat harvest and the upcoming festival.

I noticed that a number of families, who didn't have wheat fields, were bringing back bags of wheat flour from the canton market.[8] The households which had wood ovens were cleaning them and making repairs. When I asked my *mestiza* landlady about baking bread, I was invited to come on baking day. She said she would teach me how to make bread with butter and eggs, not like the tasteless bread made by the Indians, who did not know how to make really good bread. We made a large number of bread rolls, some of which she would sell in her shop to those families who did not bake their own bread. We also made some bread in the shape of dolls (called bread babies). During the night, some of her Indian neighbours, who addressed her as *comadre*[9] (co-mother) came to bake bread or to purchase rolls and bread babies. Bread baking was not the only activity. Several Indian households were brewing *chicha* (maize beer). People returned from the market with bananas, oranges and other tropical fruits which are not part of the daily diet. Some brought back elaborately decorated bread babies, sacks of potatoes and bags of peanuts.

On the eve of the festival, I visited the household of Teresa, an Indian woman. Her daughters were peeling and boiling potatoes, boiling eggs, killing and roasting guinea pigs and preparing peanut sauce. She was proud that her daughters knew how to prepare guinea pig, which is seen as a difficult culinary task. In the evening, a table was placed in a small bedroom/storage room. This was covered with food. Potatoes and eggs were heaped in a large wooden bowl and covered with peanut sauce. Roast guinea pigs were placed on top. Bread rolls and babies, bananas, oranges and cups of *chicha* were put around the wooden bowl. Empty bowls and spoons were set to one side of the table. Teresa then turned out the light and closed the door, saying that it would be dangerous to enter the room until the next morning.

Teresa explained that this food was called *la ofrenda* (the offering) and was left out all night for the souls of dead relatives and friends to eat. The bread babies were for the dead children to play with. The dead souls, who are invited by name, arrive at night when the family is asleep. Unlike the living, they do not consume the food itself, but rather the flavour or essence of the food. After eating in one house, the dead visit their other relatives to see what has been left. As they travel, they take a note of which households have remembered them and discuss the quantity and quality of the food. In return for the food, the dead are said to help in the fields. Teresa said that her fields did well because she always remembered to feed the dead and pay for a mass for their souls.

The next day, after the mass in the graveyard, the women returned to their houses. Some of the men went with their wives, but many went to the *cantina* to drink. I went to the household of Sofia, the Indian woman whose wheat I had harvested. She was putting food from her *ofrenda* into a plate. She gave the plate to a young daughter and instructed her to deliver it to the house of one of the women who had been working in the wheat fields as a share-cropper. When the daughter returned, she brought back the same plate laden with food from the share-cropper's *ofrenda*. The daughter was sent off with more of the *ofrenda* to another household. While the daughter was away, other plates of food arrived. Sofia did not ask who had sent the plates, since she recognised the children delivering them. These children were sent back with items from Sofia's *ofrenda*. Meanwhile, the food received from other households was shared out amongst the people in the house. As we ate, favourable or disparaging comments were made about the quality of the cooked food. I was also closely questioned about the food I had received in the other households I had visited that day.

Many of the plates of food seemed to be expected. However, one plate, which arrived from a neighbour, clearly was not. The plate was accepted and food was given to the child. As soon as the child left, Sofia and her daughters speculated as to the motives of the giver. When someone remembered that the neighbour had recently purchased a field, it was decided that she would probably seek their help during the next planting.

During the day, I visited other Indian households and witnessed similar scenes. However, at the house of Maria, a *mestiza*, the entire family sat down to a huge feast, which included roast chicken, roast rabbit (marinated in beer) and boiled potatoes with peanut sauce. I asked Maria if she had left out an *ofrenda* and was sending food to her neighbours. She looked horrified at the suggestion. 'No', she said, 'That is what the Indians do. We have a big meal and invite our relatives to join us'.

Commentary

During *Finados*, food is used to emphasise key social mechanisms and divisions. One of the most important social mechanisms in the Andes is reciprocity (Johnsson 1986: 118; Isbell 1977: 83). Amongst Indian households, food is exchanged not only during *Finados*, but also during Christmas and Good Friday. Food exchange defines the limits of households as well as the network of households which cooperate with each other. Women manage food exchanges and thus affect relations between households. Plates of food are sent to the households of parents, married children, married siblings, neighbours and *compadres*. However, not all relatives receive food. Women decide which kin ties they wish to reaffirm and send food to do so. The gift of food is usually reciprocated. If not, food will not be sent to that household the following year. Sending food can be the first step in creating a new relationship, such as labour exchange. Indians do not limit their network of reciprocal relations to the living. In exchange for being remembered and fed, the souls of the dead help the growth of crops. It is significant to note that *Finados* occurs just after the planting of maize. The dead are said to push the young maize plants out of the ground. This has been recorded in other parts of the Andes (Harris 1982).

The *ofrenda* is critical in the recruitment of living and dead workers. Reciprocal food exchange stresses the symmetrical relationship between households. There is, however, an element of competition in this equal exchange which indicates status and power differences. Economically successful households demonstrate their wealth by giving large quantities of high quality food. Giving a large quantity of food also indicates that the relationship that this is reinforcing is especially valued. The messages that are sent from one household to another (as well as to the dead) are non-verbal. However, as food is received and eaten, the meaning of the food becomes fixed during open discussions amongst household members. The quantity and quality of food is commented on and compared to what was sent, what was received from other households or what was received in past years.

Non-participation in food exchange is also significant, particularly as a message about ethnic identification. *Mestizos* do not participate in *rendimpa* work exchange, nor do they take part in food exchange during festivals since these are Indian activities. By having a family feast rather than exchanging food, the *mestizos* reinforce the ties between themselves while differentiating themselves from the Indians. The difference between Indians and *mestizos* is also indicated in the choice and preparation of food. Roasted guinea pigs, boiled potatoes and *chicha* are Indian foods and appear at every celebration. They are traditional foods and are used to emphasise traditional values (Archetti 1997; Weismantel 1988). The messages that are sent by making such food choices are discussed verbally. Maria emphasised the difference between herself and the Indians not only by preparing and serving her food differently, but by pointing out these differences to me and to her family. On the other hand, Teresa openly told me in full hearing of her daughters how proud she was that they could cook guinea pig.

Cooking and the exchange of food plays an important role in the creation of female identity. In some areas of the Andes, learning to weave is an important step in the transformation from Indian girlhood to womanhood (Harris 1978; Arnold 1990). In Sucre, where only men weave, an Indian girl has to be able to cook before she can be considered a likely prospect for marriage. This ability to cook is also a source of power (Arnold 1990). The meals that women make are used by women to create, maintain and manipulate social ties that are essential to the formation and survival of the household. This is seen in the importance of cooking in defining household membership and in the use of food exchange in maintaining labour exchange networks. Women also use food to exert control over their husbands.

Episode 3: photos and eggs

As soon as I had my photos of *Finados* developed, I gave away copies to the people who appeared in them. People were surprised when I said that I was giving rather than selling the photos to them. Their experience with photographers was gained during trips to the market towns, where men with Polaroid cameras earn a living by selling pictures. At each household I visited, I was thanked for the photos. As I left, the female household head or a daughter would give me two or three raw eggs (from their own chickens), saying 'here is something to add to your soup' or 'maybe you can fry these'.

Commentary

I did not really think about the raw eggs, apart from seeing them as an example of Andean reciprocity: I was given eggs in return for the photos. However, I noticed that the village doctor would also be given raw eggs and cheese after making house calls. I began to compare the situations where I was given cooked food as opposed to uncooked food. Cooked food is given after work in the fields or during festivals. Uncooked or raw food is given for non-agricultural and non-traditional services. Cooked food is given on occasions when a social tie between the giver and receiver is being emphasised. In the case of agricultural workers, people are bound together by repeated exchanges of labour as well as joint cooperation in productive activities. During festivals, such as *Finados*, cooked food is given to dead relatives, living kin and neighbours, who all help contribute to household agricultural production.

Weismantel (1988: 27) observes that cooking in the Andes is a transformation where the results of productive activities outside the household are brought inside. At the household level, cooking is the means by which the family internalises the external world. I would argue that this does not only happen at the level of consumption within the household, but also at the level of exchange between households. When cooked food is sent from one household to another (even though the recipient may consume all of the food at the household of the giver, as is usually the case with agricultural workers), what is given is something which is associated not only with the inside of their house but with the centre of the house: the hearth. Gifts of raw food, on the other hand, merely come directly from the people's fields or animals.

Episode 4: serving the Corpus Christi feast

The most important community festival in Sucre is Corpus Christi (Bourque 1994; 1995a; 1997). The main features are: costumed processions, a mass, an evening dance, and feasting at the house of a festival sponsor. After the Corpus Christi procession in 1989, I went to the festival sponsor's house to participate in the feast. I was invited into the kitchen, which was dominated by an enormous cauldron of chicken and potato soup. A woman was searching through the soup with a spoon, extracting the potatoes and chicken pieces and putting them into separate pots. A young woman entered the kitchen to announce that the band members and other participants were arriving. As the procession participants arrived, they entered without the customary request for permission. The woman at the cauldron prepared bowls of soup by selecting out an appropriate piece of chicken, adding potatoes and topping the bowl off with broth. She then handed the bowl to another woman and indicated to whom it should be served. The members of the band, who were honoured guests, were given the largest pieces of chicken and a greater quantity of potatoes than other people. Members of the festival committee, relatives of the sponsors, and members of the community council also received soup with more potatoes and meat.

Commentary

The two most important issues illustrated by this episode are the use of space during festivals and the use of food to indicate social hierarchy amongst

Indians (see Bourque [1994; 1997] for a more detailed discussion of space). During baptismal feasts, which are considered household festivals, only invited people may attend. However, during community festivals, such as Corpus Christi, any community member has the right to attend the feast. The strict household boundaries which are in effect during daily life are dissolved to embrace the entire community. The meal which is consumed does not reinforce the bond between the host household and the recipient. Rather, it emphasises the bonds between community members, just as a daily meal reinforces bonds between household members. The food that is supplied during a community festival feast is not just the produce of the host household but of other households in the community.[10]

Consuming feast food is a ritual act. It is important to eat, drink and dance during the festival or else the community will have to bear the anger of San Francisco, the village patron saint. The reward for having processions, eating, drinking and dancing is San Francisco's assistance in making next year's maize crop fertile.[11] The canton priest, who comes to say the mass for Corpus Christi, criticises the Indians for spending money on food and drink and for worshipping San Francisco above God (see Bourque [1995c] for more information of the relationship between the priest and Indians). The *mestizos* of Sucre also see the Indians' excessive consumption as wasteful. They attend the mass and watch the costumed procession, but they do not attend the feast. The community that is being united during the feast is essentially the Indian community. However, they believe that their actions will benefit the entire village. Any agricultural misfortune which befalls a *mestizo* may be blamed on the wrath of San Francisco for their lack of participation in his festival.

The festival feast does not only unite the Indian community, it also emphasises some of the differences between them. This is seen in the variations in the quality of the soup served. The creation of a bowl of soup is a socially significant event. This is particularly the case during festivals, when the components of the soup are separated to facilitate the construction of bowls of soup. In other parts of the Andes, the serving of food during festivals is more structured than in Sucre.[12] Weismantel (1988: 179–80) indicates that in Zumbagua (about two hours from Sucre) status is indicated by the order in which people are served, the positions in which people are seated, and even the size and quality of the plates used. As during *Finados*, this recognition and affirmation of status is in the hands of the women. I was told that it was very important to have a good cook, because she would understand how to direct the serving of food. In some cases, women have been known to manipulate or deny status during the distribution of food. This has also been noted by Weismantel (1988: 28, 179–80).

Episode 5: a visit from the canton officials

In April 1990, after years of lobbying and negotiation with canton and provincial politicians, state funding was approved for the construction of a secondary school in Sucre. It was announced that there was to be a special ceremony, during which the canton officials would hand the document approving the funding to the members of the community council. I was invited to this event along with the village doctor and nurse, the teachers of the primary school and the head of the parent-teacher association.

The officials, wearing suits, ties and sunglasses[13] arrived half an hour late. They made speeches which were accompanied by a series of toasts called *brindis*. These occur at *mestizo* or white public occasions throughout Ecuador. Small glasses of sparkling wine (referred to as champagne) and small finger-shaped sweet biscuits were passed around. After each speech the glasses were raised and people took a drink.

After the *brindis*, the officials were ready to leave. However, during the preparations for their visit, it was decided that the ceremony must be accompanied by a feast. Every parent who had children in school was asked to contribute something to the feast. It was decided that the first course would be chicken soup, to be followed by potatoes with peanut sauce and roast guinea pig. When the officials arrived, they clearly had not been expecting to be faced with a feast. Pressure was put on them to remain. They agreed to stay, but emphasised that they had a busy day and would not be able to stay for long.

For this meal, a number of tables had been assembled into one long table in one of the classrooms of the primary school. Everyone had a chair. The chicken soup arrived and was eaten without much comment. The various guests talked amongst themselves. When the plates of guinea pig were brought out, the officials were given whole guinea pigs, while the other guests received only a quarter of a guinea pig. No comment was made on this. All eyes were turned towards the officials to see if they were going to eat the guinea pigs. When the politicians picked up the guinea pigs with their fingers and began to eat in the customary manner, the people looked at each other and smiled.

Commentary

This episode provides an excellent example of the complex ways in which meals and certain items of food can be used by different social players. The *brindis*, the only event of its kind I ever witnessed in Sucre, displayed the Indians' awareness of the correct *mestizo* food and drink code during official public occasions of this nature. At the same time, in deciding that the politicians were to be fed a meal, the Indians of Sucre were also using their own system of cultural codes to indicate their support of the politicians. The decision to serve roasted guinea pig made it even more obvious that this meal was not only an expression of celebrations, thanks and support, but also an expression of Sucre's 'Indian' identity in a *mestizo*-dominated canton. In accepting the meal, eating the guinea pigs and using their fingers to eat the guinea pigs, the politicians were indicating that they understood and accepted the meaning of the meal and especially of the guinea pigs. The politicians, who owe their positions to the results of democratic elections, had no wish to offend potential voters, regardless of their ethnicity.

It is worth mentioning that there are differences between the way that *mestizos* from Sucre and *mestizos* from the canton and provincial capitals view certain foods. The guinea pig is a case in point. Guinea pig is seen as an 'Indian dish', yet at the same time it is also part of Ecuadorian national cuisine. *Mestizos* in the cities raise and eat guinea pig, seeing it as a typical Andean (as opposed to coastal) dish. When *mestizos* in the provincial capital cook and eat guinea pigs, they do not worry about compromising their *mestizo* identity by eating an Indian food. However, *mestizos* in Sucre are concerned about eating guinea pig because people in the canton and provincial capital see Sucre as an Indian village. When I talked about some of the Sucre *mestizos* to people in the canton capital, I was told: 'These people think they are *mestizo*, but they are really Indian. Look at their last names and the colour of their skin. They are Indian'. This ambiguity makes the *mestizos* of Sucre especially keen to avoid actions that could be seen as 'Indian'. On occasions when the *mestizos* of Sucre eat guinea pig, they try to downplay the 'Indianness' of this dish. Sometimes this is done by using special methods of preparation, such as marinating the guinea pig before roasting it. When Enrique, a young Indian man, said that some *mestizos* do not like eating guinea pig, he was not referring merely to a like or dislike of the flavour and texture of guinea pig meat. He was also referring to the association of ethnic identity that accompanies the act of eating guinea pig prepared in the Indian way.

Discussion

These episodes give an indication of the variety of contexts in which food is used as a means of communication in the Andes. The joint production and consumption of food reflects, and on occasions is used, to make statements about household and community membership as well as gender and ethnic identity. Food is used to create social ties as well as social differences. It can be used to emphasise or demonstrate affiliation with tradition or modernity, rural or urban areas, or traditional or capitalistic economic systems. This use occurs in a context where reciprocity is a defining feature of daily and ritual life. Moreover, food itself, the type of food and the actions of producing, preparing, serving and consuming food, reflect and demonstrate religious, moral and social beliefs and values. In fact, it is the importance of reciprocity and the religious, moral and social implications of food that make food an effective and powerful means of communication.

Certain foods (such as guinea pig) or the state of food (such as raw or cooked) can have multiple meanings to members of different groups. These various meanings may not be accepted, but they are certainly understood (to differing degrees) by individuals who are giving or receiving food. According to the context, individuals or social groups may borrow the food practices of another group in order to make a particular point. The adoption of the *brindis* in the episode of the visiting canton officials is an example of this. At times, this borrowing is contested. On the other hand, the acceptance of adopting borrowed foodstuffs and cooking techniques, such as frying, can lead to wide-scale change.

The use of food, the manipulation of social ties and identity, the moral values attached to food, and the impact of changes in the types, meanings and values of food, affects both men and women. However, it is clear that women are the major players in anything involving food. They are the ones who cook, prepare, serve, buy and sell food. If the men of Sucre want to make an impression on local politicians by serving them roast guinea pig, they can only do this if the women agree to butcher and cook guinea pig. If a husband wants to impress his friends by serving rice instead of potatoes, he can only do this if his wife consents. This has two major implications: first, women use cooked food to wield power; and second, women largely control the changes that take place with regard to cooked food. To some extent, this has resulted in the maintenance of many traditional food practices, meanings and values in comparison to other areas of life.[14] Clothing is an example. Many researchers have noted the importance of clothing in the Andes as an indicator of gender, regional and ethnic identity (Arnold 1990; Meisch 1987; Salomon 1981). However, in many areas (Sucre included) these differences are not as rigid as they once were, because fewer groups produce their own clothing, preferring to purchase clothes from the markets. It is usually the men, who have more access to cash, who first abandon traditional modes of dress. Even in 1989, the men of Sucre dressed the same as *mestizo* men from most other rural areas of Ecuador. Women's dress had also changed significantly, especially amongst younger women, some of whom wore trousers rather than market-purchased skirts or the even more traditional woollen wraparound skirt.

Generational differences are also seen in the use of food. It is the younger people who are introducing new crops, new foods and new ways of preparing food. It is the older people, such as Teresa, who are emphasising the importance of traditional practices, such as leaving the *ofrenda* for the souls of the dead. Now that the younger generation have more access to other people's ideas about food, via television, radio, school and working outside of the community, changes are inevitable and will probably occur more rapidly.

Conclusions

Most of the major conclusions to be drawn from this chapter have already been covered in the discussion above. However, I want to make a few additional points. First, this paper has only covered a small number of the events in daily and ritual life where food is significant. I have not addressed what happens when women go to market to sell or purchase food, I have not fully discussed the use of food during ritual, and I have not even touched on beliefs about how food affects health and the use of food in healing (see Acero and Rive 1989; Balladelli 1988; Archetti 1997; Bourque 1996). Nor have I discussed the importance of drink in the Andes.

The question also remains as to the use of food as non-verbal communication. To what extent can it be said that people in Sucre manage to communicate using food? Rapport (Chapter 1 in this volume) suggests that often what we take for communication is actually mis-communication. He notes that even if social interactions are shared, the meanings to the participants can differ. Pink (Chapter 6 in this volume) also asks how anthropologists and other social actors can impute intentionality, given the possibility of multiple and changing intentions. With regard to the use of food in Sucre, these are both valid considerations. How can one person be said to have communicated with another person if there is some ambiguity about the intentions of the person giving food? In spite of the possibility of miscommunication, people manage (in Rapport's terms) to 'muddle through'. That is, people decide what the most likely intention is and act on it.

People frequently talk about the foods that they have given, received and consumed. Discussions about food provide a forum where the multitude of possible intentions is evaluated and the appropriate reaction is agreed upon. Such discussions usually take place amongst household members or close friends. Thus the imputation of intention has both individual and group aspects (a point not covered by Pink). Moreover, past discussions about non-verbal food messages shape both the way that food is used and the interpretation that is placed on food use. Supplementary to the non-verbal nature of food messages, talking about food is an essential part of the process by which people, including anthropologists, learn about the verbal and non-verbal languages of food, and about ways that food can be used to communicate, affirm or challenge existing beliefs, practices and social, political and economic relations.

Notes

1 Fieldwork was carried out in Sucre from 1989 to 1990 and in 1996.
2 Sucre is predominantly an Indian community (that is, the majority of inhabitants see themselves as and are generally accepted as Indians). A few people who classify themselves as *mestizos* (people of mixed Indian and Spanish descent) also live in Sucre. Sucre is the only Indian community in the canton. For the Indians, interaction with people in the canton or provincial capitals essentially means interaction

with *mestizos*. Most of the *mestizos* that I have talked to in the area see themselves as superior to the Indians.

3 It is beyond the scope of this chapter to summarise the history of anthropological and sociological studies of food. Caplan (1997) and Beardsworth and Keil (1997) both provide excellent discussions of how the study of food has changed.

4 This is a common expression of thanks amongst Indians in the Andes.

5 Many households engage in labour exchange to compensate for imbalances in supplies of labour and land. The type of labour exchange that people engage in varies according to ethnicity. *Rendimpa* (called *ayni* in other parts of the Andes) exchanges labour for labour and is only usually practiced by Indians. *Partido* is a form of share-cropping utilised by both Indians and *mestizos*. It is also possible to hire labourers for wages, which is an option primarily exercised by *mestizos*.

6 The importance of household boundaries amongst Indians has been noted in other parts of the Andes (Johnsson 1986; Isbell 1977; 1978; Allen 1988). In contrast, *mestizo* families do not uphold such strict boundaries.

7 In contrast, Weismantel (1998: 179) notes that in Zumbagua, the food that is served is 'specifically understood to be her [the cook's] presentation to the person receiving the food. The recipient directs their thanks to the woman at the hearth, not to the person delivering the bowl'.

8 Sucre does not have a market. It only has a few small dry goods stores where people buy items in small quantities. There are a number of regional markets in the canton capitals and in the provincial capital which operate on different days of the week. Access to these markets is facilitated by a bus service which leaves Sucre early in the morning, goes to the market in question and returns to Sucre in the early afternoon.

9 This is a reciprocal term of address between the parents of a child and the god-parents of a child. The term is usually extended to include the spouse and consanguineal relatives.

10 In the past, friends, neighbours and *compadres* would lend agricultural produce and money to the host household to enable them to provide a feast. In 1989, a festival committee collected cash donations from most of the households in Sucre, purchased food, hired a band and appointed a cook.

11 Corpus Christi occurs in May or June, shortly after the harvest of maize.

12 See Parkes (Chapter 14 in this volume) for an example of how, in Pakistan, seating during public events is related to status.

13 In Chapter 6 of this volume Sarah Pink indicates how items of clothing, such as sunglasses, can be used to suggest an association with outsiders.

14 Compare this to Josephides (Chapter 13 in this volume) who discusses how women in Papua New Guinea challenge cultural norms by rejecting conventional forms of communication.

References

Acero, G. and Rive, M. (1989) *Medicina Indigena: Cacha, Chimborazo*, Quito: Abya Yala.

Allen, C. (1988) *The Hold That Life Has: Coca and Cultural Identity in an Andean Community*, Washington DC: Smithsonian Institution Press.

Archetti, Eduardo P. (1997) *Guinea Pigs: Food, Symbol and Conflict of Knowledge in Ecuador*, Oxford: Berg.

Arnold, Denise (1990) 'Owners, borrowers and weavers in the Bolivian Highlands', paper presented at the workshop on Gender Relations, Work and Proprietorship Among Indigenous People of South America, Institute of Latin American Studies, London, 7–8 December 1990.

Balladelli, P. (1988) *Entre lo Magico y lo Natural: La Medicina Indigena*, Quito: Abya Yala.

Barthes, R. (1975) 'Towards a psychology of contemporary food consumption', in E. Forster and R. Forster (eds) *European Diet from Pre-industrial to Modern Times*, New York: Harper & Row.

Beardsworth, A. and Keil, T. (1997) *Sociology on the Menu*, London: Routledge.

Bourdieu, P. (1986) *Distinction: A Social Critique of the Judgement of Taste*, London: Routledge and Kegan Paul.

Bourque, N. (1994) 'Spatial meaning in Andean festivals: Corpus Christi and Octavo', *Ethnology*, 33(3): 229–43.

——(1995a) 'Developing people and plants: life-cycle and agricultural festivals in the Andes', *Ethnology*, 34(1): 75–87.

——(1995b) 'Savages and angels: spiritual, social and physical development in Andean life-cycle festivals', *Ethnos*, 60(1–2): 99–114.

——(1995c) 'Priests and saints: syncretism and power in the Ecuadorian Andes, *Scottish Journal of Religious Studies*, 16(1): 25–36.

——(1996) 'Working gender: the construction of gender and the use of power in the Central Ecuadorian Andes', University of Glasgow, Latin American Studies Occasional Paper no. 64.

——(1997) 'Making space: social change, identity and the creation of boundaries in the Central Ecuadorian Andes', *Bulletin of Latin American Research*, 16(2): 153–68.

Brush, S. (1977) *Mountain, Field, and Family: The Economy and Human Ecology of an Andean Valley*, Philadelphia: University of Pennsylvania Press.

Caplan, P. (1997) 'Approaches to the study of food, health and identity', in P. Caplan (ed.) *Food, Health and Identity*, London: Routledge.

Douglas, M. (1966) *Purity and Danger*, London: Allen and Unwin.

——(1975) *Implicit Meanings: Essays in Anthropology*, London: Routledge and Kegan Paul.

Fischler, C. (1988) 'Food, self and identity', *Social Science Information*, 27(2): 275–92.

Goody, J. (1982) *Cooking, Cuisine and Class: A Study in Comparative Society*, Cambridge: Cambridge University Press.

Harbottle, L. (1997) 'Fast food/spoiled identity: Iranian migrants in the British catering trade;, in P. Caplan (ed.) *Food, Health and Identity*, London: Routledge.

Harris, O. (1978) 'Complementarity and conflict: an Andean view of women and men', in J. La Fontaine (ed.) *Sex and Age as Principles of Social Differentiation*, ASA monograph 17, London: Academic Press, pp. 21–40.

——(1982) 'The dead and the devils among the Bolivian Laymi', in M. Bloch and J. Parry (eds) *Death and the Regeneration of Life*, Cambridge: Cambridge University Press.

Isbell, B. J. (1977) 'Those who love me: an analysis of Andean kinship and reciprocity within a ritual context', in R. Bolton and E. Mayer (eds) *Andean Kinship and Marriage*, Washington DC: American Anthropological Association Special Publication no. 7.

——(1978) *To Defend Ourselves: Ecology and Ritual in an Andean Village*, Austin: University of Texas Press.

Johnsson, M. (1986) *Food and Culture among Bolivian Aymara: Symbolic Expressions of Social Relations*, Uppsala Studies in Cultural Anthropology 7, Stockholm: Almquvist and Wiksell.

Lévi-Strauss, C. (1965) 'The culinary triangle', *Partisan Review*, 33: 586–95.

Lévi-Strauss, C. (1968) *Structural Anthropology vol. 1*, Harmondsworth: Penguin.
——(1970) *The Raw and the Cooked*, London: Jonathan Cape.
Meisch, L. (1987) *Otavalo: Weaving, Costume and the Market*, Quito: Ediciones Libri Mundi.
Mennell, S. (1985) *All Manners of Food: Eating and Taste in England and France from the Middle Ages to the Present*, London: Blackwell.
Mintz, S. (1985) *Sweetness and Power: The Place of Sugar in Modern History*, New York: Viking Press.
Salomon, F. (1981) 'Weavers of Otavalo', in N. Whitten Jr (ed.) *Cultural Transformations and Ethnicity in Modern Ecuador*, Urbana: University of Illinois Press.
Weismantel, M. J. (1988) *Food, Gender, and Poverty in the Ecuadorian Andes*, Philadelphia: University of Philadelphia Press.
Willetts, A. (1997) 'Bacon sandwiches got the better of me: meat-eating and vegetarianism in South-East London', in P. Caplan (ed.) *Food, Health and Identity*, London: Routledge.

Chapter 6

Sunglasses, suitcases and other symbols

Intentionality, creativity and indirect communication in festive and everyday performances

Sarah Pink

This chapter discusses local everyday and festive representations of wealth, status and power in Guinea Bissau. Focusing on representations of self and pertinent cultural themes through public display, costume and verbal descriptions, I explore how 'direct' and 'indirect' strategies become interwoven through the creativity of communication. The fieldwork, carried out in 1997, was based in Canchungo, a town in north-east Guinea Bissau. Manjacos, the largest ethnic group in the area, are known for their powerful *iran* (forest spirits) and European migrant wealth. I discuss how locally meaningful representations of transnational connections and wealth form a continuous theme through everyday and carnival representations. Many informants 'directly' stated their desire to leave Guinea Bissau for Europe. Their aspirations and strategies were simultaneously represented 'indirectly' though the symbolism and performance of everyday life and carnival. Whilst I understood certain communications to be direct or indirect in terms of my own ability to interpret them, distinguishing between indirect/direct communication, as I argue below, is considerably more complex.

Wealthy women[1]

In this section I introduce the story of Miranda. Based on accounts related to me by local people, and on my own experience, Miranda's tale mirrors that of one of my informants. However, for ethical motives as well as issues of representation, her name has been changed.[2] In 1977 Miranda was twenty-one, a single mother with two daughters: Ana, four years old, was 'white' – Miranda told me her father was a *cooperante* (European development worker) who had returned to his country, wife and adult offspring – and Segunda, aged two, was the daughter of a local man who very irregularly fulfilled his paternal economic obligations. Her experience of working for *cooperantes*, combined with the 'natural' connections she implied by identifying her 'white' daughter with Europeans, had helped Miranda to find employment in the houses of *cooperantes*. During her 'marriage'[3] to the European, and the stay of other *cooperantes* who had showered Miranda and 'white' Ana with gifts and cash, she had been 'rich'. When I arrived in Guinea Bissau these people had left. Miranda was living from hand to mouth, accumulating increasing debts to local shopkeepers, neighbours, and her landlord. During her pregnancy and after Ana's birth, she had lived in a big house with a white man in his late fifties to whom everyone had referred as her 'husband', been surrounded by electrical appliances, eaten European food, and worn beautiful clothes. Formerly the envy of the neighbourhood women, she now sent her 'white' daughter to their verandas to beg for rice for her dinner. Miranda was bitter, not towards her 'husband' (who she said 'wanted' to send her money), but towards the father of Segunda and her neighbours who were unwilling to 'help'. Miranda worked part-time helping in our house; here she shared her aspirations, problems and strategies with me. Her Guinea Bissauan neighbours witnessed her new link with Europeans.

In February, as carnival approached, Miranda showed me photographs from previous years. She had worn full carnival costume: a short skirt, blouse, make-up, shell beads, and was photographed in the main square and in the disco. In 1997, lacking essential components for her costume, she had to beg from neighbours, attending carnival only once, wearing borrowed shorts our neighbour had worn the previous day. She spent her entire week's wages on the disco entrance fee, then requested an advance on her salary to pay a large debt to the photographer. The next week Miranda's children were begging for their dinner again.

At the beginning of April, one of Miranda's European *cooperante* friends visited a local NGO. He settled her debts, gave her cash, opened a bank account in her name and brought gifts of gold jewellery and a letter from his wife. I transcribed a letter to his wife into English dictated by Miranda in Krioulu. She asked for more gold, shoes and regular telephone calls. Miranda's new wealth was displayed the following evening. She had not cleaned our house; she was busy having a blouse tailored and buying new jeans, and purchasing hair extensions for herself and Segunda. She invested some money in a telephone call to her 'husband', arranging for him to transfer a large monthly allowance into her bank account – to make her considerably wealthier than most local people. She asked him to visit and bring gold jewellery and a bicycle for his daughter. Miranda continued to work for us, but now her daughters walked with her in view of the neighbours, breakfasting on bread sticks filled with margarine, instead of the cold rice (or nothing) that they usually consumed.

One day I visited Miranda when she was cooking meat for lunch on her verandah. Her youngest daughter swung on a post clutching a wad of *peso* notes in her fist, whilst Ana sat carefully folding each of the notes in her bundle. In reality, little of Miranda's allowance remained and the fortune from Europe would take months to arrive. The displays of wealth I have described above had exhausted Miranda's immediate resources. However, they had not symbolised what she perceived as the real extent of her wealth and status. Thus she combined another strategy to communicate her wealth. She recounted the story of her restored status to Marta, also 'white', who had recently been working in Europe. Marta's was currently the richest of the families that socialised in the neighbourhood and had manifested a range of indicators of their well-being (discussed below). Miranda wanted Marta to know that her gold necklaces were in transit.

However, a bigger prize awaited: a week later Miranda's brother arrived with the message that she must immediately go to meet 'someone' in Bissau. She left directly, returning the next evening with her 'white' aunt from Paris. She explained that her aunt wanted to take Ana and herself to live in France. Impatient to return to more developed Dakar, the aunt would telephone Miranda once she had information from the French embassy. Miranda was on the verge of a most prestigious local achievement: to be absent – a migrant. The day before her departure for Dakar the children were breakfasting on bread and margarine and a neighbour was completing Miranda's hair extensions; yet, she confided, she was having problems raising the cash for the journey.

Miranda's hair, clothes, jewellery, the cash and 'luxury' food she flaunted in her young daughters' hands, her European friends, her 'white' daughter, her prospects of migration, were variously invoked as symbols of wealth and well-being. Sometimes this was through displaying local resources, tailored clothes, bread with margarine, and *peso* notes. Others, like gold necklaces and the full bank account, must be imported from Europe and take time to be displayed. These aspects she announced verbally, thus building a framework by which the neighbours may understand why she dressed smartly and proudly walked to the bank, asking a neighbour to do her shopping since she was much too busy to go to the market.

Miranda was consistently successful in obtaining 'help' from *cooperantes*, but her benefactors were less happy with how she spent their donations: not on nutritious food and medicines for Ana, but on clothes and hair extensions for herself. But Miranda treated these Europeans as Guinea Bissauans treat migrant relatives. Her external economic support was represented locally through displays of wealth and well-being. Had Miranda spent these cash gifts on medicines and vitamin supplements for Ana she would have been no 'richer' than before. The status represented through costume and clothing is thought to increase one's access to other resources, and Miranda was concerned with translating her 'European' connections and resources into symbols that were meaningful locally.

Indirection and inter-intentionality

The 'communication' I discuss here entails a series of representations of 'self' and 'society' that refer to wealth, prestige and access to transnational resources.

In the crafting of these representations, individuals creatively draw on a range of material and cultural resources that they may intentionally arrange in particular ways in particular contexts. For instance, the intention may be to conform to particular 'conventions' of what one does with wealth, or it may be to invent a tailored strategy by which one's wealth may be displayed to particular other individuals in particular contexts.

As I have shown above, material objects, such as costume, jewellery or cash, and personal relationships, such as a 'white' child or 'friend', can be used to symbolise wealth and status. Likewise, performance, in the form of language, ritual (in this case carnival) and everyday display, becomes part of the process by which these items and individuals are referenced and made meaningful. In this analysis, indirect communication entails the intentional use or creation of symbols to produce and in which to invest meanings. Sometimes these symbols are personalised as, for example, *Miranda's* gold necklace that she spoke of to represent *her* own wealth and its source as opposed to *Marta's* gold necklaces – which could stand for Marta's personalised economic strategy. However, the meanings of these objects and behaviours are not constant: 'cultural forms such as language, ritual and other symbolic constructions are made meaningful and substantial by people's interpretations of them. They are given life by being made meaningful' (Cohen 1994: 167).

Cohen (1994) highlights certain problems associated with 'intentionality'. Discussing public speaking, he points out that 'the audience constructs the speaker's intentions as being the same as theirs: the speaker does not achieve the audience's compliance with his/her intentions' (1994: 46). This questions whether any type of (direct or indirect) communication can be intentional in that the intention of the speaker is inevitably re-invented by their audience. As Rapport (Chapter 1 in this volume) suggests, all social interaction is characterised by an 'ambiguity of exchange and a diversity of perception'. Moreover, intention is not exclusive to the communicator. Intentionality is also part of the creativity of the 'receiver' of a 'direct' or 'indirect' communication. This assumes an intersubjectivity or 'inter-intentionality' whereby individual's intentions are motivated by their interpretations of the intentions of others. This relates similarly to the communications anthropologists are involved in: we cannot get inside the heads of our informants and likewise they cannot get inside one another's heads. The intention of the communicator is inevitably inaccessible, be the communication 'direct' or 'indirect'; as Rapport points out (*ibid.*), 'miscommunication is the inexorable result of meanings being channelled through and refracted by the boundary of the individual body'. Moreover, does an individual ever have just one single intention? An individual may consciously combine a plurality of intentions in one action or representation. Such representations are flexible: even if we don't know exactly what someone else intended to mean, we do know that they may have intended a variety of possibilities. It is this very inaccessibility and indeterminacy of intention that allows symbolic meanings, and the communications and social relations in which they become embedded, to be so negotiable.

However, when a representation is interpreted though the diverse personal experiences of its 'participants and onlookers', who in Cohen's words use it to 'tell themselves a story' (1994: 164), there may not be space for negotiation: the story may remain unchallenged in the mind of its inventor. With this in mind here I draw from my own experiences of being a person from 'outside' (Europe) who became involved with a context where the outside was seemingly constantly referenced, forming part of the everyday world and conversation. Some of the stories I tell here are shaped by the stories told to me; I have used these 'local histories' to develop my own understanding of local people's intentions. Sometimes a fuller understanding of the 'indirect' nuances, or symbolic references, of a conversation can be constructed through historical knowledge of how these are interwoven with long-term narratives, relationships and strategies. This entails what Hendry (1993: 5) has called 'unwrapping', but in this case, following Hendry I have attempted to examine not only what is underneath the 'layers' but to also focus on the layers themselves (Hendry 1993). For instance, Miranda told me that several years before my arrival she had argued with Marta, who had criticised her affair with a European that 'hadn't got her anywhere'. Miranda said that in response she had accused her friend of various immoral acts, and told her that her own 'white' daughter would not be stuck in Guinea Bissau like Marta: Ana *was* going to live in Europe, go to school, have a good life and be 'better' than Marta. Shortly after, however, Marta did migrate to Europe. On her return Miranda visited her with the other neighbourhood women: she did not need to be told 'directly' that she had been wrong. Whilst the argument was not referred to explicitly or 'directly', it was not forgotten: Miranda recounted it to me the day that she nervously anticipated Marta's return. Miranda's subsequent broadcast of her own good fortune to the neighbourhood, and particularly to Marta, was also a reference to the argument, and a response to Marta's past observation that her affair with a *brancu* had brought her not the wealth she had hoped for, but poverty and little prospect of migration. Miranda found an indirect, 'diplomatic' way of indicating that Marta had been wrong. Whilst her intentionality was linked to the bitterness of the row that still simmered beneath their friendship, her response had been (to borrow Hendry's [1993] term) 'wrapped' in politeness. Now both could see the other's successful strategy, displays of wealth and European contacts to offer continuity.

In everyday life, costume, material and bodily symbols of wealth and power thus combine with linguistic narratives. 'Indirect' communication is not an isolated genre, but is used in combination with other more or less 'direct' forms of communication. Both 'direct' and 'indirect' communication may occur within the same sentence or action. These different ways of saying things combine as individuals experience them and build their own 'pictures' and narratives from the variety of interpretations they piece together. For me, the anthropological problem is how to define a communication as 'direct' or 'indirect'. In some fieldwork contexts and in everyday life the distinction appears simple. When in Spanish and English my friends speak of how they have been told something through an *indirecta*, a 'hint', the communication can be defined as 'indirect' in terms of the 'route' by which it is represented, or coded. But a direct/indirect dichotomy is problematic: an action, word or performance seen through one pair of eyes as 'direct' may have a different 'indirect' meaning for another. Direct/indirect communications are not a pair that can be simply identified and compared. Instead I treat the 'indirect' as a constant possibility. Below I concentrate on how local discourse and constant themes of wealth, migration and consumption are 'indirectly' (and sometimes 'directly' as I have described above) referenced in local, everyday and festive carnival representations. Both everyday and festive representations will be interpreted as *strategies* and as *representations of strategies*.

Carnival and transnational concerns

Carnival is, in the words of several informants 'the biggest festival in Guinea Bissau'. Historically it was introduced by the Portuguese and institutionally appropriated by subsequent governments. Whilst carnival is celebrated in most smaller cities and towns as well as rural villages, the main focus of carnival is in the capital, Bissau, where the event receives international attention. In 1997 in Canchungo the carnival competitions (for groups, carnival queens and masks) were not supported by prize money from the Ministry of Culture, therefore the competitive and 'officially' structured aspects of carnival were abandoned. Nevertheless, my informants predicted, 'the people will still have carnival'. Indeed, many people were unaware that the formal carnival had been cancelled until carnival had begun. Here my interest is in how individuals represent discourses on wealth, migration and consumption in carnival. I do not attempt conclusively to define this (or any) carnival: I believe that carnival is interwoven with society and culture in multiple ways and thus expresses a range of possibilities. As Schechner proposes, it is an event in which people celebrate 'life's fertile possibilities'. In doing so, 'they put on masks and costumes, erect and wave banners, and construct effigies not merely to disguise or embellish their ordinary selves, or to flaunt the outrageous, but also to act out the multiplicity that every human life is' (Schechner 1993: 46). Individuals are inspired by their personal understandings of carnival. Their representations and interpretations both become part of an event called carnival and are performances that are inextricably interwoven with each individual's personal narrative, agenda and circumstances. The aspects of carnival discussed here are part of the wider spatial and social choreography of carnival which, we need to remember, is enacted in public and shared space where performances are shaped by the intersubjectivity between performers and audiences. The interdependencies and continuities created by the carnival at any one moment are also key to understanding how in this setting people enact fragments of their identities, aspirations, perspectives on things, on self and other.

The origins of this carnival can be seen in a 'tradition' that was historically invented and performed through the interaction between local creativity and the structures of Portuguese carnival and colonialism. As such it is a festivity that has always had 'transnational connections' (see Hannerz 1996: 22–3). During my fieldwork these links were made explicit through media references to carnival in Brazil and Portugal, and are integral to many performances. The local and personal implications of migration, migrant remittances and abilities to consume represent some of the concerns of local people. As Comaroff and Comaroff suggest, imported artifacts, commodities, behaviours or rites 'may serve to situate people in wider regional, national and international landscapes'. In this imported carnival, imported goods are owned and activities performed, in relation to 'traditional' ones. Once woven into local performances, practices and costumes, they have the power to impart a sense of presence though which distant horizons become tangible realities' (Comaroff and Comaroff 1993: xxi). It is these realities that individuals are constantly reaching out to grasp, at the same time emphasising the importance of personal experience.

Textiles, tailoring and second-hand clothes

In Canchungo wealthy women exhibited an appropriate range of clothes for each occasion. For example, a smart European suit would be appropriate to wear to the Portuguese bank in Bissau; to visit sick relatives a summer dress, perhaps with a locally made *pano* wrapped around; in the neighbourhood or at home, a loose African dress; to a European party jeans and a blouse; and for first of May celebrations, shorts and a T-shirt over a bikini. In the homes of even the poorer Guinea Bissauans, the second-hand European clothes sold in the market were used as floor cloths.

Panos, locally woven cloth, are an important aspect of local costume that have various uses in both ritual and everyday domains. 'Traditionally' *panos* are worn at Manjaco weddings, funerals and other life-cycle rituals, and are important prestige items: the number of *panos* a man is wrapped in on burial is directly related to his wealth and importance when alive. At around 400,000 pesos each, *panos* are costly, ownership of them represents wealth, and to give *panos* at life-cycle rituals constitutes a display of wealth. My women neighbours often wore *panos* in the morning before dressing, but in my urban neighbourhood men did not wear *panos* in everyday life. There are no absolute rules for *pano* use: the *pano* maker told me that people could use them for 'whatever they like'. A Manjaco woman from a village some twenty kilometers away laughed at a man crossing the square of another village: 'look at that man wearing his *pano* as if it was a skirt'. In that village I frequently saw men and women wearing *panos* as 'skirts' during the day and as shawls in the early morning chill. In her village, she told me, women wear *panos* similarly, but men reserve them for rituals.

However, *panos* are worn in Canchungo's city streets for carnival. My Manjaco women neighbours described it thus: you wear a pano around your waist as a skirt, then a T-shirt or short blouse with strings of shell beads, then you wear make-up on your face and put talc on your face and chest. Often just one strip (six of which make up a *pano*) is worn by children. In carnival, *panos* as both ethnic symbols and indicators of wealth may represent both general and personal Manjaco wealth. But many Manjaco women discarded the iconography of 'traditional' wealth for transnational icons of consumption.

During the days prior to carnival the neighbourhood's tailor made more profit from the many young women needing short blouses and skirts for carnival than he normally took in a month. Throughout the year women informants wore both West African and European fabrics and styles. My younger neighbours tended to wear their older African clothes for relaxing or working around their houses, and European styles – jeans, skirts, blouses, T-shirts – for school, the market or the disco. Older women stuck more closely to 'African' fabrics and styles. In the words of a middle-aged Guinea Bissauan woman business-skills trainer, 'it's alright for young girls with slim bodies to wear short skirts and tight trousers, but when you get to our age, and you are bigger, you want to wear comfortable larger clothes'. Her own silk trouser-suits and embroidered dresses exuded her wealth and status. The popular culture of the teenager and women in their twenties favoured the tight jeans and short skirts that she spoke of. The significance of these European styles may partially be understood in terms of the connections with Europe that they imply. Informants frequently requested clothing from migrant relatives in Europe and other West African countries. Their requests are usually specific, representing ideas of availability and local popular culture. When I made my first return trip to London my teenage neighbour called to put in her order: 'I want you to bring me something from England', she told me – 'a blue blouse with short sleeves and a gold necklace with a heart on it'. Several local women wore gold earrings with small hearts hanging from them. These had been sent by relatives from Lisbon.

In contrast to imported new clothes, imported used clothes are not presti-gious. Used clothing is called *ropa descoitadu* in Krioulu, meaning spoiled, poor clothing, and also used to refer to one's own old clothing. When Miranda complained that we had unsuitable cleaning cloths she instructed me to buy *ropa descoitadu* from the imported used clothes stall in the market. A certain stigma is attached to used European clothes (although not when they are gifts from European friends). They indicate poverty, as do one's own old clothes. In contrast, informants said that wealth, represented through one's physical appearance, can facilitate access to other resources. Elena, a cook at a local

NGO, made clothing central to her point about local hospital provisions. Speaking of how hospital services were regulated, she described how she arrived early one morning to wait for a consultation, sitting on the hard seats, with fever, headache, wearing her old clothes with no shoes and hugging her aching body, crying. Whilst she waited, others arrived from Bissau, with their high-heeled shoes, straightened hair and expensive clothes, to be ushered directly into the consultation room. The discussion group I was running at the time confirmed her story. I asked if they thought a means-testing system could help. They shook their heads ironically; one man explained that if free treatment was offered to poor people then everyone would pretend to be poor − they would dress in old *descoitadu* clothes for the consultations. If someone was too ill to seek out old clothes their family would find some and dress them. In this discourse second-hand clothes were made meaningful in a particular way, their symbolic cargo was made explicit through their association with poverty and the powerlessness that goes with looking as if one cannot afford a bribe. My informants identified clothing as a symbol used indirectly and intentionally to communicate about wealth. Simultaneously they used the example of clothing to speak by analogy about the privileges of the wealthy and well connected and the powerlessness of the poor.

The other context in which *descoitadu* clothes emerged was in carnival. As a man drifted past wearing a woman's transparent nightdress, a VSO volunteer observed to me that this was one of the few uses that Guineans she knew had for the used clothes sent by European charities: they were only suitable for cleaning the floor or performing the outrageously ridiculous in carnival and thus implying that they were inappropriate for everyday wear.

Icons from imports

The week before carnival, those young women in my neighbourhood who could afford to bought hair extensions, and hair-plaiting on the verandah became even more intense than usual. By carnival most had fashionable long plaited *rastas*. Wearing *rastas* is not solely a carnival theme, but part of a wider body project, in this case attaching a symbol of one's power to consume to the body as a symbol of beauty. On becoming 'rich' Miranda bought hair; as soon as migrants returned their daughters had *rastas*. Hair extensions cost at least 40,000 pesos for a head of hair and require several long afternoons of cooperative plaiting. A glimpse of young women's spending patterns indicates the importance of *rastas*. Their prevalence in carnival similarly implies their importance within women's popular culture and consumption patterns. Whilst *rastas* alone are not a symbol of extraordinary wealth, their relative costliness, and women's tendency to invest money in *rastas* and thus in the transformation of their bodies rather than in healthcare and schooling, illustrates their prioritisation of symbolic well-being and its public display.[4]

The carnival costumes of young women in my neighbourhood were extraordinary combinations, creative and personalised, drawing on both popular culture and fashion and 'traditional' carnival themes. Some wore jeans, shorts and bra-tops for carnival, others *panos* with blouses and beads. The personal was inscribed on clothing as my informants drew and wrote on their shorts and jeans, borrowing imagery from imported materials, reproducing cartoon characters, consumer labels and foreign words. One teenage woman wrote 'love' and other words on her shorts, admitting to me that she didn't know their meaning but had copied them from her school exercise book. I had seen the glossy slogan-covered exercise books on sale in the main street. She insisted I photograph her in her carnival outfit. Another day she had worn a brightly coloured short skirt and top with her face painted and hair wild. I remembered the first time I had photographed her: she had arrived at my house immaculately dressed in a skirt and T-shirt and posed at my table as if writing in my notebook.

'Give me your glasses'

'I want your glasses', said Lucinda, handing me the change for the tomatoes she had sold me. Since arriving in Canchungo I had been approached by strangers, neighbours and my husband's students, all asking for my glasses. I explained that they were useless to her, and I would be unable to see without them. 'But you've got two pairs', she insisted, referring to the prescription sunglasses she had seen me wearing. I wondered what she would say if she knew I also had two spares. Sight tests are available at the hospital in Bissau, but spectacles are not made in Guinea Bissau. Acquiring spectacles depends on one's access to personal and cash resources extending outside the country. Guinea Bissauans send their prescriptions to Europe along migrant networks whilst imported sunglasses are sold locally from boards or tables by street vendors. Having sight glasses represents wealth and implies the theme of possession of things from 'outside', and their acquisition requires the willingness of a migrant to submit the prescription and pay for them. One informant suggested 'rich' people wear spectacles as an adornment, thus displaying an item that can only be accessed from 'outside'. In carnival this image was reproduced constantly, but I interpret it as a representation of the discourse on glasses and transnational connections rather than personal displays of wealth. For both photographs and festive costumes my informants borrowed and shared sunglasses. In carnival borrowed glasses invoke a general theme about the connections, cash and material wealth that is associated with their possession. Simultaneously they situate their wearer by indicating that they are in a position to borrow. This connects with the theme of migration and European friends – of access to 'outside' and of the power to consume the icons of fashion and popular culture represented on television and by immigrants' accounts.

The men in suits

During carnival I photographed a neighbourhood teenager who had disguised himself by shaving his head as if balding. Several months after carnival I took a copy of the photograph to his sister's house. First I passed the photo to his sister, who had missed carnival; she roared with delight seeing her brother dressed in a shirt, his head half shaven and gleaming like that of a balding businessman. He had been carrying a briefcase and maintained a very serious gait and expression. When he had arrived in the *rua*, where people were beginning to congregate after the Mission school's carnival procession, the other teenagers pointed him out to me. He was performing a local image of economic success. With his skin whiter than many local people, the image he had presented had become more forceful, allowing the contrast between his forehead and hairline to be quite striking and perhaps unconsciously refer- encing the local association of whiteness with wealth. However, he was enacting what he was not; aged around fifteen years old, he worked doing odd tasks for people about their homes.

Other men and boys dressed equally 'smartly'; some wearing suits and hats walked the street carrying suitcases. 'Are they migrants?' I asked one of my informants. 'Of course!', he smiled, implying the centrality of migration to local culture and images of well-being. They were in fact returning migrants, their bags bulging with goods and cash. The return of a migrant does not simply refer to an injection of European resources, but also to the contracts Manjaco migrants make with local *iran* forest spirits, thus reaffirming the power of these spirits of 'the land' to ensure that migrants fulfill their obliga- tions 'at home' (cf. Van Binsbergen 1988). 'Real' migrants also played roles in carnival. But rather than carrying old worn-out suitcases to represent the goods they brought from Europe, they carried functioning icons of wealth and migration, as for instance one man stood on the central pavement of the *rua* viewing carnival through his new video camera. Whilst he recorded, a teenager surveyed the scene through a cardboard model of a hand-held video camera.

Other carnival representations contrasted with the theme of migration and external sources of wealth. Whilst migrant remittances flow into the country to individuals, families and ritual specialists, local flows of money are under- stood differently. One carnival afternoon I encountered a group of young men. One, dressed in a suit with odd shoes, with *rastas* in his hair, danced to the drum beat played by his friends. The others surrounded him wearing a variety of costumes that parodied smart imported everyday clothing: jeans worn back-to-front, suit jackets, etc. As the dancer began to take money from his friends, stuffing the crumpled notes into his mouth, the young man standing beside me explained: 'He is the President of the Republic, he is taking our money and eating it'. In Guinea Bissau anyone in a position to accept bribes, or pocket money paid them for official purposes, is said to 'eat money' – *kume dinhiero*. This carnival skit can be interpreted as an enactment

of a Guinea Bissauan discourse on the powerlessness of individuals faced by a
system in which they feel they cannot succeed, but must participate in and
thus perpetuate in order to survive. For example, the plight of teachers, whose
salaries are paid irregularly and often only as a result of strike action, represents the frustrations of many public sector employees. Many teachers support
themselves through a variety of informal practices. By representing the higher
levels at which money is eaten, these performers were simultaneously
enacting the participation of workers like teachers and health workers, who as
distributors of exam passes and health services, can 'eat' other people's money.
The situation of teachers offers a stark contrast to the earning power of
migrants. Significantly, many teachers entered their profession because it
secured their eligibility for a scholarship to study overseas in the ex-Soviet
Union, East Germany, Cuba or Brazil. Ironically, the collapse of communism,
the 'opening up' of Eastern Europe and development of a market economy
has effectively closed these countries to Guinea Bissauan scholarship seekers.
Thus teachers' strategies to gain access to outside resources have been spoiled.

As my informant finished speaking, two more young men approached
dressed in the same style as the rest of the group. One carried a bulging suitcase. 'Who is that?' I asked, anticipating that he would be a migrant, but as the
couple came into earshot my informant, for both my and their benefit,
pointed to the carrier of the suitcase and announced 'he is the President of
Burkina Faso, and he is the bodyguard. They are going to the airport'. The
'President of Burkina Faso' put his suitcase down for a few moments whilst
he shook hands with the 'President of the Republic', myself and several others
and then continued on his way. Apparently he had not known he was the
President, and his performance had been inspired by his friend's direct statement of it. In the former case, similarly the performance I was viewing had
been given meaning by my informant's direct description of it. However, it is
not certain that my informant was directly representing the intentionality of
the performers. Had they planned to represent politicians? or were they
simply enacting a common social practice? In other words, was my informant
speaking directly? or was his explanation another type of allegory: the performance represented an activity that anyone in public office may practise.
Therefore it could have been the President, or anyone else for that matter.
Although I will never know precisely what he intended, I am sure that in this
instance of the direct and indirect being combined, more layers of meaning
were at work than I initially realised.

Transnational intentions

The contemporary significance of the transnational in local Canchungo
culture becomes interesting when compared with Crowley's (1989) description of carnival in Bissau in 1987. This carnival, ten years previously, was
organised and sponsored by the Ministry of Culture. Crowley's text and

photographs (see also Ross 1993) report monster masks, representations of African tricksters, and masks referring to the official carnival theme of vaccination. He estimates that half of the 'at least one thousand' participants wore 'elaborate masks and costumes', the others wearing 'clown-like or other traditional festive costumes' (Crowley 1989: 80). In Crowley's description, transnational links were represented by the Ministry of Culture playing a tape of Brazilian music, the possible Chinese influence in mask designs, the development worker presence in the audience, and of course the carnival appropriations of the modern project of health education. In contrast, in Canchungo ten years later, an area of high migration, in a context where private enterprise is permissible and more consumer items are available, the transnational flow of artefacts, ideas and people is a greater everyday concern. The transnational and the national are significant themes in everyday life and carnival in Canchungo. Whilst my informants insisted that during carnival 'people wear masks', in Canchungo in 1997 they noted a significant absence of masks. This is partly explained by the absence of a cash prize. The winning mask of 1994 retained in the Regional Department of Culture is very similar to those reported by Crowley and Ross; similarly the masks produced in 1997 were those of the children's carnival at the mission primary school: created in a structured context with a particular brief. The most impressive adult mask on show was worn by children, revived and borrowed from a past carnival. Significantly, it represented a television screen with the President's face on it. However, perhaps the decline in masks has another significance: perhaps monsters have little to do with the experiences and imaginations of many local people whose dreams are of donning their sunglasses, picking up their suitcase and stepping off the plane in Lisbon.

Notions of transnationalism and 'transnational habitats of meaning' are central to my anthropological understanding of Canchungo culture and society, and to the aspirations and strategies of my informants. For most of my informants who defined their own country as 'no good', insisting that they would prefer to live in Europe, transnational resources were central concerns in everyday life as well as long-term strategies. The 'indirect' communications I have discussed in this paper are situated in this 'transnational context', and it is within this framework that I have endeavoured to make them meaningful. People reference the transnational and wealth in a network of interconnected meanings that are indirectly (and intentionally) implied in communications. No doubt they are always talking about other things at the same time. Here I have drawn out a strand from their festive and everyday concerns and projects and compiled this narrative out of context. It is of course in reality immersed in a multiplicity of other cultural themes and implicit to many local discourses. My intention has been to indicate how, as an underlying concern, transnational agendas permeate everyday lives and carnival performances. Through these forms of indirect expression local people use their transnational notions to give meaning to their experiences.

Notes

1 Note that the mothers of white children, and women migrants discussed here, are in somewhat extraordinary positions *vis-à-vis* the gendered division of responsibilities of most Guinea Bissauan households.
2 Miranda's story is developed further elsewhere, in the context of a discussion of the relationship between local people and development workers (see Pink 1998).
3 In local Krioulu she was *casadu* with this man because she lived with him in his house (*casa*). This terminology both follows the Portuguese base of Krioulu, and represents local marriage whereby a couple, unable to afford marriage ceremonies, simply set up home together.
4 For instance, during a health research project nearly all interviewees (particularly women) indicated they would prioritise their children's health before other family expenses (see Pink 1997). However, ethnographic examples show women choosing to buy false hair in place of medicines, health treatment and meat.

References

Cohen, A. (1994) *Self Consciousness: An Alternative Anthropology of Identity*, London: Routledge.
Comaroff, J. and Comaroff, J. (1993) Introduction to *Modernity and its Malcontents: Ritual and Power in Postcolonial Africa*, Chicago and London: University of Chicago Press.
Crowley, D. J. (1989) 'The Carnival of Guinea-Bissau', *The Drama Review: A Journal of Performance Studies*, 33(2): 74–86.
Hannerz, U. (1996) *Transnational Connections*, London: Routledge.
Hendry, J. (1993) *Wrapping Culture: Politeness, Presentation and Power in Japan and Other Societies*, Oxford: Clarendon Press.
Pink, S. (1997) 'Willingness and ability to pay for health services in Cacheu region, Guinea Bissau: the potential for cost recovery', report prepared for UNICEF and the Direcção Regional da Saú de Pública de Cacheu (in English and Portuguese).
——(1998) 'The white "helpers": anthropologists, development workers and local imaginations', *Anthropology Today*, 14(6): 9–14.
Ross, D. H. (1993) 'Carnival masquerades in Guinea-Bissau', *African Arts*, 26(3): 64–71.
Schechner, R. (1993) *The Future of Ritual*, London: Routledge.
Van Binsbergen, W. (1988) 'The land as body: an essay on the interpretation of ritual among the Manjaks of Guinea Bissau', *Medical Anthropology Quarterly*, 2(4): 386–401.

Chapter 7

Trust, privacy, deceit and the quality of interpersonal relationships

'Peasant' society revisited

Ursula Sharma

The nature of trust has been a salient theme in recent theorising about the relationship between self and society in 'modernity' (Giddens 1990: 79; 1994: 89; Lash 1994). In this chapter I consider some issues of trust, deceit, and personal relationships, stimulated by anthropological work on the quality of interpersonal relationships in peasant societies. In spite of much difference in theoretical objectives, both the literature on modernity and the older work on 'peasant' society pay considerable attention to the subjective quality of relationships, taking into account what it 'feels like' to interact and communicate as a member of a certain kind of society, and the ways in which the self is constructed in relation to others. I shall make a preliminary attempt to relate these strands of theorising. The data I shall use to do this are generated by means of an exercise in reflexivity, drawing on experiences in an Indian village.

My very first piece of field research was conducted in 1966–7 in a Himalayan village to which I have given the pseudonym Ghanyari, the ancestral home (if that is not too grand a term for it) of my father-in-law. I visited Ghanyari many times subsequently, but never again for research purposes. Curiously, I find that many of the things that puzzled me as a first-time researcher, in particular those relating to the nature of neighbourly relationships, seem less puzzling now that I have abandoned any research persona and visit the village only as a non-resident member.

I will illustrate this with three snapshot scenarios.

Scenario 1 Not letting on about where you are going: in which the anthropologist appears as a naïve research student, in India for the first time

In 1966 Ghanyari was difficult of access and there were no shops. We would make an expedition to the nearest town (about fifteen miles away) about once a month. We would plan the trip a few days in advance, but my father-in-law would often instruct me, 'No need to tell people we are going, no need for them to know'. I could see no reason for such secrecy other than perhaps to avoid requests to bring back this, that or another item from the market, or run other time-consuming errands for neighbours. Villagers were always asking me 'where are you going, where are you off to?', as I tramped around the neighbourhood interviewing people. I found this inquisitiveness tiresome at times but it seemed easier to satisfy it than to invent subterfuges.

As well as instructing me not to divulge my intentions, my parents-in-law and others who felt themselves to have some responsibility for me constantly warned me 'take care' and 'don't trust people here'. They would recount cautionary tales in which jealous kin and neighbours connived to commit harm to the unsuspecting individual, through magic, murder or more prosaic means. Neighbours would darkly hint at the motives of those who seemed to me perfectly innocuous and open.

Scenario 2 Mystifying your neighbours: in which the writer reappears in Ghanyari as a mature widow visiting her affinal 'home' after some years absence

I was travelling to India in 1996. Shortly before I left I was approached by friends in Birmingham who hailed from Chhalli (a village very near to Ghanyari), and whom we knew well. Indeed Prabha, the wife, was related to several people in Ghanyari by marriage. Prabha asked me if I would take £2,000 to India and hand it to Kishori, a young man from our village whose wife was a kinswoman of hers. Kishori had opened an 'investment' company (a euphemism for a moneylending business) and Prabha wanted to 'invest' some of the money she had saved stitching garments as an outworker. I advised her to send a draft, but she said that she did not trust the bank and it would get to Kishori quicker if I were to take it. As she had helped me in the past I felt that it would be churlish to refuse to help her. So, somewhat against my better judgement, I agreed.

I encashed the travellers' cheques at a bank in town and took the bus to Ghanyari with the cash stashed in my money belt, hoping that the bulge under my clothing would not be too conspicuous. I was quite anxious about having such a large sum of someone else's cash about me, and planned to get it to Kishori as soon as I could. Back in Ghanyari I considered how to deliver it to him without anyone knowing. It was easy enough to call at Kishori's house, as he lived nearby. The main problem as I saw it was that (a) my mother-in-law might be curious to know why I was visiting Kishori, and (b) it would be unlikely that I would have a private moment with Kishori to slip him the package of banknotes, since doubtless his relatives and neighbours would crowd into the room to greet me or just see what was going on (and in particular whether I was bringing presents for anyone).

But dark winter evenings are a good time to go on discreet visits, since few people are about and the village alleyways are unlit. After supper, some neighbours came to sit with my mother-in-law in the kitchen, so I made an excuse that I wanted to go into the main room of the house to write some letters. I slipped out into the courtyard and went down to Kishori's house with the money in a plastic carrier bag. I was welcomed into his main room and, as I had expected, a stream of curious relatives and neighbours breezed in and out. After half an hour of chat I was beginning to feel that I would not be able to deliver the money without anyone seeing, and felt that I must return home as it was getting late and my mother-in-law would worry when she noticed I had gone. I got up to go, thinking that I would have to find some other pretext to see Kishori the next day. He evidently divined this and said loudly to the couple of neighbours who were still sitting there that he had better escort Aunty some of the way home – she had not brought a torch and the path was slippery with mud from recent rain. Out in the alleyway I shoved the carrier bag into his hand and he muttered an acknowledgement. At home I saw that my mother-in-law was still chatting in the kitchen and had not noticed my absence. What a lot of letters I must have managed to write that evening!

Why did I feel so proud of myself after this exploit? It was only later that I realised that this feeling of a job well done arose from a sense of having acted just like the villagers who had puzzled me in earlier visits. I had kept counsel about intentions, exercised caution and suspicion, been secretive. Yet what were my motives for secrecy and deception?

I was certainly anxious about the possibility of theft, but this was not the whole story. I was deceiving my own mother-in-law who was unlikely to steal from me. Why did I not want her to know what I was up to? She might scold me for involving myself in other people's business, criticise me for naïvety in getting mixed up in Prabha's affairs. I could handle that. But she might also tell others about what I had done, even if only to the extent of bragging affectionately about how I needed her to protect me from my own innocence, or complaining about the habit of people like Kishori of involving other people in risky or dubious activities. And, not having visited the village for some time, I was unsure about Kishori's current standing in the village or how his enterprise was regarded (I certainly was sceptical about it). It was none of my business if my friend Prabha chose to put her trust in Kishori and his 'investment company', but I did not want to seem either stupid, or involved in a racket. Furthermore, I felt I was protecting Prabha. I assumed that she would not necessarily want people in Ghanyari or her own village to know what she did with her savings in case they pestered her for loans. And even if they did not, there were always people who loved to conspire to bring down those who seemed successful, or who might feel offended that she had not spent the money to benefit them rather than Kishori. I wanted to protect Prabha because I liked her, because she was useful to me in various ways, and because there was a link between our families which I valued. In spite of all the suspicion I have described, there could be islands of trust in the village, often the product of multiple links between members of two familes, each link serving as some kind of guarantee for the others. In such an environment her trust of me seemed like a precious commodity, a giant risk she had taken. It was to our mutual interest that it be honoured.

Scenario 3 Giving with discretion: in which the researcher fulfils further assignments

On another occasion Prabha asked me to take some presents to people in Chhalli, her husband's village, including her husband's widowed sister Sushila, and a sister of her own, Simran, who was married there. These two were not on good terms. I visited Chhalli in the company of a classificatory 'brother-in-law', Gopal. Gopal was married to a kinswoman of Prabha's and his own daughter was married to a man in Chhalli. He was effectively an extension of the 'island of trust' which Prabha, myself and our families constituted. We had lunch at Sushila's house and she seemed pleased with Prabha's gifts. It was difficult to get away as she seemed unwilling that we should visit other houses in the village. Yet I had to get the rest of the presents to Simran without Sushila being aware of what had been given. In such a tiny hamlet, with all the houses facing onto the same street, secret visits were impossible. Sushila insisted on accompanying us to Simran's house, as did a number of neighbours and a raggle-taggle of small children who had gathered as they saw us leave her courtyard. I was frantic to see Simran for at least a moment on my own so that I could hand over the gifts without the scrutiny of Sushila and the rest of the village. Gopal had grasped the situation without being told and attempted diversionary tactics. Why didn't I take a photo of everyone standing in front of Simran's house, he suggested. It would be a nice memento of the visit and everyone could be in it. He would take it himself if I gave him the camera. Everyone rushed out on to Simran's verandah, with Sushila at the front, determined not to let Simran have pride of place. Gopal lined everyone up and took a good deal of time fussing and positioning people. This gave me time to stuff the bag of presents under a quilt lying in Simran's front room; she acknowledged the manoeuvre with a knowing grin and we joined the crowd on the verandah. Gopal's diversionary tactics had worked a treat, and again my duty as intermediary was complete.

Why were such devious tactics needful? Why make such a drama out of a simple errand?

I understood why Prabha might not wish Sushila to know that Simran was getting gifts from abroad as well as herself. Sushila could be jealous that she was not the only one to get presents, and this might exacerbate their already tense relationship. Or she might become dissatisfied if she thought Simran's present was better than her own. Of course, Simran might do the same if there was any chance for open comparison of the gifts; I knew from my own experience that in such circumstances gifts were very likely to be compared by the recipients or by other witnesses, and any perceived differences in value attributed to definite motives on the part of the giver. I liked Prabha and did not want to be responsible for sowing discord between her sister and sister-in-law. Prabha did not like Sushila, but I presumed that she wished to retain her goodwill or she would not have sent her expensive presents. And given that an affine of my own (Gopal) had a daughter married in the village, I had a further reason for not wishing to stir up trouble there, even if with the best of intentions. Gopal was also someone whom I liked and who was moreover very useful to me in a number of ways.

On the bus back to Ghanyari, I reflected that I did now understand why my parents-in-law had told me not to tell others of my business, even to be devious about my intentions if necessary. Sometimes reflexivity is a better research tool than any amount of field notes or observation of others. In relation to the discussion that follows, I am not claiming that what I felt and understood was exactly what other people in Ghanyari would have felt and understood in the same situation, only that my thoughts and feelings helped me to interpret something that I had found hard to comprehend on earlier visits to Ghanyari.

Trust, deception and social relationships in 'peasant' societies

I recognised in myself and in others around me a pattern of behaviour which has been very well documented in a literature on the nature of social relationships in 'peasant' societies, mainly written between the late 1950s and early 1970s. Given the interest in the nature of sociation and intimacy in modernity which is manifest in much contemporary sociology, and the interest on the part of both sociologists and anthropologists in what might be called the management of the self, it is perhaps curious that this literature is not referred to more often than it is. I will briefly review some of its main themes.

In 1965 George Foster published a famous paper entitled 'Peasant society and the image of the limited good', based largely on his observations in rural Mexico. He described a 'cognitive orientation', with concomitant norms of conduct, according to which peasants tend to view their social economic and natural universe – their total environment – as one in which all the desired things of life such as land, wealth, health, friendships and love, manliness and honour, respect and status, power and influence, security and safety, exist in finite quantity and are always in short supply, as far as the peasant is concerned (Foster 1965: 296).

There is no way open to the peasant to increase the supply of these good things, therefore a gain on the part of one person in the community must mean a loss to others. Where love and friendship are concerned this means that a favour given to one person is seen as potential diminution of what the giver is prepared to do for others. The conduct of friendship, and even of affective relations within the family, is stalked by the potential for grief and resentment. If Prabha gave a desirable gift to her sister, then this was liable to be perceived as a slight to her sister-in-law; it was better that each should not know what the other was given than that comparisons should be made. Concealment, even deception where necessary, is the better strategy for maintaining control over social relations.

Indeed, in the literature I have in mind, jealousy and envy appear as major components of interpersonal relationships in peasant societies. In a relatively self-contained social environment people compare themselves with their neighbours, and are loath to see those who should regard themselves as peers flaunt superior resources or good fortune. In the case of India, Pocock's perceptive account of beliefs about the Evil Eye tells us that 'it is most to be feared when those who ought to be equals are not so in fact' (Pocock 1973: 39). Foster notes that one common means of containing envy among those who regard themselves as status equals is the concealment of one's riches: explicit displays of wealth and success are limited to ritualised occasions. There is a kind of surface egalitarianism among peasants who resent the intrusion of differentials of wealth or pretension, even though each is privately concerned to maximise their own advantage (Banfield 1958). Colclough notes that in an Italian village 'The socially mobile are a constant source of danger to those around them, for their success is achieved at the expense of others, and thus they are subject to sanctions, the mildest of which is gossipy denigration of their good fortune' (Colclough 1971: 225). 'Cutting upstarts down to size' (Bailey 1971: 282) is a common preoccupation. Migrants in particular need to tread a careful path between not displaying the wealth they have earned abroad at all (and thereby risking being deemed as failures) and flaunting it too ostentatiously, exciting envy. Thus for Prabha it was better discreetly to send suitably pleasing gifts to her kin whilst secretly investing her savings as she thought fit.

The need to conserve and (if possible) maximise personal or family resources in an environment which has traditionally been experienced as insecure – either because of the inherent insecurity of subsistence agriculture or because of the inscrutable and unpredictable demands of the state or its local representatives – engenders a situation where the emotional and the strategic aspects of social relationships are seldom distinct. Individuals in the neighbourhood are constantly engaged in building and maintaining useful alliances with others. But living at close quarters also means that disputes and tensions are common; trust is hard to maintain, relationships with neighbours and kins may veer between close alliance and enmity, and sometimes this manifests itself in a kind of village factionalism. In his description of honour and conflict in a Sicilian town, Schneider describes the anxiety which people experience in balancing the need to maintain useful alliances with the need to maintain one's reputation:

> The issue is not only one of personal power – the control over people and things – but also the dignity and integrity of the self, and this is not to be taken lightly. Indeed it is difficult to describe the predicament in which people find themselves, the anxiety which accompanies working out the problem of honor in the context of competition and conflict. ... Few people are completely confident that they can in fact protect themselves when the chips are down, that their allies will remain allies and their strategies will succeed.
>
> (Schneider 1969: 153)

In this environment the politics of reputation become all-important. In some of the societies under consideration this takes the form of a well elaborated ideology of honour. But even where this is not the case, in order to secure the best advantage for oneself and one's family one needs to maintain the reputation of being difficult to con, liable to retaliate if crossed, and well connected with influential allies. In Ghanyari 'simplicity', i.e. straightforwardness and directness, is only valued when allied to a genuine otherworldly piousness, a reputation for utter moral rectitude. If you are not sure that you can reach such moral heights, then a reputation for simplicity could be a serious disadvantage. It would carry the same weight as the term 'fesso', translated by Colclough as 'soft-witted', and applied to Italian villagers who had allowed themselves to be duped or manipulated by scheming others (Colclough 1971: 224). Impression management therefore becomes crucial. It is considered wise to be guarded, even to mislead others about what one is doing and what one might do in future. Du Boulay describes how deception and lying in a Greek village is used to protect the individual from mockery and to maintain the proper kind of reputation. The lie plays a vital part in mediating relations between the individual and the community so that deceit, therefore, and the avoidance of mockery, appear as phenomena intimately connected with the structure of the value system and as part of the legitimate means by which the honour of the family is preserved and the prosperity of the household maintained (Du Boulay 1976: 405–6).

This applies to Ghanyari too, though I would point out that deception can just as readily be practised against members of one's own household (my mother-in-law never came to know about my visit to Kishori). This may be because the individual feels better able to control the flow of information if members of their own family are not privy to everything they do or know, or because even the family or household itself is the site of conflict and strategic alliances. Family honour is not irrelevant in Ghanyari, but personal reputation can be distinguished from it to a large extent.

Academics have applied the term 'lying' to deceit practised in the interests of guarding personal or family reputation. But Greek and Indian peasants would call it minding one's own business and resisting the curiosity of those who might (who knows?) wish you harm. 'Lying' does indeed seem an inappropriate term – not because people do not sometimes deliberately state what they know to be untrue, but because the word marks outright deceit off from the various other forms of indirection and prevarication which serve the same purpose – to conceal the speaker's intent and to maintain personal reputation.

In Scenarios 2 and 3 I experienced my secretive behaviour as an attempt to maintain privacy. In villages like Ghanyari, and indeed many rural locations, it is hard for the individual to maintain any kind of bodily privacy. Individuals are not expected to claim personal space within the home for sleeping, keeping their possessions or entertaining their friends, though senior men may be better placed in this respect than the rest of the family. The house itself is permeable to the gaze of others – neighbours making casual calls, children running in and out. In many Indian villages those who can afford it live behind high walls and relax in sequestered courtyards which are not overlooked but, even then, unglazed windows permit the sounds of quarrels to flow out onto the street. In Ghanyari there are no private places for bathing or excreting; bodily discretion can only be maintained with effort and, to a degree, through the cooperation of others. The requirements for modesty and bodily self-control weigh most heavily on women, for whom the opportunities to control space and the timing of household and community activities are the weakest. However, for both men and women, a sense of personal integrity and privacy is maintained less through the use of space than through the use of information – in particular, control over information about one's intentions and those of persons with whom one is allied. Such information is not vouchsafed lightly, even to close friends and kin. Lying, indirection and mistrust of others are the means by which one retains some sense of control over what one can do, keeps options open and protects oneself from the control of others. Some control over time may be bought through the control of information about intentions. Vague promises or proposals which the individual may or may not intend to carry out (Barnes 1994: 66) can be given in the expectation that they will retain goodwill, even serve as a token of respect (Bailey 1991: 6), for the time being. Some time will elapse before the person to whom the promise is made gradually realises that the service offered will not be delivered or the plan proposed not acted upon (assuming that they ever took it at face value in the first place). The strategies which Gopal and I practised in Chhalli were designed to give Prabha time – eventually her kinswomen would in all probability each discover what gift the other had received, make comparisons and come to conclusions about what the gifts represented. If her gifts fuelled misunderstanding between the women, the consequences of this would not be evident for some while, by which time other considerations might, with any luck, be more important than this little drama.

All this involves a degree of self-reflexivity inasmuch as individuals must monitor their own behaviour with a view to judging how far it does or does not close off options for the future. There are no simple formulae by which

successful living is ensured. Certainly the straightforward observance of traditional norms is not enough. But this reflection is not the confessional
reflexivity which writers on modernity have noted. On the contrary it must
be practised in the privacy of the individual's own mind. Judgements about
others' performance will be fed into the local flow of gossip, contribute to
'what people say'. But to wonder aloud about the quality of one's own
'performance' would be to appear other than discreet and in command of
one's reputation. It may even be that the kind of privacy achieved through
secrecy and lying enables one to construct a 'real' interior self which is inde-
pedent of the 'social biography' constructed for you by others' judgments (as
Gilsenan [1976: 204] suggests in his study of playful lying behaviour in a
Lebanese village). In any case, 'take care' in Ghanyari does not mean 'be kind
to yourself' but 'monitor your behaviour with a view to managing relationships and events to your best advantage'. Indeed, the release of information of
any kind (not just about one's inner thoughts about oneself or one's future
intentions) could be risky. If the notion of the limited good applies to information, then useful information imparted represents advantage lost to oneself.

Discussion

The 'peasant' literature I have referred to presents a cumulative account of
what is clearly a widespread mode of inhabiting society, a way of conducting
and monitoring oneself and one's performance in relation to others and
constructing a sense of self in the process. Indeed, we have something which
might be described as a 'condition' to set alongside sociological descriptions
of the 'conditions' of modernity and postmodernity. In pursuing this line of
exploration I found it interesting to relate my material and reflections to
Giddens' account of modernity, this being a detailed and well substantiated (as
well as very influential) account of a 'condition' of modernity. What happens
if we situate Foster's observations within Giddens' problematic? And if what
we have is some kind of 'peasant' condition, then what are the aspects of
'peasant' society that generate and sustain it?

Foster sees peasant society as constituting

> communities that are the rural expression of large, class-structured,
> economically complex, pre-industrial civilisations, in which trade and
> commerce, and craft specialisation are well developed, and in which the
> market disposition is the goal for a part of the producer's efforts. The city
> is the principal source of innovation, and the prestige motivation brings
> novelty to the countryside.
>
> (Foster 1960: 175)

There has of course been much debate about the nature of the category
'peasant' since then, and there was at the time much disagreement about how

the 'quality of interpersonal relations' in peasant communities might properly be evaluated. But anthropologists who wrote in this mode in the 1950s and 1960s showed considerable agreement in treating it as a matter of moral outlook. Banfield saw 'amoral familism' as a set of values. Foster regarded the notion of the 'limited good' as a concept which was implicit in peasant behaviour and modes of association.

Foster identified the limited supply of land in peasant communities as an important factor making for a view of life and a way of conducting relationships which valorised strategic calculation of the way in which the gains and losses of others impinged upon one's own chances. But he stressed that the behaviour he associated with the idea of the 'limited good' could be found among other kinds of community, and even sometimes in modern cities. Certainly it seems to flourish in the kind of agrarian community which has not yet experienced a high degree of what Giddens calls 'disembedding'. Social relations, organised in terms of place, are crucial and relatively stable, and have not yet been 'lifted out' of their local contexts through the distanciation of time-space relations (Giddens 1990: 21ff.). A high degree of an individual's interaction will be with known persons, face-to-face, with minimal reliance on 'abstract systems' of knowledge and organisation. Migrants like Prabha, of course, have experienced the process of disembedding or 'deterritorialisation' (Appadurai 1990) of their social relationships and cultural values. Yet they continue to return to and relate to a community where relations are still largely embedded in the concrete realities of local land tenure, physical communications, demographies and use of space, as do people from Ghanyari and Chhalli who have ventured only as far as the nearest market town to find work. Gossip can only constitute a means of social control when it is the stuff of conversation in concrete localities – coffee-shops, the village well or parish pump, the bus stop or the school gates.

Perhaps in these accounts of peasant social relations we have a rich description of what both modern and classical sociologists have called 'traditional' or 'pre-modern' society, that state that precedes modernity, ever more shadowily described as we move further from Weber's classical accounts of traditional authority and legitimation. The mode of conducting relationships which I have described does not entirely fit Giddens' idea of the 'pre-modern'. He characterises pre-modernity as a condition in which ontological security is achieved through the reliability and trustworthiness of certain institutions. In particular, kinship provides a framework for relations which, though also generating tension and conflict, have a certain stability across time and space. Likewise, the local community represents a grouping of known persons which is relatively immobile and isolated. On the whole I can recognise Ghanyari in this characterisation, at least the Ghanyari of my first visit. Yet while the relative stability of social relations may breed trust, in the general sense of trust in institutions, it does not breed trust in individual people. Indeed, as we have seen, mistrust and concomitant dissembling and deviousness are the order of the day. We can see behaviour in Ghanyari as governed by tradition in Giddens' sense of 'formulaic truth', the 'organizing medium of collective memory' (Giddens 1994: 64) but it is not the formulaic truth of authoritative religion, only that expressed in a number of general observations which do not even have the punch and wit of proverbs ('expect trouble from your co-parceners', 'don't trust anyone', 'showing off your good fortune always gets you into a mess', 'there is always jealousy among sisters-in-law', 'be careful of the Evil Eye'). Nor does this 'tradition' have any ritual guardians, other than perhaps the senior women who know a lot about countering sorcery and warding off the effects of the Evil Eye; it is the formulaic truth of canny common sense embodied.

But the lack of trust in individuals need not undermine Giddens' basic theory. Under conditions of modernity, he says, individuals need to establish trust in the abstract systems which are crucial to social life. For example, in the case of medicine we need to establish trust both in the system of scientific knowledge that underpins modern medicine and in the professional probity of the doctor who administers it, as guaranteed by professional education and codes of conduct. Alongside this we find the search for emotional intimacy, the arena where persons can discover trust in each other – but this trust is worked upon through a process of mutual disclosure (Giddens 1990: 121; 1991: 186). We might counter this by pointing out that 'working on interpersonal trust' is not exclusive to modernity. In villages like Ghanyari, relations of trust are certainly 'worked upon'; Gopal, Prabha and I trust each other as a result of effort put into our mutual relationships, albeit in each case work laid down on a foundation of basic liking, prior family connections and proximity of different kinds. However, the work described in the scenarios I have recounted was not so much a matter of building trust as dealing with mistrust. The work which Giddens attributes to individuals in the condition of modernity is designed to construct trust in the *absence of trust*; the work which takes place in Ghanyari is designed to deal with and domesticate active *mistrust*. Prabha does not trust abstract systems over much, which may in part be the product of her poor access to them as a non-English speaking migrant. She preferred to send her money through me rather than through the bank, but she does not mistrust banks as much as she mistrusts her husband's sister.

The more we look at it the more we become aware that Ghanyari does not really fit into either Giddens' modernity, nor into sociological conceptions of 'traditional' society. Of course, anthropologists never bought into this dichotomy. Giddens could allow !Kung Bushmen to stand for the entire pre-modern order (Giddens 1994: 61), but anthropologists know better. Prabha lives in a modern European city and Gopal is no stranger to modern social and economic forms outside the village, having worked in the Gulf for some years. From the common rooms of Cambridge or LSE, the behaviour of Prabha and Gopal looks like a throwback, an archaic form. Indeed, Prabha's children probably will not acquire the skills to negotiate relationships in

Chhalli as competently as their mother. On the other hand, the pattern of migration in which urban migrants retain an interest in their rural places of origin, investing money in land or other ventures there, maintaining ties of obligation (and sometimes of enmity as well) is a regular and inherent feature of social and economic organisation in labour reserve areas like Ghanyari. The local economy of Ghanyari is heavily reliant on remittances and pay checks brought in from employment outside, and its social relations are not as 'embedded' as they first appear. From that point of view, perhaps it does not matter if Prabha's children fail to reproduce the relationships she is involved with and merge with the modernity of urban British youth; another set of families will find themselves in the disembedded but mediating positions in which Prabha, Gopal and myself were conducting ourselves.

Indeed, Foster speculates that what have been identified as 'peasant' inter-personal relations are actually the product of the disturbance of older peasant communities. Whereas the 'limited good' idea was a fairly accurate perception of the state of affairs in hypothetically stable peasant societies, it is character-istic of peasant societies in the modern world that they are not stable. Labour migration allows some members to import new goods, capital, information. Yet the 'productive pie' is still small – it is hard to add to the village stock of workable land or improve its productivity. Furthermore, the supply of consumer goods and cash may increase, and the potential for flux and distur-bance in local status systems is enormous. Prabha was cautious about making her gifts and investments public for this reason. She aimed to slip her new wealth into the local system quietly and without making uncontrollable ripples. Such a strategy would bear more fruit, as was evident from the example of a family in Ghanyari who had earned irreversible unpopularity in the village by flaunting the wealth they had earned in the Gulf too openly. So perhaps what Foster identified was actually a pattern of behaviour which is associated with the convection currents which are inherent in the conception of 'peasant' communities which he uses, and which are simply speeded up with contemporary globalising trends.

I suspect that the 'consequences of modernity' are as Giddens says they are for a large number of people in the West. But I suspect that modernity enfolds within it subsets of experience and behaviour, such as that of the modernising peasantry of which Prabha and Gopal are members – perhaps also the urban 'cultures of poverty' which have been (controversially) identi-fied by social scientists working in Third World cities, also the cultures of calculated reciprocity identified by Stack among poor urban African Americans (Stack 1974).

If this chapter has a message it is really about what anthropologists and sociologists may learn from each other when they theorise the 'quality of interpersonal relationships'. Giddens' theoretical approach to identity and rela-tionships suggests that notions like 'moral ethos' employed in the 1950s and 1960s, or the 'culture' of more recent anthropological theorising, are weak ones when divorced from rigorous consideration of the general and formal structural features of contemporary societies. Yet the experience of anthropologists suggests that notions like 'modernity/pre-modernity' or 'traditional/post-traditional' need to be opened up and simple dichotomies discarded.

Acknowledgements

I am grateful to Effie Delmouzou, Sarah Pink and participants at the ASA Annual Conference 1998 for helpful comments on this paper.

References

Appadurai, A. (1990) 'Disjuncture and difference in the global cultural economy', *Theory, Culture and Society*, 7: 295–310.

Bailey, F. (1991) *The Prevalance of Deceit*, Ithaca NY: Cornell University Press.

Bailey, F. (ed.) (1971) *Gifts and Poison: The Politics of Reputation*, Oxford: Blackwell.

Banfield, E. (1958) *The Moral Basis of a Backward Society*, Glencoe: Free Press.

Barnes, J.A. (1994) *A Pack of Lies: Towards a Sociology of Lying*, Cambridge: Cambridge University Press.

Colclough, N. (1971) 'Social mobility and social control in a southern Italian village', in F. Bailey (ed.) *Gifts and Poison: The Politics of Reputation*, Oxford: Blackwell.

Du Boulay, J. (1976) 'Lies, mockery and family integrity', in J. Peristiany (ed.) *Mediterranean Family Structures*, Cambridge: Cambridge University Press.

Foster, G. (1960) 'Interpersonal relations in a peasant society', *Human Organization*, 19(4): 174–8.

——(1965) 'Peasant society and the image of the limited good', *American Anthropologist*, 67: 293–315.

Giddens, A. (1990) *The Consequences of Modernity*, Cambridge: Polity Press.

——(1991) *Modernity and Self-Identity: Self and Society in the Late Modern Age*, Cambridge: Polity Press.

——(1994) 'Living in a post-traditional society', in U. Beck, A. Giddens and S. Lash, *Reflexive Modernization: Politics, Tradition and Aesthetics in the Modern Social Order*, Cambridge: Polity Press.

Gilsenan, M. (1976) 'Lying, honor and contradiction', in B. Kapferer (ed.) *Transaction and Meaning: Directions in the Anthropology of Exchange and Symbolic Behaviour*, Philadelphia: Institute for the Study of Human Issues.

Lash, S. (1994) 'Reflexivity and its doubles: structure, aesthetics, community', in U. Beck, A. Giddens and S. Lash, *Reflexive Modernization: Politics, Tradition and Aesthetics in the Modern Social Order*, Cambridge: Polity Press.

Pocock, D. (1973) *Mind, Body, Wealth: A Study of Belief and Practice in an Indian Village*, Oxford: Blackwell.

Schneider, P. (1969) 'Honor and conflict in A Sicilian town', *Anthropological Quarterly*, 42(3): 130–54.

Stack, C. (1974) *All Our Kin: Strategies for Survival in a Black Community*, New York: Harper & Row.

Chapter 8

The temple and the theme park

Intention and indirection in religious tourist art

Terry D. Webb

Although anthropologists have examined the capacity of tourist art to express cultural, national and ethnic values (e.g. Shenhav-Keller 1995; Harrison 1992; Silver 1979), its capacity to convey deeply religious sentiment among its producers is not well documented. Nevertheless, religious tourist art may be remarkably common. I have argued elsewhere that the Polynesian Cultural Center (the Center, or PCC), an ethnic theme park owned and operated by the Mormon church in Laie, Hawaii, is laden with religious significance. In fact, as one of Hawaii's most popular tourist attractions, the Center annually conducts nearly a million visitors through a forty-acre enterprise that is as much a monumental work of Mormon art as it is a work of tourist art (Webb 1994a; 1994b). This paper probes the depth of the PCC's religious content by examining the formal and symbolic similarities between the Center and the Mormon temple ceremony, which is the most sacred of Mormon ordinances.

The temple and the PCC both embody a powerful aesthetic that extols commonplace, quotidian human existence. This is accomplished by creating a sense of crisis through a presentation of the inescapable effects of sinfulness: social decay, human suffering, and the odium of death. The resolution of this crisis is the exaltation of the quotidian, as the commonplace is lifted to a paradisiac, immortal stature. This is also the aesthetic of the *Book of Mormon* and other Mormon scriptures, and it is used in rendering Mormon art and history. It is the Mormon aesthetic, and it differs from the common pattern of rising action, conflict and resolution, in that it replaces resolution with nothing less than apotheosis.

The aesthetic sum of these expressions is to make heaven in the image of families, daily toil, and normal human sensibilities and understanding, and follows naturally from Mormon theology. According to O'Dea, Mormonism transformed conventional American Protestantism

> into a theological liberalism, in terms of which human effort and constructive activity in the world advances men toward eternal glory and even to 'Godhood.' … Common secular American notions were theologized,

while theology itself was secularized. The temporal was equated with the spiritual, the mundane with the holy.

(1957: 56)

Unintentional audiences

The PCC denies that it is only a tourist attraction, and claims to be a 'living museum' in which skilled artisans transmit to young novices the traditional performing arts, customs and history of Polynesia. Nevertheless, enormous crowds of tourists are the PCC's intended audience; its art and performances cater to their stereotypic expectations of Polynesia as an exotic paradise; and the Center's sizable revenues attest to its success as a commercial enterprise.

This chapter, however, puts aside issues of commercialism and intended audiences, and instead considers the Center's effect on its unintended audience, the Center's Mormon performers themselves, who were the informants for this study. They, too, experience the Center's art, but in a way that subtly and indirectly isolates them from their heritage, from the outsiders they entertain, and from the church they believe in. For while the Center is indulging the tourists' fantasies, it delivers the performers an ulterior significance. Somewhat like the Irula's festival séances described by Neil Thin (Chapter 12 in this volume), the PCC detours its Mormon performers from their usual unambiguous religious expressions, to a place that exposes their beliefs to disrespect from the tourists and to doctrinal equivocation on the part of the Center's own administration. From this dislocation, the employees must seek a return to blessedness.

For various reasons, it was not appropriate to suggest to my informants that the Center resembles the temple. Comparing the PCC with sacred ordinances required discretion; I could not probe these matters too deeply because that might have affected the interviewees' willingness to speak freely. Furthermore, as a Mormon, I have sworn to observe the secretness of temple rituals, even in the company of other Mormons.

Oaths of secrecy, then, have been a perplexing problem in completing this study. I have tried to resolve the dilemma by relying on descriptions of the temple ceremonies that outsiders have written based on the accounts of informants. These descriptions are readily available and generally accurate, but they lack an awareness of the degree to which the temple ceremony – everything from its form and costuming to its vocabulary and innuendos – conforms to the Mormon aesthetic. Only an insider can identify these motifs, even if divulging them then becomes problematic.

The PCC as an aesthetic construction

The PCC has two main aesthetic components: the 'villages' at one end of the grounds, and the 'night show,' which is staged at the opposite end of the grounds in a 3,000-seat theatre. The seven villages are set amid coconut palms, lagoons, and well kept lawns and walkways. They feature replicas of dwellings characteristic of the societies for which they are named: Samoa, Tonga, Fiji, Hawaii, Tahiti, the Marquesas, and Aotearoa, which is the Maori name for New Zealand.

Several costumed 'villagers' in each setting perform Polynesian songs and dances, give brief lectures about customs of the respective island societies, and demonstrate simple activities of daily life that were practiced in ancient Polynesia, such as husking coconuts, pounding poi, carving traditional implements in wood and stone, and so forth.

Most PCC performers are students at Brigham Young University, Hawaii, another Mormon institution in Laie. Indeed, a primary reason for building the PCC in 1963 was to create jobs in tiny Laie so students could pay for their schooling (Britsch 1986: 186; Stanton 1989: 248). The student performers are youthful Polynesians, zesty, good-humoured, and very popular with the tourists. For many of these students, the Center is their first significant contact with the traditional ways of their ancestors. According to a Maori from New Zealand,

> Everything that I know now [about Maori culture] I learned at PCC. I learned about each building, what it meant. I learned how to sing certain songs we have, like for Waitangi Day [annual observance of the 1840 treaty between the Maori and the British]. I learned how to pronounce the language properly, I learned how to move properly the way they did when you do the poi [lightweight balls on strings used in dancing] and when you dance. I became more proud of my culture than I was in New Zealand.

In its brochures and publicity, the PCC portrays itself as a preserver of Polynesian cultures that are quickly fading. The tourists do not realise that a restoration of lost greatness is an important Mormon religious and aesthetic motif, but it is certainly not lost on the Mormon Polynesian performers. The *Book of Mormon* specifically mentions their progenitors, and promises that the Lord will remember His people on the scattered isles of the sea and return them to greatness (1 Nephi 19:16; 22:3–12; 2 Nephi 11:21).

The villages are open in the afternoons, and guests are encouraged to arrive early enough to sample the cultures in all seven. Brochures promise them that they will 'explore 7 Polynesian nations in a single day' (PCC 1997: n.p.), and see 'All of Polynesia. All in one place' (PCC 1995?: n.p.). This levelling of Polynesia's social diversity only generalises the threat of extinction that the Center is preventing.

The programmes of the different villages are very similar, except for costuming and a few other culture-specific touches. Tourists try the dances, taste coconut milk or poi, or learn to weave simple souvenirs from palm fronds. The lectures and explanations avoid complicated or unpleasant details about traditional Polynesian social life and religion that would conflict with Mormon teachings. Nor is mention made of the very real social, economic and political issues presently confronting the region. Instead, the villages portray the innocent, simple, casual life of Polynesia familiar from countless movies, books and paintings, and which the tourists expect to see. A PCC brochure promises that visitors will experience 'the islands as you always hoped they would be' (PCC 1986: n.p.). The 'natives' are young, robust and happy in their leisurely naïvete, and apparently untouched by hectic modern pressures. But again, the simple bliss presents a fundamental Mormon belief that greatness lies not in grand achievements, wealth, or celebrity, but in the methodical accomplishment of the unspectacular duties of a simple life.

The villages close in time for the tourists to dine in the Center's eateries and then attend the night show. In contrast to the simple village programmes, the night show is a staged and choreographed extravaganza. Like the villagers, the night show dancers are mostly young Polynesians in traditional dress, but here the costumes are lavish and dazzling under bright lights, and the performances are exuberant and spectacular, with up to 150 dancers on stage. A narrated text, taped orchestral music, and stage effects such as waterfalls and a fiery volcanic eruption, embellish the performance.

Nevertheless, the night show reworks the simple village motifs into a spectacular recapitulation. The programme includes a separate set for each of the village societies. Each set is composed of dances that enact such activities as welcoming guests, playing games, fishing, food preparation, making tapa cloth from tree bark, husking coconuts, and making leis.

Taken together, then, the villages and the night show are variations on the theme of Polynesian simplicity and innocence, which evoke popular conceptions of Polynesia, the false culture expected by the tourists. It is this pattern of theme and variation between the separate villages, and between the villages and the night show, that gives the Center its unity as a single, complex artwork. In the night show, however, the Polynesians are lifted to a higher state of admiration in the eyes of the tourists. The simple, clever villagers are portrayed in the night show as polished performers, reputedly the finest Polynesian troupe in the world. The underlying message, another tenet of Mormonism, is that proper training and sponsorship can transform simplicity into the sublime.

Humour and diplomacy

In his account of carnival in the Caribbean (Chapter 11 in this volume) Jonathan Skinner alludes to the power of tourists to influence calypso music despite their failure to grasp fully its local idiom. In James Carrier's terms, this is the type of social gap that special languages of indirection and diplomacy, or some other social product, may bridge. Because of the PCC's religious content, the social gap between its performers and the tourists is chasmal. The tourists are unsuspecting of the religious devotion the PCC evokes in its employees, and many of my informants exhibited outright disdain for tourists, whom they regarded as ignorant, patronising or rude. One villager stated:

> I find that the worst tourists we have are Americans. They're the most spoiled brat people in the whole world. When they come, a lot of them have this image of themself of how the [white] people really helped improve Hawaii. 'Oh, it's lucky they're modern now.' ... I say, 'We have a million people in Hawaii now. We have welfare. People do not have homes and people do not have jobs. Who's better off? Are we better off because of what you introduced? Or was my ancestors better off because they all had something?' And this kind of clicks, and they go, 'Gee, we never thought of it that way.' And I say, 'Yeah, because it's not your past.'

Yet these same villagers enliven their demonstrations with infectious vitality, and often quip with the tourists. In fact, amusing the audience is valued as a sign of showmanship, and the young employees often try to out-perform each other in entertaining the tourists. Not surprisingly, however, much of the comedy at the PCC is hardly complimentary to the visitors.

For instance, one jokester raises the wooden stake he uses in his coconut husking demonstration, and says to the audience, 'In Samoa, we call this – ', pausing to draw his audience in, 'sharp stick'. And the audience laughs heartily for being tricked by him. But he is not finished: 'In Japanese, it's called "chop stick" ', and in his pidgin, the two punchlines sound just alike. The non-Japanese members of the audience laugh particularly loudly at this because they think they are not still laughing at themselves as well. In another village, a guide tells his tourist group that they will see many unusual sights, and instructs them that whenever he asks 'What do you think about that?', they must respond loudly with 'That's incredible!', which of course they do, and then laugh obligingly each and every time he gives the command.

Meanwhile on the lagoon ride, a smiling canoe steersman hands a rope to a passenger, then devilishly tells him to hold it tightly and plunge into the water when he yells 'drop anchor'. Other steersmen splash each other when they pass in the narrow lagoon, engage in mock jousts with each other as they stand on the rear of their canoes, and even pretend to get knocked or fall into the water to amuse their passengers.

In his analysis of Irula séance, Thin observes that joking often amounts to insider collusion and outsider exclusion, but with an indirectness that approaches politeness and diplomacy. But at the PCC, the banter, jokes and feigned clumsiness, by provoking laughter, I think serves more as a levelling device to dispel the performers' feelings of servility and establish a sense of indirect equality with, or even superiority to, the wealthy, powerful tourists. Aside from their mutual interest in Polynesia, which shapes up quite differently for the leisure-seeking tourists and the devout PCC employees, humour is about the only thing they can have in common. Yet some informants, on the other hand, objected to the comedy because it demeaned ancestral ways.

Because the night show performers are onstage and inaccessible for conversation with the tourists, the narrator speaks for them. And here the communication is highly theatrical and diplomatic. The narration stresses the Center's role as cultural preserver; extols Polynesian virtues; praises Laie as a cultural crossroads; and credits the church for cultivating 'the best' of Polynesian culture. The narrator's role as a Polynesian 'Everyman' is to blend Polynesia's cultures and ultimately bring credit to the church (see Ferre 1988: 175–6).

As a diplomatic discourse at the crowning moment of the Center's day-long ceremony, the night show narration epitomises the diplomacy of the entire PCC. In Carrier's terms, the PCC becomes wholly visible as a social product to cross the gap between the Mormons and the tourist outsiders. But the crossing never completely occurs because the tourists are as unaware of the religiously explicit personal dimensions the PCC has for its Mormon performers as most listeners were of the horrific meanings in Saltfish's award-winning calypso song on Montserrat (see Skinner, Chapter 11 in this volume).

Sacred spaces: the temple

Unlike the chapels and meetinghouses of the Mormon church, the temples are so sacred and their ordinances so elevated that outsiders are prohibited even from entering a Mormon temple once it has been consecrated. Only adult Mormons may participate in the major ceremonies, and to do so they must be annually interviewed by church leaders to assure their worthiness to attend the temple, as measured by their adherence to the church's beliefs and standards. Persons can be initiated into the temple ceremonies at about the age of nineteen, and they are then encouraged to participate in the ceremonies as often as possible.

The ceremony

The temple ceremony is unlike any other rite or experience in the church. It is dense with symbolism, and follows a narrative text that can be considered holy scripture. Trained temple workers act as guides for the participants and as officiators in the ceremony.

Lasting several hours, the ceremony begins with a symbolic purification that figuratively separates the participant from his previous transgressions and from behaviours that are inconsistent with the gravity of temple oaths. The main part of the ceremony then incorporates the initiate into the most select and covenant-bound of the faithful. To reach this high station, participants are led through a series of rooms representing periods of the earth's history, stages of mortal life, and afterlife rewards. Because the rooms have several symbolic meanings, they have different names that are used in different contexts. As described by Dolgin,

> the core of the rites involves a ritual drama. The creation of the world and the 'Fall' of man are enacted in the 'Creation Room' and the 'Garden of Eden Room,' respectively. In the 'World Room' … there is a recognition of the restoration of the 'gospel' to earth through the Prophet Joseph Smith. The culmination of the sacred dimension occurs in the 'Celestial Room' ('heaven') which is entered through a sacred veil from the 'Terrestrial Room.' This veil is the ultimate link, or alternately the boundary, between heaven and earth.
>
> (Dolgin 1974: 536)

Speaking of the temple attender, Leone observes,

> Narrated before him by supernatural personages is the whole of human history comprising the creation, the fall and redemption of man. At one point there is actually verbal and physical contact with God himself and then God actually invites the purified to enter and experience heaven. Throughout the narrations people are listening to God the Father and Christ talk, not as read by a reader out of the gospels, but by people playing the heavenly beings. And for additional emotional impact the audience overhears private off-stage conversations between God, Christ, Peter and others making plans to redeem man based on his worthy performance. If he believes what he is hearing, the Mormon is hearing a level of reality not present even in *Revelations*.
>
> (Leone 1977: 52)

Within the last several years, the number of rooms used for the ceremony has been reduced so that more ceremonies can be conducted simultaneously. The content of the ceremony has not been significantly altered, however, and movement between rooms is still required to complete the ceremony.

Temple clothing

To signify their purity, participants wear white for the entire temple ceremony. And with biblical allusions, they are instructed always to be modest in their dress. They also receive sacred undergarments that are to be worn next to the body at all times and throughout one's life. Although these garments are seldom spoken of, they remind participants of the oaths made in the ceremony, and of the lofty promises of salvation to which they now are entitled if they remain worthy. Furthermore, these garments, if worn properly, assure by their design and cut that those who have participated in the temple ceremony will dress modestly at all times thereafter.

Time overcome

After an initiate has participated in the temple ceremony the first time for his own edification, he may experience the ceremony perhaps hundreds of times throughout his life, because Mormons believe that performing the temple ceremony vicariously for deceased progenitors, even from the very distant past, can help achieve salvation for the deceased.

The Mormons' affinity for ancestors springs from the doctrine that salvation will not be bestowed individually, but according to lineages (Church 128:15–18). This is the reason for the church's extreme interest in genealogy. Using the church's vast genealogical resources, Mormons search for the names of their progenitors and perform the temple ceremony for those who did not receive them in their lifetimes. Establishing an unbroken line between the present and the past, therefore, is a task that is constantly before the Mormons as a duty to the deceased. In this way, the temple ceremony dismisses the anonymity of ancestors; they become near-tangible personalities to whom the participant joins himself.

To heighten the nearness of the past, the temple ceremony abolishes worldly time as the acts of God among men are ceremonially superimposed with little regard for chronology; old and new testament Christologies are combined; and biblical epochs collapse into a timeless uniformity that makes the Edenic and the early Christian periods contemporaneous with the modern. This anachronistic dismissal of time becomes highly personalised for the temple participant through the ancestor motif and the dramatisation of his own entry into heaven. Again, Leone:

> All this elevates the temple experience to one that is unique ... and makes the temple a place of total security, for in it the faithful Mormon is in contact with both his deceased relatives and his own future. Time stands still in this building; or better, it is compressed. Time is overcome.
>
> (1977: 46)

He adds,

> The temple and its rites are about order; they create a continuous line of relatives stretching back through the otherwise personally meaningless epochs of history and do this through [temple ceremonies] projecting the family forward to infinity. The temple guarantees order in history, and reduces the future to a function of acts performed now.
>
> (1977: 47)

Thus the temple ceremony does not lend itself to logical understanding, but to an affirmation of peace and orderliness. In highly ecclesiastical language and sacred surroundings, it enacts the belief that common human relationships and activities are the makings of salvation and the eternities. That is, the ordinary is the substance of the extraordinary.

Mormon sacred space and time at the PCC

The grounds

The characteristics of space and time that make the temple ceremony an extraordinary experience for the Mormons are also fundamental to the content and presentation of the PCC. The Center, like the temple, ushers its participants through a sequence of preliminary spaces and activities. In each village, costumed guides playing islanders teach participants a mixture of history and popular belief, and initiate them into simple activities that dramatise the exotic allure of Polynesia. Along the way, they are informed repeatedly that these traditional activities are disappearing and would already be lost if not for the intervention of the PCC.

After this progression comes a spectacular culmination that elevates the Polynesians and their pure and simple lifestyle to an unparalleled level of sophistication and admirableness. In the temple, the culminating experience is beyond a veil-like boundary. At the PCC, the resplendent night show can be witnessed only by crossing a narrow bridge over a branch of the lagoon that surrounds the theatre.

Anachronisms and ancestors

In its efforts to preserve Polynesian culture and tradition, the Center is purposely anachronistic, and follows equivocal concepts of time and culture. Stanton observes that

> It is virtually impossible to place all of the buildings, costumes, material items, and live demonstrations ... within the same specific time-frame. The PCC tried to tie all portions of 'village' exhibits into a functionally integrated whole, with the full realization that an artifact might be removed two hundred years in authenticity from the house where it is located.
>
> (1989: 254)

According to Ferre, the Center's creators

> realized that the articles of incorporation had not identified any specific era in the history of the island cultures that the Center was to preserve,

only that they were to preserve Polynesian culture. ... [They] pointed out that, since culture was not a static thing, ambiguity had always existed as to what period of time in each of the cultures the Center ought to preserve. ... [They] therefore did not feel bound to represent any one period in particular ... [and] felt that determining authenticity in culture was a matter of relativity, and that island cultures disagreed among themselves over points of authenticity.

(1988: 165)

This equivocation of chronology allows the Center to be selective and provide an uncomplicated, timeless rendition of Polynesia the tourists delight in, but one which the Mormons also are pleased to lay claim to, for they believe that Polynesians are descended from the ancient civilisations whose histories are contained in the *Book of Mormon*. One village manager even refers to Polynesia as '*Book of Mormon* Land.' One night show performer told me:

[The instructor] will get up and give a strong testimony and the relationship with the Hawaiian people and the Book of Mormon and with Christ. He knows a lot about Hawaiian genealogy, and he'll just [recite] the names that go all the way back to Book of Mormon times, and we'll just get goosebumps listening to him because he's got all the genealogy. He'll name Book of Mormon names, except it won't be like 'Nephi,' 'Lehi.' He'll name them in Hawaiian, and then say, 'This is Nephi, this is Lehi.' We'll just go 'Wow!'

The PCC, then, is invested with scriptural stature, as is the temple. But here the source is not the *Bible*, but the *Book of Mormon*. In fact, this sacred book of scripture recounts the destruction and promises the restoration of a number of ancient American societies, which heightens the aura of holiness attached to the Center's mission to preserve Polynesia's cultures.

So while the tourists' PCC experience consists of spectacle mixed with a little education and contact with 'ancient' Polynesians, to the Mormon employees who work there, the Center reenacts their ancestors' way of life. Even though they know that only certain aspects of traditional Polynesian culture are represented there, learning about the ancestors and portraying their dress and customs at the PCC engages the same devotion to ancestors that is more ceremonially invoked in the temple. According to one Maori respondent,

This piece of land, the building, and everything [i.e. the Maori village] belongs to our tupuna [i.e. ancestors], and we're upholding those principles in this latter-day. We're upholding the principles that they upheld, and this makes us feel good.

A Hawaiian village supervisor said

As I taught theater, my first [priority] was for them to take pride in who you represent. We represent our kapunas [ancestors]. Our ancestors worked hard for us to be where we are.

A former night show performer said

I think it's still there, the affinity with ancestors because from the scripts that we share with the tourists we're always talking about, you know, anciently Hawaii was like this, our forefathers performed fishing this way, and this way, and that type of thing. [The scripts] used those types of words, 'anciently,' and 'early history.' So I think in that way it does bring them closer together. ... [Some students are] almost meticulous in how they prepare. It's just got to be the best. It's almost a feeling of reverence, I'd say, in their preparation. There must be some feeling of that genealogical [concern], you know, going back.

In some ways, honoring the ancestors by recreating their customs and traditions at the Center is even more satisfying than performing temple ceremonies for them because the results of one's efforts are more tangible. The personal journal of one villager reflects her satisfaction as she performed for the Maori queen and her retinue visiting from New Zealand:

I could really feel the spirit of God with us today as we performed. I think that if we had not asked Him for His presence and thanked Him for all He'd done for us, we would not have performed as well as we did. Everyone put their faith in Him. I felt as we were performing that I was actually back in the days of the ancient Maori. I felt fear as the trumpet was blown announcing strangers into our village. I felt proud of our Maori warriors as they challenged them, and I felt happiness when they made known to us that they came in peace and were welcomed into the village. I think everyone today performed at their best and really showed our queen that we are proud of our heritage and respect it.

Clothing at the PCC

Modelled after traditional styles, the Center's costumes evoke the past and create a perception of authenticity for the tourists. The Center's costumes also delineate the PCC as an extraordinary place for its performers, but for them it is because the outfits are so contrary to acceptable Mormon standards of modest dress. The costumes are certainly not prurient, but they are clearly outside the standards of modesty set by the church and articulated in the temple ceremony. Even the university where most of the employees are students would discipline and perhaps suspend those students if they wore clothing on campus as revealing as the costumes they wear when they work at the PCC. Some Mormon visitors to the Center have found the costumes objectionable (see Forester 1986: 64), and a Hawaiian PCC performer told me,

> If you go to Waikiki and you see the shows, a lot of the times they wear hardly anything at all. For somebody who's never saw a show in town, they'd say that maybe some of our dancers, the way they're dressed, they might not [approve].

Precisely because performers cannot wear the temple garments while wearing their PCC costumes, the costumes recall by negation the vows of modesty enacted in the temple. The costumes, therefore, are a structurally equivalent reversal of the temple clothing that establishes the Mormon dress standards from which the PCC costumes deviate so blatantly.

Sacred reversals: the anti-temple

Immodest clothing is not the only reversal. The PCC has all the elements of a temple ceremony: the simplicity motif; costuming; scriptural foundations; audience participation; reverence for ancestors; dismissal of conventional chronologies; the threat of social and personal loss; and a final glorious reaffirmation of cherished social values and structures. These elements are arranged at the PCC into activities and exhibits that pay respect to ancestors, and correspond thematically to the temple ceremonies performed for the dead. The threats of culture loss, which only the Center can forestall, correspond to the temple's portrayal of the violence, pestilence and death in the sinful post-Edenic world. In contrast, the night show, because it glorifies Polynesian arts and society, is the counterpart to the temple's rendition of heaven and its rewards.

At the PCC, however, it is the tourist outsiders who experience the aesthetic fullness of rise, fall and deification. The Mormons stay in their places as guides, tricksters, interlocutors and performers in the Polynesian dramas. And while the Center inducts tourists into a manifestation of a legendary Polynesia, it separates its employees from their faith by reducing them to immodesty and drollery for the amusement of tourists who are often rude, belligerent and uncomprehending of Polynesian tradition, reverence for ancestors, and the religion that places a sacred value on Polynesia. For instance, a female performer told me,

A lot of tourists ask really dopey questions. It's not so much what they ask; it's how they ask. You kind of feel insulted when people talk to you, 'Oh, what's that?' 'Hey, you.' You really get annoyed. A lot of them are like that. They don't understand what in-depth culture is. So a lot of people will ask questions in an insulting way, or else they'll come out and ask insulting questions. It really offends. I have to constantly get myself used to them.

According to a male night show performer,

I guess we felt like we were like people in a zoo. Here's a nice performer, and you got to smile to them all the time, and it starts with our bosses. They tell us to perform, 'Smile! Look good! Look happy!' It's hard to keep the kids like that every night constantly for the whole year. Sometimes I come with a bad attitude, or if you had a bad day and you go out dancing, and sometimes you look at the crowd and you go, 'What, you're just paying here to look at me, and you think you can get a good performance?' So sometimes it's like the animal in a cage kind of bit.

Another performer complained that when the tourists become rude,

You're not allowed to retaliate. You have to hold it in, and sometimes it's really difficult because some tourists, because they're anti-Mormon as well. I don't know why they come if they're anti-Mormon, but a lot of them try and pick at you about the church more than about the culture.

Like an anti-temple, the PCC reverses the sacred. Instead of preserving their obligatory modesty, the PCC places its performers in a state of undress; instead of treating their objects of reverence with solemnity, they must resort to comedy; and instead of being the dignified faithful, the performers perceive themselves as curiosities on display.

Polynesia lost and regained

Although my respondents praised the PCC instructors, and were deeply grateful for the traditions they learned there, I also found among them high levels of dissatisfaction and outright hostility toward the tourists' disrespectfulness and the administration's blatantly commercial motives. Yet these same respondents clearly indicate that for them the Center is an extraordinary space with religious significance. Furthermore, instead of blaming the church itself for allowing and even fostering the PCC's contradictions, they consider the Center only a quasi-religious subsidiary of the church, and focus their discontent on the Center's management.

Like the Irula festival séances Thin analyses, the PCC elicits a sort of quasi-worship from its performers, but it places them in circumstances of contradiction and ambiguity in the presence of the divine. And like the Irula with their séances, the PCC performers distinguish between the Center and the formal, reverential worship services provided by the church. One difference, however, is that the Mormon Polynesian performers at the PCC do not find the Center entertaining in the way the Irula are entertained at the séances. Again, the PCC's entertainment is for the tourists. In Thin's schema, the PCC performers are more like the priest-headmen who are the brunt of the public humiliation that is part of the Irula séances.

Humiliation seems to propel the PCC performers back into the formal offices and activities of their church. Nearly all of my respondents reported high activity in the church, even those who displayed the most animosity toward tourists and the Center. It seems that the enormity of the reversals that occur at the PCC separates the performers from their guests and reinforces their strong Mormon identity. The quasi-sacred place where they preserve the ways of their kapunas becomes polluted, like Eden, through the invasion of outsiders who force them into displays of immodesty and servility. And since the Center provides them no reintegration because the PCC's 'saving' ordinance is intended only for the tourists, the employees must seek their rites of reintegration outside the Center in the official workings of the church and in the larger Mormon community of Laie, including its temple.

It is almost as if the PCC designers had intended the place to be a rite of separation from outsiders, who now flood Laie, and reincorporation into the church; however, there is no evidence that the similarities between the PCC and the temple were intentional. But neither are they likely to be purely coincidence or happenstance. They are both Mormon cultural expressions, after all. Comparison of the form and content of the Center with the elements of the temple show that the Center serves a function not only for the tourists. It is an expressive restatement of the temple ceremony; it plays on temple themes, and reinforces Mormon beliefs. But in so doing, it imposes reversals on the employees, who then must return to the unambiguous sacraments and services of the church for resolution, perhaps absolution.

Among the Irula, according to Thin, séances provide a catharsis of lingering ambiguities through the open but indirect questioning of their religious values in a quasi-religious setting. But the séances give voice to the Irula's own ambiguities in an extemporaneous ceremony of their own devising. In contrast, the PCC is a rigidly programmed domain for outsiders, although it is a Mormon property. Because of that great difference, the Center itself creates ambiguities for its Mormon employees that must be quelled outside the Center.

The PCC is successful as a tourist attraction and a Mormon anti-ceremony because both the tourists and the Mormons share a deep interest in Polynesia. The PCC demonstrates that this international style of art – tourist art – can carry a complex religious significance for its producers, and transfer this significance to tourists. When tourist art becomes more than an economic endeavour, when it becomes an expression of the artisan's sense of form and significance, it has entered the aesthetic realm, with all the capacities to carry meanings that art can carry.

References

Britsch, R. Lanier (1986) *Unto the Islands of the Sea: A History of the Latter-day Saints in the Pacific*, Salt Lake City: Deseret.

The Church of Jesus Christ of Latter-day Saints (1981) *The Doctrine and Covenants*, Salt Lake City: The Church. References are cited by section and verse.

Dolgin, Janet L. (1974) 'Latter-day sense and substance', in I. I. Zaretsky and M. P. Leone (eds) *Religious Movements in Contemporary America*, Princeton: Princeton University Press, pp. 519–46.

Ferre, Craig (1988) 'A History of the Polynesian Cultural Center's "Night Show": 1963–1983', Ph.D. dissertation, Department of Theatre and Film, Brigham Young University.

Forester, Rubina (1986) 'The Polynesian Cultural Center: the realization gone far beyond the dream', *Proceedings of the Seventh Annual Conference, Mormon Pacific Historical Society*, pp. 60–72, Laie HI.

Harrison, David (1992) 'Tourism to less developed countries: the social consequences', in D. Harrison (ed.) *Tourism and the Less Developed Countries*, London: Belhaven Press, pp. 19–34.

Leone, Mark P. (1977) 'The new Mormon Temple in Washington, D.C.', in L. Ferguson (ed.) *Historical Archaeology and the Importance of Material Things*, Washington DC: Society for Historical Archaeology, pp. 43–61.

O'Dea, Thomas F. (1957) *The Mormons*, Chicago: University of Chicago Press.

PCC (Polynesian Cultural Center) (1986) 'Passport to Polynesia', brochure, Laie HI: The Center.

——(1995?) 'What to see & do in Polynesia: official guidebook', brochure, Laie HI: The Center.

——(1997) 'Polynesian Cultural Center: all the spirit of the islands, all in one place', brochure, Laie HI: The Center.

Shenhav-Keller, Shelly (1995) 'The Jewish pilgrim and the purchase of a souvenir in Israel', in M-F. Lanfant, J. B. Allcock and E. M. Bruner (eds) *International Tourism: Identity and Change*, London: Sage, pp. 143–58.

Silver, Harry R. (1979) 'Beauty and the "I" of the beholder: identity, aesthetics, and social change among the Ashanti', *Journal of Anthropological Research*, 35(2): 191–207.

Stanton, Max E. (1989) 'The Polynesian Cultural Center: a multi-ethnic model of seven Pacific cultures', in V. L. Smith (ed.) *Hosts and Guests: The Anthropology of Tourism*, 2nd edn, Philadelphia: University of Pennsylvania Press, pp. 247–62.

Webb, T. D. (1994a) 'Highly structured tourist art: form and meaning of the Polynesian Cultural Center', *Contemporary Pacific*, 6(1): 59–85.

——(1994b) 'Missionaries, Polynesians, and tourists: Mormonism and tourism in Laie, Hawaii', *Social Process in Hawaii*, 35: 195–212.

Part III

Bodily possibilities

Chapter 9

Dance, dissimulation and identity in Indonesia[1]

Felicia Hughes-Freeland

This chapter explores embodied forms of politesse through Javanese ideas about dissimulation and avoidance in court dance, and the implications of these ideas for our understanding of identity at the personal, social and national level. Within the colonial court, dancing was an education in techniques of politeness which have been elaborated beyond the more generally instilled patterns of polite Javanese social interaction, and this very specific and select education was able to become an exemplar in ideologies of national identity which were developed after Independence as state policy. At a previous ASA conference, David Parkin asked 'How far do we now view "meaning" not as given us by signs but as placed by ourselves on and through the objects and acts we see and experience?' (1992: xiii). The definition of meaning which reifies culture is used by the Indonesian government in a cultural politics which creates difference through the category of 'Asian values'. My analysis is between political and semantic anthropology, and questions the universalist approach to the embodied nature of communication, and explores how physical action, like speech, is also subject to indirection and dissimulation: we can lie and strategise with our bodies as much as with our tongues. Embodied performances are as vital for imagining society as Gilsenan has suggested are verbal lies (1976: 210ff.).

Truth, lies and stereotypes

The contradictions inherent in polite lies present a challenge to rationality in its different forms (Wolfram 1985). Take for instance the ethnographic contrast between 'the' Javanese tendency to lie and 'our' inclination to tell the truth promulgated by Clifford Geertz:

> When we tell white lies, we have to justify them to ourselves ... we usually have to find some sort of reason for telling a lie. For the Javanese (especially the *prijaji*),[2] it seems, in part anyway, to work the other way around: the burden of proof seems to be in the direction of justifying the truth. ... In general, polite Javanese avoid gratuitous truths.
>
> (1960: 246)

Geertz's formulation prioritises style or surface over morality, and produces what I call a semiotic orientalism, dramatically illustrated by Roland Barthes' discussion of Japanese semiosis. For Barthes, the value given to corporeal gestural precision 'has nothing which is rational or moral ... the logic of Occidental morality is to be impolite, is to be true' (1994: 778, 790).[3]

Positive socio-cultural evaluations of a person who is 'sincere' and 'natural' whose behavioral style shows what they are 'really like' have often led to a mistaking of different presentations as morally suspect. But 'Orientals' do not necessarily have a monopoly on dissimulation. Take this moment from a novel by John Le Carré:

> ... the privately educated Englishman – and Englishwoman ... is the greatest dissembler on earth. ... Nobody will charm you so glibly, disguise his feelings from you better, cover his tracks more skilfully, or find it harder to confess to you that he's been a damn fool. ... He can have a Force Twelve nervous breakdown while he stands next to you in the bus queue, and you may be his best friend, but you'll never be the wiser.
>
> (1991: 29)

Indirection as social style

The practice in polite Javanese social interaction of dissimulating fact and feeling in social interaction (*ethok-ethok*) is not necessarily 'other' as a form of presentation. Goffman's approach (1956) brings Javanese and English behaviour into a single frame, where politeness conceals 'the dirty work' (Goffman 1956: 28), and everyday life is a performance, organised in contexts classified as 'front stage' and 'back stage', to which styles are adapted to appropriate degrees of formality. Polite Javanese social interaction is well known for its use of elaborate and nuanced speech 'levels' which are used to manipulate relative social statuses. The concealment of intention by using deferential language codes gives the user power over the one being offered such codes (Dewey 1978). These 'levels' or 'codes' become less exotic and morally suspect when treated as 'styles' in a 'matrix of face-saving practices' (Goffman 1967, cited in Errington 1988: 238). Politeness, for the Javanese, is 'the management of meaning', a 'fundamental property of political interaction' to be explained with reference to the 'phenomenological realities of situations ... [it is] an essential aspect of power' (Cohen and Comaroff 1976: 87–9).

Javanese language is performative as well as informative. Ordered behaviour depends on a knowledge of 'the relative values of language', *unggah-ungguh*. Nine levels are used, according to whether an interaction is formal (*krama*), semi-formal (*madya*), or basic (*ngoko*) (Koentjaraningrat 1985: 234). The correct use of levels is crucial for expressing polite deference. For example, a Yogyakartan Prince was quick to correct me when I mistakenly asked him if he had seen (*ningali*) a recent shadow play, using the plain polite level (*krama*) instead of giving him the self-abasing *krama andhap* word for 'see' (*mirsani*). Politeness is used forcefully, and speech styles are more than verbal acts. The intertwined relationship of being Javanese, speaking Javanese, and Javanese manners was nicely expressed by a court musician, who explained that however perfect one's linguistic skill, it is only complete (*jankĕp*) when accompanied by the appropriate gestures. He demonstrated 'complete *krama*', accompanying a sentence with a gentle forward inclination of the shoulders. *Krama* is melodious, measured, 'muted gesturally' (Errington 1988: 245), and is used for first-impression management and distance-preservation, for keeping on the safe side. When speaking Javanese it is better to be overweeningly polite than sorry. The rhythms of *krama* are the rhythms of dance-measures as they are practised in the court; these do not exclude the possibility of violence but it is kept under a strict rein. By contrast, people using the informal and semi-polite codes (*ngoko* and lower *madya*) have a bickering, insolent tone, a ragged, fraying texture. *Ngoko* is rich in word play for comic effect; its pungently derisive or ironic effects are exploited in comic performances of all kinds. *Ngoko* expresses a hint of contempt, a hostility, a proximity to open physical violence which tends to be overlooked if one concentrates on polite areas of speech behaviour. The difference, in short, is that where *ngoko* has a screeching nasal laugh, in *krama* a smile is quite enough.

'A person's speech and comportment are strategically adapted relative to the status of the addressee, as a means to social ends extrinsic to norms of etiquette' (Errington 1988: 228). In these terms, Javanese people become agents instead of being constrained by codes. For instance, a speaker can use indirection to subvert the rules governing a situation by directing the speech to themselves away from the addressee by using the familiar code, *ngoko*. This 'as if' internalisation frees the utterance from constraints and gives it licence to be daring, blunt, shocking and funny, and is often used by noted comedians. Comedy is thus able to deal with political matters which can only be articulated by virtue of indirection and humorous framing. It makes it possible to say things which the normal rules of Javanese discourse – and current Indonesian politics – make it otherwise impossible to say.

As linguistic data have been given priority over embodied action, and studies about the effect of power and social effectiveness on the Javanese self have focused on speech,[4] I will concentrate on the behavioural significance of physical gesture and movement in social interaction, and show why embodied behaviour has come to have particular importance in the state's view of culture and identity.

Dance and everyday life

The boundary between formal performance as an event and the performance of everyday life is deliberately blurred by Javanese experts on court traditions and educationalists. Since the late colonial era in the sultan's palace in Yogyakarta, court dance training has been a form of socialisation which promotes socially approved behaviour by developing the self-control which is necessary for harmonious social interaction. These codified movement systems have maintained significance in the post-colonial Indonesian Republic of which Java forms a part.

Dance movement is the enactment of *ĕmpan-papan*, best understood as a Javanese version of Goffman's 'impression management'. The dance *sĕmbah* (salutation with joined palms, thumbs just below the nostrils), is also used in daily court life to show respect to the sultan. Dancing is thus both art and exemplar. This relationship between dance and manners (*tata-krama*) was explained to me by Prince Suryobrongto, a dancer who was later responsible for court protocol.[5]

> In *trapsila*, every movement is ordered ... Everything is in dance move-ment: how to stoop so as not to be taller than someone you are passing in front of; how to do the sitting walk; how to sit cross-legged, how to sit in *sila marikĕlu* ('broken rice-stalk', the masculine position of respect to the sultan, cross-legged with the knees close to the ground, with the hands folded – see Figure 9.1) without fidgeting and shifting around, which may be for hours in dance drama; how to hold the front pleat of one's *bathik* with your left hand so that the fold does not flap open in the wind, which would be sloppy (*ngĕlomprot*); how to sink to the ground holding a tray so that the glasses don't spill; how to hold one's arm so that your armpit does not show indecently. *Subasita* is being polite, having a friendly attitude, and being modest, not arrogant, respectful and consid-erate of others. In Yogya the Princes express this by using *krama* to people, not *ngoko* like they do in Surakarta ... *Unggah-ungguh* is language use. ... These kinds of *tata-krama* all come into dance. ... In the dance is reflected the character of the person.

Formal politeness is fitting for certain occasions and places, although ethnography presents politeness as normative behaviour. Indeed, one theme in Orientalist images of the Javanese is their essential grace. 'Few peoples are more naturally sensitive to rhythm than the Javanese' wrote Van Lelyveld in his text about Javanese dance, published for the colonial exhibition of 1931 (1931: 47). This sort of cultural stereotyping has given 'The' Javanese an ethnographic reputation for being graceful *by nature*. Individual Javanese people may find this stereotype useful to hide behind, and words like sensi-tivity, refinement, and self-control come up in local discourses as well that of outsiders, and play their part in defining and shaping national programmes of identity production.

This *effect* or ideal should not be confused with actuality. Being Javanese is not naturally given, but the result of socialisation or training. Before this one

Figure 9.1 Refined male dancer sits in *sila marikělu*. Dance drama by Siswa Among Běksa, Yogyakarta, 1983.

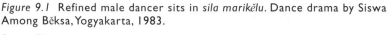

Source: Photograph by author.

is 'not yet' Javanese (*dhurung Jawa*), a phrase applied to children under five, foreigners, or insane people (Geertz 1961: 105), and glossed by my Javanese teacher as 'not being able to think yet'.[6] As the well known Javanese poet and dramatist W. S. Rendra writes,

> It may be that Javanese civilization has consciously balanced the violent character of its masses. Their insights, psychologism (*kěbatinan*), language and arts are directed primarily towards controlled sensibilities.
>
> (1983: 11, author's translation)

The Javanese do not value behaviour as 'natural' in any general sense, so no movement may be understood as 'everyday and normal' in contrast to those used in dance situations. The regular observation of formality in movement, speech delivery and styles, in the palace may generate an ease within the constraint which might appear 'natural'.

The catch-all term in Javanese which summarises this effect is *alus* (refined, gentle), a word as ubiquitous in Javanese conversation as 'nice' is in English, and as vague. And where English people oppose 'nice' with 'nasty', Javanese say *kasar* (rude, harsh). *Alus* describes behaviour which is appropriate to context: it is not *alus* to behave with excessive formality at informal events.

Court appearances require that people feel at home (in all senses) in the formal codes of etiquette, so that these codes *appear* natural, unconstrained, and graceful.[7] Rather than simply denoting the show of manners which is etiquette, they refer to the prior knowledge and sense of appropriateness necessary to know about when and how to put on such a show and when to play it down. Effective competence and performance of *ĕmpan-papan* is *alus*. This includes judging the time and the place as appropriate for informal behaviour. Misplaced or excessive manners are not *alus* at all; they are mannered, badly performed. In the broader context of the potential chaos of Javanese everyday life, *alus* is a kind of rationality or morality for Dutch-educated Javanese *priyayi*, for whom its absence produces barbarism. But *alus* also refers to a gentleness of spirit which can only be acquired through stringent self-examination and discipline. Prince Suryobrongto's generation puts a value on honesty, and included speaking the truth as a fourth point of court etiquette:

> *Udhanĕgara* is politeness in general … if you say 'yes' you should mean 'yes'. *Ethok-ethok* (polite dissimulation) is not in keeping with *udhanĕgara*, which means 'a king is as good as his word'.

He explained the absence of masked dance forms from the Yogyakartan palace as the result of an ethos of openness: the dancer's eyes carried the role, and a mask would conceal the truth of that gaze. This view counters nicely a favourite Western image of so-called Oriental inscrutability, and also reminds us that we need to be careful of how we use metaphors of masking with reference to different styles of face-saving.[8]

Dancing develops physical balance consistent with the claim that there is a cultural preoccupation in Java with keeping one's balance (Geertz 1961: 149). This principle is not theoretical but at the forefront of consciousness, and there was general agreement in Yogyakarta that the dance movement is 'always on one leg'. Learning the feminine mode was learning how to effect the subtle shifts of weight between the feet. Taking the body's centre of gravity down to the pelvic girdle but *not* into the turned-out knees, and then shifting it slowly from one side of the body to the other for eight counts of the gong in a movement called *ngoyog*, described and demonstrated as the most difficult movement (Hughes-Freeland 1988). Skill is required to control the constant shifts of weight from one leg to the other which, together with detail in the movements of the head, neck, arms, wrists, fingers and dance sash, completes the figure.

The expressive power of all Yogyakartan dance movement rests not on the élancé style of classical western ballet, but on a sustained control over any desire to take off. Dance rhythms in the feminine dance mode are cautious, tentative, assessing, without abruptness; there is an unbroken flow subsuming the individual poses. Dancing is about keeping on the ground, and keeping within the limits. Apart from the footwork, this style of court dance is noted for its strict convention in the control of the arms and elbows which are held in a square shape. The muscles of the upper and lower arms need to be supplemented by a fluid and supple wrist and precise control over the fingers which must be neither tense not relaxed.

Just as effort is dissimulated in polite strategic social interaction, in dancing the appearance of the movement conceals the work that produces it to produce the effect of refinement and grace. But dancing is not simply a form of disciplined physical practice. It is the acquisition of social resources which produce possibilities. As a training it instils Javanese values and a sense of rhythm and measure, but the performance of dance movement goes beyond control. The experienced dancer ceases to experience the doing of the movements: the experienced dancer reaches the point where the acquired habits of movement have their own momentum, independent of the performer's intention (Hughes-Freeland 1997a).

Competence in dance is not only a matter of balance and control of one's own movements, but the interaction with others, which is expressed choreographically through avoidance and learning to be in place (*mapan*). Once trainees develop a better balance they are then faced with problems of orientation. The matter of avoiding the pillars which support the roof in the dance pavilion is complicated enough, but things become worse, because most dance forms are for groups of two, four, or nine. To lose control of one's orientation is to run the likely risk of collision, especially in fighting sequences. Most difficult are the complicated transitions in the asymmetrical floor patterns in the complicated Bĕdhaya dances for nine experienced female dancers, which demonstrate the greatest logistical skill in Javanese choreography, especially in the changing of formations which are achieved by the dancers running swiftly on tiptoe to reform without interrupting the sustained rhythm of the dance, impossible without control and coordination.

Orientation and positioning are thus closely linked to etiquette and *ĕmpan-papan*. There is a close connection between movement, manners and identity, which serve to articulate ideas about order and coherence (Suseno and Reksosusilo 1983). Dancing expresses a Javanese theory of space and is a metaphor for Javanese ideas about behaviour, both in regard to a person's own occupation of space and their interrelations with others. Dancing thus represents fundamental orders of practised behaviour appropriate to person and place which form part of the practical knowledge about being Javanese (*cara jawi*) (see Figure 9.2). These Javanese semantics resonate with analytical concepts such as De Certeau's notion of 'practised place' (1984).

Javanese people are polite in situations where it is strategically expedient to be so, but in ongoing situations, the equivalent in everyday polite social interaction of not bumping into other dancers or pillars (and the prolonged lead up to danced conflicts), a process of complete evasion in the form of avoidance and not-speaking is common – for example in a household I often

Figure 9.2 Formal politeness and non-interaction at the exchange of rings in a household in the palace enclave, Yogyakarta, 1983.

Source: Photograph by author.

visited, this was the only means to allow fifteen siblings to co-habit. Being in place can also mean avoidance, in the sense of maintaining 'nonrelations' (Gilsenan 1976: 211). Enforced sociability in Java's crowded communities tests everyone's patience. Javanese people are also trained to be fearful (*ajrih*) and awkward (*sungkan*) as children: 'each time that he faces an unfamiliar *alter ego*, a Javanese individual will either evade the situation and run away, or remain inactive and wait to see how the situation develops' (Koentjaraningrat 1985: 250). Evasion is one way to maintain dignity and clout. Without these, society breaks down.[9] Social interaction is performed in an evasive and defensive style to deflect anger which incompetently managed behaviour may incur. When anger is shown and impression management breaks down, Javanese manners rapidly disintegrate. Accusations of hypocrisy (*munafik*) are often heard, and there are degrees of acceptability about kinds of lies: presenting a false reality disguise; deceit; trickery; gossip. There is a difference between saying something intentionally to be patently false (and verifiable as such), with the intention to deceive and make mischief for someone, and not saying what you think or feel, which is classed as controlling your feelings, not reacting to provocation, not showing your hand, and also not saying how bad things are (i.e. not complaining). Once people break this polite distance, the interaction is no longer *à la* Javanese culture – though the withdrawal after intimacy and confidence sharing is done in a very distinctive manner, and often disseminated through true and false rumours by gossip, itself a form of generalised indirection.

Court dance in Indonesia

This account of dance describes a historically situated system of skill, techniques and discipline. Dancers danced for the sultan's eye, particularly that of Hamĕngkubuwana VIII, the last colonial sultan of Yogyakarta, who was famed for his searching gaze and for establishing the norms of what is now classical Yogyakartan dance. He extended ceremonial dancing in the colonial court beyond the ritual frame to the more general sphere of manners and personal development, and supported the foundation of the first dance association (Kridha Bĕksa Wirama) where court dancers trained outsiders. In this way Javanese court dance came out of the palace as exemplary centre to become a national cultural resource which also serves the diverse interests of particular individuals, moving into dance associations and state academies to contribute to the production of Javanese and Javano-Indonesian identities (Hughes-Freeland n.d.).

As a significant embodied practice, dance is often overlooked as a factor in the construction of national identities, due to the emphasis on language-based rationalities in Western thought. Anderson, for example, has famously suggested that nations are 'imagined communities' constructed out of journeys and print technologies (1983). At the heart of Anderson's argument is the claim that languages are not '*emblems* of nation-ness', but have agency: the power to generate 'imagined communities building in effect *particular solidarities*' (1983: 122). These imagined communities may be given 'echoed physical realization' on occasions of 'unisonality' such as, in the case of Indonesia, the singing of the national anthem, Indonesia Raya (1983: 132). Anderson's 'disembodied' approach may more specifically reflect his extensive knowledge of Javanological traditions. There is congruence between the priority he has given to spoken forms in the construction of Indonesian and other nationalisms and the privileging of language in official representations of Javanese culture. For Anderson, the embodied action of dance – and 'folk dance' at that – has a merely emblematic status, along with flags, costumes 'and the rest' (1983: 122). I would suggest, *contra* Anderson, that Javanese court dance has become an important part of Indonesian culture precisely because it is *more* than an emblem. Dancing literally embodies ideas about acceptable forms of behaviour and being. The sense which Javanese people bring to court performance traditions is constituted by recent history and projective interests: performance, in Javanese culture, is valued for the futures it allows groups to imagine. But more than this, it also allows groups and individuals to embody present identities. Attempts by Javanese people to make sense of practices such as court dancing orientate identity because dancing starts in the body, rather than writing or making visual or aural images.

As we know, court dancing is an education of the sensibilities and teaches a person how to be Javanese. Today, court dance contributes to the creation of a Javano-Indonesian identity, and is still valued for its power to instil 'controlled instincts'. Dance can change you, can give you access to practices and to systems which are potentially empowering. Dance movement is valued for its improving and educative capacities. It is a means of socialisation into the Javanese way of behaving. Unruly individuals or groups, such as Javanese children being brought up in the Indonesian capital Jakarta, learnt Javanese dance and became controlled, quieter, and compliant. As a senior courtier said, 'I didn't recognise her. Could this be the same person?'. The change is not profound, but manifestly visible. Being Javanese is not an arcane and secret state, but something which can be *seen*. A person is constituted by the behaviour they bring to the world of social interaction. It is in this context that we need to understand the social significance of dance. It is a particular practice in which knowledge is incorporated – in the sense of literal embodiment – and then displayed. Dancing in this sense is the Javanese way in practice. However, its visibility is only one side of its social relevance, as will become clear. In independent Indonesia, court performance is taught in many venues and has become mainstream. Unlike Western training in classical ballet, people who learn court dance are neither isolated nor marginalised. People of all ages participate in dance/drama, either for fun or as part of formal education, from kindergarten through to professional development programmes. And in Yogya in the early 1980s, the police training fitness programme offered a choice between volleyball, the martial arts and dancing.

Dance educationalists acknowledge that contemporary ideas about dance derive from the educational ethos of Haměngkubuwana VIII's reign. The cultural policies of the Ministry of Culture and Education are based on those of the modernist nationalism of the 1920s and 1930s, which aimed to develop a process by which Indonesian nationhood would grow, not to produce professionals or artists. It was the cultivation of a national Javanese identity (*kepribadian* Ind.) which concerned both the nationalist pedagogue, Ki Hadjar Dewantara, and Indonesia's first President, Soekarno (Lombard 1990: I, 200). Indonesian character building continues to use early Javanese nationalist vocabulary:

> An arts education is a means to raise the interest or appreciation of arts and culture of the Indonesian people, which needs to be related to Nation and Character Building, in the name of National Security, so arts education needs to be continued, with the people joined together as a subject together represented in artistic activities.
>
> (Dinusatama 1983)

Court dance is an 'education in sensibilities [*rasa*]'; Javanese 'culture' is 'the results of character [*budi*] given form in various media', and is always education in disguise; finally, rather than developing Indonesian culture, the state should develop and preserve 'local peaks' (*puncak daerah* Ind.), in the spirit of the Indonesian state motto, 'Unity in diversity'. This policy re-emerged after the political crisis of the mid-1960s as the foundation for New Order cultural politics, and the assertion of the state philosophy, the Pancasila, as a moral code (Watson 1987: 37ff.). Problems have arisen in the slippage between the Javanese references for the early nationalists, and the Indonesian objectives in the post-colonial situation.

Culture as self-citation

Since Indonesian independence, the terms of the committed struggle for independence and the establishment of the republic have become abstracted and formulaic in the contemporary Indonesian state (McVey 1967: 133). Some see this process as a re-Javanisation of the nationalist spirit (Anderson 1990), although Javanese people such as Prince Suryobrongto might object to this view of Javaneseness, and would claim that Javanese values, including those embodied in movement styles, are being imposed on other groups which form part of the Indonesian Republic.

In Indonesia's New Order regime, culture is politeness and dissimulation, while politics is opposition, which includes plain speaking as well as confrontation. Culture is part of a political agenda to preserve tradition and develop a nation. Since independence, the state has promoted dancing as an education to form citizens, and also to control them. In one sense, dancing is prevalent in Indonesia today because it is a form of discipline. Javanese dancers distinguished dance from the other (visual) arts on the grounds that, despite costume, music and so forth, the only material a dancer has is their own body, and the skill of dance movement lies in self-presentation and control. This direct contact with the person's physical body (*lahir*) is a means to control their spiritual body (*batin*). Javanese thinking recognises that the inner is not only a private place for avoidance of externally imposed and contingent constraints, but place of collective identity, the *aku* or 'I' in a collective, relational, socio-centric sense. The New Order control of bodies, labour and discourse is the basis of socio-political order. It transposes the social values which give significance to court dance as a force for socialisation to a formula for cultural patterning which is implemented to create illusions of the new society, the new nationhood (Hughes-Freeland 1997b).

The Indonesian state controls the activities of its citizens through surveillance and censorship.[10] It is easier to obtain police authorisation for dances than for performances which use language. Verbal drama is an overt threat to stability, despite sporadic government announcements of 'openness'. In contrast to theatre and poetry, dance messages are ambivalent, and to a certain extent elude censorship. Closely related to censorship is standardisation, and a tendency to aim at reducing ambiguity by standardising messages and genres by means of competitions which set the standards for forms and styles, incorporating active bodies into organised performance and sports. These act as a mechanism of control. Potentially disruptive energies are channelled into such events organised by the Ministry of Culture and Education, directing energies which might otherwise run wild. The regime legitimises such contests to save itself from becoming the object of a different kind of contest: as any official of the Ministry of Culture and Education will tell you, organising competitions is time-consuming and exhausting. In a classic functionalist manner, competitions formalise, contain and defuse conflict, keeping it in a state of immanence, not imminence – or have done for the past thirty years.

Dance is excellent for spreading and standardising culture *as appearances*. Culture reifies front stage: culture *becomes* front stage. This front-stage presentation is an aspect of abstracted 'culture' in Indonesia (and other post-colonial states). Culture in Indonesia is a word which dissimulates other terms which, from the state's point of view, are too risky to articulate: culture is a word which conceals processes which might otherwise be called politics or religion. This separation extends to the relationship of form and agency, as social deference becomes political deferral, putting off confrontation. This abstracted, front-stage concept of culture can be illuminated with reference to De Certeau's concept of citation. By dint of saying that something is so, of citing something *as fact*, it becomes so. Citation metamorphises messy realities into truth/authorisation (1984: 171–2). Citation produces a form of truth which dissimulates the processes of everyday life (*ibid*.: 188–9). Citation is another way of thinking about reification. Culture becomes a 'thing', to be packaged and controlled. Culture in New Order Indonesia may be understood as a self-parody of Javanese culture which is represented as truth in an exaggeratedly dissimulated pseudo-Javanist style. Culture in these terms is lie, a misrepresentation, which nonetheless allows expedient survival under dysfunctional circumstances. How long this can continue, and how much counter-claims to the construct of self-citation (such as those of liberal Islam) can support is anyone's guess.[11]

Dance as dissimulated agency

Despite the top-down policies of Indonesian cultural politics, I will close with an argument for optimism. New Order culture might appear to be an analytically determinist category at a distance, but the experiencing of work and research in Indonesia makes it seem less monolithic, and more a dysfunctional anarchy, where communication and control do not work, and the paper projects do not represent the experiences and aspirations of the public. Although Indonesian culture as self-citation produces a collective effect, culture is a process of individuals working, planning, training, choosing, learning. Culture does not just happen because someone signs a piece of paper in an office in Jakarta. State developmental plans (REPELITA) are not inevitably realised. Cultures are made by the actions of individuals (Alexander 1989: i).[12] In the current political climate, education might to the outsider seem repressive, but for Indonesians, education is a means to develop a person's opportunities for survival. Furthermore, people may go through the motions of doing what the state endorses, but for reasons which are nothing to do with state policy. Official state policy is often added on as a rationalisation. Performance is not necessarily the enactment of classifications in some constraining, limiting, and reductive manner. Performance is made up of practices which people do as agents, and *generates* the stuff of classifications in interaction with previously inscribed classifications, actualising other versions which may or may not be 'new'. The dance does not have deep structures but dense proliferations of reference, which may be mobilised in various versions and degrees in terms of completion and awareness by participants and viewers.

The extent of what people may choose to do, however, is constrained. The avoidance of confrontation which was discussed as a matter of politesse is also a matter of political expediency. The attitude has been eloquently put by Selosoemardjan: 'there was no demonstration of overt rejection, but neither was there any enthusiasm to co-operate' (1962: 80). This attitude of passive non-cooperation is a well known 'weapon of the weak' (Scott 1985), but given Indonesia's relatively recent stability, there has been a widespread social preference to play things safe, rather than be confronted with an armed policeman or a subversion charge. Such caution may be historically determined, an adaptation to living under colonial and, today, New Order surveillance.[13] For this reason, then, we might be cautious in attributing to politeness and impression management a universality which transcends history.

The concept of indirection discussed earlier helps us to understand how dancing is more than a form of social control which is exercised on the body of the dancer. As noted, politesse is a form of power, and discipline also empowers the dancing body. Yogyakartan people born in the 1920s who experienced the nationalist movements and the war against the Dutch inscribed dance in a specific socially constructed history of resistance. Dance was valued because it carried messages of revolt within the movements it made visible, and unified those who shared in that knowledge. This generation values court dancing for developing a militaristic perseverance (*ora mingkuh*). The competitions of the New Order could be interpreted in a similar way to the fighting dances of the early Yogya court; the apparent aestheticised control of persons in the movements of dance is the political confrontation, on hold, pending.

The feasibility of the analogy between the self-discipline of the dancer and the soldier was sustained during the reign of the ninth sultan (d. October 1988), who had maintained his political credibility in the republic because of his nationalist activities. This identification has become increasingly anachronistic under the New Order, where struggle and sacrifice are idioms for submission to the difficulties of forging a viable economy for the twenty-first century. Heroism today resides in service, not revolt. The star of the hero is given to those whose work helps to consolidate the unitary republic, not to revolutionaries who attempt action of a radical kind. It would seem that today the space for resistance is gone, and the martial ethos of the Yogya court and its self-image based on rebellion and heroism have been normalised. Revolutionary acts may not be on the agenda for now, but this does not mean that Javanese Indonesians have lost all agency and simply become puppets in the hands of state culture. The person who performs Javanese dance is not only danced *by it*, regimented into obedience. That person is invoking the powerful forms of Javanese deference and dissimulation which allow for manoeuvre and manipulation of those in power. The discipline of dancing is more than control, and is not in itself a completion. Rather, it is a beginning, because it opens up the dancers's *rasa*, their sensibility, consciousness or imagination. The constraints of disciplined physical practice is the prerequisite for a liberation of the imagining spirit. Movement is not controlled by a possessing spirit which obtrudes from outside. The dancers that dance the dance slip between the rules and elide impossible conjunctions. Dance's silence *may* make it vulnerable to cultural manoeuvres, but this same silence gives it a resistance to policing and control. The disciplined silence of dance movement may seem passive; but just as hierarchical language codes permit the subversion of the order they comprise, so too does dance's silence also allow it to speak of things which cannot be voiced. This is recognised in one way in the Yogya story of dancing being a secret way of keeping in training. While giving all the appearances of an elaborate cultural disciplining of the body, to perform court dance is to remember rebellion: dancing is a form of social memory, embodied but not to be articulated in words. The dancing body is neither the enslaved body nor the enchained body. To dance is to perform actions which subvert constraints, or transcend them. Dance movement produces a field of significance which is expressive not of meanings, but of connections. Embodied knowledge which cannot be made conscious in words is nonetheless a form of understanding which consists in 'being in touch with reality … it is our embodied understanding that manifests our realist commitments' (Johnson 1987: 204).

Intentions to 'standardise' dance movement ignore the crucial fact that each performer brings their own unique qualities to the enaction of movement. These are personal physical proportion and *rasa*, elements which are resistant to standardisation. Javanese people live their lives, as do the subjects of any nation state, with room for experience and response which is beyond control in most cases.

Observer models may negate the experience of being: we all inhabit nooks and crannies between our inheritance, our talents, our communities and our governments' rulings. But those nooks and crannies, like the inwardness of the Javanese dancer, open up unbounded horizons of hope through the action of the imagination. A top-down system of cultural programming relies on the passion and energy of the producers and performers themselves. The current developmental ethos in Indonesia today strives to incorporate individual creators who in Western society might be marginalised. However, the modern conditions of reproduction of performers entail expectations about future roles in society as well as on stage. It is the personal commitment of artists and impresarios in urban and rural settings that makes performances happen, not simply government policy acting on a void or on passive pawns. Dance practitioners may also have roles as civil servants, but in Yogyakarta it is their passion for theatre rather than power which makes them active. As a retired member of the Ministry of Information pointed out, career-minded civil servants do little for theatre: it is artists who become civil servants who do the work that counts. The current situation is not one which coerces people into performing: rather, people are motivated by enthusiasm and interest.[14]

Conclusion

The controlled formal behaviour noted by foreigners as characteristic is recognised by the Javanese themselves as arising from training or practice. Court dance continues to be valued as an effective means to instil 'controlled instincts', and to produce a person who knows how to be Javanese, within the context of the Indonesian state. Fluid connections allow diverse interpretations to co-exist, and can undermine cultural constraints. The value ascribed to movement, both socially and aesthetically, lies in its elusiveness and fluidity, in its resistance to being contained and categorised. Communication in this style, then, is the art of concealment rather than revelation or expression. It is the indirection of sense, not the directed imparting of information. It is not the sign, but the way it is placed, and thus constituted, which produces social sense (to answer Parkin's question raised at the start of this paper).

Dance training thus goes beyond the instillation of the unconscious actions which constitute the habitus. Apart from socialising a person into the group, it develops personal skills which, though defined by collective concepts, create a space for imagination and aspiration. The effect of learning dance well is to achieve personal liberation and empowerment by means of physical discipline which embodies polite dissimulation. Javanese courts have become symbolic centres, but the dancing which remains associated with them is not merely a symbol of action, it is real action, embodied action. Human performance is of a different order from puppet theatres, because it is accessible to participation of bodies of individuals in a way that puppet plays are not. It is literally incorporative. Its reality includes ideal representations of the Javanese self and its actions. As such, it has implications for the construction of identity. It is theoretically a practice which serves as a model for action/human activity as a balance between agency and structure.

Silence and concealment, then, have two sides; whether or not wrapping is revealing or concealing depends on strategies, which may be conscious, or may be from habit. To suggest that either is necessary is to prejudge situations. In a similar vein, the 'otherness' often inscribed in 'lying' and style, as suggested by semiotic Orientalists, may be countered with a more general account of style and evasion which is impression management. However, we should be cautious about imputing universality to evasion (Gilsenan 1976). Historical conditions give a particular force to evasiveness. Javanese dissimulation in part is manners, but it is also a question of survival in a more brutish sense. The situation I have described includes different levels of dissimulation which invite different kinds of judgement, which, again, anthropology feels required to dissimulate. In the final analysis, though, I would conclude that whereas politeness may appear to be the effect of external control (and in the Indonesian case, a mandatory strategy for survival), politeness is also a way of doing and being, between the rules, before the rules, and after the rules.

Notes

1 *Editors' note*: This chapter was written prior to the extraordinary political upheaval which occurred in Indonesia in 1998 and which led to the downfall of President Suharto and the break-up of the New Order. Rather than attempt to alter the political references, we have decided to let the chapter stand as it is and allow the reader to enjoy the prescience of many of the comments which reflected on repression and resistance in the New Order.
2 Post-colonial urban administrative officials and intelligentsia (Koentjaraningrat 1985: 233).
3 'Cette précision n'a rien de raisonable ou de moral … être impoli, c'est être vrai, dit logiquement la morale occidentale'.
4 For example, Keeler (1987); indeed, there is a Javanese discourse which underplays and conceals the embodied aspect of Javanese identity.
5 Suryobrongto was the leading dance expert during the time of my fieldwork. The son of the eighth sultan, he had performed in dance drama during this period. After the struggle against the Dutch and the achievement of Indonesian independence, he taught dancing in the organisation set up outside the court on the ninth sultan's instructions in 1950, and subsequently in Yogyakarta's Academy of Dance, founded in 1963. He also acted as secretary to his brother, the ninth sultan.
6 I experienced how rude Javanese people can be to those whom they see as infantile foreigners in my relations with a certain Yogyakartan Prince. On patterns of socialisation in urban contexts, see Koentjaraningrat (1985: 233–42), and for rural ones see Koentjaraningrat (1985: 100–21) and Keeler (1987: 51–84).
7 These are the Javanese equivalents of Goffman's 'false fronts', 'tact', and 'manipulation' (1956: 38, 146, 162).
8 Compare views on masking and face-saving in Bali (Wikan 1990: 112–13) and the Pacific atoll of Tokelau (Hoem 1998: 36).
9 Other examples of everyday Javanese avoidance are Jay (1969: 204); H. Geertz (1961: 136); and Sullivan (1980: 22–3).
10 Embodied powerful performance such as political oratory in the east Indonesian island of Sumba may be banned, and retained as culture in 'literary' school texts, again separating culture from religion and politics (Kuipers 1990: 174–8).
11 Since originally writing this chapter, developments in Indonesia raise uncertainty to new levels. President Suharto resigned on 21 May 1998, but for now it remains unclear whether the New Order will survive, or become something different.
12 'Cultures are seen as historical products which are continually being created and recreated in daily life. As with any other system of meanings, cultures are inherently ambiguous and are always open to alternative interpretations. Humans are

not captives of culture or ideology, every society contains iconoclasts, and while radical cultural changes are often reactions to outside events, in the absence of such events cultures are not static'.
13 A celebrated account of New Order surveillance represented through the Dutch policies of the early twentieth century is Pramoedya Anata Toer's *Rumah Kaca* (1988); this novel also includes an important discussion of Javanese opportunism by Indonesia's most celebrated censored author.
14 Writing this paper I received news of the death on 27 December 1997 of one of Yogya's leading male dancers. Ben Suharto had taught at ASTI and had recently been working on his own kind of meditative dancing, which he had been developing with people in other countries, including the UK, who are interested in the healing powers of dance. While Ben was at the heart of Javanese culture, a quintessentially refined Javanese gentleman, he was also a creative individual whose work extended beyond anything which could be imposed or contained. I could name any number of other individuals whose contributions it would be an insult to label as 'culture' in the official sense.

References

Alexander, Paul (ed.) (1989) *Creating Indonesian Cultures* (Oceania Ethnographies 3) Sydney: Oceania Publications.

Anderson, Benedict O'Gorman (1983) *Imagined Communities*, London and New York: Verso.

——(1990) 'The language of Indonesian politics', in *Language and Power*, Ithaca NY: Cornell University Press.

Barthes, Roland (1994) [1973] 'L'empire des signes', in E. Marty (ed.) *Oeuvres Complètes*, tome II, 1966–1973, Paris: Seuil.

Certeau, Michel de (1984) *The Practice of Everyday Life*, trans. S. Rendall, Berkeley and Los Angeles: University of California Press.

Cohen, A. and Comaroff, J. (1976) 'The management of meaning: on the phenomenology of political transactions', in B. Kapferer (ed.) *Transaction and Meaning*, Philadelphia: Institute for the Study of Human Issues.

Dewey, Alice (1978) 'Deference behaviour in Java: duty or privilege?', in S. Udin (ed.) *Essays Presented to Sutan Takdir Alisjahbana on his Seventieth Birthday*, Jakarta: Dian Rakyat.

Dinusatama, R. M. (1983) Speech before the annual anniversary concert of Siswa Among Běksa. Yogyakarta: mimeograph.

Errington, J. Joseph (1988) *Structure and Style in Javanese*, Philadelphia: University of Pennsylvania Press.

Geertz, Clifford (1960) *The Religion of Java*, Chicago and London: University of Chicago Press.

Geertz, Hildred (1961) *The Javanese Family*, New York: Free Press.

Gilsenan, Michael (1976) 'Lying, honour and contradiction', in B. Kapferer (ed.) *Transaction and Meaning*, Philadelphia: Institute for the Study of Human Issues.

Goffman, Erving (1956) *The Presentation of Self in Everyday Life* (Monograph no. 2), Edinburgh: University of Edinburgh Social Sciences Research Centre.

Hoem, Ingjerd (1998) 'Clowns, dignity and desire: on the relationship between performance, identity and reflexivity', in F. Hughes-Freeland and M. Crain (eds) *Recasting Ritual*, London: Routledge.

Hughes-Freeland, Felicia (1988) *The Dancer and the Dance*, 16mm film. © Royal Anthropological Institute and National Film and Television School.

——(1997a) 'Consciousness in performance: a Javanese theory', *Social Anthropology*, 5(21): 55–68.

——(1997b) 'Art and politics: from Javanese court dance to Indonesian art', *Journal of the Royal Anthropological Institute* (n.s.) 3(3): 473–95.

——(n.d.) 'Performance from a Javanese Palace', manuscript.

Jay, Robert R. (1969) *Javanese Villagers*, London: MIT Press.

Johnson, Mark (1987) *The Body in the Mind*, Chicago: University of Chicago Press.

Keeler, Ward (1987) *Javanese Shadow Plays, Javanese Selves*, Princeton: Princeton University Press.

Koentjaraningrat (1985) *Javanese Culture*, Singapore: Oxford University Press.

Kuipers, Joel (1990) *Power in Performance: The Creation of Textual Authority in Wejewa Ritual Speech*, Philadelphia: University of Philadelphia Press.

Le Carré, John (1991) *The Secret Pilgrim*, London: Hodder and Stoughton.

Lelyveld, Th. B. van (1931) *La Danse dans le Théatre Javanais*, Paris: Librairie Floury.

Lombard, Denys (1990) *Le Carrefour Javanais*, Paris: Editions de l'Ecole des Hautes Etudes en Sciences Sociales.

McVey, Ruth (1967) 'Taman Siswa and the Indonesian national awakening', *Indonesia*, 4: 128–49.

Parkin, David (ed.) (1992) *Semantic Anthropology*, London: Academic Press.

Pemberton, John (1994) *On the Subject of 'Java'*, Ithaca NY: Cornell University Press.

Pramoedya Ananta Toer (1988) *Rumah Kaca (The Glass House)*, Kuala Lumpur: Wira Karya.

Rendra, W. S. (1983) *Mempertimbankan Tradisi*, ed. Eneste Pamusuk, Jakarta: PT Gramedia.

Scott, James (1985) *Weapons of the Weak*, New Haven: Yale University Press.

Selosoemardjan (1962) *Social Change in Yogyakarta*, New York: Cornell University Press.

Sontag, Susan (1967) [1961] *Against Interpretation and Other Essays*, New York: Farrar, Strauss and Giroux.

Sullivan, John (1980) 'Back alley neighbourhood: kampung as urban community in Yogyakarta', Centre of Southeast Asian Studies Working Paper 18, Monash: Melbourne University.

Suseno, Franz Magnis and Reksosusilo, S. (1983) *Etika Jawa dalam Tantangan*, Yogyakarta: Kanisius.

Watson, C. W. (1987) 'State and society in Indonesia: three papers', Centre of South-East Asian Studies Occasional Paper 8, Canterbury: University of Kent.

Wikan, Unni (1990) *Managing Turbulent Hearts*, Chicago: Chicago University Press.

Wolfram, Sybil (1985) 'Facts and theories: saying and believing', in J. Overing (ed.) *Reason and Morality* (ASA monograph 24) London: Tavistock.

Chapter 10

Don't talk – blend

Ideas about body and communication in aikido practice[1]

Tamara Kohn

This chapter discusses the communication and embodiment of notions about practice and learning through the practice of aikido, a Japanese martial art, in the northeast of England. It illustrates how many practitioners there feel themselves drawn into what they perceive to be 'other' or 'new' ways of speaking, moving, thinking and feeling through their practice, and how they often struggle with making these new aspects of 'self' integrate smoothly with other transforming aspects of their working and social lives. 'Practice' (*keiko*) in martial arts discourse is something less associated with the attainment of a hard won goal (as in the sayings 'practice makes perfect' or 'no pain no gain') and more associated with a way of living or a path with no end.

The *dojo* (place of practice) becomes an instructive and fascinating place to watch collisions and blendings of culture and negotiations of self-identity as they are communicated through bodily practice. When these non-verbal performances are combined with aikido students' spoken and written reflec-tions about their progressions and struggles along 'the path' of self-disciplined practice, it becomes possible to contextualise and hence to interpret the body talk more closely.

One thing that this body talk appears to tell its audience, which departs significantly from much of the extant literature on bodily practices (e.g. sports), is that through practice the body develops meaning afresh; meaning of 'culture', meaning of 'self', meaning of 'self in society'. Wacquant's study of professional boxers in Chicago makes this point clearly when he describes the passion and skill wrapped up in the 'game and its stakes, inscribed deep within the body through progressive incorporation of its core tenets' (1995: 493). By demanding a restructuring of the 'self', boxing 'becomes part of their inside' (*ibid.*: 507–8). The layer of significance that a study of aikido practice in England reveals *beyond* this is found in the way the self is transformed by what is seen and felt to be a 'foreign'/'other' practice (cf. Bell 1996). Unpacking this multicultural learning process and the 'bricolage' of shifting identities and understanding expressed in it is the exercise presented here. I would suggest that many of the people who live in England and practise 'Japanese' arts are not dabbling in 'otherness' momentarily, nor are they delineating two separate 'cultures' in their practice, but they are basking in what Rapport has called 'the ubiquitous, desiring and creative resort by individuals to the contradictory' (1997: 658). They are allowing diversity to triumph as 'part of their inside'. For many practitioners it is irrelevant that the art originates in Japan – it only matters that others, who speak the same language of the body regardless of their national or class backgrounds, are available for practice.

Social analysts and linguists tend to peripheralise or even forget the body when they attempt to understand human communication and social learning. For most of them, language found in the spoken word is the most powerful and hence most meaning-rich of sign systems (e.g. Berger and Luckmann 1966: 49ff.). Spoken language has been presented through Western education systems as the most sophisticated and hence 'direct' vehicle available for transmitting meaning. Anthropologists attempt to master their informants' spoken language because they have been taught that the other's words about his/her lived experiences are closer to some cultural 'truth' than the anthropologist's bodily attempts to feel the other's experiences through participation, empathy and imagination (Kohn 1994). The way in which individuals learn the principles of a bodily art through touching, feeling and moving is no less 'direct' than learning them through the spoken word.

To understand this it is no doubt best to practise such a 'thinking' bodily art oneself, but for the reader who cannot do so, I will attempt a short written introduction. The next section introduces the uninitiated to aikido, describes the method and sources used for this study and introduces the prime research site – the place of practice, or *dojo* – and the people in it.

Aikido

Aikido is a 'modern manifestation of the Japanese martial arts (*budo*)' (K. Ueshiba 1984: 14) which requires one to 'blend' or 'harmonise' with and then redirect the energy of an attack to throw or pin an attacker. It is generally practised 'empty hand',[2] but as its techniques and movements are derived from the art of Japanese swordsmanship, students also practise with weapons. Coordination and athleticism is required through paired practice, and yet unlike most 'sports', there are no winners and losers resulting from its practice. Aikido was founded by Morihei Ueshiba (1883–1969), also known as 'O-Sensei' (Great Teacher) to his students. *Ai* may be translated as 'harmony', *Ki* refers to 'spirit', and *Do* means way – hence aikido can be translated as the way of harmony of spirit. With aikido, even a small physically weak person can learn to redirect the energy of a strong attack if they learn to apply basic principles of movement. Circular or spiralling movements are key in the understanding of how to execute aikido techniques. Later in this chapter we will see how spiralling rather than linear concepts about 'learning' itself confront students of the art. Aikido practice is centred on learning a series of forms/movements (*kata*) in which the student must participate as the executor of the technique and the receiver in paired exercises. Unlike other martial arts *kata*, emphasis is placed upon the correct 'feeling' of execution rather than visual correctness. It is often said that receiving the technique (*ukemi*) is the key to understanding aikido, for in *ukemi* one conditions the body and learns the art of blending with and absorbing the energy of an attack.

The Durham 'big dojo' is a room in a local sports hall which is set up with wall-to-wall mats two evenings a week for aikido practice. The 'little dojo' covers a smaller area, but is permanently matted (with canvas-covered tatami) and available to dojo members for informal and formal practice any day of the week.[3] The people who practise aikido in these dojos are almost entirely male (perhaps two out of twenty regular practitioners are female). They also come from a range of occupational backgrounds (from mechanics to hairdressers, firemen to nightwatchmen, builders to anthropology lecturers).[4] Occasionally students at the local university join the club, but they tend to be transient members who move on by the end of their course. The majority of regular/long-term members are local – born in the northeast of England – and come from working-class backgrounds. I was surprised, therefore, to find that there is a popular mythology about aikido being the martial art of the 'new petty bourgeoisie' (Bourdieu 1990: 157).

Bourdieu has suggested that sport is 'consumed' (like food or leisure) in socially predictable ways *vis-à-vis* class – that 'relation to body ... is associated with a social position and an innate experience of the physical and social world' (1990: 157). Social standing, according to Bourdieu, affects the 'taste' that a person will have for one activity over another and for a particular type of body cultivation (1993). He has explicitly used aikido as an example of a sporting practice which appeals to 'bourgeois' tastes. He says, 'one can immediately sense the privileged relation that is today established between wrestling and members of the working classes or aikido and the new petty bourgeoisie' (1990: 157). Interestingly enough, this does appear to be the case from my experiences at courses held in France. Many practitioners there are doctors, lawyers, academics and the like. Why is this not true in England? Why are so many 'members of the working classes' treading on the élite Samurai path? Is it because of the way aikido was introduced in this country? (Chiba Sensei, one of O-Sensei's students, arrived in the 1960s in Sunderland, a working-class industrial town.) Is it because of the time of arrival? (One of my informants sent me an e-mail suggesting it was a '60s awakening anti-class thing'.)

Better than surmising is to listen to what people practicing in the Durham *dojo* have had to say about their own practice. Often they had already practised one or more of the other martial arts until injury, boredom or discontent sent them looking for something new. They might have had a friend who introduced them, or might have spotted a flyer advertising an aikido course. Virtually all keen beginners speak of their attraction to the non-competitive aspects of aikido. They speak negatively of the way arts such as karate and taekwondo have become 'Westernised' and 'spoiled', and have even been reconsumed in the 'East' as competitive sports (appearing in the Olympics, etc.). Aikido is a highly effective, practical martial art which various informants have had to apply in real-life conflicts, but it is 'consumed' as far more than a craft or skill by people from a large range of occupational and class backgrounds. It appears to break down social class barriers in its philosophy and its practice both on and off the mat. As one friend put it, 'the job you have is the last thing people find out about. Aikido is a great leveller'.

Evening classes are held three to five times per week, and most committed students attend at least two of these. In addition, some students from that club travel twenty miles away to practise with a respected teacher in a dojo in Middlesbrough, or an equal distance in the other direction to train with a senior instructor in Newcastle. Whenever a visiting aikido instructor comes to town, a special weekend course is arranged and attended by students from all over the region. Serious students who can afford the time and/or money also attend week-long international summer schools in England and abroad where they can gather with well over a hundred other students and learn from senior Japanese masters – *shihan* – who in their youth may have been students of O-Sensei. The chief instructor of the Durham dojo was one of the first students taught by Chiba Sensei, a shihan who established aikido in the north of England over thirty years ago. Chiba Sensei's dojo is now in San Diego, California, and many senior students and instructors travel there to study with him and bring his evolving understanding of the art back to their home dojos.

Aikido is a global or transnational phenomenon, but I intend here to concentrate on its manifestation in Durham as an example of anthropology 'at home'. I came to 'think (anthropologically) with' aikido through my own practice of the art and my involvement in the British aikido community over the past six years. My informants are primarily from the northeast of England, although I have shared practice and ideas with aikidoists from elsewhere in the UK, from France and other areas of Europe, from America, and from Japan. I have begun to feel my own body and mind transformed through practice and I have considered both the natural reflections of other club members in social contexts (e.g. in pubs after practice) as well as the ideas expressed in *yudansha* essays – essays written by any students wishing to grade for any level of black belt in the art. These essays, often composed by people who have little experience of writing reflexively for an unknown audience, are rich repositories of people's thoughts about their own progression along 'the Way of Harmony'.[5] This path begins at one's first lesson.

Aikido practice: please don't talk on the mat

Aiki cannot be exhausted
By words written or spoken,

Without dabbling in idle talk,
Understand through practice.
                        O–Sensei (quoted in *Aikido Today*, Jan/Feb 1998)

The new student tentatively enters the dojo, unsure of how to behave. He is welcomed by the instructor and any senior students at the practice. The class begins with the teacher (*sensei*) clapping, the students lining up kneeling (in *seiza*) in order of seniority of grade, and the teacher kneeling in front. First the teacher will turn away from the students, bowing to a picture of O–Sensei placed by the wall in the room of the sports hall, then will bow to other teachers, and finally teacher and students all bow, saying 'Onegaishimasu [please teach me]'. This is used as an audible cue that practice is about to begin. Both teacher and pupil say 'onegaishimasu' to indicate that they learn from each other. Then the teacher generally leads the class in a gentle stretching warmup which involves a number of exercises peculiar to the art (for example stretches in an elongated forward posture, and stretching manipulations of ankles and wrists). The new students may be told in a five-minute introductory speech something of the history and basic principles of the martial art, but then the teacher quickly suggests that aikido can only be understood through practice with the body.

Practice begins with the instructor demonstrating a technique on a senior student. This will usually be a stretching and balancing technique, such as a basic *irimi* (entering) movement. The *uke*, or person receiving the technique, must learn to keep a firm hold while also relaxing the body and letting it be moved into a position from which she can recover. The move is demonstrated a few times with as little verbal description as possible. Then the students pair off to practise that technique, taking it in turns to 'uke' until the instructor interrupts for corrections or moves on to a new technique. On an assistant coaching course offered by an aikido instructor from Birmingham, we were told that body language is by far the most effective means of communication, followed by 'paralanguage' (tone of voice, etc.) and finally 'words'. He also put up an overhead that suggested that for skill retention, only 10 per cent of the things one is taught verbally would remain after three months, whereas 65 per cent of the things told, shown and also practised oneself would remain. While it remained unclear how and where such statistics were obtained, it is true that 'sports' pedagogy would reinforce aikido principles about the power of 'doing' over 'talking'.[6]

One exercise often offered in the very first lesson (but rarely repeated) is designed to prove to novices the power achieved by extending one's energy (*ki*) through the fingers and across the room (known as 'unbendable arm'). Students are often greatly impressed by the simplicity and the tremendous strength that the mind can offer to the weaker body. This serves to foster the sense of 'mystery' and hidden knowledge that attracts many students to take on the study of a martial art (or as one student told me, the 'feel the Force,

Luke' experience).[7] That 'ki extension' exercise and the challenge of learning to roll safely out of aikido throws, etc., serves to lure people into a wish to know more.

They are also attracted by the formality and etiquette of practice – the rituals of bowing at the beginning and end of the practice, and also greeting and then thanking the partner for practicing. 'It [the ritual] gives the practice a clear shape and cuts it off from the stresses of the day – I feel like I'm entering another world in the dojo', said one beginner. 'To me it's about respect and trust. One can only enjoy and grow through practice when you trust your partner not to hurt you', said another. Another once suggested that it's good to feel 'part of a long tradition', shared with others on the mat and around the world – 'it's an international language of respect'. So the ritual of bowing and exchanging words of thanks, etc., joins together a group of otherwise unconnected people into a bond of trust and 'tradition' while demarcating the time of practice as being qualitatively apart from other times of day. Hendry (1993: 153), following Kondo (1985: 302), would call these 'unfoldings' of ritual time and space.

From the first few practices, one begins to recognise a clear hierarchy within the dojo. Different depths of knowledge and expertise are displayed in variable solidity of stances and differing abilities to execute and receive techniques with grace and agility. It is also communicated by wrappings of dress (Hendry 1993). Senior students wear *hakama* in the dojo – black or dark blue long divided 'skirts' traditionally worn by Samurai. The hakama are put on over the white cotton *keiko gi* (practice clothes) on the mat in the dojo before practice, and are carefully folded on the mat at the end of practice. The state of a practitioner's hakama and the black belt worn beneath it expresses something of the seniority of the student. With years of practice, the knees of quality indigo-dyed cotton hakama begin to fade, and the blackest of belts becomes greyer and greyer until it is almost white again. Lower grade students look up to anyone in hakama, while hakama-wearing students look out for wear and tear as a possible mark of seniority. Generally, *kyu* grades (*mudansha*) are encouraged to practise with their 'seniors' (*yudansha* = *shodan*/first degree black belt and above), but arranging this can be seen as a skill in itself at large courses with many unknown people on the mat. Ideas about hierarchy are not just observed, but they are reinforced and illustrated through bodily practice. These result from different levels of experience, different ranking and training, and political wranglings between senseis and students from different dojos. They are not, however, seen by practitioners to have resulted from activity in a 'competitive' arena – the experience of practicing technique is still perceived to be free of combat, winners and losers.

Students new to aikido often ask questions of their more senior partners during practice, and some students tend to offer advice to others, but the teacher will sometimes discourage the noise and distraction of verbal exchange on the mat. Part of martial art philosophical reasoning is that the techniques need to be absorbed bodily rather than being talked about, cognised, and translated back into movement.[8] The mat should resound with the sounds of bodies falling and rolling, but not with voices speaking. Silence is seen to reflect politeness towards the teacher as well as to the special space of the dojo. One of the most common criticisms of certain instructors is that he or she 'talks too much' – keen students feel that they learn more from doing and want to fill the time they have in the dojo with bodily practice rather than with too many words of wisdom. When Chiba Sensei and other Japanese shihan teach in English dojos, they tend to talk less and demonstrate more, showing the movements at different speeds and angles, with bodily emphasis placed on particular details of alignment, posture and hand position. At large summer school classes, the Japanese instructors rarely speak, maybe in part due to the problematic acoustics in large sports halls, and partly, perhaps, following a tradition that they remember from their training with O-Sensei, who rarely spoke as he instructed. Silence is clearly one of the most powerful non-verbal communicative devices available when meaningfully filled with action. The power of silent communication features also in the paper by Christensen *et al.* (Chapter 4 in this volume). Miller usefully writes of the generation and maintenance of Japanese 'myths' and 'antimyths', and it is perhaps significant that the Japanese antimyth he describes is the preference for and worship of silent communication (1982: 85–6). Several aikidoka have suggested to me that one's body cannot 'listen' as carefully to 'contact' with other bodies during practice if speech is being interpreted at the same time.

If students complain of too much talk, they also sometimes reflect negatively about certain instructors who seem to take up too much of the class time with demonstration (whether augmented with speech or not). Mori, in her book about Americans studying the Japanese tea ceremony, makes a similar observation that the non-Japanese student is not willing to learn as much from observation as from participation, and gets frustrated with lessons that lack enough practice. She attributes this to the inability of the 'Western' student to give the teacher full authority for decisions of study (1992: 150). This seems to be only one of a number of possible reasons. Another factor which goes beyond teacher/student relations, and is most relevant for this chapter, could be that time 'spent' in the dojo, when seen to be competing for space next to other life demands, is monitored differently than when viewed as an experience contributing to a lifelong pursuit of practice for practice's sake. Students who can only attend one or two evening classes a week because of demands away from the dojo may feel that to prepare for a grading they will need to use those practices well. They may become frustrated when 'too much time' is spent watching demonstrations and not practicing. We will return to different notions of 'path' shortly, but suffice to say that varying assessments of 'good practice' reveal much about students' placement of their art in their lives as a whole, as well as culturally informed ideas about 'learning from doing'. Most English aikidoka would agree with Mauss that 'The body is man's first and most natural instrument' (1979: 104).

Here, then, we see in aikido a bodily practice which often expresses an ideology of silence in practice while at the same time inviting an excess of written and spoken language in reflection. Silence and language communicate in cooperation with one another. Or, as Merleau-Ponty suggests, the 'lived' (if silent) body which experiences the world is entirely expressive, and this allows for speech (Matthews 1996: 105). The two genres of expression are inextricably linked and incomplete without the other. Now, having looked at some aspects of aikido bodily practice, we shall consider some of the principles and experiences revealed in instances of 'aiki talk'.

Aikido talk: how to traverse the path

At the heart of aikido and other 'Asian' martial arts like judo, karate, and taekwando, as well as the zen arts of calligraphy, flower arrangment and the tea ceremony, is a sense of *do*, which means 'way', or 'spiritual path'. 'The Way draws us into the domain of the potential self: self-realization, self-cultivation, and self-perfection' (Lowry 1995: 18). Learning to read meanings embedded in the surface forms of a martial art like aikido, in the rituals of formal practice, the dress, and the attitudes about talking and doing during practice, tells us something about the rules and 'traditions' about interaction on the mat. It tells us something of the 'culture' of what it is one has to know in order to behave appropriately in the dojo (external components of practice), but not how to traverse a path and 'feel' transformations of self along the way (internal aspects of practice). These personalised links between practice and lifeway seem to be articulated most explicitly through key descriptive/evocative words and concepts that are mulled over in the pub and other arenas for aiki talk that generally takes place off the mat.

It is interesting to note, in keeping with the theme of this collection, that while body communication is often classified as a prime example of 'indirection' from the linguistic scholar's point of view, and while in my estimation all forms, both verbal and physical, may be seen as 'indirect', for many aikidoists verbal communication is the 'indirect' form. Talking is often seen as a supplement to communication on the mat with the body, or is about the reflection on bodily practice and how it impacts upon people in different social contexts. To study transformations of self at more than a superficial level, however, it is essential to listen to people's words.

Commitment

'Commitment' is one of the most common words used to describe people's involvement in aikido practice. So-and-so 'lacks commitment' – is a common refrain used to refer to people who do not come to enough practices or practise with what is seen as the 'wrong attitude'. 'Commitment' in this context is about duty to a community of other members of the dojo, and a lack of commitment implies a selfishness in a person's motives for practicing.

If 'commitment' is about duty to others, it is also about an individual's acceptance of aikido practice as a life project. Acknowledging the long path ahead and a future of 'continuous training' (Kamata and Shimizu 1992: 97) is an indication of one's commitment to any of the martial arts. As Zarrilli suggests,

> The encoding of body-consciousness is viewed as a long-term process, part of a 'path' or 'way.' Without romanticising the daily drudgery involved, it is assumed that such a path must be followed if one is to approach mastery ... the 'path' is not a 'course of study,' but a totally absorbing way of life.
>
> (1990: 132)

This message seems to resonate in most yudansha essays I have collected. One ends by saying, 'I enjoy my aikido practice which brings me face to face with my limitations. If aikido is more a process than a goal oriented system then that should be enough'. Another concludes with, 'The journey, for me, is also the end'.

Implicit in 'traditional' Japanese notions of *do* is commitment to one master. This can be problematic in contexts where there is a variety of instructors helping a student along, and in a cultural context where one has tended to doubt the absolute authority of any instructor (cf. Mori 1992). It is clear that local practitioners may feel a strong commitment to a community of others in a dojo without necessarily feeling strong commitment to any one instructor. The *do* is constantly redefined by people traversing it rather than the *do* determining the directions and allegiances that people take. Practitioners in England may be 'committed' to practice as 'path', but redefine the qualities of relationship found along that path.

Conceptualising the learning process

> The body should be triangular, the mind circular. The triangle represents the generation of energy and is the most stable physical posture. The circle symbolizes serenity and perfection, the source of unlimited techniques.
>
> (M. Ueshiba 1992: 78)

Accepting an idea that the path leads on *ad infinitum* is a challenge to people who are accustomed to learning new skills in 'courses' which have discrete beginnings and ends. Even more challenging is coming to understand the circularity of the learning process – the way the body takes you back to basics over and over again – along the 'way'. I would suggest that learning tends to be conceptualised in the Western mind as a linear process; one builds upon knowledge and expertise in an ever upward journey. But the notions of 'way' that are not just spoken about philosophically but are constantly enacted on the mat, demand long repetition of kata (form) and repeated breaking down of techniques into the most basic exercises. The learning path is circular or spiralling, just like the movements embodied in the art of aikido. It means that advanced students happily practise at beginners' classes, and that the most basic techniques are still tested at high levels. It is assumed that one returns full circle to experience the beginning with new levels of understanding. The focus, therefore, is on the process of learning rather than on the object of learning. As Bethe and Brazell say of the performance of *noh* theatre, 'To follow a way is to immerse oneself in an activity, to practise it until one attains mastery. What one masters is not as important as the process of mastering' (1990: 185). The path along the 'way', then, is by nature one of 'indirection', a spiralling route that never reaches a goal, rather than a 'direct' or straight one which does.

During the time that I was beginning to get 'into' my aikido practice and was reading about 'the ways' of various martial and other zen arts, my five-year-old boy was starting to learn violin with a teacher who followed the Suzuki method. She gave all the mothers copies of books written about Suzuki and his philosophy of music learning. He urges his students to develop excellence through repetition:

> The reason that we chatter freely in Japanese is that we use it daily. … It is a matter of 'Ease comes with training.' We simply have to train and educate our ability, that is to say, do the thing over and over again until it feels natural, simple, and easy. That is the secret.
>
> (Suzuki 1983: 42–3)

And so I was urged to not feel impatient as my boy played variations of 'Twinkle twinkle little star' daily for well over a year before adding anything new to his repertoire. His teacher said that even her students who can play the Bach double violin concerto will also be sure to play 'Twinkle', but will do it with a different understanding.[9]

In aikido, with this spiralling model in mind, everything on the grading syllabus, from the easiest to the hardest techniques, can be asked of students during higher-level gradings because what matters is *how* you demonstrate 'understanding' of aikido principles and body movement through the techniques. Greater quality and depth are what indicate progression on the Path, along with the humble conviction that the process of learning anything in the art is never done. What matters is practice and then more practice.

'Understanding' and 'personal development' of the self

Students often reflect on the performances of their instructors, and the word 'understanding' often features in these discussions. 'Skill', 'awareness', 'sensitivity' and 'effectiveness' are other descriptive words used frequently, but 'understanding' encompasses all of these other attributes. 'Understanding' is judged both by watching the way a person moves, by witnessing the way the instructor observes others, and by feeling the way the instructor connects with you in the practice of techniques. While 'skill', 'awareness', 'sensitivity' and 'effectiveness' may be discussed at length with ample illustrations of each, 'understanding' defies narrative illustration. Other people demonstrate 'understanding' – it is a deeply aesthetic observation of others, but it is not an attribute one would give oneself, for in that context it would imply a mastery that an acceptance of aikido as a never-ending spiralling path would not allow. Little bits of 'understanding', therefore, are embodied consequences of long years of practice, but 'Understanding' with a capital U is not a personal 'goal'. 'Personal development', however, is.

Personal development takes many different forms and is spoken of in many different ways by people. On one level it is about confidence and alertness in order to *find* or *discover* a 'self' that may have always been there, but was hidden or clouded over. On another level it is about *changing and improving* a self, as in the following quote from another essay:

> As I became more serious about practice and eager to know more, training became more of a habit and less a leisure activity. I began to be aware that subtle changes were taking place in my attitude and behaviour outside the dojo. It was gradually noticable that I was getting better at handling stressful situations at work, particularly when dealing with 'difficult' people.

On a third level 'personal development' is about *transcending* or *abandoning* the self.

> In aikido, we do not initiate attacks. The ultimate purpose of the art is to evade an opponent's attack, to abandon the mind and renounce the self. Self-abandonment, or *sutemi* in Japanese, is advocated in Zen. ... [K]illing the self which has been living in delusion ... means to make the self into nothing. Herein lies the philosophy of nothingness in aikido.
> (Kamata and Shimizu 1992: 37)

Similarly, in Zarrilli's study of kalarippayattu, the Keralan martial art, it is suggested how 'in-body' encoding of techniques repetitively practised leads to a state of 'accomplishment, control and transcendence of "self"' (1990: 131). And yet the mastery required for an abandonment of self is akin to the mastery wrapped up in the attainment of 'understanding', and consequently transcendence of self is not easily illustrated in the lifestories of my informants.

From a review of some of the abundant literature on Japanese notions of 'self', it is tempting to suggest that Western practitioners do not so readily recognise a sense in which they 'transcend self' while a Japanese student might, because of essential differences between Japanese and 'Western' notions of self. For instance, according to Rohlen (1976), Japanese are said to find 'individuality' in their participation in activities which build their spirit (e.g. in the practice of zen arts, perhaps), and hence 'growth toward individuality consists of aesthetic polishing that builds toward the final unity of non-self rather than individualism in a sense of essentialism and consistent identity' (Rosenberger 1992: 13). This assumes, of course, that the English student of Japanese martial arts does not imagine his identity to be transformed through participation in that art, and we know that is not the case from the examples given above. Surely this assessment polarises two of many cultural possibilities into stereotypes of Japanese and non-Japanese individuality, and it avoids looking at situations where Japanese practices are experienced through bodily practice by non-Japanese people.

Perhaps a focus away from social homogeneity and national stereotype and towards a more general understanding of the relationships of bodies and selves is more helpful. For instance, Johnson suggests that

> the 'who I am' shaped in practice cannot be divorced from the 'who we are'; that is, individual experience and collective identity form a dialectic that *is* the arena through which the 'self' is forged *in practice*
>
> (1986, cited in Zarrilli 1995: 189).

This seems to work for me in trying to understand the ways people talk about personal and internal change while also talking about their transforming selves within particular social environments.

Discussion: bodies and selves

There has long been an interest in understanding the ways that 'society' becomes embodied in the self. For example, in the 1930s, Mauss attempted to lay out an anthropology of the body, stressing the way that 'techniques' of the body are learned differently from society to society (1979). Benedict's work (1946) on the Japanese is of this genre. Later, there was interest in seeing how significant differences between people within societies would likewise inscribe themselves on the body. Gender would be one point of difference (as illustrated by M. Mead's chapter 'Ways of the body' in her book *Male and Female*) and individuals' movements through different stages of the lifecycle would be another (as illustrated in the work of van Gennep) (Synnott 1993: 245–9). The fact that these inscriptions are there is undisputed, since the body 'is at the heart of social life and social interaction' (*ibid.*: 262). But how they get there, and how 'society' changes with the changing body, and the multiplicities of possibility available in their form and meaning, is less clearly discussed.

The Japaneseness of aikido is not necessarily what etches itself on the practitioner's body – it is the changing multicultural and diverse experience of practice which does so, and the most common transformations discussed are not immediately apparent to the untrained eye. Some 'committed' students comment about their pursuit of physical fitness and are pleased about the way their practice firms up and strengthens the body. And as discussed earlier, different levels of 'understanding' may be seen etched on the body's movements by those who are also traversing the 'path'. But the most striking transformations are spoken of in terms of changes in 'character', 'attitude', and 'dealing with life events' differently than before – internal aspects of self. These changes may push and pull the practitioner in different, sometimes invigorating and sometimes disturbing, directions. They can make life less stressful at work or in situations of conflict, and they can also cause the aikido student to feel more stress at home or with friends who are felt to not understand what they are going through. If it were just about body fitness, this complexity of shifting sociabilities would fall away.

Another clue which suggests that, for most aikidoka, shaping the body's exterior is not of central interest, is the consumption of greasy pizza and curry and several pints of beer in the pub immediately after hours of practice. Such consumption is commonplace after regular practice, as well as during weekend or week-long courses elsewhere in the country or abroad. In fact, the development of a good 'centre' is enhanced, some suggest, by a bit of a firm beer belly which many of the leading male practitioners of the art display over the tops of their hakama. The preference for the wide base as opposed to the 'swelling chest' has been pointed out as a significant difference between Japanese and Western ideas of athleticism since the early 1900s (e.g. Harrison, cited in Ratti and Westbrook 1973: 401), but most people in the Durham dojo do not explain their body shapes in terms of the emulation of Japanese masters, but rather in terms of 'having a good time' in the pub and filling a hungry spot with the closest available food.

Taking this back to concerns with body and society, there are many activities which are clearly designed and promoted to sculpt the body into a form which 'society as a whole' may deem desirable at a particular point in time. The body is often physically shaped into society's image. Aikido, on the other hand, is an activity which variably shapes the 'centres' (encompassing body, 'mind', and 'spirit') of those who travel the 'path', regardless of whether or not the society the practitioner is institutionally and intimately involved in outside the aikido community understands the value of such changes. One's belly might grow unseemingly, but the centre it houses might be that much more grounded and powerful on the mat. The body is etched in mysterious ways by practices like aikido. Knowledge is created through it and communicated to others in several different ways. Society itself is what becomes transformed by the planting of such exotic seeds in familiar places.

This chapter has attempted to show how the practice of aikido in the northeast of England is clearly something which defies constriction – constriction to class, to national 'roots', to prioritised forms of communication, etc. Possibilities have been seen to expand through its practice. Social circles extend; travel to distant places becomes a reality to many who never travelled much before. One yudansha essay concludes: 'On arrival at the dojos up and down the country there is always a warm welcome, excellent practice and a bed for the night. Where else could this happen except for the circle of Aikido practitioners?'

To study aikido practice anthropologically in England, it is not enough to look at surface levels of form and ritual, nor to stereotype the art *vis-à-vis* other activities (such as sport) and social 'class', but to look at a deeper experiential level at individuals and how they see their participation in their practice affecting their inner selves and their personal and social worlds. Such a view questions the way that bodily arts are made into static cultural 'forms' which slot in predictable ways into people's structured lives. People cannot casually insert a martial art or any other 'in-body discipline' into a 'foreign other' space within an 'English', 'French' or any other core identity, in the way that they might place an 'Oriental carpet' on the floor next to their old English sofa in their Victorian terraced house. 'Selves', 'culture', 'society', 'class', are all qualified through practice, whether or not the 'otherness' of that practice's origins are celebrated or not. It is at the interfaces of social experience, which I have tried to exemplify here with some ideas about how aikido is practiced in the northeast of England, and how the art's principles are indirectly communicated with both bodies and words, that one can glimpse how individuals' different selves may happily traverse 'paths' of their own creation.

Notes

1 This paper emerges from a seminar paper presented at SOAS in Feburary 1998, followed by the ASA paper presented at Kent later that spring. I am grateful to the participants of both, who gave me lots of useful feedback. I am also grateful to members of the Durham and Middlesbrough aikido dojos, particularly my teachers: Arthur Lockyear, Steven Magson, Joe Curran, Malcolm Blackwood and Roy Bennington. Special thanks for people who answered queries and/or offered comments on the draft: Luisa Belaunde, Sandra Bell, Tom Cahill, Sara Connor, Coryl Crane, Eamonn Devlin, Chris Reid, Andrew Russell, Noriko Sato, Bob Simpson, Pauline Squire, Dave Stevenson, and the editors of this collection.

2 In common with karate – *kara*/empty + *te*/hand.

3 A permanent dojo will comprise a rectangular matted area or *tatami*. At one side is a raised platform or 'table', the *kamiza*, which is the focus of the dojo. It is decorated with a picture of the founder and other items such as calligraphy, weapons, floral arrangements, and is treated with respect. The other three walls of the dojo may contain dojo noticeboards for course details and messages, etc., a student rank board, and weapons racks.

4 Note that since the time of writing this descriptive section, there have been significant changes in the dojo. Several senior students left to establish their own dojos,
   and the 'big dojo' was taken over by two of these, leaving the Durham chief
   instructor with a smaller group in the 'little dojo'. A number of senior students
   'joined' the Middlesbrough instructor's dojo (myself included). The 'politics' of
   aikido and the patterns evident in dojo change could fill a large book.
5 The writing of essays as part requirement for yudansha gradings was only started
   in the last twenty years or so by Chiba Sensei. One of Chiba Sensei's first students
   in Britain recalls his own first yudansha grading in which he was required to stand
   up and answer, off the top of his head, a question posed about the philosophy of
   aikido (e.g. what is the relationship between aikido and nature, etc.). This gave
   way to the less frightening but no less demanding requirement to produce an
   essay. When Chiba Sensei was recently asked why he asks for this, he replied 'To
   get to know the student better'. He continued to say that he was often disap-
   pointed with essays that are full of quotes from what other people have written
   and do not put aikido together from their own lived experience of it (Crane,
   personal communication).
6 Elsewhere I have looked at the ways in which action can speak louder than words
   in certain ethnographic contexts.
7 I have been told that the action in the film *Star Wars* derives from many Japanese
   martial art traditions, including aikido, and that the story itself was based on
   Kurosawa's film *The Hidden Fortress*.
8 This resonates with Japanese ideas about bodily communication in other contexts.
   Research on the ways small children become socialised in Japan has been particularly concerned with the way people absorb knowledge and learn to
   communicate through their bodies (see Hendry 1986; Ben-Ari 1997).
9 A wonderful visual representation of this sort of spiralling development of understanding can be found in the Nintendo 64 game of Super Mario, also developed
   in Japan. As the player improves her skills (collecting coins and stars along the
   way), she gains access to new 'rooms' in the game but may also return to previously played landscapes in which much more complexity and possibility emerges!

References

Bell, S. (1996) 'Change and identity in the Friends of the Western Buddhist Order',
   Scottish Journal of Religious Studies, XVII(2): 87–107.
Ben-Ari, E. (1997) *Body Projects in Japanese Childcare*, Richmond: Curzon Press.
Benedict, R. (1946) *The Chrysanthemum and the Sword: Patterns of Japanese Culture*,
   New York: Meridian.
Berger, P. and Luckmann, T. (1966) *The Social Construction of Reality*, Harmondsworth:
   Penguin.
Bethe, M. and Brazell, K. (1990) 'The practice of Noh theatre', in R. Schechner and
   W. Appel (eds) *By Means of Performance: Intercultural Studies of Theatre and Ritual*,
   Cambridge: Cambridge University Press, pp. 167–93.
Bourdieu, P. (1990) *In Other Words: Essays Towards a Reflexive Sociology*, Stanford: Stan-
   ford University Press.
——(1993) 'How can one be a sports fan?', in S. During (ed.) *The Cultural Studies
   Reader*, London: Routledge, pp. 339–56.
Harrison, E. J. (n.d.) *The Fighting Spirit of Japan*, London: W. Foulsham and Co.
Hendry, J. (1986) *Becoming Japanese: The World of the Pre-School Child*, Manchester:
   Manchester University Press.

Hendry, J. (1993) *Wrapping Culture: Politeness, Presentation, and Power in Japan and other Societies*, Oxford: Clarendon Press.

Johnson, R. (1986) 'What is cultural studies anyway?', *Social Text*, 16: 38–80.

Kamata, S. and Shimizu, K. (1992) *Zen and Aikido*, English translation, Tokyo: Aiki News.

Kohn, T. (1994) 'Incomers and fieldworkers: a comparative study of social experience', in K. Hastrup and P. Hervik (eds) *Social Experience and Anthropological Knowledge*, London: Routledge.

——(1995) 'She came out of the field and into my home: reflections, dreams and a search for consciousness in anthropological method', in A. P. Cohen and N. Rapport (eds) *Questions of Consciousness*, London: Routledge.

Kondo, D. (1985) 'The way of tea: a symbolic analysis', *Man* (n.s.) 20: 287–306.

Lowry, D. (1995) *Sword and Brush: The Spirit of the Martial Arts*, Boston MA and London: Shambhala.

Matthews, E. (1996) 'Phenomenology and existentialism: 2. Merleau-Ponty', in *Twentieth-Century French Philosophy*, Oxford: Oxford University Press.

Mauss, M. (1979) 'Body techniques', in *Sociology and Psychology: Essays*, London: Routledge and Kegan Paul.

Mead, M. (1964) *Male and Female*, Harmondsworth: Penguin.

Miller, R. A. (1982) *Japan's Modern Myth: the Language and Beyond*, New York and Tokyo: Weatherhill.

Mori, B. L. R. (1992) *Americans Studying the Traditional Japanese Art of the Tea Ceremony: The Internationalizing of a Traditional Art*, San Francisco: Mellen Research University Press.

Rapport, N. (1997) 'The "contrarieties" of Israel: an essay on the cognitive importance and the creative promise of both/and', *The Journal of the Royal Anthropological Institute*, 3(4): 653–72.

Ratti, O. and Westbrook, A. (1973) *Secrets of the Samurai: The Martial Arts of Feudal Japan*, Rutland VT: Charles E. Tuttle Company.

Rohlen, T. (1976) 'Promises of adulthood in Japanese spiritualism', *Daedalus*, 105: 125–43.

Rosenberger, N. R. (ed.) (1992) *Japanese Sense of Self*, Cambridge: Cambridge University Press.

Shioda, G. (1968) *Dynamic Aikido*, Tokyo, etc.: Kodansha International.

Suzuki, S. (1983) *Nurtured by Love*, Smithtown NY: Exposition Press.

Synnott, A. (1993) *The Body Social: Symbolism, Self and Society*, London: Routledge.

Ueshiba, K. (1984) *The Spirit of Aikido*, Tokyo, etc.: Kodansha International.

Ueshiba, M. (1992) *The Art of Peace*, trans. J. Stevens, Boston MA: Shambhala Press.

Wacquant, L. (1995) 'The pugilistic point of view: how boxers think and feel about their trade', *Theory and Society*, 24: 489–535.

Zarrilli, P. B. (1990) 'What does it mean to "become the character"? Power, presence, and transcendence in Asian in-body disciplines of practice', in R. Schechner and W. Appel (eds) *By Means of Performance: Intercultural Studies of Theatre and Ritual*, Cambridge: Cambridge University Press, pp.131–48.

——(1995) 'Repositioning the body: practice, power, and self in an Indian martial art', in C. A. Breckenridge (ed.) *Consuming Modernity: Public Culture in a South Asian World*, Minneapolis and London: University of Minnesota Press, pp. 183–215.

Part IV

Intricacies of language explained

Chapter 11

Licence revoked

When calypso goes too far[1]

Jonathan Skinner

Introduction

> Calypso a ah we culture,
> We'll be proud o' um forever.

So ended David Edgecombe's review (Edgecombe 1975) of the Calypso Competition 1974–5 on Montserrat, a small English-speaking Caribbean island of 10,000 in the Eastern Caribbean, a Leeward island of the Lesser Antilles, a colony sharing more than language and parliamentary democracy with its British mother country. 'Calypso is our culture, We'll be proud of it forever'. Writing at the start of the new year, Edgecombe was paraphrasing a part of the chorus line from the New Year Calypso King's winning entry, the Mighty Arrow (1994) with his calypso 'Montserrat English' ('Dis is Montserrat culture/We'll be proud of it forever') to make the point that calypso defines and draws people together, that calypso is an intrinsic part of the people's Montserrat culture.

On a small island where social networks are dense, in a 'muted society', as local poet, English teacher and calypso judge Jamaal Jeffers once described the oppressive and guarded nature of life in a small community; on Montserrat, where known and unknown social and kinship ties cut and cross-cut each other, it is often necessary to resort to indirect means of communication and expression for fear of retaliation in the immediate or distant future. Whilst undertaking fieldwork on Montserrat from 1994–5, I found that the publication of poetry in papers and booklets, and the singing and performing of calypso songs were two significant strategies for passing comment in society without engaging in direct criticism (Skinner 1997): Howard Fergus (international poet and organiser of the Maroons group, island historian, Montserratian Deputy Governor, Speaker in the House of Parliament, and University of the West Indies Resident Tutor), for example, is a private man who presents several contradictory public personas and who often resorts to poetic narratives to make sense of various occurrences in his life. In some circumstances Fergus publishes his poetry in local newspapers to comment upon national events as a poet, when to offer such opinions acting as impartial Speaker in the House of Parliament would not be appropriate (Skinner 1997: 65) Perhaps this is as to be expected for society is, after all, constituted by the coming together of such indirect communication interaction as Rapport has argued elsewhere in this volume.

Poetry and calypso are both diplomatic strategies, opportunities to present an opinion, or a 'social commentary' in the words of the calypsonians I interviewed. Indeed, on Montserrat there was a unanimous chorus amongst calypso writers, singers and audiences that calypso was a form of 'social commentary' itself. These social commentaries – certainly the poetic – serve the same purpose as the poetry Lila Abu-Lughod came across amongst the Beduin in Egypt (1988): it is the diplomatic veiling of sentiments in everyday life. In 'high' society this veiling – or 'wrapping' (after Hendry 1993) – of direct commentary, of direction, has become the expected norm, certainly in diplomatic circles (see Black, Chapter 15 in this volume). These examples I consider to be 'indirections', a feature, one might add, of many enclosed communities such as the small islands in the Pacific and the Caribbean where indirection has become a necessary strategy for dealing with egalitarianism in a wider system of hierarchy (Brenneis 1984; 1987). In her comparative study of politeness and presentation in Japan and other societies – where the ability to distinguish between the front (*omote*) and the real opinions (*ura/honne*) is much valued as a social skill (Hendry 1993: 163) – Hendry concluded by casting indirection alongside dissimulation (1993: 162). Here, however, in the context of music and performance in the Caribbean, indirection, I shall be arguing, is less about dissimulation or deception, than deflection, veiling and masking.

On West Indian islands – where a person is often on show more than in European countries; where image, style and 'respect' are sought and maintained by verbal duels, multiple sexual unions and public performance – Paula Burnett (1986) has identified a strong oral tradition of social commentary and social protest which stretches through time from the first slave work songs of Africans transplanted to work on the Caribbean plantations between the sixteenth and nineteenth centuries, through to her interesting inclusion of popular calypso songs with performance and dub poetry in the twentieth century (see also Markham 1989). Calypsonians both sing and perform their songs, marginal figures on centre stage during calypso competitions, creating and maintaining their own dramaturgical space. They play and project a character to the audience like actors presenting their character in a social drama which can be both reflexive and therapeutic. Talking about such social drama in another context, Victor Turner argues that the theatre is a liminal place where the audience can undergo a part of the performance – 'a redressive ritual' – by being swept up in the *communitas* of the experience (1986: 41, 43). So too for the audience of a calypso competition performance. However, in some circumstances the various audiences are lost by the performer as the performance or calypso song fails; in many cases the suspension of the moment disappears leaving behind no chord of harmony between self and objects, but disharmony. In 1987 and 1990, for example, the Trinidadian calypsonians Mighty Trini and Denyse Plummer, respectively, were jeered and bombarded with rolls of toilet paper and orange skins by unruly crowds attending the preliminary rounds of the Trinidad Calypso Monarch Competition. Keith Warner (1993: 275) explained these reactions to the calypsonians because 'the feeling that calypso is the exclusive province of the black section of the population': Mighty Trini was from a Syrian family, and Denyse Plummer was a white woman born on Trinidad 'venturing into what is virtually a black man's territory, and [they] did not fit'. In these two situations the predominantly 'black' audience did not identify with the calypsonians' ethnicity; their publicly perceived ethnicity jarred with what the audience expected. Analysing such public performances as a form of rhetorical text (Patton 1994: 61), we might say that the usual 'shared meaning' failed due to a breakdown in the rhetorical signature between 'rhetor – text – audience'; or, that, as in the case with other examples, the calypsonian exceeded the accepted and expected nature of the calypso performance.

It is when the calypso song and/or the performance goes too far, when it is too direct, when it is undiplomatic, when it jars the audience and judges, when it oversteps the mark, or crosses the unstated line or boundary, that I wish to consider in this chapter. It is when the ambiguous and equivocal nature of the social commentary breaks down, when it approximates everyday communication, that indirection is lost – along with 'the licence in ritual' to use Gluckmans' term for the rite of protest which does more to bless social order than change it (1966: 133, 134). For it is when things go wrong that we get an indication of what is expected in a calypso song, and from a calypso performance – though ironically it is perhaps when the regularity of calypso indirections are lost that we see the true subversive potential and disordering possibilities of calypso. During the 1974–5 Calypso King Competition on Montserrat, Edgecombe reported no such untoward happenings. This was not the case during many other calypso competitions on Montserrat; calypsos and calypsonians are given a special licence to licentiousness, but on some occasions even they can find themselves criticised, ridiculed and even physically assaulted as their licence is revoked. Before examining some of these *faux pas* of social commentary in the context of indirection and calypso licence, let me first situate calypso in its social, historical and indirect context.

Licensed to licence: Carnival, canboulay and calypso

> I say, 'Do, do come in town Jou'vert morning;
> Find yourself in a band,
> Watch the way how the natives moving;
> Hug up tight with ah man,
> Sing along with the tunes they playing,

And now and again you shouting,
"Play mas! Carnival!"
Miss tourist, that is bacchanal'.[2]

This is the advice of Trinidad calypsonian Aldwin 'Lord Kitchener' Roberts to an imaginary young female tourist visiting his island. Cited by Burnett as a part of the oral tradition in the Caribbean (1986: 41–2), Kitchener's song was chosen for the Road March in 1968, the catchiest calypso which will be played through town so that there can be dancing in the streets. This is a calypso chorus which encourages the tourist to join in with the local celebration, the Carnival – 'mas' as it is also known in Trinidad – a two-day street festival leading up to Ash Wednesday.[3] 'Play mas!', join in with the free-spiritedness and *bacchanal* – a term which Daniel Miller translates as the 'general level of excitement and disorder, as well as the expressive sexuality' (1994: 24); a term which for Birth refers to the 'violent disorder', the 'fights and the wild, sexual and drunken revelry of Carnival' (1994: 167). This state of bacchanal, so Miller informs us, relates to J'Ouvert morning – the official beginning of Trinidad's Carnival (Jour Ouvert – opening day [the local abbreviations vary]) which is followed by Mardi Gras ('Fat Tuesday') (Campbell 1988: 9) – when bands and dance troupes come together before dawn, dressed in mud and ashes, to reveal themselves in the first light as the 'truth' (Miller 1994: 112). Miller thus rightly characterises Trinidad Carnival as 'a time of rudeness' and profanity in opposition to the sacred time of Christmas (1994: 82, 107–33). It is a time when social rules and conventions are subverted, the pretensions of existing social orders exposed, and the formal and hierarchical structure of social relations ritually inverted.

The time following Christmas is a special time, be it the rite of passage into the new year (see Leach 1979), or the 'betwixt and between' (Turner 1979: 234) period between Christ's birth at Christmas and his death and resurrection at Easter. In this way, Carnival has always been a part of the Christian calendar as the excessive lead-in to the lenten religious period of abstinence (a recreation of Christ's fasting in the wilderness). It is thus a time when carnal behaviour is sanctioned by religion, described in Rabelais' representation of medieval European Carnival as a 'joyful hell' (Bakhtin 1984: 133, 123). Both Carnival and calypso in their present form in Trinidad also have other symbolic associations – namely, with resistance and the subordination of domination. The European 'religious' Carnival was traditionally celebrated by the Spanish and British colonisers of Trinidad (*c.*1500–1802, 1802–1962) until post-slave emancipation in 1838 when the former slaves in Trinidad's capital, Port of Spain, came to dominate and overturn the white colonial minority's genteel masquerade celebrations through the streets. By the 1860s the former slaves had brought African songs and dances, instruments and customs, and far more overtly suggestive masquerades to the Carnival holiday (Campbell 1988: 18). They introduced marchers in transvestite costumes (*Pissenlit*) to their flaming processions (*canboulays*), and stick fighters (*batoniers*) accompanied by *kalindas* – men who rallied the crowds to the side of their *batonier* by singing obscene songs and improvising insults against his opponents (the early calypsonians).

The ruling colonial authorities disliked this potent cocktail of revelry and rioting, *communitas*, egalitarianness and 'anti-structure' amongst the former slaves on the streets. But when they introduced the Peace Preservation Act (1884), banning the use of the African drum on the streets, the result was a backlash as processionists improvised a beat by striking bamboo tubes, blocks of wood, strips of metal or the ground ahead. Carnival became a regular – if disorderly – festival, a social and anti-colonial protest, a class and ethnic struggle (Campbell 1988: 1) as Port of Spain's neighbourhoods took to the streets in costumes and disguises. The role of the *kalindas* especially developed in the twentieth century as they took to satirising society: releasing topical songs throughout the year, popularising them for the Carnival; competing against each other in calypso tents, and attracting tourists to the island (Birth 1994). Outside of Trinidad, elsewhere in the English-speaking Caribbean and in West Indian migrant communities such as New York or London, present-day examples of Carnival and calypso are just as much techniques for mass mobilisation and ways of expressing cultural power in the people: both Chris Searle and Gail Pool have demonstrated the insurgent role of calypso and poetry in the Grenada Revolution (1979–83) (Searle 1984: 199; see also Pool 1994), an example which suggests that Carnival and calypso indirections can be more than the 'ceremonials of rebellion' which Gluckman identified in African rituals of licence (1966: 134, 135); and, generalising from the Notting Hill Carnival, Abner Cohen has noted that 'Carnival is ... politics masquerading behind cultural forms', an activity which has retained its traditional symbolic capital of emancipation and protest, protest and triumph (1993: 132, 27).

As sexually direct as many aspects of Carnival are, so too are many of the calypso songs, 'the music of the masses' (Rohlehr 1970: 87). As both the medium and mode of social expression, of social situations, social issues, ills and opinions, calypso is explicitly a form of social commentary, and calypso as social commentary can be very explicit in its content. Mighty Sparrow, an international calypsonian from Trinidad, is accepted as one of the international Kings of Calypso, notorious for his songs of carnivalesque ill repute: 'Wood in the Fire'[4] for example plays upon a shared understanding that references to 'wood' can in fact be slang references to the penis; and his 'Sell de Pussy'[5] can be interpreted either as a song about a cat, or as a clever parable about prostitution that is only disambiguated at the very end of the song. Historically, such songs on Trinidad in the nineteenth century would have ended with the words '*sans humanité*' to absolve the singer from responsibility for their *risqué* remarks (Lewin 1980; see also Campbell 1988: 20); such was the desire of the calypsonian to maintain as much of his performative indirection as possible by drawing disapprobation to the song rather than the singer. Similarly, the calysonians' titles which they create for themselves, like the writer's *nom de plume*, also act as techniques of indirection by protecting the calypsonians' character from public criticism. These techniques still persist as unacknowledged – and sometimes unknown – parts of the traditional calypso licence, whether on Trinidad or Montserrat.

Calypso as Montserrat culture

> People think that it's wrong
> To talk real Montserratian
> They say it ain't right – grammatically
> Day can't find them words in no dictionary
> Call it bad language
> Despising we heritage
> But don't care if dey call we foolish
> Dis is Montserrat English[6]

Calypso – capoeira with the kick in the song rather than the foot – and Carnival came to vary slightly from island to island in the English-speaking Caribbean as each island adopted and adapted their own distinctive hybrid version often using it as a 'symbol of national culture' (Young 1993: 172–9). On Montserrat, both calypso and Carnival have become an integral part of the islanders' cultural and national consciousness. 'Calypso, the commonest song-form of the Caribbean', so Montserratian cultural artist Ann Marie Dewar states, 'is one of the most communicative forms of music, enabling the composer to comment on any situation with a freedom of expression and language' (Dewar 1977: 75). It thus has revolutionary potential (Pool 1994: 84). In the above extract, the Montserratian calypsonian Arrow is drawing attention to the hybrid mixture of Montserratian and English – to what Edgecombe refers to as 'Monglish' (1987e: 4) – suggesting that it is a 'nation language'[7] in its own right rather than a pidgin English[7] or debased dialect[8] which retains a sense of identity in relation with the colonial metropole (Angrosino 1993: 74). Arrow continues in his calypso 'Montserrat English':[9]

Gee me lee – wha you ah yete dey
(Give me a little – of what you are eating there)

Dat ah wa we just say
(That is what we just said)

Pick um up – han um gee me
(Pick it up – hand it to me)

Dats de Montserratian way
(That's the Montserratian way)

Com – ma sisah – fetch me de poh
(Come here – my sister – fetch me the potty)

Wan pain na me belly yah so so
(I have a pain in my belly right here)

Dis is Montserrat culture
We'll be proud of it forever [10]

With reference to this calypso and others equally socially and politically informed, Howard Fergus has described Arrow as a part of Montserrat's national conscience (1994: 252). Where a politician might communicate to their public on Montserrat in English or Monglish, using imagery and allusion in their speech for rhetorical purposes, Arrow communicates to his masses by maintaining the allusion and imagery throughout the whole of his calypso, as is expected of a calypso. This is the difference between everyday communication which can be direct or indirect and has little licence, and calypso communication which is largely indirect and has much more licence granted to it. The licence of the latter, I should point out, comes from the nature and circumstances of calypso as much as from its emphasis upon word-play, punning and deliberate openness to various interpretations, its ambiguity.

Montserrat's Carnival differs from that of her neighbouring islands. Nevis, for example, has celebrated Culturama at the end of July since 1974 (Nevis Culturama Committee 1994: 55), a time for calypso competitions, Miss Culture Talent Contest, and J'Ouvert Jump Up dancing in the streets, all disconnected entirely from any religious festivals. Montserrat, in contrast, has been holding its Carnival (called Festival) over Christmas and the beginning of the New Year since 1962. Carnival had been proposed in 1958 but had been resisted by individuals fearing such 'calypso and cutlass' dangers from cosmopolitan Trinidad (Fergus 1994: 253–4), consequently restricting calyp-sonians to junior high school competitions and trade union dances (Flasher n.d.; Dewar 1977: 75–80); it should also be noted that Montserratians had achieved adult suffrage in 1952 by using the trade unions to break the stranglehold of plantocracy landowners, and many of the calypsonians were drawn from the same working-class trade unions. Nonetheless, a period of musical growth ensued on Montserrat in the 1960s and 1970s: calypso was performed to large audiences, joining the 'fife and drum' music made for the traditional masquerade dancers (see Figure 11.1); and at the same time on Montserrat, at George Martin's AIR Studios, Stevie Wonder cut a version of 'Ebony and Ivory', Duran Duran recorded 'Rio', and Elton John recorded 'Jump-up' (Hanley 1984: 48).

Considered an art form, with the 'advantage' that it does not necessitate literacy or specialist training, calypso places calypsonians into the category of cultural artists, heritage brokers accounting for the highlights of each year as they lyricalise present social concerns. The result is a social history which most Montserratians are intimately connected with. From the 1960s calypso was dominated by young men such as the Cassell brothers – Justin 'Hero' Cassell who has won approximately thirteen crowns (the first in 1962), and Alphonsus 'Arrow' Cassell who competed from 1968 to 1974 before going to Trinidad to make his fortune. Winning these calypso competitions involves passing through three heats at two-week intervals: Eliminations early December, Semi-Finals mid-December, Finals at the end of December. One band, comprising of bass and acoustic guitars, drums, synthesiser and a section

Figure 11.1 'Playing mas' on the streets of Plymouth, Montserrat.

Source: Photograph by author.

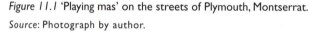

of trombones and trumpets, plays for each of the thirty or so Eliminees' two songs which are judged according to four criteria: lyrics (35 per cent), melody (35 per cent), rendition (20 per cent), presentation and performance (10 per cent) – all judged in 1994 by Jamaal Jeffers. Approximately half will be eliminated at each heat, narrowing the number down to ten calypsonians in the Finals. In the second heat the calypsonian is allowed to enter an alternative song to his original selection. As with all the songs, however, they cannot have been sung in any previous year, yet they can have been released on the radio during the competition year so as to gain public support and notoriety. In practice, calypsonians will try to keep exciting the crowds by improvising some of their lyrics, by dressing in glittering costumes, or by acting out the storyline of the calypso in the finals, appealing to the unknown quantity of the performance points (see below). Only the King or Queen of the previous year's Festival Calypso Competition is exempt from the elimination rounds.

Any person on Montserrat has the opportunity to become Calypso King or Queen and win a pair of holiday flight tickets to another island, a trophy with $5,000EC (£1,500) cash, celebrity status around the island and the opportunity to represent Montserrat at the inter-island calypso competitions. The other competitors also receive Festival Committee financial prizes ranging from $150EC at the Eliminations to $400EC at the Semi-Finals, and between $1,000 and $1,600EC at the finals. Calypso on Montserrat is thus highly socially egalitarian and financially rewarding on a relatively poor island bound by an hierarchical colonial administrative system. Pat 'Belonger' Ryan, for example, a Trinidadian woman who migrated to Montserrat where she married a Montserratian and thereby gained 'belonger' status on the island, has entered the calypso competitions several times. She was an immediate success, achieving third position in the controversial 1988–9 Calypso Competition with 'Bring Dem Back' (Edgecombe and Burns 1989: 6). This calypso was a complaint about the recent loss of island-known cultural practices and characters such as John Bull and Miss Goosie – both popular 'mummers', a bull dressed in sack-cloth, wearing horns and carrying the devil's forked stick, and a very tall wooden puppet manipulated by a masked person on foot (see Figure 11.2; Fergus 1992: 52, 53; see also Sarah Pink's chapter on Carnival costume in Chapter 6 of this volume).[11]

Belonger's concluding lines in the calypso make reference to other masked

Figure 11.2 Belonger in costume with John Bull and Miss Goosie, 1988–9 Calypso Competition.

Source: Photograph by Dem Pollock.

dancers on the streets who come out in troupes at celebrations; for her, they should all be the celebrated:

> Culture shouldn't be a mask
> That we wear on Festival day
> Take it to the classroom
> Parade it in every way
> Let's be proud and glad
> Of a heritage that's our own
> Foreign culture bang water come here
> Is here we tradition born[12]

Ironically, Belonger 'bang water come here' herself in her migration to Montserrat. As a belonger, Belonger's acceptance on Montserrat contrasts with the rejection of Mighty Trini and Denyse Plummer back home and is testament to the benign and welcoming nature of Montserrat society. In the next section, I hope to show that occasionally Montserrat calypso, a form of social commentary and an integral part of the national conscience and culture, can in fact cause controversy, resulting in a form of social failure which can be understood in terms of indirection: they fail because in various ways they all exceed the levels of indirection – or break the implicit contract of indirection between calypsonian and Carnival audience – traditionally understood and accepted as a part of the calypsonions' ritual licence to licentiousness. In each case their failure leads to the calypsonians' 'licence' to licence being partly or wholly revoked.

Calypso controversies

> Ah say a jam to the left
> Wail to the right
> A make a wine to the centre
> Push back to the rear[13]

The calypsonian, described by Patton as 'a voice for pent-up feelings, frustrations, and attitudes of the people affected by social and economic problems' (1994: 60), produces calypsos which are social and symbolic actions. During the performance, a time of 'conscious intent' (Schiefflin 1998: 196) when performer is accountable to audience and attempts to close the gap between the two, the aim of the calypso is to articulate and symbolise the thoughts and values of the audience, to 'become the means for defining and redefining issues of central importance to the shared cultural world of performer and audience' (Patton 1994: 55). It is on the stage that, we might say, after Richard Bauman, the calypso verbal performance becomes '*constitutive* of the domain of verbal art as spoken communication' (1984: 11, author's emphasis). In the calypso contests the audiences and judges need to identify with the calypso performances (lyrics, rendition, meaning, and all). The calypso and calypsonian can fail if the audiences does not feel that the calypso, the calypsonian or performances is 'speaking' to them, or if this indirect form of communication is not in keeping with the ordered disorder and general licence given to the occasion, in other words the audience's expectations or the government's strict interpretations of the calypso. What is also interesting about the calypso in its performative state is the possibility of bacchanal and mayhem in the rendition. Literally, anything can happen Before, During and After a live performance, as the following controversial examples go on to show.

Before: Cupid and the election box

Herman Francis is a school teacher, a civil servant for the Montserrat Government, and a popular calypsonian known as 'Cupid' or 'Q-pid'. Always a serious contender for the Calypso King title, Cupid entered the 1987 competition with the song 'What's Inside de Box'. The year 1987 was an exciting calypso competition year, one in which the current monarch Justin 'Hero' Cassell and the former monarch Everton 'Reality' Weekes were not competing – between them they had won the title for the past eleven years (Anon. 1987b). Cupid's song satirised a controversy surrounding the re-election of the People's Liberation Movement (PLM) led by John Osborne in the 1987 general election, and is a good example of the government's withdrawal of the calypso 'licence'.

Nine respectable Montserratians signed affidavits to the effect that the names of the candidates in the election had not been printed in the correct order on all the ballot papers, thereby arousing suspicions as to the legitimacy of the entire ballot. Justice Albert Redhead was flown in from Antigua and was persuaded by a Crown legal representative (Attorney General) defending the electoral officials, such as Howard Fergus (Supervisor of Elections), not to open the boxes and examine the stored ballot papers. The boxes remained closed even when the Attorney General later decided to campaign – less vigorously, in the eyes of *The Montserrat Reporter*'s editor (David Edgecombe) – for the election boxes to be opened and the case of the suspicious ballots resolved (Edgecombe 1987c: 4). Cupid made this political problem the subject of his calypso with his song repeatedly running the following lines in its chorus, 'Whats' in the Box, Redhead?/Redhead, open the box' (ll. 9–10). The calypso was subsequently banned from being played by ZJB Radio, the government-run radio station, whilst, ironically, the song was passed on to the very same Attorney General for an official ruling about the nature of its contents (Edgecombe 1987e: 4; Staff reporter 1987). As expected, the ban on the calypso elevated the level of attention focused upon the Calypso Competition performances when the calypso could be heard live.

One verse expressed explicit criticism for the culprits and for the democratic process on the island:

Some got promise, others got threats

I hear some even sold their 'X'
Governor needs to investigate
The culprits, they must not escape
True democracy must be upheld
Any breaching must be repelled[14]

In this way the lyrics approximated 'everyday' communication, straight talk, direct speech without imagery, metaphor, allusion or the distance of story: the indirection of calypso communication was lost. Despite all the controversy that the calypso caused, the only sanction available towards the calypsonian and his song was to ban it from the government-run airwaves just as they do to overly political calypsos on Trinidad (Birth 1994: 171). Cupid's song was not played, just as two years earlier ZJB Radio had withheld airplay of 'Long Grass', another of Cupid's calypsos.

Furthermore, the reported responses to the informal ban of Cupid's 'What's Inside de Box' are telling indications of the perceived nature of calypso. David Edgecombe, editor of *The Montserrat Reporter* and critic of the PLM, questioned the ban, playing upon Montserratian dialect with his rhetorical question – 'Why is the regime, to use a lovely Monglish phrase, so touchous bout de box?' (1987e: 4). Edgecombe continued with this answer:

> Q-Pid is exercising his artistic right to explore an issue which affects, and is the concern of, thousands of people. If anything, in this age of jam & wine, he should be congratulated for so consistently selecting themes of greater substance, for choosing subject matter of relevance which so closely touch on what it is like to live on Montserrat in the 1980s.

Q-Pid, himself, when interviewed about his song's disadvantage as an unknown in the calypso competition, had the following to say about the nature of calypso on Montserrat (Edgecombe 1987d: 1):

> [w]e need to go back to the roots of calypso. It is an art form which has traditionally been used to reflect and comment on the lives of people socially and politically.

The government's ban, placed upon the calypso broadcast but not the calypso performance, highlighted the importance of the song in the public's ears, a prohibitive strategy which failed to quell the government's embarrassment. Finally, what this example does show is that the song rather than the singer was the target (reiterating the *sans humanité* Trinidadian calypso tradition), and that indirection and calypso/Carnival licence can be easily lost.[15] Despite all this controversy, Q-Pid eventually finished as first runner-up to Cepeke, the new Calypso Monarch of Montserrat 1987–8 (Edgecombe and Chambers 1988: 12), who was himself to be the focus of a calypso storm in later years.

During: Cepeke, Hero and the hooligans

Ostensibly, during the Montserrat calypso competitions, there are few, if any, instances of sexual discrimination against the female calypsonians (Calypso Bee, Singing Maro, Rachel Collis and Belonger are all highly respected); nor is there supposed to be any discrimination against the ethnicity of the entrants, though I have yet to witness an expatriate 'white' entry. A calypso commotion was caused, however, by reigning monarch Cecil 'Cepeke' Lake's unsuccessful 1992 entry 'White Man's World', a song criticising the white man's perceived domination of the world. This calypso was an uncomfortable entry by a publicly perceived 'black' Montserratian with a 'white' father from England, Peter Lake, a poet who worked as an agriculturalist for the British administration on Montserrat and eventually settled on the island, marrying a local 'black' Montserratian. Cepeke's calypso song is another example of calypso indirection and licence lost, an example that did not work for the crowd (as opposed to the local government) who, in this case, judged the singer and his song together and did not like to hear specific comments about ethnic relations coming from a man with a mixed ethnic background. In this instance the traditionally neutral position of the calypsonian, his *sans humanité* status, could not be maintained and, because of Cepeke's background which he failed to overcome, the gap between the audience and the performance could not be closed. In the end Cepeke's performance was tolerated though resented. Nothing untoward occurred bar some heckling and public disapproval. The performance ritual went awry because the usual calypso licence could not be recognised or accorded. This atypical example shows that the indirect nature of the calypso communication broke down because Cepeke took his calypso just a bit too far: despite the friendliness of Montserrat society, there are inter-ethnic tensions and concerns on Montserrat such that black/white relations can be tense, too tense to be able to enjoy the traditional licence in calypso ritual (cf. Gluckman 1966: 132).

Another awkward calypso performance, equally jarring in some respects, an example of Carnival bacchanal, was made by Hero in the 1986–7 calypso finals when he acted out a version of his song 'Body-to-Body', *wining* (gyrating hips and waist) – in a skin-tight costume – with a much younger woman. Hero won the competition (his sixteenth crown) but was strongly criticised in the press for appearing 'paunchy-paunchy' rather than the 'sexy-sexy' which he sang (Edgecombe 1987a; see also Edgecombe 1987b; Anon. 1987a). In this example the power to grant or withhold the calypsonian's licence lay with the public and not with the government. Again, like the previous example, the calypsonian went too far: in this example, however, it was due to the awkward performance of the calypso which could not sustain the lyrics rather than to the lyrics themselves.

The most consternation caused by calypso on Montserrat, however, occurred at the 1988–9 finals when the audience disagreed with the judges' decision to crown Earl 'Hustler' Browne, place Drago second and Belonger third, thereby dethroning Monarch Cepeke to fourth place. Bottles and stones were thrown onto the stage in anger at what many considered to be a bad decision omitting Cepeke from the top three (Edgecombe and Burns 1989: 6), or for the misplacing between first and fourth place (Galloway 1989). The press also seized upon this event, criticising such an excessive reaction to the judges' decision. What is interesting about this final example from the stage is that the crowds on Montserrat reacted to the judges' decisions more violently than to any calypsonians' possible offence or effrontery, showing that they had clear expectations in their minds as to the order of the calypso finalists, and that calypso is indeed the music of and for the masses.

After: Saltfish and the 'Socialism Jam'

Saltfish – his nickname derived from his favourite subsistence food – Archibald 'Lord Alfredo' Mills has been singing calypso since 1972. Alfredo is a simple man: a part-time construction worker, he helps unload ships when they arrive and plays in a steel band for tourists on Wednesday nights. Though not often a contender for the calypso finals, Alfredo's great gift for music has led to the production of some very popular and memorable songs, for example 'Socialism Jam', winner of the 1980 Road March Competition, a very danceable and memorable calypso which is now referred to as 'Push to the Rear'; the song's chorus runs with instructions to 'jam to the left', 'wail to the right', 'make a wine to the centre' and 'push back to the rear'. These calypso words, set to a fast and lively tune, continue to catch the public's imagination: certainly during the calypso competition, Montserratians danced in the streets to this song, performing – with relish – the suggestive actions described, encouraged and sanctioned in the calypso.

Not long after the calypso competition, the public found out the 'true' meaning behind Saltfish's calypso and the significance of the words which they had been dancing to. On this occasion many felt that calypso had gone too far; they were horrified that they had been dancing to Saltfish's woes. In this calypso case study the indirection turned out to be wholly inappropriate for many – in the wrong direction. In an interview with Alfredo, during which he revealed to me his sentiments, hidden behind his personal veil or mask, he admitted that the song was a very personal expression of an experience that he had had, and that the chorus instructions had, in fact, been directions for a very unfortunate type of sexual movement:[16]

> One night in 1979, you know, that time the Jimmy Cliff picture came here. 1979. So I know, I took a walk around the island, you know, you know, around St John's and Roche's, because I really believe in the Marines, you know. So I had on the full combat – knapsack, helmet, and everything. ... And when I came back, you know, I felt sleepy but I wanted to see the movie – the Jimmy Cliff that – a Saturday night. So I now went over in

Grammar School. And when I went, I met people, you know. That time some people from Guadeloupe were camping down by the establishment. And I, now, um, went over from Grammar School to Sturge Park and went in the last bench, you know – cooling out. And this guy came up there, you know, and put a lock around my neck, right. ... And it's the first time that um, I believe that the heart is more on the left side because there is a kind of beating, the heart beating, you know. We call it a kind of frightening, you know, and so. And he held me in the um, in the local way ... and raped me.

And, and, that's what the song's about?

Yeah.

Did he – did he go to jail?

Well um, after that, you know, he continue raping people. So one time, you know, he rape an old woman who is cripple. And, ah, he spent ten to fifteen years in jail.

So, it sounds like the Rasta guy last year; similar, similar kind of person. And you, you, built this into a song the same year, or later on?

The next year.

A version of this song called 'Push To The Rear' is now included on the cassette *Emeral City Festival Volume 1* (Duberry n.d.) as a tourist souvenir. About this particularly memorable calypso controversy, I would like to suggest that it was a cathartic number for Saltfish, evoking poignant memories of the rapist's instructions – move to the left, to the right, *wine* and push back. However, it encourages a very different response from the listener who is at first unaware of the sexually explicit personal dimension, the painful significance, of the dance lyrics. Once the background to the calypso was made public, the equivocal nature of the interpretive veil lifted, the calypso continued to be played, sung and danced to, albeit with some reservation. Public disapprobation was rife once indirection had given way to explicitness, but not to the degree that the calypso was banned and censored. Where previously it was acceptable to dance out the movements as an acceptable parody of the sexual act, now it was frowned upon and not copied by all. The lack of any sanction being placed upon the calypso or the calypsonian suggests that, perhaps, this calypso is now interpreted as a revelation in keeping with the calypsos of the past century on Trinidad. The disapproval and moral outrage associated with the calypso arises not just from the brutality of the activity upon which it is based, but also from its close connection to the reality of the rape: whereas most calypsos are about social and political topics close to home, in this case, the connection between the calypso and the act upon which it was based was too close to local notions of decency and sexuality for comfort. Finally, I can think of no stronger example to support the thesis that calypso is an implicit commentary – often with explicit themes, personal expression as well as public performance.

Conclusion

Calypso is as much public, social commentary as it is private, inner commentary – for the singer as much as for the listener. I would even go so far as to argue that people repeat calypso to each other, play and parody the songs, and make sense of their lives by recourse to calypso. Yet calypso communication is different from everyday communication in its indirect nature, with its imagery, allusion, and story-like removed narrative. These qualities, along with its Carnival setting, contribute to calypso's licence to be so explicit. With such possibilities, calypso has the capability to be much more than a public tune, public expression, end-of-the-year phenomenon. Calypso is thus also able to maintain a position in both public and private spheres: calypso narratives are internal and external, both inner and outer. V. S. Naipaul demonstrates this in the novel *Miguel Street* (1971: 98, my italics) where the character Hat continually quotes calypso advice to Eddoes and the narrator. When Eddoes has to come to terms with his girlfriend's unexpected pregnancy, Hat externalises and finds ground for the calypsonians' public commentary:

> Hat said, 'The calypsonian was right, you hear.
> > *Man centipede bad.*
> > *Woman centipede more than bad.*
> I know the sort of woman. She have a lot of baby, take the baby by the fathers, and get the fathers to pay money. By the time she thirty-five, she getting so much money from so much man, and she ain't got no baby to look after and no responsibility. I know the thing'.

In this way calypso is-and-can-become mother wit, social counsellor, whereby the lyrics internalised over the years come out at opportune moments to guide and assist with the present situation: calypso, expression of public values, is turned into proverbial expression of private situations. Pithy, apt and quotable lyrics make a song memorable, popular and useful, and can be found in constant use in conversation: Teknikal's competition calypso-line 'a news dem a look' stood the test of time far into the new year of 1995; so too, Top Secret's line 'come better dan dat' in his calypso 'Tropical Gal' (1994) is used frequently on the streets as a humorous put-down. Other Montserrat calypsonians have equally explicit messages which have entered the collective memory and conscience of the islanders; many of them are apparent from the calypso and calypsonian titles such as 'Nation' (Cutter 1982), 'Save this Country' (Patriot 1982) and 'Montserrat is for Montserratians' (Rockamaya 1993). In this way, lines from calypsos which capture the public's attention are internalised, and surface as personal commentaries; so too the calypso controversies which often return as coarse memories – Hero's *wining* body and Saltfish's dramaturgical confession, for instance.

The calypso medium and message certainly acts as a fragment of national culture on many Caribbean islands, turning calypsonians into culture brokers who use their expressive and evocative performance tools to leave behind an oral heritage. In my presentation and discussion of my exceptions to the calypso norm, moments when calypso indirection and licence is lost, I have also high-lighted two additional observations about the calypsonians' deliberate attempts at indirection, namely by use of calypso name and the traditional use of the *sans humanité* expression. More significantly I have noted that much calypso exempli-fies Gluckman's idea about the 'licence in ritual'. As an important release valve, a means of intentional indirection, calypso and Carnival – though increasingly divorced from their more genteel roots – have emerged in this century as insepa-rable partners in a carnal dance, a *wining* jump-up which performs, each season, a controversially joyful heaven and hell on earth. I have shown in this chapter that this indirection strategy found in calypso communication on Montserrat and other English-speaking islands in the Caribbean is less about deception than deflection, and more about the veiling of sentiments than the dissembling of diplomatic indirection; further, with its strong emphasis upon imagery, story and illusion, calypso communication also differs slightly from everyday communica-tion. Finally, I have argued that this indirection strategy in calypso communication is highlighted by examples of when it is lost, indirection lost, so to speak. Many of the examples of calypsos which go too far, significantly, lose their licence to licentiousness; a calypso which has its license revoked (by national government, Carnival audience or local islanders), does so because it has lost its indirection – in Patton's terms it has failed to close the performative or aural gap between the calypsonian with his or her calypso and the audience.

Notes

1 I am grateful to those calypsonians, judges and members of ZJB Radio who helped me whilst I was on Montserrat. I would also like to acknowledge some useful discussions with Chadd Cumberbatch and Nigel Rapport on the nature of Carnival, calypso and communication.
2 'Miss Tourist' (Lord Kitchener 1968: ll. 9–16, chorus).
3 This term derives from 'masquerades', masked dancers (mummers) who dance from house to house or street to street on special occasions, traditionally during Carnival time (Fergus 1994: 241); this activity has its origins in the European tradition of the masquerade (Hebdige 1990: 35).
4 'Wood in the Fire' (Sparrow 1992).
5 'Sell de Pussy' (Sparrow 1992).
6 This transcription is from a modern soca version, 'Ole Time Calypso Medley' (Arrow 1994: ll. 5–12, first verse excluding the introduction).
7 A *pidgin* is 'a simplified language containing vocabulary from two or more languages, used for communication between people not having a common language'. This is different to a *creole* language which is 'a mother tongue formed from the contact of a European language with another' (Thompson 1995: 1033, 317).
8 A *dialect* is 'a subordinate variety of a language with non-standard vocabulary, pronunciation or grammar' (Thompson 1995: 372).
9 'Montserrat English', winning song for Calypso King The Mighty Arrow, 1974–5, contained within 'Ole Time Calypso Medley' (Arrow 1994; see also Edgecombe 1975: 2).

10 (Arrow 1994: ll. 13–20, first chorus; my translation in brackets).
11 Unsourced photograph given to the author by Belonger, artwork by Dem Pollock. In the 1995–6 Carnival procession Chadd Cumberbatch cleverly designed, built and reincarnated Miss Goosie.
12 'Bring Dem Back' (Belonger 1988: ll. 48–55). Belonger translates 'bang water' from the Montserratian dialect as 'to cross the seas' (i.e. to migrate).
13 'Push to the Rear' (Lord Alfredo 1980: chorus).
14 'What's Inside the Box' (Q-Pid 1987: ll. 9–16, second verse).
15 Another question, which lies beyond the remit of this chapter, is whether or not this calypso licence was intentionally or unintentionally lost.
16 Transcript of an interview between the author and Archibald 'Lord Alfred' Mills, 7 June 1995.

References

Books and articles

Abu-Lughod, A. (1988) *Veiled Sentiments: Honor and Poetry in a Beduin Society*, London: University of California Press.
Angrosino, M. (1993) 'Dub poetry and West Indian identity', in P. Benson (ed.) *Anthropology and Literature*, Chicago: University of Chicago Press, pp. 73–88.
Anon. (1987a) ' "In Bad Taste" says Hero', feedback letter to the editor, *The Montserrat Reporter*, 23 January 1987, p. 4.
——(1987b) 'M/Rat will get a new calypso monarch', *The Montserrat Reporter*, 23 December 1987, p. 1.
Bakhtin, M. (1984) *Problems of Dostoevsky's Poetics*, ed. C. Emerson, Minneapolis: University of Minnesota Press.
Bauman, R. (1984) *Verbal Art as Performance*, Prospect Heights IL: Waveland Press.
Birth, K. (1994) 'Bakrnal: coup, carnival, and calypso in Trinidad', *Ethnology*, 33(3): 165–77.
Brenneis, D. (1984) 'Straight talk and sweet talk: political discourse in an occasionally egalitarian community', in D. Brenneis and F. Myers (eds) *Dangerous Words: Language and Politics in the Pacific*, New York: New York University Press, pp. 69–84.
——(1987) 'Talk and transformation', *Man*, 22: 499–510.
Burnett, P. (ed.) (1986) 'Introduction', in *The Penguin Book of Caribbean Verse*, London: Penguin, pp. xxiii–lxiv.
Campbell, S. (1988) 'Carnival, calypso, and class struggle in nineteenth century Trinidad', *History Workshop Journal*, 26, Autumn: 1–28.
Cohen, A. (1993) *Masquerade Politics: Explorations in the Structure of Urban Cultural Movements*, Oxford: Berg.
Dewar, A. (1977) 'Music in the Alliouagana (Montserrat) cultural tradition', unpublished M.Phil thesis, Montserrat Public Library.
Edgecombe, D. (1975) 'Night of the invisible artistes', *The Montserrat Mirror*, 10 January, p. 2.
——(1987a) 'Hero reigns again', *The Montserrat Reporter*, 16 January. No other references available.
——(1987b) 'No skin-tight outfit for Hero', *The Montserrat Reporter*, 30 January. No other references available.

——(1987c) 'The case of the suspicious ballots', *The Montserrat Reporter*, 23 October, p. 4.

——(1987d) 'ZJB is not playing Q-Pids song', *The Montserrat Reporter*, 18 December, p. 1.

——(1987e) 'Let Q-Pids song be played', editorial, *The Montserrat Reporter*, 18 December, p. 4.

Edgecombe, D. and Burns, A. (1989) 'Hustler is the new Calypso Monarch', in D. Edgecombe and A. Burns, 'Festival 88 highlights', *The Montserrat Reporter*, 13 January, pp. 6–7.

Edgecombe, D. and Chambers, B. (1988) 'Cepeke is the new Calypso Monarch', *The Montserrat Reporter*, 23 January, p. 12.

Fergus, H. (1992) *Montserrat – Emerald Isle of the Caribbean*, London: Macmillan Caribbean Guides.

——(1994) *Montserrat: History of a Caribbean Colony*, London: Macmillan Caribbean.

Flasher (n.d.) 'The history and evolution of calypso in Montserrat', unpublished lecture, Montserrat Division of Culture, probably by the calypsonian Desmond 'Flasher' Daley.

Galloway, W. (1989) 'Our culture is dying', letter to the editor, *The Montserrat Reporter*, 13 January, p. 5.

Gluckman, M. (1966) *Custom and Conflict in Africa*, Oxford: Blackwell.

Hanley, C. (1984) 'Island studio attracts rock stars', *The Sunday Cape Cod Times*, 5 August, 48.

Hebdige, D. (1990) *Cut 'n' Mix: Culture, Identity and Caribbean Music*, London: Routledge.

Hendry, J. (1993) *Wrapping Culture: Politeness, Presentation, and Power in Japan and Other Societies*, Oxford: Clarendon Press.

Leach, E. (1979) 'Two essays concerning the symbolic representation of time', in W. Lessa and E. Vogt (eds) *Reader in Comparative Religion: An Anthropological Approach*, New York: HarperCollins, pp. 221–9.

Markham, A. (ed.) (1989) 'Random thoughts', in *Hinterland – Caribbean Poetry from the West Indies & Britain*, Newcastle upon Tyne: Bloodaxe, pp. 13–42.

Miller, D. (1994) *Modernity – An Ethnographic Approach: Dualism and Mass Consumption in Trinidad*, Oxford: Berg.

Myers, H. (1980) 'Trinidad and Tobago', in S. Sadie (ed.) *The Newgrove Dictionary of Music and Musicians*, London: Macmillan, pp. 146–50.

Naipaul, V. S. (1971) *Miguel Street*, London: Penguin.

Nevis Culturama Committee (1994) *Nevis Culturama Anniversary Magazine 1974–1994*, Nevis: Nevis Printing Ltd.

Patton, J. (1994) 'Communication and cultural identity through calypso and poetic discourse', *Bulletin of Eastern Caribbean Affairs*, 19(3): 53–68.

Pool, G. (1994) 'Culture, language and revolution in Grenada', *Anthropologica*, XXXXVI(1): 73–107.

Rohlehr, G. (1970) 'Sparrow and the language of calypso', *Savacou*, 2: 88–99.

Schiefflin, E. (1998) 'Problematising performance', in F. Hughes-Freeland (ed.) *Ritual, Performance, Media*, London: Routledge, pp. 194–207.

Searle, C. (1984) *Words Unchained: Language and Revolution in Grenada*, London: Zed Books.

Skinner, J. (1997) 'Impressions of Montserrat: a partial account of contesting realities on a British Dependent Territory', unpublished Ph.D. thesis, St Andrews University, Scotland.

Staff reporter (1987) 'Francis looks inside de box', *The Montserrat Times*, 23 December. No other references available.

Thompson, D. (ed.) (1995) *The Concise Oxford Dictionary*, 9th edn, London: Oxford University Press.

Turner, V. (1974) *Dramas, Fields, and Metaphors: Symbolic Action in Human Society*, New York: Cornell University Press.

——(1979) 'Betwixt and between: the liminal period in *Rites de passage*', in W. Lessa and E. Vogt (eds) *Reader in Comparative Religion: An Anthropological Approach*, New York: HarperCollins, pp. 234–43.

——(1986) 'Dewey, Dilthey, and drama: an essay in the anthropology of experience', in V. Turner and E. Bruner (eds) *The Anthropology of Experience*, Chicago: University of Illinois Press, pp. 33–44.

——(1987) *The Anthropology of Performance*, New York: PAJ.

Warner, K. (1993) 'Ethnicity and the contemporary calypso', in K. Yelvington (ed.) *Trinidad Ethnicity*, Knoxville: University of Tennessee Press, pp. 275–91.

Young, V. (1993) *Becoming West Indian: Culture, Self and Nation in St Vincent*, London: Smithsonian Institution Press.

Music

Arrow (1994) 'Ole Time Calypso Medley', calypso, Alphonsus 'Arrow' Cassell, Montserrat, from *Arrow – Classics*, Plymouth: Montserrat; containing the calypso 'Montserrat Culture' [1974].

Belonger (1988) 'Bring Dem Back', calypso, Pat 'Belonger' Ryan, Montserrat.

——(1989) 'Buy Local', calypso, Pat 'Belonger' Ryan, Montserrat.

Cepeke (1992) 'White Man's World', calypso, Cecil 'Cepeke' Lake, Montserrat.

Cutter (1982) 'Nation', calypso, Ishmael 'Cutter' Skerrit, Montserrat.

Duberry, E. (n.d.) (arranger) *Emeral' City Festival Volume 1*, undated compilation of Montserrat Festival hit songs, Rome, Italy and St Michael, Barbados: Mango Media Organization.

Hero (1986) 'Body-to-Body', calypso, Justin 'Hero' Cassell, Montserrat.

Lord Alfredo (1980) 'Push to the Rear', calypso, Archibald 'Lord Alfredo' Mills, Montserrat.

——(1980) 'Socialism Jam', calypso, Archibald 'Lord Alfredo' Mills, Montserrat.

Lord Kitchener (1968) 'Miss Tourist', calypso, Aldwin 'Lord Kitchener' Roberts, Trinidad.

Mighty Sparrow (1992) 'Wood in the Fire', 'Sell de Pussy', calypsos, Francisco 'Mighty Sparrow' Slinger, Trinidad, in *Mighty Sparrow – Volume Two*, Ice Records. No other references available.

Q-Pid (1985) 'Long Grass', calypso, Herman 'Q-Pid/Cupid' Francis, Montserrat.

——(1987) 'What's Inside the Box', calypso, Herman 'Q-Pid/Cupid' Francis, Montserrat, *The Montserrat Reporter*, 18 December, p. 4.

Rockamaya (1993) 'Montserrat is for Montserratians', calypso, Charles 'Rockamaya' Weekes, Montserrat.

Teknikal (1994) 'A News Dem a Look', calypso, Sean 'Teknikal' Martin, Montserrat.

The Patriot (1982) 'Save this Country', calypso, Lenroy 'The Patriot' Tuitt, Montserrat.

Top Secret (1994) 'Tropical Gal', calypso, Neville 'Top Secret' Greenaway, Montserrat.

Chapter 12

Indirect speech

Heteroglossia, politeness and rudeness in Irula forest festivals

Neil Thin

Introduction

Worship exaggerates politeness, even to the point of caricature. Imaginary entities are flattered in ways that parody the obsequious and pseudo-obsequious behaviour and talk of everyday life. In the effervescent festivity of forest-dwelling Irula people of the Nilgiri mountains in southern India, indirectness in general is both indulged and parodied, and this involves a jumbled complementarity of politeness and rudeness. Politeness phenomena generate and maintain those aspects of 'face' (of deities, people and society) associated with order, hierarchy and social distance. Rudeness generates disorder, equality, and social proximity. There is more to rudeness than the fun and laughter of festive occasions. It is part of the work which, as Parkes has shown (Chapter 14 in this volume), people in relatively and relationally egalitarian 'enclave societies' must put in to counter tendencies towards hierarchy.

In an influential article on ritual language, Tambiah made the broad statement that 'in ritual, language appears to be used in ways that violate the communication function' (1968: 179). If the function of communication were to convey messages by the most efficient means possible, this would be undeniable. Scholars studying conversation have for over twenty years been influenced more than anything else by Grice's notion of the 'co-operative principle', which he assumed to be based on nine maxims which constitute expected norms of conversation (Grice 1975: 45). Following Grice, we would expect people normally to speak truthfully, sincerely and economically, avoiding ambiguity and obscurity – not the kinds of quality we expect in ritual language.

It is not surprising that ritual language is an orgy of maxim-flouting, given that religion more generally flouts maxims of cognition, defying logic, categories, and rationality. But scrutiny of almost any everyday utterance will reveal that in some respects it disobeys Grice's maxims insofar as it does not convey meaning as economically and unambiguously as possible. Austin, who provided the main source of inspiration for Tambiah's analysis of ritual language, has himself been criticised by Bauman for his 'failure ... to recognise that the notion of strictly referential, 'literal' meaning has little, if any, relevance to the use of spoken language in social life' (1984: 50). Ritual language, then, offers a caricature rather than an antithesis of normality.

Based on analysis of fourteen Irula festivals in 1988, I showed in my Ph.D. thesis (Thin 1991) how this festivity, Irula peoples' most important collective activity, mixes formal ritual structure and respectful worship with informal play and versatile disrespect. The playful improvisations in the festival séances offer striking illustration of how sceptical subversion of divinity and formality can be allowed relatively free rein in religious worship. This poses a challenge for the understanding of worship: why would people imagine entities worthy of worship, and then be so rude to them that they question not only their power but even their existence?

Irula festive mockery of deities and of formality differs from the inversions of politeness among the Kalasha people as described by Parkes (Chapter 14 in this volume). Like them, Irulas are an enclave minority in a hierarchical wider society, but for Irulas the term 'egalitarian' would fail to capture the essential ambivalence of their value system. The Irula people are known in India as a 'scheduled tribe' (or *adivasi jati*) – an administrative and folk classification denoting some degree of separation from Hindu caste society by virtue of their long-term residence in inhospitable mountainous forest areas. While Irulas are neither wholly outside the caste system nor 'non-Hindu', they are somewhat separate from mainstream Hindu caste society, and display degrees of independence, egalitarianism and uncertainty about values that are rarely seen in caste society. For Irulas, attitudes to egalitarianism and to the associated values of informality and scepticism are ambivalent and contrapuntal, reflecting their ambivalent attitudes to the perceived values of hierarchy and formality in the Hindu society which encapsulates them but from which they also distinguish themselves.

Though highly egalitarian in practice, following a pattern common to forest peoples in India and elsewhere, Irula people have adopted a ritualised formal veneer of hierarchy, with headmen deriving their legitimacy through association with village and lineage deities, the formal collective worship of which is considered essential to the well-being and constitution of villages and lineages. During worship, the deities, as well as the formal institutions of worship and headmanship, are subjected at times to extreme disrespect and sceptical mockery which occurs within a frame of respectful worship, obedience to the headman, and formality. But both these institutions are (at least in part) dependent on festivity for their existence. Also during worship, séance consultations through spirit-mediums offer indirect ways of debating village politics and of arriving at decisions important to everyday life for individuals and for the community.

Festivals and séances

The festivals described here are organised around worship of a main local deity, usually a goddess, who is associated with a social unit such as a village or a lineage and whose worship is coordinated by the headman-priest, who calls the worshippers together and keeps images and emblems of the deity in his house. The festivals typically last a full day, starting with a summoning of the goddess from within the centre of the village, followed by a lengthy excursion into the forest and often up a hill, then several hours of sporadic worship involving vegetarian offerings, at least one lengthy séance, sacrifice of goats and chickens, offering and collective consumption of a cooked meat meal, and finally a return to the priest-headman's house in the village and concluding vegetarian offering.

Festivals always include at least one séance at which a spirit-medium, sometimes several in series, induces in himself (aided by the manipulation of ritual symbols and by vocal support of bystanders) a state of trance in which occult entities enter his body, speak through him and hold heated discussions with worshippers. The ideal spirit-medium is an affine of the priest, i.e. not of the priest's lineage and preferably from a different village too. It is also important that the medium is selected in an apparently ad hoc way and with a show of resistance by an unwilling medium. This selection process also would make it hard for anyone to use mediumship to further their own political ends. Mediumship is thus systematically contrasted with priesthood in terms of kinship, residence and formality/informality, much as the séance itself, unpredictable and chaotic, is contrastable with the encompassing formal ritual.

Possession requires noisy assistance by a crowd of shouting onlookers, and may take a long time to happen, but when it does it is announced suddenly with a dramatic display of shaking, hissing, bellowing, stumbling around and self-flagellation. Musicians play to accompany this irregular movement, until the medium raises an arm to silence them and begin the séance. Sometimes also the medium's possession may for some time be echoed by more peripheral possession-trance, typically involving women and young men who are temporarily possessed but don't speak.

The séance discussions may last up to a couple of hours, punctuated into what might be called 'chapters' and shorter 'verses', each with a different theme. These are divided up by interludes in which the medium takes a break from talking and returns to paralinguistic shouting and throwing himself around. Sometimes a 'client' – an individual whose problems have been discussed – shakes the medium's hand and/or prostrates themselves in worship, indicating that some kind of argument or negotiation has been resolved. Usually the first client is the priest-headman, and the discussion may concern the relationship between all of the worshipping group and the goddess, or may primarily concern the priest-headman as an individual.

Indirectness, ambiguity, and deceit

A séance is a special kind of linguistic event or frame, offering unique opportunities and challenges for the study of linguistic strategies and for the interpretation of ritual. While allowing relatively non-intrusive, non-interventionist observation of linguistic phenomena, séances pose peculiar challenges for interpretation because of the numerous and compounded ambiguities of both the content and the frame. Elaborately wrapped in multiple quotes, the séance is a heteroglot babble in diverse codes.

The following forms of indirectness are particularly striking in Irula séances:

- speaking to an imaginary and generalised addressee (the deity, etc.) whose identity is not clearly ascertained, thereby rendering ambiguous the speaker/addressee relationship;
- articulating (through mediumship) and listening to the voices of imaginary speakers, thereby displacing and denying authorship of utterances;
- referring vaguely or ambiguously to human referents (e.g. as 'some child or other' or 'that child');
- using elaborate metaphors which can be interpreted, with varying degrees of ambiguity, as commentaries on relationships, livelihoods, well-being and philosophy;
- making thinly veiled insults by using irony and disrespectful terms of address and reference;
- paradoxically portraying solidarity with deities through versatile displays of joking disrespect.

Addressing an imaginary addressee is the verbal equivalent of feeding an inanimate entity. Both are common worldwide in children's play, in psychotic behaviour, and in worship. Both are essentially ambiguous, articulating doubts about what constitutes a 'real' relationship, and questioning the boundary of the self. In various ways Irula people reveal their acknowledgement that the practice of talking to imaginary beings through mediums can be seen as absurd. Articulation of these doubts takes various forms. The truth of utterances, and of specific instances of possession, is questioned during and after the performance, and an entire séance can be dismissed as a sham. Also questioned – and rarely answered unambiguously – is the identity of the voices that speak through the medium: the medium is at times like an ill tuned radio, with numerous voices being received during the same event, leaving bystanders to guess who it may be. Many festival participants simply ignore the séance, and many deny its ritual importance. Bystanders occasionally disrupt the proceedings with jocular comments, and it is not uncommon for drunken parodies of spirit-possession to cause sufficient hilarity to put an end to the proceedings.

The séance offers a complex parody of communication, and particularly of indirectness. This is underlined by the ambiguities of the authors', speakers' and addressees' identities. It is never clear who is speaking, who is being quoted, or who is being addressed. In contrast with other séances in southern India, Irula séances are often followed through with no precise identification of the speaker. Many bystanders appear to care little whether it is a goddess or an ancestor or a roaming spirit that is speaking, while others may entertain contradictory assumptions about who is speaking.

Indeed, uncertainty of the speaker's identity in séance discussions is empha-sised by both worshippers and the medium, in such phrases as 'I don't care whether you're a goddess or an ancestor or a spirit', and 'whoever you may be'. Terms of address also reveal ambiguity: the medium often addresses the client as 'father-child', and both are likely to address each other using both familiar and respectful terms of address in the same utterance.

The drunken parodies mentioned above point to common ground between mediumship and inebriation. Drunkenness itself is a form of indirec-tion which is closely analogous to trance-mediumship as a strategy for allowing the voice of unreason to speak under the licence of inebriation. Another example is offered by Van der Walde's discussion of hypnosis as an institutionalised shifting of authorship (1968: 62).

More fundamentally still, séance debates include frequent references to the potential deceitfulness of the medium or the voices. This and the drunken parodies of spirit-possession imbues the whole festival with a tension between illusion and reality. Trust and transparency are not on the menu.

When a séance begins, the voices from beyond tend to talk evasively in parables, riddles and paradoxes, and people reciprocate by talking in vaguely allusive terms of their troubles. Both parties frequently accuse one another of telling lies:

Client   No-one's to tell me anything, I don't want any deities, it's all lies! You're just testing me out, why bother? Just tell me what deity has been bringing me down for so long.
Medium   So am I supposed to humble myself to you only?
Client   Then why did you tell me lies when you came to my veranda?
Medium   If I was lying then, am I lying again now?
Bystander He thinks the whole lot is just lies, so don't bother talking to him. Just give us some answers to our questions and we'll go.

The Irula term for the séance is *jaaya*, a term which has no other referent and which refers both to the event, the form of talk, and its contents. A contrasted term for another form of talk is *naaya*, which refers variously to any kind of negotiation, particularly talk aimed at publicly resolving a dispute, and to truth and justice. In *jaaya* talk, all parties, particularly the various enti-ties speaking through the medium, are likely to be obscure and ambiguous at best if not downright deceitful. Exceptionally, when a goddess, for example, has said something that is reasonable and comprehensible, people will say 'adu naaya' – 'that's true'. The implication is that whereas *naaya* as a form of talk presumes a rational progression towards agreement and truth, *jaaya* presumes no such thing but revels in obscurities and untruths which are not usually resolved.

Uncertainty and ambiguity are referred to in such utterances by the medium as 'I don't care whether you think I'm lying or telling the truth' or 'I could be lying, I could be telling the truth.' Generally, the séance is replete with metacommunication – explicit or implicit discussion about features of the communicative event. A favourite image used in séance discussions to refer to the link between humans and divine beings is the path to the temple, which like the séance dialogue offers a link, but a difficult one which needs to be cleared of thorns and branches. The path and the séance dialogue simultaneously show both the possibility of human-divine linkage and the tenuousness of it, and the ultimate separation of humans from the spirit world. There are always hints that the link may be illusory, and it is not surprising that worshippers often wonder whether dreams may be a more reliable way of communicating with deities and ancestors. Individuals who brought an offering to the temple often told me that they had been instructed to do so in a dream rather than in a séance, and it is clear that communication in dreams, elusive though it maybe, is not necessarily any less reliable than séance communication:

Medium   Bring your piles of offerings, bring lorry-loads, I don't give a damn whether you do or not. That's just what the rules are.
Client   You should tell us in dreams what those rules are.
Medium   I'll tell you now. You don't need dreams or any nonsense like that.

Like the dream, the séance expresses a dilemma: it's good to talk with spirits, but the conversation will be plagued with insincerity or incomprehensibility, and promises may not come true. The entire rite is ambiguous – entertaining and playful, but also deadly serious. There are life-and-death issues at stake, and amid all the joking there is serious business to transact:

Medium   Are you playing games with me? I'll show you here and now, I'll bring witnesses.
Client   Why would I want to play games?

Arbitration, code and privacy

An obvious hypothesis about the reason for the existence of the séance is that it facilitates indirect airing and arbitration of disputes which are too socially sensitive to discuss directly. Perhaps so, but this function is explicitly denied by frequent reminders that worshippers should not hold festivals until they have resolved all their disputes. Still, there are hints in séance discussions that deities may be expected to arbitrate and resolve disputes:

Medium   Whatever the problem may be, I'll look at it from all points of view, so all you need to do is say the word.
Client   You must only listen if it's true. Say that's right.
Medium   I'm the one who'll show you.
Priest   And what if you don't?
Bystander You'll see no-one in any of your temples.
Medium   If you people have any arguments, don't bother coming to this temple next year.

In this instance, the phrase 'don't bother coming' looks less like a prohibition than an insistence that if the deity fails to solve disputes, humans need not reciprocate by coming for worship.

Ancestors, too, are explicitly associated in séances with dispute settlement and the maintenance of social order. Worshippers frequently respond to deities' and/or ancestors' accusations of laxity by saying 'you need to tell us the rules'. Sometimes the ritual cutting of coconuts, goats, and chickens that are offered to deities and ancestors are linked with the divine/ancestral role of dispute settlement:

Medium   As soon as a dispute breaks out, we break it apart for you, don't we? We don't want any arguments, any quarrelling or any fuss. Just as you break things for us [make offerings] we break things up [solve disputes] for you.

There are occasions when people become possessed as a political manoeuvre. When this is done too blatantly, however, either the séance will simply be stopped, or its content will be dismissed as 'lies' (*poyyi jaaya*) – as, for instance, when an Irula man used the local goddess festival on the tea estate as an opportunity to demand higher wages.

Unlike the relatively simple séance quotations reproduced here, many of the séance utterances are heavily encoded and require convoluted explanations of both specific and more subtle semantic resonances. Most participants in Irula séances understand little of what is being said, and many utterances are the verbal equivalent of abstract art. Specific clients can hold private discussion with a deity in public, in a code which only they can understand – or at least pretend to do so. Also, since the priest-headman is always on hand offering occasional interpretive suggestions and helping out when the discussion becomes wayward, code offers an opportunity for the priest-headman to display his special relationship with the deity.

Long-standing quarrels are a favourite séance topic, grievances being aired in public but indirectly, and unspecified people accused of occult aggression through witchcraft or deities:

Client   Does this trouble come from my wife's side, or if not my wife's side, then has somebody else set a deity against me? … does that deity belong to my wife's side or to somebody else?

Medium   Look here, that's not good enough, you've been saying one thing to your wife, you've been saying another thing to your own children, and something else again to your cross-relatives, and you've confused me.

Although I witnessed many similar discussions, most were in vaguer and more indirectly allusive terms than this, with specific kin categories rarely mentioned and individuals never specified by name. Indeed, the degree of required indirection is policed by the bystanders: when particular quarrels are more than vaguely alluded to – as does happen from time to time – anyone introducing such a topic too blatantly will be interrupted. On two occasions I witnessed a séance being stopped when this happened.

In general, then, the séance dialogue expresses a variety of uncertainties about personal relationships, ranging from the vague expression of doubt about the goodwill of consanguines and affines, to the thinly veiled public criticism about the anti-social behaviour of a particular relative. Instead of the psychobabble in which people in post-1960s Western countries discuss one another's personalities, Irulas strive to articulate personalities and personal relationships in the language of ill-will and occult struggles. Vague expression of uncertainties can be cathartic, but open discussion of arguments is likely to lead to more arguments. And open arguments between humans have no legitimate place in the Irula festival.

Insults, proximity, and 'face'

Irula worship calls into question the common assumption that worship is all about reverence towards superior divine beings. Irulas insult their deities during séances, using an impressive repertoire of swear-words and insulting epithets, addressing them with familiar rather than respectful pronouns, and employing heavy irony in pseudo-respectful addresses. They also criticise their deities' poor sense of justice and their dishonourable conduct in human-divine transactions, they mock at their powerlessness vis-à-vis other deities and spirits, remind them of their dependence on human worshippers (for food, attention, status, and earthly habitation and form), and even question their existence. All of this is a normal part of their worship, not just deviant and tangential behaviour.

On one occasion, when the deity had threatened to withhold rain as a punishment for a poor turnout at the festival, the priest-headman upbraided him for such an unjust intention:

Priest   Look here, they [these worshippers] came and fell at your feet, didn't they? Can't you send rain to their gardens only? You show us. … Get your umbrella and prevent the rain from falling on the gardens of those who didn't come.

Hearing this, the worshippers' laughter made it clear that they interpreted this as a heavily ironic request: of course the deity isn't clever enough to deal out such selective punishments to wrong-doers. This is a logical inversion of the kind of politeness strategy discussed by Brown and Levinson (1987). In a politeness strategy, you exaggerate an addressee's benevolence and power by disguising a request as a question with an implied 'no' answer: 'You couldn't possibly pass the salt, could you?' As Robin Lakoff puts it (1973: 297), being polite involves making the addressee 'feel good'. By contrast, the above example looks like a rudeness strategy designed to make the (imaginary) addressee feel bad: a request is made which the requester knows perfectly well the addressee can't comply with.

A more widespread use of irony in séances is the subversion of the respect that worshippers formally show to deities, as in the following exchange:

Medium   You can't ever fool me. I've got a thousand eyes, and you've only got two.
Client   Right! Can a two-eyed man answer a thousand-eyed woman? No indeed!

Deities are frequently reminded in séances of their dependence on human worshippers, as in the following exchange, where the goddess' bombast is deflated with a typically cutting remark:

Client   He must roll [i.e. the (imaginary?) enemy must be killed] within eight days.
Medium   If I am the thousand-eyed goddess, if I'm the one who makes a thousand districts dance, I'll cut him to ribbons.
Bystander Otherwise there'll be no-one following you, we'll just tell you to bugger off.

Subversive joking during the rite is not simply there as a prelude to a return to seriousness and humility. Often, the goddess may be sent on her way with a parting insult. On one occasion, the medium ended a séance with the grandiose statement: 'I must go and join all my people'. This was responded to with merciless derision: 'Yes, it's about time too. We humans are all bored stiff'. Someone else joined in with a comment on how little had been achieved by the séance:

Bystander 'Just put up with whatever storm comes your way', that's all they said. What big rules they talked about. What a shit-awful séance.
Priest   Saami, if you've any other grudges, then say so, otherwise [let the medium] get up, what's the point in boring us with the same old stuff?

So what does the jocular, even abusive style of séances tell us about how Irulas characterise their deities? The deity is someone who is close enough to people to share a joke with them, and on equal enough terms to be poked fun at. There is, of course, a vital ambivalence in acts of jocular irreverence: to test someone out with a bit of cheek is to force that person either to cross the threshold into the in-group or stay with the out-group, those who can't be joked with. To insult can be a form of friendliness, whereby speakers assure addressees that they are 'of the same kind', as Brown and Levinson put it (1987: 71–2).

Euphemistic flattery paradoxically insults the deity with its ironic hyperbole, but inversely the ritual invective of Irula séances paradoxically flatters the deity by portraying her as an in-group member. Deities are addressed in familiar terms, yet honorifics are consistently used in Irula conversation between members of the opposite moiety. Irulas put their deities firmly in the familiar we-group at the same time as subverting the normal superiority of the deity by using irony, rhetoric, and the deliberate manipulation of ambiguity. The sociology of religion elsewhere tends to show, by contrast, that in religious dialogue it is generally deities (or mediums who speak for them) and religious leaders who are allowed to use the ambiguous and abstruse language of parables, and that devotees and disciples are not expected to reciprocate in a style other than the straightforward confession of faith.

In Irula séances, the deity uses complex metaphors whose meaning the hearer has to work out. This would be consistent with an assumption that the deity is superior to, more powerful than, the worshippers. But this is subverted by the almost continual use of heavy irony on the part of those addressing the deity. People are constantly trying to out manipulate the deity in the game of forcing implicatures. This implies that it is in fact humans that are more powerful, because they can get away with using irony.

Goffman's analysis of 'face-work' (1972: 12ff.) points the way towards understanding the linguistic strategies that respond to the need, throughout all everyday interpersonal encounters, to 'save face' (our own and that of others). The kinds of cooperation involved in the maintenance of 'face' are encapsulated in Brown and Levinson's all-embracing term 'politeness' (1987), which provides a coherent framework for showing how relationships are linguistically constructed and maintained. As a theoretical rather than normative concept, politeness is concerned with impolite behaviour too. Brown and Levinson assume that the best way to 'make sense' of conversation is to assume that participants are 'rational face-bearing agents' (1987: 58). Grice's discussion of 'conversational implicature' likewise emphasises that assumptions have to be made about rationality and cooperation if conversation is to make sense despite apparent oddities (1975: 43ff.).

It would be rash to assume *a priori* that Irulas regard their deity as a 'rational face-bearing agent'. Indeed, such an assumption about relations between people seems unwarranted. A major difficulty with the Gricean conversational maxims is that it is quite unclear whether there is such a thing as a template of rationality from which utterances might be said to deviate. Grice (1975: 45) evasively assures us that his 'cooperative principle' is observed '*ceteris paribus*'. He thus side-steps altogether the question of whether other things ever are equal – whether, that is, there is is some baseline vantage-point of normal conversational cooperation from which people come to understand conversational deviance. At any rate, all of the maxims which go together to form the cooperative principle are flouted repeatedly throughout the Irula séance.

Séances usually involve public humiliation of both the deity and the priest-headman. The latter is done indirectly through the spirit-medium and never with direct insults. In terms of Brown and Levinson's theory of the performance of 'face-threatening acts', the act of becoming possessed is a linguistic strategy which allows the medium to criticise publicly the headman or anyone else in the village while at the same time saving face by making the goddess do the criticising. Since mediumship is not a hereditary role, and since it is usually not the priest-headman who acts as medium, the séance is itself potentially a subversive act. Should anyone want to make public criticisms without seeming to do so, this is obviously the way to do it.

More generally, the priest-headman publicly affirms his own dependence on mass support indirectly, with frequent reminders that deities only turn out for festivals if there's a good crowd. A gesture of humility before the deity is also a gesture of humility before the crowd of participants, as is the gesture made in public avowal of repentance at a village council. Durkheim's 'god-is-society' formula may be vague, reductionist and overgeneralised, but the Irula deity constitutes a fairly fundamental social process to the extent that she facilitates transactions (linguistic or material) between humans while minimising threats to the face of the transactors. In séances, the deity facilitates negotiation and theorising of relationships in a fairly safe frame, in which inter-personal hostility is kept in check by laughter and by the shifting of responsibility for actions or utterances.

Séances might also be said to insult the formal institutions of worship, through cynical questioning of whether tangible offerings and structured acts of worship achieve any influence over divine grace. This warns us of the danger inherent in two assumptions which have been dominant in the analysis of religion:

- that ritual acts are 'rational' because the practitioner believes them to be efficacious;
- that they thereby give the practitioner confidence.

If the formal acts of Irula worship indicate a belief and confidence in the efficacy of human–divine transactions, séance discussions remind us that sceptical subversion is never far away (i.e. Irulas recognise the irrationality of ritual), and that Irulas are far from confident either about their deities' power or about the efficacy of worship. The séance is a licentious frame within a more formal frame of reverential worship, which allows contrapuntal and even iconoclastic subversion. Icons are illusions – symbols which stand for something else – and if the subversive irony, the exaggerated flattery, and the outright obscenities hurled at the deity do not actually smash the illusions that are created by reverential worship, they certainly remind participants of the value of questioning the icons they worship.

My own interpretive hunch about this is that Irula people are doubtful about the value of formal ritual officiated by specialist priests. They employ such a structure in emulation of higher castes, but feel the need to poke fun at it in the ritualised humiliation of the séances.

Divinity, worship and society

Durkheim would have loved the Irula word *toga*, which means 'deity', 'assembly' and 'festival'. He would particularly have liked the phrase for worship, which is *toga maaDugeemu* – 'we make/do the god/festival', which hints that Irulas share Durkheim's understanding that god is (in part) a euphemism for society. Irula worship, particularly the séances, repeatedly emphasises the close association and mutual interdependence of deities and human congregations. The deity will not appear without vociferous calls in unison from a crowd of worshippers, and a deity who fails to ensure the well being of the village can be threatened with dismissal. Séance conversations with deities allow indirect commentaries on general as well as specific aspects of relations among humans and the fabric of society.

Criticisms of Durkheim's reductionism are justified (there is surely a great deal more to divinity than the personification of society), but he did provide an important explanation of the process whereby collective worship generates and expresses emotional attachments of individuals to groups. This is fundamental to the sociology of religion. Equally fundamental is the acknowledgement, at least implicit in Irula theology, that deities are created by acts of worship and dependent on them for their periodic regeneration.

Irula worship shares with all worship the property of indirectness whereby something is expressed about oneself or one's society via the invented concept of an invisible divine entity. In psychological terms, worship brings to mind G. H. Mead's (1934) theory of the indirect processes whereby individuals come to understandings of themselves by 'taking the role of the other'. By extension, the community seeks an understanding of itself by invoking and worshipping an imagined other, much as a child does with an imaginary friend or enemy. In spatial terms, the whole festival involves strategic dislocation and relocation: the worshipping community returns to a new sense of its own social centre – the village – by detour of the forest. The festival is an *excursion* in the full etymological sense.

The dominant motif in the negotiations of the séances is the question of justice or injustice of divine retributions and rewards, and this facilitates commentary on the relationship of the individual to society. Since some divine punishments (drought, theft of domestic stock by wild animals) fall on the just and the unjust alike, and since these punishments are related to human morality, evidently the misdemeanours of individuals are of concern to the collectivity.

Although superficially the deity may be blamed for treating sinners and the righteous indiscriminately, it is also the fault of the headman if he fails to bring the ungodly to the temple. The séance often begins with a complaint by the deity about poor attendance, and this is countered by a complaint from the headman–priest that it is up to the deity to ensure good attendance:

Medium   You've been thinking about this and preparing for a long time. Will they come? Will they not come? Have I only got two children? Won't anyone else come?

Priest   That's what you have to think if you lack people. Who is there to support us? It'll only work if there's a reasonable number of people. ... So are we to blame you, or blame the villagers? ... Are you going to give a good word or a bad word to those who've come? ... I'm the one who'll control the village. You're the one who must see to that.

There is nothing particularly complicated or surprising in discussions like these. Two questions are expressed and left ambiguous: whether it is up to the deity or the headman to bring people to the temple, and whether the misdemeanours of the individual are the concern of that individual or of the collectivity.

In Irula society, which is formally hierarchical and role-centred but informally egalitarian and person-centred, such questions cannot be unambiguously answered. Formally, the headman is responsible for everyone's correct behaviour and temple attendance, and relationships with the deity are mediated through the priest-headman. But informally, it is up to individuals to act as they see fit, and they are therefore directly answerable to the deity. So the issue of temple attendance must simply be expressed as a miasma of ambiguities and dilemmas.

What is portrayed in séance debates, then, is a qualified version of the individual-oriented morality of more isolated forest peoples of southern India like Paliyans, among whom 'individuals rather than the group create order' (Gardner 1988: 439) or Chenchus, who

> have no belief in collective responsibility, nor do they believe in the polluting effect of deviant behaviour. In their view every individual is only responsible for his own actions, and a man's misdeed cannot jeopardize the well-being of his kinsmen or neighbours.
>
> (Fürer-Haimendorf 1967: 21)

and in whose view 'divine injunctions do not, on the whole, refer to social relations, deity is appealed to for practical assistance only' (ibid.: 23).

The point of crooked talk

Let us not over-emphasise the search for a 'point' to Irula festivity in general or to the indirections of the séances in particular. Though it would be absurd to say that intentions are absent from Irula festivity, we must recognise the importance of escapism and entertainment in festivity. We should not shy away from ludo-theology and the anthropology of fun in over-zealous pursuit of more functionalist interpretations. Perhaps the most important lesson I learned during many months of trying to extract exegesis of séance discussions from Irulas, was that for the most part, the idea of *post hoc* interpretation seemed pointless to them. They might as well have quoted Northrop Frye at me:

> A poet's intention ... is directed towards putting words together, not towards aligning words with meanings. ... What the poet meant to say, then, is, literally, the poem itself.
>
> (Frye 1957: 86–7)

The séance dialogue would be of little interest to the analyst or to the participant, were it not full of puzzling ambiguities and thought-provoking contradictions in the presentation of the character of the divine. As we saw earlier, the deity is precisely *not* a single coherent person, but a multiplicity of metaphors or, to use the language of postmodern literature, a multiplicity of *voices*. These voices are often mutually contradictory. Considered as a game, the séance consists in the competitive manipulation of ambiguous identity.

Defying Fortes' assumption that people tend to communicate with ancestors via tangible offerings rather than talk because 'there can be no dialogue and no appeal to reality' (1976: 10), the Irula séance affirms the possibility of communicating with all spiritual beings in a real dialogue. Spiritual beings answer prayers with words as well as actions. Verbal communication is sometimes explicitly said to be more effective than communicating with ritual symbols:

Priest   If you can't understand what we're saying, do you expect the banana leaves [i.e. the ritual food offering] to say it any more clearly?

This is a cunningly ambiguous reference to the two uses of banana leaves in ritual − as the plate on which offerings are made, and as a gag which the priest, during offerings, must keep stuffed in his mouth. This allusion to the difficulties that humans have in communicating with divine or spiritual beings through words or objects is a favourite topic in Irula séances.

Irulas are well aware that conversations with deities, like conversations among people, involve what Rapport (Chapter 1 in this volume) calls 'miscommunication'. But this ethnography questions Rapport's assumption that miscommunication results from imperfect translation between private selves via the medium of publicity. We should not assume that people communicate, inadequately, in order to transfer information and generate agreement and understanding. Nor, *pace* Turner, do they use symbols, metaphors and other forms of indirection only as 'parsimonious' devices for expression of difficult topics (1967: 26). People need entertainment, and for this purpose ambiguity, indirection, bafflement, and the avoidance of mundane obviousness are essential ludic strategies.

Parables, metaphors and elaborate or obscure ritual language are great fun for the anthropologist to unravel. But whether we see purpose or purposelessness in Irula séances, and whether we assume that their aim is to communicate with the spirit world or to communicate with people and above all to resolve arguments, the same question must be answered: why do Irulas not discuss things in a more straightforward manner? For the analysis of the séances I have described, each of the following reasons is valid:

1   *Elaboration as entertainment* Linguistic elaboration is indulged in for the sake of entertainment; the séance could thus be seen as the linguistic corollary of the deliberate construction of obstacles and adversaries which we so often find in play and ritual. Since a major aim of the festival is to entertain rather than to solve problems, the central debate over human misfortune and divine assistance is elaborated in linguistic play. The repetitiveness of the séance dialogue is a paradoxical kind of obliqueness: the redundancy of ritual utterances should make us acknowledge that they may be being used without reference, uttered simply for the sake of the utterance, for the pure pleasure of making noises.

2   *Heuristic device* 'By indirections find directions out' (*Hamlet*). Discussion in parables is a heuristic device which makes the content of the discussion, once unravelled and understood, more memorable (this was the explanation Christ gave for his own use of parables). The obscurity of the language involves the audience as participants in the construction of meaning.

3   *Mnemonic device* Typical of oral tradition (parallelism). The use of semi-scripted abnormal speech is a mnemonic device which enables the rules of how to communicate with non-human beings to be passed down intact through the generations. This has often been noted with reference to oral literature, where rhyme, rhythm, parallelism of ideas and conventional metaphors all serve as devices for minimising alteration as myths, epics, poems and songs are passed on orally. In *The Singer of Tales*, Lord also observes that this style is in part a function of the instability and variability of the audience, and the performer's need to keep their attention while not losing a grip himself (1968: 16); this explanation would certainly fit for the constantly fluctuating group of Irulas who listen to the medium.

4   *Indirectness is a politeness strategy* used by both deities and humans alike, aimed at saving the face of both hearers and speakers.

5   *Privacy* Discussion in obscure language keeps the meaning of a public discussion at least partially private; the full meaning is only available to the person discussing with the medium. Like jokes, parables function to include and to collude with the in-group (those able and willing to participate in the unravelling process), and to exclude the out-group (those unable and/or unwilling to unravel meaning from the utterances).

6   *Polyvalency* Communication in parables and in difficult language allows for a variety of interpretations, not all of which will suit the requirements of the hearer. It encourages the audience to participate in the construction of meaning rather than passively accepting meaning which is forced on them.

7   *Multivocality* Communication in parables produces a multivocality which gives evidence of the multiple authors of the séance (the goddess, spirits, the medium, the headman, the players whose complaints are being voiced) and addresses the multiple listeners simultaneously (the client, the interested listeners, the relatively disinterested witnesses, the anthropologist).

8   *Medium as message* Obscurity and ambiguity convey the message that the human-divine link is difficult and elusive, dramatising relationships with the tensions of misunderstanding while sometimes allowing worshippers the satisfaction of feeling close to the deity by having understood one of her metaphors. The heteroglossia of the séance conveys the elusiveness of the deity by the bewildering variety of frames in which communication takes place. It is possible to identify both direct and reported speech, as

well as unacknowledged mimicry (presence and absence of quotation marks), metaphor and simile, a variety of dialects, seriousness, joking, anger, friendship, proximity and distance.

References

Bakhtin, Mikhail (1968) [1965] *Rabelais and His World*, trans. Helene Iswolsky, Cambridge MA: MIT Press.

Bauman, Richard (1984) [1977] *Verbal Art as Performance*, Prospect Heights IL: Waveland Press (reproduced from *American Anthropologist*, 77(2): 290–311).

Brown, Penelope and Levinson, Steven (1987) [1978] *Politeness: Some Universals in Language Use*, Cambridge: Cambridge University Press.

Elwin, Verrier (1955) *The Religion of an Indian Tribe*, Oxford: Oxford University Press.

Fortes, Meyer (1976) 'An introductory commentary,' in William H. Newell (ed.) *Ancestors*, The Hague: Mouton, pp. 1–17.

Frye, C. Northrop (1957) *Anatomy of Criticism: Four Essays*, Princeton: Princeton University Press.

Fürer-Haimendorf, Christoph von (1943) *The Chenchus: Jungle Folk of the Deccan*, London: Macmillan.

Gardner, Peter M. (1988) [1972] 'The Paliyans', in M. G. Bicchieri (ed.) *Hunters and Gatherers Today*, Prospect Heights IL: Waveland Press, pp. 404–47.

Goffman, Erving (1972) [1967] *Interaction Ritual: Essays on Face to Face Behaviour*, New York: Doubleday (Anchor Books).

Grice, H. P. (1975) 'Logic and conversation', in P. Cole and J. L. Morgan (eds) *Syntax and Semantics: Speech Acts*, vol. 3, New York: Academic Press, pp. 41–58.

Lakoff, Robin T. (1973) 'The logic of politeness: or, minding your p's and q's', *Papers from the Ninth Regional meeting of the Chicago Linguistic Society*, Chicago, pp. 292–305.

Lord, Albert B. (1968) *The Singer of Tales*, Cambridge MA: Harvard University Press.

Mead, George H. (1934) *Mind, Self and Society*, Chicago: University of Chicago Press.

Tambiah, Stanley J. (1968) 'The magical power of words', *Man* (n.s.) 3: 175–208.

Thin, Neil (1991) 'High spirits and heteroglossia: forest festivals of the Nilgiri Irulas', Ph.D. thesis, University of Edinburgh.

Turner, Victor W. (1967) *The Forest of Symbols*, Ithaca NY: Cornell University Press.

Van der Walde, Peter H. (1968) 'Trance states and ego psychology', in Raymond Prince (ed.) *Trance and Possession States*, Montreal: R. M. Bucke Memorial Society, pp. 57–68.

Chapter 13

Straight talk, hidden talk and modernity

Shifts in discourse strategy in Highland New Guinea

Lisette Josephides

In a recent visit to the field I couldn't help noticing that many Kewa people often equated their rich and flexible communicative practices, which were based on a form of indirection, with deceit and tradition, while they associated straight, direct talk with modernity. During one dispute, Simon, the local Evangelical Church of Papua pastor, interrupted the debate with these words:

> This is the sort of talk that will consign us to the flames. God is not happy with the way we talk, we say the same thing over and over again. We don't express ourselves clearly and truthfully. Lisette and Marc [the anthropologists] are waiting to hear the real point of our talk, but instead you talk rubbish. We are a really rubbishy clan. Others in Papua New Guinea have learned good ways, but you carry on with this rubbishy talk. Lisette and Marc know we are just wasting time, repeating the same bad arguments. White people don't waste time like this.

Conciseness, economy of speech, simplicity, and directness are here presented as values, veiled speech as deceptive and repetition as a waste of time. Even allowing for the possibility that Simon was influenced by the presence of the anthropologists, his speech nonetheless revealed a real perception of differentially evaluated communicative styles, one associated with tradition and the other with modernity. In this essay I begin with an examination of traditional Kewa language use and the pragmatics of speaking, particularly as expressed through indirection, then I consider local perceptions that different lifestyles require different communicative practices.[1]

Eliciting talk: veiled and direct speech[2]

In common with any other people, Kewa use language both propositionally and rhetorically. Joy Hendry (1989) describes the Japanese 'wrapping' principle as a linguistic feature which extends into the material and spatial world. Among the Kewa, metonymic substitution and metaphor replace wrapping, and something stands for something else without necessarily containing it. Kewa speakers extend these linguistic practices into Tok Pisin, the Papua New Guinea lingua franca, revealing them to be pragmatic aspects of their language use rather than intrinsic features of the Kewa language.[3] The broadest feature of Kewa language use is 'eliciting talk', a form of indirection that consists in a disguised negotiation of meaning. The use of *siapi*, a 'veiled' speech based on metaphor, openly signals this negotiability.[4] Less obviously, in apparently direct talk speakers may also advance opinions or claims which they are ready to modify at the sign of strong opposition.[5]

Siapi ('to put', 'as on a shelf', people explained) was not just an alternative language, understood by all who had been initiated into it, but a metaphorical use of language whose meaning had to be worked out on the occasion of the speech event itself. It was a way of negotiating meaning and of signalling unexpressed intentions and desires, rather than a secret code or polite, face-saving formula (Brown and Levinson 1987). Siapi was also the formalised language of ritual, courting songs and dirges, political oratory, and ceremonial exchanges at pig kills. Formalisation did not, however, result in the restriction of political options or a diminution of the potential for communication (Bloch 1989). As in the case of the Wana of Indonesia (Atkinson 1984), coercion was inappropriate in the general Kewa context of fierce male egalitarianism, competitively achieved status, and fragile political relations and influence. Yet Kewa men did not as a result develop the seductive, flirtatious ways of speaking which Atkinson describes for the Wana (1984: 59). Kewa men are far less concerned with not giving offence by the use of strong words, especially in the initial interaction, and their aggressively confident claims are more in line with the flamboyant swagger of warriors of the previous generation, before the onset of colonial pacification. Unlike the Chinese, who 'first establish a shared context, then provide the relevant details and finally make a request' (Hendry 1989: 631), Kewa put the cart before the horse, hoping that the force of their claim will conjure up a horse (or a shared context) in the listener's imagination. A Kewa big man, after all, was successful to the extent that he could convince others that his interests and point of view coincided with those of the whole clan (Josephides 1985).

Competitive male egalitarianism was offset by another culturally salient feature: gender asymmetry and female exclusion from prestigious ceremonial activities. Though siapi was the language of formal political interaction, it was also a basic linguistic form used by everyone. Unlike *kiyori*, by means of which Wana created political relations (Atkinson 1984), siapi was not a specialised genre denied to women. Kewa women were not debarred from creating political relations because they did not use siapi, but because they were excluded from the political arenas in which siapi was the main mode of linguistic interaction.

Nonetheless, women made less use of siapi than men did. In everyday exchanges women tended to speak more plainly, both to each other and to men, and their statements rarely gave rise to debates over their meaning, as in the case of the faintly menacing men-to-men retorts. This is not to say that women made no use of indirection, only that it was in the form of metonymic substitution. While siapi is metaphoric speech which invites inter-pretation and signals the possibility of negotiation, metonymic utterances are delivered in apparently direct talk but nonetheless leave the door wide open for complete withdrawal. That women often do not avail themselves of this escape route is indicative of female tactics in general, and is a cautionary reminder that readiness and ability to negotiate are not always present. Brothers locked in disputes over the fairness of exchanges continue to main-tain the spirit of negotiability while they scrape the depths of bathos, but feuding cowives see no room for negotiation or space to backtrack, their words are stinging arrows laced with the bile of their own frustrated claims or desires. They know that they are fighting for their place in the social world.

Yet the mere fact that feuding wives were talking kept them on the side of creative sociality. Direct talk could never entirely block all avenues for compromise. Hiding talk, on the other hand, repressed grudges, a practice considered to make people sick or even kill them. Speaking in veiled form created a sort of information exchange forum for negotiating meaning, as well as of signalling unexpressed intentions and desires. Most interactions combined elements of these different communicative strategies, as the following incident illustrates.

> Rimbu's house was becoming overcrowded. In addition to himself, his wife and five children, the following were staying there: his brother's wife-to-be, her child and her mother, and Ragunanu, an old woman married to the most senior clan member living in a neighbouring settle-ment. Ragunanu moved to Rimbu's house when she changed church affiliation and had differences with her husband and his son. One day Rimbu complained publicly about the dirty and untidy state of his house. Ragunanu was furious when the complaint was relayed to her. She retorted that she had been invited to stay, yet now she was accused of 'destroying the house'. Rimbu immediately pacified her with assurances that he wasn't singling her out, other people were also responsible.

Several interacting tactics were at play here. By letting Rimbu know how she would respond to a direct accusation, Ragunanu preempted and averted Rimbu's direct accusation of her. At the same time, Rimbu put *her* on check, by letting her know what kind of behaviour he would consider unacceptable. At this stage of the proceedings, the suggestion of shared responsibility ('other people were also responsible') took the edge off the criticism.

To sum up, what I gloss as 'indirection' incorporates three broad practices: the use of metaphor, metonymic substitution, and elicitation. Elicitation is the larger category under which I classify Kewa discourse strategies, metaphor and metonymic substitution being the form taken by eliciting talk. Common everyday exchanges are elicitations in the form of claims.[6] What initially seems to be a confident or even aggressive claim evolves into a conciliatory negotiation intended to ascertain how far the elicitator's project can be made into a shared project. Each proposition is a bait thrown to the interlocutor. Kewa communicative exchanges seem almost to be seeking their own meaning, yet at the same time by their mode of delivery they belie this semantic and tactical flexibility. These complex communicative strategies are not signalled solely by the use of siapi, but are advanced also by apparently direct talk, when opinions or claims are made by speakers who are ready to retreat at the sign of strong opposition. Other claims, or other reasons, are substituted for unsuccessful ones, with no concern to retain an argument that carries no weight so as to avoid appearing fickle or self-contradictory. Moreover, intentions develop in the interaction itself, adapted to responses, so that people can never be sure in advance exactly how things will turn out (see Josephides 1998). Eliciting talk is often a strategy for understanding what is left unsaid in siapi.

Below I examine two forms of indirection: metaphor and metonymic pragmatics (or metonymic substitution). While the first proclaims its non-literalness and invites interpretation, the second may have the form of a literal proposition, yet neither its message nor meaning is to be found in the interpretation of its content. What is said is merely a vehicle for a different kind of claim or utterance.

Metaphor

As any other language, Kewa has a rich reservoir of stock phrases that refer indirectly to various activities. The innovation is in the way a speaker puts the phrases together, to create cryptic and allusive meanings that have to be worked out by the listener on the occasion of their use. When an unmarried man responded to the question of whether he would be killing pigs at the forthcoming pig kill with the words 'Never mind about eating pork, I want to eat sweet potatoes first', I knew that sweet potatoes were a woman's crop and that eating them was a metaphor for marriage. (Describing the first days of their marriage, women told me how their husbands approached them in their gardens and prefaced the consummation of their marriage with the words 'You cook my sweet potatoes'.) I also knew that 'eating pork' referred to killing pigs, and since pigs were also used in brideprice it was easy to work out that the young man was saying that he wanted to marry before participating in a pig kill. The new meaning created by the juxtaposition of the stock phrases was the implication that participating in pig kills had an adverse effect on one's ability to get married. Thus the young man was opposing prestige politics to domesticity.

Metaphor immediately declares itself as requiring interpretation, but at the same time it leaves many clues for its decoding. For instance, if a man says he has found a wildcat in the forest when he means he caught a stray pig, those listening will guess that he is intending to indulge in some secret, transgressive behaviour, such as kill the pig and eat it, and they are addressed as potential co-conspirators. Or when a man welcomes his rival's death with the words 'a stinking pig came floating on the river, I smelled it and was happy', listeners can have little doubt about his feelings or the effect he intends to produce. Nor was it too difficult to decode the same man's meaning when, on the purchase of a clan truck, he bragged: 'One man on his own can't easily catch a cassowary in the bush. If he shoots and hits it, he will get it. I shot this cassowary and put it in my house. Who will cut it?'. Those addressed may have been affronted by the slighting of their own contribution to the purchase, but they would have understood the allusion, and its culmination in the call for a driver.

Self-aggrandisement can go too far, however, and invite such retorts as 'you eat spinach with pitpit'. The speaker explained to me that the bigman he was thus addressing 'wanted to have everything in his name', first the truck financed by the whole clan and then the impending pig kill. 'You always go first and I follow behind' was the speaker's Tok Pisin translation. The retort was an accusation of political greed that expressed resentment and foreshadowed a more serious challenge. In a more graphic interaction, P gave R an uprooted piece of sugarcane with the words: 'When you eat this sugarcane, you must plant its root in Y [the speaker's village]. If it grows well we must bind it. If it dies, we'll both be the losers'. The occasion was R's pig kill, which had been brought forward with the result that P was unable to hold a concurrent pig kill in his own village, as previously agreed. R understood P's meaning well: 'We'll kill pigs here now, but then you'll build your pig-killing house in Y. Killing pigs here now must lead to killing pigs in Y later, otherwise there will be trouble'.

The foregoing examples all concern men's strategies, expressed in political, social and transgressive behaviours. Thus there is a whole spectrum of social relations in which men employ metaphoric speech. Often they adopt an aggressive tone of delivery, but in itself this does not give offence as it is men's normal tone on public occasions. Because the meaning of metaphoric speech may be revised, a metaphoric statement does not bind people to specific action, thus allowing for the affront contained in any of its interpretations to be righted. For instance, when Rimbu did not give Roga a share of the payment he received for the loan of his rifle, Roga complained, 'I never eat.' Rimbu angrily switched into direct speech, retorting that he constantly made gifts to Roga which amply repaid his small contribution to the purchase of the rifle. Thus challenged, Roga changed his tune: 'I do eat, but you are attacking me now that I am old and sick'. Switching into direct speech is an unmasking device that allows respondents to show the limits of their tolerance, while also allowing the negotiation of meaning to continue.

Metonymic substitution

I use 'metonymic substitution' to denote a speech event in which a whole statement is intended to achieve something unconnected or obliquely connected with its ostensive content. As mentioned earlier, what is said is merely a vehicle for a different kind of claim or utterance, and neither its message nor its meaning is to be found in the interpretation of its content. In linguistic theory the instructive contrast is between semantics and pragmatics. Semantics is the meaning expressed by the linguistic properties of the proposition, while pragmatics includes intentions, references and contextual implication – the 'unsaid' which the listener must calculate in order to understand the meaning of the proposition (Brown and Levinson 1987: 49). Metonymic substitution is a sort of pragmatics, when the whole of the 'said' is really a vehicle for saying something else. Consider the following four speech events.

1   His own successful pig kill over, Rimbu persistently asked his clan brothers 'what they meant to do'. This was understood as a question about when they would hold their own pig kill, and worse, as a rhetorical taunt about their inability to match him in pig killing. When his intent was exposed by a senior clan brother, who switched into direct speech and told him he had no business to press them about their pig kill, which in any case would surpass his own display, Rimbu immediately gave a different account of his intention: 'I didn't mean to push you, I just wanted to know what you were planning so that I would be ready to help you'.

2   I was talking with Liame and Lari, two women who often clashed. Having first ascertained that Lari had given me the single rubber band I wore on my wrist, Liame, who wore no rubber bands at all, disdainfully remarked that she wouldn't wear just one band. It was clear to Lari that the remark was not intended as a criticism of me. It was intended to criticise Lari, by suggesting that she had been insufficiently generous in giving me only one rubber band.

3   Following her discovery of her husband locked in an embrace with another woman, Lari told him that a grown man should not be groping surreptitiously with a 'no longer young' woman. If he 'intended anything' he should marry her. Despite her words, Lari's real intention was not to encourage her husband to marry the woman; it was to shame him into giving up what she described as unseemly behaviour.

4   At the death of clan elder Wapa, Roga told Wapa's son, Rimbu, that the various festivities Rimbu had planned for the impending pig kill would have to be foregone. With these words Roga, who was Rimbu's senior, was claiming authority as next clan elder. His proscription, the whole of the 'said', was thus a statement about authority, an announcement that the mantle of Wapa had fallen on him.

The last speech event can be seen as an example of Bloch's (1989) formalised language, whose purpose is not to communicate a specific content but to make a statement about authority and intent. Following Searle (1969), Bloch refers to this form of communication as perlocutionary force. In the Kewa case, however – and this is what unites the four speech events above – the rhetorical use of metonymy, rather than formalised language, conveys (or contains) the perlocutionary force. While the meaning of metaphoric speech can be found in the proposition itself, by interpreting the words used, metonymic substitution works by means of a different kind of association, and a statement that makes a rhetorical claim can be more difficult to interpret. To the contrast between semantics and pragmatics, I add the correlation between semantics and illocutionary force on the one hand, and pragmatics and perlocutionary force or effect on the other. Metaphor belongs in the first set, and metonymy in the second. An examination of the difference between illocutionary and perlocutionary acts will clarify my definition of 'metonymic substitution'.

Illocutionary acts and perlocutionary effects: doing things with words[7]

In his *Speech Acts* (1969) Searle warns us not to confuse illocutionary and perlocutionary acts by defining meaning in terms of intended effects.[8] For Searle, saying something and meaning it is a matter of performing an illocutionary act, not necessarily intended to elicit any state or action in the hearer, who merely understands. To recognise someone's intention that I should believe something does not necessarily lead to my believing it. When a hearer recognises what I am trying to do, it does not mean that I have done it, that she experiences the 'effect' of my intentions. From Searle's discussion I deduce that, strictly speaking, there are no perlocutionary acts, only perlocutionary effects. An act can be registered as perlocutionary only after it is established that it has had the desired effect on the hearer.

Searle's first concern, that meaning should not be defined in terms of its intended effects, is followed by a second concern, that accounts of meaning should not ignore the conventions of meaning in language. Analyses of illocutionary acts must therefore capture 'both the intentional and the conventional aspects [of meaning]' (*ibid.*: 45). Searle uses a typical philosopher's 'counter-example' to argue his case.

An American soldier is captured by Italian troops in World War II. He wants them to believe he is a German soldier, but does not know the German or Italian for 'I am a German soldier'. So instead he uses the only bit of school German he remembers, a line from a poem, hoping it will do the trick. 'Do you know the land where the lemon trees bloom', pronounced in German, does not mean 'I am a German soldier', but this is what the speaker intends to convey. For Searle, the soldier's strategy raises a serious problem of dissonance between the meaning of the words and the speaker's intention.

I would argue that the hypothetical scenario admits of at least another possibility. Granted that the American soldier did not know the German for 'I am a German soldier', it does not follow that he intended the Italian soldiers to believe that this was the literal meaning of his utterance. His act was intended to be perlocutionary. He might even have thought that a line from a German poem would have more perlocutionary force than the statement 'I am a German soldier', in either Italian or German. If such was his belief , this would be the sort of statement to which I referred as 'metonymic substitution'. The problem with this speech act is that it is not accessible to linguistic analysis, for it concerns only perlocutionary effects. Propositional meaning and intention are kept separate. What one means, and what the words one uses mean, are not the same thing. In my earlier Kewa example, the man who expected to succeed to the position of clan elder following a death did not say 'I call the shots now', or 'I am now lineage elder'. Instead, he gave a list of injunctions which were contingent on his new authority.

As noted, perlocutionary intent does not lead automatically to perlocutionary effect. When, in the Kewa example, Lari found her husband embracing another woman and told him that he should marry her, her intention was really to shame her husband and stop their lovemaking. Her husband understood her, but still married the woman. This was an illocutionary act that did not have the desired perlocutionary effect. Moreover, Lari did not *think* it would have the effect she desired, so she did not *intend* it in the sense of expecting it to happen. Her meaning, as desire, was understood, but did not have the effect of averting the marriage.

To sum up, a listener may recognise what the speaker is trying to do when uttering a proposition. This is illocutionary effect. Whether the utterance has the desired effect in the listener is another matter. Intentions are from the speaker's side, but effects concern the hearer. The speaker can only propose; it is up to the listener to take on the disposition and experience the effect. Although there are no perlocutionary acts but only perlocutionary effects, I argue that when perlocutionary effect is intended in Kewa practice, metonymic substitution is likely to be used.

Modernity: from warriors to diplomats, or from veiled talk to straight talk

To what extent have these characteristic forms of language use and communication changed with modernity? By 'modernity' I mean a new local discourse, which does not take for granted any conditions that exist in countries where modernity is locally believed to hail from. As a local event, modernity is the product of local people's agency on that external thing, and their activity is what accounts for the divergence between the global and its local manifestation (see Miller 1995: 3).

I argue that there *has* been a shift in language use. In various degrees, it can be seen in the use of Tok Pisin and English; in the formulaic objection to traditional veiled speech, which is denounced as deceitful, uneconomic, and inefficient; in the collapsing of modernity, Christianity and 'white ways' with direct and straight talk; in young women's pragmatic, intentional talk which uses statements and propositions designed to reconceptualise male/female relations; and in the development of a diplomatic, mediating talk that looks beyond village life and deals with relations outside the local context. I examine this shift by considering, briefly, three modern forms of authority: religion, the police force and politics.

The 'straight talk' of pastor Simon, itself hardly concise, was to a large extent based on an authoritarian revelation of God which did not so much offer explanation as demand belief and commitment. Onlookers said that they couldn't argue with Simon because he was holding the bible, which contained the word of God. Another local pastor, speaking at a funeral, expressed this dependence on apocalyptic faith. 'If you don't think the dead can rise again, then Jesus didn't rise up. If Jesus did, all the dead can'. The first premise, that Jesus rose from the dead, had to be accepted before anything else followed logically. (This was by way of a reprimand to a layman with an agnostic, empirical bent, who said on his mother's death, 'If her devil will stink or her god will stink, we don't know'. He meant that he could not know whether her spirit [devil or god, depending on whether it was viewed negatively or positively] would die just like her body.)

The Christian church, for all its fideistic authoritarianism, was a voluntary institution that drew villagers in as participating human beings with souls worthy of salvation. The police force, locally the most prominent agent of modern state power, had no such pretensions. The language of this executive arm of the law was brutal, straightforward, terrorising, and with no recourse to indirection. In one incident, a visiting affine accused villagers of beating him up and robbing him. His complaint resulted in a visit from the police, who drove up to the village and asked for the culprits to be given up. When nobody came forward, policemen seized a pig and carried it away. The next day they seized another pig, and announced through their megaphone: 'If you don't give up the rascals we'll kill a pig every day, lay waste your gardens and burn down your houses'.

What distinguished police action from traditional tribal warfare was that the legitimacy of police power was not in dispute, and therefore could not be contested in open warfare.[9] The language of its commands was accordingly non-negotiable, direct and authoritative. In the incident just recounted, when the plaintiff was found out to be a liar he was beaten mercilessly. At times villagers may, out of sheer frustration, respond in symbolic terms to the brutality of authority. One young man, whose wife had been roughly handled and her garden laid waste by the police, did just that. He placed at the entrance of his settlement a palisade of intertwined canes, as a public statement of the insult and a reminder that reparation was outstanding. His action could be seen as registering another feeling, a nostalgic backward glance to a time when clansmen were at liberty to take action to defend themselves.

Never having enjoyed political freedom, women could not now miss it. As the forms and political arenas that excluded them become replaced by new economic, educational and social opportunities, women adopt strategies that pursue personal liberties and bypass the constraints of local conventions and forms of interaction. Despite disadvantages *vis-à-vis* men in terms of opportunities, legislation and political advancement, in their strategies women embrace the modernising process. They do so, moreover, without experiencing the existential angst or political compulsion that appears to plague men, who, in order to legitimate modernity as a form of knowledge, need to appropriate the knowledge source of the new practices by linking it to their traditional world-views.

National politics entered the village most visibly through the electoral practices of campaigning and voting. Representational, parliamentary democracy was in many ways a continuation of colonial rule. People were now always aware that in acting they are responding to forces outside as well as within local conditions, and this spurred them on to a new diplomacy which would in turn shape those external forces.

I distinguish two types of political actors: parliamentary candidates, who were often mavericks increasingly more out of than in the community, and local people who saw themselves as mediators. They had in common their use of apparently direct speech. The hopeful parliamentarian was usually visible only as a campaigning politician. Publicly, he (no women candidates ran for the elections in this part of the highlands) used the seductive language of persuasion, peppered with plans for 'development' projects. Privately, he made promises of gifts of money and expensive equipment to influential individuals. The campaigner's speeches were not like the pig killer's orations, expressed in siapi. A typical manifesto contained the following items: 'I undertake to build a road from x to y. I undertake to establish an aid post in z. I undertake to bring q form of development'. Rather than interpretive skills, what the electorate needed was the oracular power to divine the extent of a candidate's exaggeration, bad faith, or plain, deceitful dishonesty.[10]

The new diplomacy of those who mediated between the local and the global was also expressed in straight talk. Rimbu for one was skilled in practising this diplomacy with the anthropologist.

> I once attended with Rimbu's less politically adept clan brother a ceremonial pig exchange in a neighbouring settlement. I found myself in the midst of a potentially explosive situation, which, alas, I was also responsible for creating. The hosts had hired dancers, whom I proceeded to photograph.

I had not taken more than two shots when a man who acted as the dancers' manager began to shout and gesticulate, saying that I did not pay for the performance and had no right to take photographs. My companion retorted angrily, and afraid of a fight, I dragged him away. On the walk back we discussed the implications of the episode. Had the impresario insulted us? Had the hosts insulted us? I had always taken photographs before, why not this time?

Rimbu came to see me as soon as he heard of the incident. He established the facts carefully through close questioning, and then explained the situation to me. Our neighbours had paid for the dancers, and could take as many photographs as they pleased. When the impresario began to shout at us we should have told him calmly that we would obtain the hosts' permission, and done so right away. Our neighbours were not to blame because they were not aware of the altercation, and the impresario was not to blame because it was the business of his group to dance for payment. There had been no affront, and there was no call to read into the situation any other intention or message.

Such instances of diplomacy in relations with the anthropologist were common. I was always aware of the contrasting styles of 'warrior talk', veiled, indirect and negotiable yet at the same time aggressive, and the direct talk of diplomacy, which I now observed extended to relations with representatives of powers from outside the local context.

It did seem, at times, that by adopting what they dubbed the straight, concise talk of modernity, people thought they were making themselves more like Europeans, with 'lives more fully integrated into the white global world' (Robbins 1997: 25). This is not to say that Kewa were not aware of the subterfuges, deceit, and specialised vocabulary of modernity. Many told wry, self-deprecating stories of their own gaucheness and ignorance in the past, the occasions on which they were thoroughly perplexed, cheated, ignored or made into figures of fun.

One young man recounted how his father had lost his mother. The local mission aid post could not deal with her breech pregnancy, and she was driven and flown from hospital to hospital, to end up in a different province from her own. When her husband finally tracked her down the hospital orderlies pointed to a fresh grave and told him that she and the baby were buried there. He did not have the vocabulary, conceptual or linguistic, to ask how she had died, or to request to take the bodies home. So instead he took a clod of earth from the grave and carried it to the village, where a wake was held over it in traditional fashion. The son believed that his mother was still alive somewhere in the world, but the orderlies simply could not be bothered to deal seriously with his father.

To sum up, what do the communicative practices of the three modern forms of authority reveal about language change with respect to directness and indirection? Simon's speech, with its reliance on the authority of a bible inextricably linked to modernity, left little space for more egalitarian negotiation of meaning. People could reject the premises of those meanings, but between their source and their expression there was no room for argument.[11] Simon and the other pastors gave 'straight talk', but its dependence on an original premise metonymically substituted an appeal to faith with an appeal to truth, goodness and efficiency. It was indicative of this substitution that symbolic and metaphoric stories in the bible were taken literally, and treated with the sort of immediacy that led people to ask me if I had known Jesus, or seen a photograph of him.

Police power was uncontestable for more visibly persuasive reasons. Though the language of its commands was unmistakably direct, police behaviour itself resembled, and was received as, a traditional form of punitive payback. Yet the new distinctions between juridical and law enforcement powers, politics, and social relations, opened creative spaces, especially for women. Siapi use declined as occasions for its use were transformed, but elicitation through metonymic substitution continued. As a form of indirection, the latter was less open to negotiation, and while it left the door open for retraction it also carried a more strongly perlocutionary intent.

Conclusion

Most Kewa people were well aware that modernity had its own vocabulary, its own forms of indirectness, its own deceit and its own asymmetries. They never claimed that the white people with whom they had had official dealings were 'straight' talkers. But they struggled to find the key to successful communication with the new powers. Though they used the metaphor of indirection versus straight talk, their quest seemed rather to be for linguistic forms of interaction appropriate to particular lifestyles. Language use had become more differentiated, split to match the forking of authority. There was far less negotiation of meaning at the level of authority, and metaphoric speech was used on a less grand scale. Conversely, metonymic substitution and perlocutionary, seductive use of persuasion were very much in evidence. Kewa language use seemed rich with possibilities.

Notes

1 Kewa communicative practices and their transformations are discussed at length in Josephides 1999.
2 Strathern (1975) first wrote about veiled speech in the Papua New Guinea Highlands, but he describes different aspects of Hagen practice from the Kewa ones described here.
3 Substitution is also a conventional practice in the material and spatial world, as when sticks stand for pigs, or the invocation of one place evokes another.

4 There are many commonalities between Zande *sanza* and Kewa 'eliciting talk' in the form of *siapi*. Evans-Pritchard describes sanza as so frequently used among the Azande, 'that one may say it is a characteristic mode of speech, an indication of their mentality' (1962: 227). As with siapi, what is important in the use of sanza is to 'keep under cover and to keep open a line of retreat' (ibid: 222). However, there are also differences. While siapi is also 'a circumlocutionary form of speech or action in which words and gestures have hidden meanings different from their manifest meanings' (ibid: 221), these meanings are not necessarily malicious. When Kewa avail themselves of a line of retreat, it is not because, like the Azande, they want to conceal their affairs (ibid: 227), but because they want to give their interlocutors a chance to negotiate meaning, and thus avoid undue offence.

5 Kewa also have a 'dialogic' etiquette of social interaction (Parkes, Chapter 14 in this volume), but it goes in the opposite direction from the Kalasha, from traditional indirection to the direct talk associated with modernism. Similarly with the Kalasha, this etiquette conceals and contains intentionality and instrumental reason (Parkes).

6 Nigel Rapport (Chapter 1 in this volume: 28) writes that the farming people of Wanet wanted to talk 'in order to realise their expectations and see their worldviews fulfilled in each other's actions and reactions'. Kewa also talked for this reason, but at the same time they expected to have to negotiate their world-views rather than just satisfy their expectations.

7 *How To Do Things with Words* is the title of a book by Austin (1962).

8 Searle criticises Grice for confusing illocutionary and perlocutionary acts when he '[defines] meaning in terms of intended effects' (Searle 1969: 44). 'To say that speaker *S* meant something by *X* is to say that *S* intended that utterance of *X* to produce some effect in a hearer *H* by means of the recognition of this intention' (Searle 1969: 43).

9 At times villagers did refer to the police force as a 'line', that is, a clan, and held it collectively responsible for its punitive actions. However, villagers never questioned that the legitimacy of the police came from the state.

10 Ministers in office in the capital engage in more sophisticated forms of rhetoric, but here I am concerned only with electoral tactics in rural areas.

11 See Bloch (1989) on rebellion versus revolution.

References

Atkinson, Jane Monnig (1984) ' "Wrapped Words": poetry and politics among the Wana of Central Sulawesi, Indonesia', in Donald Brenneis and Fred R. Myers (eds) *Dangerous Words: Language and Politics in the Pacific*, Prospect Heights IL: Waveland Press, pp. 33–68.

Austin, J. L. (1962) *How To Do Things with Words*, Oxford: Oxford University Press.

Bloch, Maurice (1989) 'Symbols, song, dance and features of articulation: is religion an extreme form of traditional authority?', in Bloch, *Ritual, History and Power*, London: Athlone Press, pp. 19–45.

Brown, Penelope and Levinson, Stephen C. (1987) *Politeness: Some Universals in Language Use*, Cambridge: Cambridge University Press.

Evans-Pritchard, E. E. (1962) '*Sanza*, a characteristic feature of Zande language and thought', in Evans-Pritchard, *Essays in Social Anthropology*, London: Faber, pp. 204–28.

Hendry, Joy (1989) 'To wrap or not to wrap: politeness and penetration in ethnographic inquiry', *Man*, 24(4): 620–35.

Josephides, Lisette (1985) *The Production of Inequality*, London: Tavistock.

——(1998) 'Biographies of social action', in Verena Keck (ed.) *Common Worlds and Single Lives: Constituting Knowledge in Pacific Societies*, Oxford and New York: Berg, 137–67.

——(1999) 'Disengagement and desire: the tactics of everyday life', *American Ethnologist*, 26(1): 139–59.

Miller, Daniel (1995) 'Introduction: anthropology, modernity and consumption', in Miller (ed.) *Worlds Apart: Modernity through the Prism of the Local*, London: Routledge.

Robbins, Joel (1997) ' "When do you think the world will end?" Globalization, apocalypticism, and the moral perils of fieldwork in "Last New Guinea" ', *Anthropology and Humanism*, 22(1) special issue: 'Fieldwork revisited' pp. 6–30.

Searle, John (1969) *Speech Acts: An Essay in the Philosophy of Language*, Cambridge: Cambridge University Press.

Strathern, A. J. (1975) 'Veiled speech in Mount Hagen', in M. Bloch (ed.) *Political Language and Oratory in Traditional Society*, London and New York: Academic Press.

Chapter 14

Unwrapping rudeness
Inverted etiquette in an egalitarian enclave

Peter Parkes

Introduction: unwrapping rudeness

Politeness appears to be widely conceived in images of clothing, concealing and containing, as a conspicuous artifactual *façade* decorating the surface of social interaction. What is clothed, concealed and contained is presumed to be naked intentionality or instrumental reason, including the rudely impulsive reasons of the body (Elias 1978). Just as ritual symbolism is largely recognised through its superfluous deviation from instrumental action, implicating a surplus 'wrapping' of expressive meanings (Leach 1954: 12), so verbal and behavioural politeness is necessarily gauged against a Gricean touchstone of *direct* ('unwrapped') communicational efficiency. But as Brown and Levinson (1987) ironically demonstrated, this rude register of perfectly unambiguous communication – their 'bald on record' strategy – is itself perforce symbolic of differential status and power within normal social communication, which always needs to attend to the reciprocally sensitive 'face needs' of socially sensible interlocutors. From its outset, human communication is thus inflected by socially efficient considerations of politeness or face-saving indirection. Hence rudeness paradoxically becomes another kind of symbolic 'dressing' – albeit a conspicuous 'dressing down' – of expected social norms of polite communication, often expressive of alternative kinds of social solidarity or mutuality to those of hierarchy or social distance typically conveyed through express politeness.

In this chapter, I address – or metaphorically 'undress' – such aversions and inversions of overt politeness that seem characteristic of what Mary Douglas has termed 'egalitarian enclaves', i.e. minority communities encapsulated within hierarchically organised polities. Like the Irula of southern India described by Neil Thin (Chapter 12 in this volume), the non-Muslim Kalasha of northern Pakistan are just such an egalitarian community. And just as features of Irula religious culture become comprehensible as 'heteroglossic' emulations of Hindu hierarchical values, combined with their parodic subversion in ritual, so Kalasha political culture may be comprehended as a similarly 'dialogic' *absorption-rejection* of the alien tributary regime in which they have been subordinated. I therefore start with a synopsis of this 'polite' culture of

Chitrali hierarchy – itself derived from archaic Turco-Persian tributary regimes – in response to which alternatively 'rude' domains of Kalasha discourse and practice are contrastively distinguished.

Indo-Persian hierarchy and courtly etiquette in Chitral

In their comparative survey of politeness, Brown and Levinson oddly neglected honorific speech styles sensitive to social status characteristic of Islamic civilisations throughout Central and South Asia. William Beeman's (1976) 'Status, style and strategy in Iranian interaction', examining Goffmanesque strategies of deference inherent in Iranian *ta'ārof* manners, foreshadowed their own subsequent analysis of 'negative politeness' strategies (Brown and Levinson 1987: 5.4; see also Beeman 1986). *Ta'ārof*, the prestation and deferral to others of verbal compliments and gestures or material tokens of honour, is

> the active, ritualized realization of differential status in interaction. It underscores and preserves the integrity of culturally defined status roles as it is carried out in the life of every Iranian every day in thousands of different ways. ... Every time tea is offered to a group, every time a group of persons wish to proceed through one door, every time friends meet on the street, every time guests proceed to the dinner table at a party, the constant unceasing ritualization of the assessment of climate of relative status occurs and recurs.
>
> (Beeman 1976: 312–13; cf. also 1986: 11)

Beeman particularly examined *ta'ārof*'s manifestations in verbal interaction: where such basic verbs as 'to give' are substituted with refined stylistic variants such as 'to make an offering', in self-deprecation, or 'to make a favour, an indulgence or a kindness' with reference to status superiors. Similarly, verbs for 'saying' are rendered as 'making a petition' or 'giving a command'; while active verbs for coming or going have at least three further levels of status inflection, ranging from 'taking or bringing (one's) presence' to 'conferring (one's) presence' to 'commanding (another's) honour'. Conversely, in self-reference for verbs of movement, one 'makes a pilgrimage' or 'is of service' and ultimately 'becomes a (passive) recipient of honour' to successive status superiors (*ibid*.: 316–18). As Beeman indicates, such honorific registers give rise to complex linguistic manoeuvres of status jockeying – including reciprocal displays of self-abasement 'to get the lower hand so to speak' (cf. Irvine 1974) – which are labelled with idiomatic names. Excessive *ta'ārof* flattery is thus known colloquially as 'to make a donkey (of someone)', while inappropriate verbal intimacy with an inferior is glossed as 'giving (away) face' (319–20).

Such status-inflected idioms have a wide distribution in Central and South Asia, partly as a result of the adoption of classical Persian as an official administrative language by early Ottoman and Mughal as well as Iranian empires (Canfield 1991). Many of the verbal honorifics noted by Beeman are therefore also evident in Urdu and Hindi (Bahri 1960). In the Hindu Kush mountains of northern Pakistan, where semi-autonomous kingdoms persisted up to the late 1960s or early 1970s, such Persianised styles of status etiquette appear even more elaborate in verbal and behavioural expression than in modern Iran.

In such principalities as Chitral, now the northernmost district of the Northwest Frontier Province of Pakistan, whose sovereignty was only dissolved in 1969, this verbal etiquette was associated with a complex system of ranking linked to tributary feudal services owed to the ruling Mehtar (Persian 'owner'). British colonial accounts and Chitrali sources document several named status grades or quasi-'castes' grouped within three broad classes: those of the nobility or *adamzāda*, literally 'descendants of man' or true humans; a yeomanry of middle peasants, variously referred to as *arbābzāda*, 'descendants of officials' or *yuft* 'the yoke'; and a large lumpen-category of enserfed peasants, called *fakir miškin*, literally 'miserable poor', who provided the basic tribute in agricultural produce and manual labour upon which the whole state depended. Interlinking these classes and ranked grades were alliances of hypergamous marriage and of fosterage or tributary milk kinship allegiance.[1] Women from lower-ranked families might marry 'up' as secondary wives and concubines to their social superiors, while infants were passed 'down' to be fostered by subordinate families. Affinal alliance, milk-kinship, and subinfeudated tributary services thus comprised an elaborately nested hierarchy of social segments, where households of all degrees were symbolically encompassed within the *mahraka* 'court' of the reigning Mehtar. As Frederik Barth noted:

> Political and administrative life centered around the *mahraka* – receptions in the audience room of the Mehtar's palace, where he, surrounded by prominent chiefs and administrative officers, made his decisions public, granted favours or disgraced, dismissed, or condemned people, all in [a] complex system of traditional regalia and idiom.
>
> (Barth 1956: 81)

The 'traditional regalia' was that of Turco-Persian courts of earlier Timurid and Mughal dynasties, where political subordination was expressed through prestations of tribute in exchange for ceremonial gowns or other sumptuary tokens of honour (*khelāt*); and the 'traditional idiom', expressed in archaic Persian as the official court language of Chitral, was a local variety of *ta'ārof*. Indigenous accounts of *mahraka* ceremony indeed explicate the behavioural protocols of court ritual, from which *ta'ārof* idioms were metaphorically derived (cf. Cohn 1983: 635–37, after Abu al Fazl 1927):

> The ruler used to have his meals in the company of the notables twice a day. This system was called *mahraka*. It would be wrong to consider the *mahraka* as only taking of meals as it conceals in it many important secrets of government. ... Here the ruler encouraged and honoured his favourites by giving the higher position in precedence. ... In case someone sat at a seat lower than his status, the ruler would notice it and call him up to a seat according to his rank. The person involved would, taking it as an honour, first kiss the hand of the ruler and then take the seat assigned to him. ... At the end of the meals those desirous of making some petition would do so. This was known as *khowsik* [beseeching].
>
> (Hussam-ul-Mulk n.d.: 82–4)

Such courtly etiquette still characterises the regal sport of polo in Chitral (Parkes 1996b), while comparable ceremonies of deference and precedence orchestrate public dancing (cf. Tahir Ali 1981). The rituals of the royal *mahraka* are also still echoed within every Chitrali household: more or less informally at ordinary meals according to the status of guests present, but with more meticulous attention to courtly 'regalia and idioms' at wedding celebrations (Aseer 1996). The traditional architecture of the Khó house was indeed a conceptual microcosm of the *mahraka* 'state room' of the Mehtar's court. Domestic space was partitioned into a series of named levels and platforms on either side of a central hearth, connoting relative rank, which a household head could use to choreograph his favours precisely like the Mehtar at court:

> Within the household the father may temporarily promote a son or nephew who has distinguished himself, and on occasion may even give the honoured guest's *kloop* [highest status seat beside the hearth] ... If a visitor takes too high a place in the sitting area it is much resented. ... [O]n extraordinary occasions, such as marriages, the allocation of seats is so strictly observed that, it is said, if a stranger goes to a room where members of both parties are present he can tell the relationships of those present from where they are sitting. For example, the maternal uncle of the bride, who accompanies the bride from her own home to her husband's, sits on the *nakh* [elevated side platform]; while her foster-brother or foster-father, who may also accompany her, sits on the *bend* [lower side platform].
>
> (Hussam-ul-Mulk and Staley 1968: 108–9)

Kin terms for the bride's mother's brother and fostering milk-relatives were customarily replaced by such domestic-spatial metonyms of relative rank: i.e. respectively, 'he who sits on the *nakh*' and 'he who sits on the *bend*'; while marriage prestations to these kin were correspondingly termed 'for sitting on the *nakh*' or 'for sitting on the *bend*' (Staley 1982: 89–96; Illi 1991). Deferential idioms – representing motion as a 'petition' (*arzī*) summoned by a commanding 'order' (*hokm*) – also characterise the appropriate verbal address of differentially ranked relatives on such occasions. Khowar, the Indian language of Chitral, thus has an elaborately stratified social lexicon of honorifics, as well as grammatical calques of Persian verbal-deictic idioms, which are also bodily enacted in deferential greeting, such as an attempted kissing of the hand in symbolic vassalage to status superiors (cf. Goody 1972).

Chitrali mores of status sensitivity thus encode a refined hierarchical regime of fractal *emboîtement*, corresponding to a tributary regime of multiple subinfeudation, which persists as an ideological template of social distinction even thirty years after the dissolution of the Mehtar's principality. The Khowar language also abounds in colloquial glosses for conventional strategies of dissimulation through elevated status flattery and ingratiation (*iṣkalī*), including equivalents of the Persian expressions noted by Beeman, referred to above.

The Kalasha enclave: rude reversal?

Incorporated within such hierarchical polities are subordinate ethnic groups internally organised on contrasting moral principles of egalitarianism. Such are the Kalasha ('Kalash Kafirs'), whose legendary kingdoms in southern Chitral were conquered by Mehtars commanding the Islamised Khó tribes of the north around the early sixteenth century. Conversion to Islam, accompanied by the adoption of Khowar language and culture, gradually reduced the non-Muslim Kalasha population to its present refuge of three small valleys in the southwest. Kalasha were enserfed as a subordinate category of tributary peasants within the *fakir miškin* class of 'miserable poor', subject to heavy taxes and arduous corvée labour services. This oppressive regime of serfdom and tributary extraction persisted until the mid-1950s, still bitterly recalled by Kalasha as 'the time when the rulers were eating the very skin off our backs'.

Kalasha culture seems well characterised by Mary Douglas' ideal-typical depiction of what she terms an 'enclave culture' (Douglas 1993; 1996: xix–xxi). This is the political culture of an encapsulated and embattled minority community, whose social institutions have become selectively shaped to ensure communal solidarity, and particularly to discourage the 'defection' of its members to a dominant and morally alien universe outside its localised domain. The religious culture of such enclaves tends to be preoccupied with ritual criteria of purity and pollution, demarcating a distinctive group boundary that distinguishes insiders from outsiders, although these symbolic boundaries are inevitably breached in quotidian social practice. Despite performative rites of separation and purification, no enclave can ever actually be autonomous, being constituted within – and indeed expressly *against* – its encompassing hierarchical regime; for it is in reactive response to hierarchical encompassment that its enclaved culture is cumulatively instituted as a moral barricade, being contrastively defined as *egalitarian* in principle. This anti-hierarchical ethic also poses distinctive institutional contradictions according to Douglas (1987: 38–43): especially surrounding consensual leadership, necessary to protect communal interests against external coercion and internal defection, which receives little institutional support in a political culture where, as it is vigorously insisted, 'all Kalasha are poor, all are equal' (*saf kalāṣa gharibān, saf barabār*).

Douglas' ideal-typical depiction of the fractious 'enclave culture' captures several salient features of Kalasha indigenous understanding of local organisational problems surrounding episodic factionalism (Parkes 2000a). A historical shift from relative hierarchy to enclavement is also suggested by oral traditions concerning 'caste-like' grades of artisan slaves (*bāira*) and other features of rank stratification in the past, comparable with the more hierarchical chiefdoms of the neighbouring non-Muslim Kafirs of eastern Afghanistan observed by Robertson (1896). Yet Kalasha have also evidently retained organisational features of what Douglas terms 'proto-hierarchy' (i.e. diffuse segmentary authority), evident in ceremonial lineage organisation and competitive feasting, which provide at least some symbolic support for representative 'eldership' and ceremonially ranked leadership. Like many other encapsulated minorities, Kalasha communities therefore comprise *tensile* social systems of variously opposed tendencies, in which enclavism is a dominant but not entirely absolute aspect (Flanagan and Rayner 1988; Flanagan 1989: 261).

Kalasha discursively contrast their social order and culture with that of the majority Khó of Chitral, ironically depreciating themselves as rude 'wild people' (*jaŋgalī muč*) in contrast to its 'civilised people' (*šāhrai muč*). Kalasha also typically refer to themselves as 'poor Kalasha' (*gharīb kalāṣa*) or 'simple Kalasha' (*sadā kalāṣa*), even sometimes mockingly adopting such gross Chitrali disparagements as 'stinking Kalash' (Khowar *ghōṇḍa kalāṣ*) or 'Kafir' (*kaphēr*, from Arabic *kāfr* 'unbeliever'). Such reflexive meiosis or self-depreciation is also a more general feature of social rhetoric: where, for example, great wealth accumulated for feasting is personally referred to as one's 'poverty' (*gharībī*). Self-representation as 'simple Kalasha' also has ambivalent reference. Used internally, the notion of a 'simple person' (*sadā muč*) has generally positive connotations of unscheming sincerity: someone who is 'straight' (*sīḍha*) and 'true' (*ūjak, sahī*). In collective self-reference, however, the 'simple Kalasha' often alludes to a cunning ploy of enacted stupidity, celebrated in recollections of the feudal era, where feigned simplicity is hilariously shown to have outwitted credulous and greedy Khó Chitralis (Parkes n.d.). As another observer noted:

> Kalash[a] generally are very aware of the need for techniques specifically intended to beguile outsiders and … Kalash[a] language is particularly

rich in idiomatic expressions of the type which describe these subterfuges. An example is [a] perjorative word which means someone who outwardly is as sweet as 'candy' [*haliwāi*] ... and inwardly is manipulative and inquisitive in intent. In this same vein is an expression ... meaning a person who, being unnoticeable as 'water flowing between the roots of wheat plants' [*tuṣ nə̌runa uk*], works his or her way into another's good graces. Similarly, someone ... who cleverly works him or herself into favour with an unsuspecting person [is] like 'water being blown through the coiled intestines of a slaughtered animal' [*čākuruna uk*].

(Darling 1979: 10, transcriptions emended)

Such strategies of ingratiation (*iṣkalī*) and dissimulation (*lawēk*) are similar to those recognised in the related Khowar language of Chitral, which all Kalasha speak fluently, their own colloquial glosses being intentionally 'coded' in obscure imagery further to beguile outsiders. As petitioners and servants at the court of the Chitrali Mehtars, Kalasha indeed needed to master its niceties of regal etiquette, and they were even renowned for their especially skilled deployment of cryptic allegory (*nākul*) or artful indirection in Khowar. As a court historian remarked:

Kalash ... are very humble in their behaviour. While greeting they bow low. Notwithstanding this, they are extremely intelligent and surprise the courts with their witty remarks when they appear in connection with their cases.

(Ghulam Murtaza 1962: 48)

Externally, Kalasha were thus well embraced within the tributary regime of Chitral. But internally, their enclaved egalitarianism and mistrust of authority conditioned a culture of determined rudeness or 'wild custom' (*jaŋgalī dastūr*), which downplays or evaluatively 'inverts' the hierarchical formality of Khó Chitrali culture.

This rude reversal of status grading is visibly evident in Kalasha domestic architecture and everyday family manners. Unlike the Khó house, with its elaborately ranked internal partitions, Kalasha houses have a minimal differentiation of internal space, lacking any distinctive lateral or vertical markers of age, status or gender, beyond an overall topographical (back-front, up-down) orientation in terms of ritual purity and pollution (Parkes 1997: 30–3). Compared with a somewhat stern atmosphere of patriarchal authority characteristic of other Chitrali households, Kalasha domestic relations also appear markedly informal, where men and women of all ages chat and joke and tease one another quite freely around the hearth. Only when senior elders or Khó Chitrali guests are present at mealtimes is there a faint echo of courtly deference to authority: a senior elder is then invited to take the first loaf of bread and divide it for others, who each salute him, touching their caps, as they receive their portions. Otherwise, codes of greeting – including reciprocal hand-kissing by opposite-sex relatives – are inflected solely by recognised kinship status.[2]

Kalasha egalitarianism is also characterised by markedly casual styles of address and directness in conversation: unadorned 'straight talk' (*siḍha mun*) or 'true talk' (*sahī mun, ūjak mun*), contrasted with the 'crooked talk' (*křõřõk mun*) or 'empty talk' (*khalī mun*) of ingratiating flattery typical of Khowar speech registers (cf. Katriel 1986). All persons of equivalent age are thus normally addressed (by default of kinship recognition) as 'brother' or 'sister' in Kalasha, whereas in Khowar unrelated coevals are likely to use such honorifics as 'noble' (*lāl*) to a status superior and 'man/person' (*muš*) or 'son' (*žāu*) to a male inferior, while reciprocal sibling terms alternatively convey a marked intimacy (or indeed subaltern disrespect). The prominence of 'nursery words' (*Lallwörter*) for primary kin among Kalasha also seemingly conveys an egalitarian 'infanto-centric' perspective in relational discourse.[3] Male seniority is acknowledged only through an ambiguous honorific for 'eldership' (*gaḍērak*, literally 'senior' or 'elder', derived from *gāḍa* 'big, tall', through the comparative *gaḍāra* 'older, bigger', with a diminutive suffix *-ak*), which may be used respectfully to address almost *any* adult man on formal occasions.

Directness and overt rudeness in Kalasha speech is most prominently expressed in sexually flirtatious banter: in what is called 'shame(ful) talk' (*lač mun*), expected in virtually all encounters between people of opposite sex who are not related as potentially incestuous consanguines (*nerawā*) or defined as senior-generational affines (including a spouse's elder siblings), with whom all reference to sexuality should be avoided. In contrast to Khó Chitrali (and general Islamic) status values surrounding sexual honour and female chastity (*izzat, namūs*), Kalasha gender relations appear remarkably informal (Parkes 1997: 55ff.). It is the prominent 'freedom' (*azatī*) of women, especially in festival celebrations, that is most frequently remarked upon by Kalasha men and women, as well as by outsiders, as a distinctive feature of their non-Islamic culture (Maggi 1998). Sexuality is also a bawdy motif of everyday conversation, as my own daily fieldwork experience may convey:

> Rising in the morning, one struggles across the village to relieve oneself in the communal 'pissing-place' (*mūtra-garikäin*) down by the river. Just before reaching this meadow, I am invariably accosted by village girls coyly asking 'Where are you going, brother?' (*e bāya, tu kawāi parā?*). To avoid an unacceptably inelegant truth (**a mūtra-garikäinai parīm*, 'I am going to the pissing-place'), one answers 'I'm just walking (for no reason), sister' (*e bāba, mič kāsim daî*), which may well delay urgent matters with a further enquiry, 'But where are you just walking, brother?' and so on. An expected response in shameful talk would be, put crudely, 'I am going into your vagina, sister' (*e bāba, a tai gušíkuna parīm*); or more subtly, 'Oh sister, I am (going to) your, your …' (*e bāba, a tai, tai …*), with perhaps a

rude lunge; or more flirtatiously, 'Oh *prejä* (wife's younger sister, a licensed joking relationship), I am (going to) your, your ...', etc. – which should have the desired effect of scattering the girls in mirthful embarrassment (*lač jōnin*, 'they know shame'), yet which might still encourage older women to riposte with further lewd innuendos, such as 'Oh brother-in-law, just *how* will you ...?' (*e jhamōu, tu khē kai* ... ?), and so on.

Similarly obscene banter – e.g. 'I shove [it] up your arse' (*a tai darāli thūkim*), 'Eat shit!' (*rič žu!*), or 'Eat *that!*' (*šāma žu!*), shaking a phallic fist – characterises male camaraderie in the exclusively masculine domain of the goat stables and mountain pastures; and I am informed that comparably abusive 'shameful talk' is typical of women's conviviality in the exclusively female domain of the *bašāli* 'house of retreat' (cf. Maggi 1998: ch. 5).

Egalitarian denial of status distinctions and 'directness' of both speech and behaviour could be illustrated in many other domains of Kalasha culture, including dance and music (Parkes 1994; 1996a), which all deny or evaluatively reverse distinctions of status etiquette characteristic of hierarchical Khó culture elsewhere in Chitral. Yet this status aversion should not be regarded as a chaotic shedding or literal 'unwrapping' of all social decorum. As Rayner (1988) indicates, egalitarian social institutions often paradoxically entail far *more* elaborate rules and regulations to ensure moral equity than those required for the simple replication of status distinctions in hierarchical regimes. Enclaves also tend to have distinctive etiquettes of social respect, primarily expressed through kinship gift-exchange, which duly acknowledge the socially sensitive 'face needs' of others, even while they deny or denigrate claims to any more permanent status differentiation. Kalasha parents thus seem just as anxious as Khó parents to instill a habitual sense of 'politeness' (*adyapī*, from Arabic-Persian *adab*, 'courtesy') or respect among their children, albeit mainly concerning appropriate terms of verbal address for kin, and the proper uses of their honorific extensions, or of teknonyms, according to specifically defined ceremonial contexts. Below, I briefly summarise such verbal and behavioural 'alternative etiquette' in three distinctive arenas of ceremonial performance, which are referred to as 'the three great customs' (*tre ghōna dastūr*) of Kalasha – those of prestige feasting and renown (*namūs*); of compensation in wife-elopement feuds (*doṇ-grōm*); and the ritually obscene midwinter festival of Chaomos – all of which variously emulate, exaggerate or 'invert' the cultural institutions of dominant neighbours.

Alternative etiquette in three ceremonial domains

I   *namūs: festal renown and reciprocal eulogy*

As indicated above, Kalasha are reluctant to acknowledge status differences in a moral context where supposedly 'all Kalasha are poor, all are equal'.

Seniority is perpetually contested by rival elders; and as Douglas' model of the enclave culture suggests, the practical politics of Kalasha communities therefore tends to be factional. Yet 'proto-hierarchical' authority is at least symbolically legitimated in Kalasha prestige feasts (*namusī çaṣṭ, jirē*), whose performance is itself a marked reversal of everyday egalitarianism, albeit still distinct from Khó Chitrali status hierarchy.

Kalasha prestige feasts are evidently similar to those of the 'Katir Kafirs' of eastern Afghanistan observed by Robertson (1896), from whom ceremonial procedures and rank symbols have been overtly adopted, together with oratorical loan-phrases of festal renown (Parkes 1992). The performance of such feasts also draws upon a common symbolic legacy of Turco-Persian regality comparable with the Mehtar's *mahraka* court ceremonies. Thus sumptuous clothing and regalia denote festally achieved emblems of rank, often awarded by a feast-giver to other senior elders like the Mughal investiture of *khelāt* robes of honour to nobility (Cohn 1983: 635–6). At major prestige feasts, the feast-giver is even conducted on horseback 'like a king' to the sacrificial sanctuary, where he supervises the proceedings seated on a carved throne or 'chair of renown' (*namusī kursī*). Praise oratory similarly portrays the feast-giver as a 'king' (*badšāh, mer*) ruling over dependent subjects who have assembled to feed off his bounty (Parkes 1992; cf. Darling 1979: ch. 5).

Such symbols of sovereignty were more elaborately displayed in the prestige feasts of the Afghan 'Katir Kafirs' of Bashgal, where Robertson (1896: 472–4) described a series of festal grades culminating in Mir (*mer*) 'kingship', associated with quasi-chiefly government. But even in these ceremonially ranked communities, practical leadership was still ultimately based upon competitive factional 'eldership' (Strand 1974). Among Kalasha, symbols of rank and regal sovereignty are further circumscribed within the ritual arena of prestige feasts, where, as among Kachin, 'it is as if anyone might be king for a day' (Leach 1954: 120). Moreover, festal renown is not emblematised in any overt privileges of rank outside of the ceremonially circumscribed arena of feasting or festival celebration. Such renown is properly the collective property of lineages, whose members should ideally collaborate in sponsoring feasts that reaffirm those of their common ancestors, rather than being the wholly personal 'symbolic capital' of any feast-giver.

Kalasha egalitarian mistrust of assertions of authority or self-aggrandisement does, however, still conflict with a performative focus on the ceremonial personality of feast-givers and senior elders as sovereign embodiments of group identity. But this potential contradiction of enclaved and proto-hierarchical moral claims is effectively resolved through the dramatic staging of praise recitation or 'name-naming' (*nom-nomēk*) in Kalasha prestige feasts and festivals, particularly through the carefully choreographed device of 'reciprocal eulogy' (Parkes 1994: 172f.). This entails alternating cycles of praise circulated between lineage elders according to strict protocols of balanced mutual admiration. Praise songs and oratory are also characterised by a highly stylised formulaic language, relying upon tacit background knowledge of ancestral traditions to implicate lineal renown indirectly (Parkes 1996a), often through an opaque collage of idiomatic intertextual 'quotations' (cf. Barber 1991). Such formulaic conventions also provide a protective veil of ambiguity for the disguise or distancing of personal opinions, which again may only be inferred with the aid of tacit contextual knowledge. Implicated criticism, as well as allusive praise, is thus conveniently communicated through the expressly indirect language of panegyric. Far from being 'empty vessels' of depersonalised authority (Bloch 1974; cf. Irvine 1979), the seemingly constrictive formulaic media of Kalasha song and oratory are therefore well suited to *implicate* privately critical as well as flattering opinions, within an oral context of extensively shared mutual knowledge, while at the same time conforming to a traditional repertoire of conventional imagery. They thus tactfully evade overt contradictions of prestige ranking and egalitarian rivalry inherent in Kalasha feasting.

2   *Doṇ-grōm: rude antagonism and indirect diplomacy in wife-elopement compensation*

While prestige feasting provides ceremonial authorisation for Kalasha eldership, effective political authority is rooted in the successful arbitration of disputes and inter-lineage feuds, particularly those of wife-elopement (*alaṣīṇ*).[4] After the elopement of a married woman, the lineages of the aggrieved ex-husband and the abductor become opposed in a state of formal hostility (*dušmanī*) or quasi-feud. Following several weeks of such hostilities, peace-making (*pruṣṭēk*, literally 'making good') is initiated by outside elders acting as mediators from lineages unrelated to the belligerent parties, who should help to arbitrate the 'work of compensation' (*doṇ-grōm*) in the form of a double repayment of bridewealth goods due to the ex-husband. After the bargaining of active (younger) lineage elders (*gaḍērak*), negotiating an always disputed amount of inflated bridewealth, senior (older) ceremonial elders (*gāḍa baṣāra*) are called in to impose an impartial communal settlement.

This 'work of compensation' is properly regarded as one of the 'three great Kalasha customs'. It is an elaborately orchestrated and performed 'social drama' of enacted antagonisms between lineages, whereby group eldership is expressly legitimated through diplomatic mediation. The performance of elopement, of interlineage hostilities, and of the cumulative arbitration of antagonisms, is indeed conducted according to an implicitly 'scripted' scenario of opposition and mediation at successively senior levels of segmentary authority, in which 'proto-hierarchy' is effectively enacted in an idiom of feud and peace-making (Parkes 1994: 162–4; cf. Black-Michaud 1975). Despite occasional outbreaks of violence, such group antagonisms are also discursively conceived as a kind of 'game' or ludic 'performance' (*labřē , tamašā*).

Yet such performances of abusive hostility and diplomatic mediation emulate the genuinely aggressive bloodfeuds (*badalā*) of neighbouring Pakhtuns, whose violent culture is considered even more 'wild' (*jaŋgalī*) than that of Kalasha themselves. Not only are conventional terms of inter-lineal abuse primarily adopted from Pashto obscenities (e.g. such bestial or incestuous expletives as *xinzir!* [pig-eater!] and *bančōt!* [sister-fornicator!]), but an entire honorific lexicon of (sexual) 'honour and shame' (*nāŋ, izzāt, ghairāt, šarm*, etc.) is peculiarly appropriated in the histrionic discourse of wife-elopement feuds, being otherwise wholly alien to Kalasha disregard for sexual modesty. Indeed, the widespread south Asian notion of patriarchal 'honour' (*izzāt*), marked by the sexual propriety of one's women, is never elsewhere employed in Kalasha egalitarian discourse (which rather alludes to distinctions of festal 'renown' as liberality, *namūs*: an Arabic loanword that significantly denotes female sexual chastity in both Pakhtun and Chitrali Islamic culture). Gestures of reconciliation in the 'work of compensation' are also seemingly modelled upon Pakhtun ceremonies of submission (Pashto *nanawatī*) in the context of bloodfeud (cf. Ahmed 1980: 90); while reciprocal elopements (*badēl alaṣīŋ*) between lineages are conducted expressly in terms of bloodfeud revenge (Pashto *badalā* 'exchange'; cf. Grima 1992: ch. 5).

The entire arena of rude abuse and mediation in Kalasha wife-elopement thus represents a ludic *simulation* of bloodfeud: but one in which, despite murderous words and histrionic indignation, nobody is ever actually killed, nor is sexual honour ever seriously at issue; yet which serves as a convenient forum of feigned violence for proto-hierarchical political influence to be tested in negotiations between elders, and for their symbolic authority to be demonstrated through diplomatic peace-making.

3   *Čaomōs: a festival of shameless and direct obscenity*

If the etiquette of festal renown is largely derived from the chiefly institutions and 'proto-hierarchical' idioms of the Afghan Kafirs, while that of wife-elopement compensation is modelled on Pakhtun bloodfeud and honour rivalries, a third arena of alternative and truly 'inverted' etiquette seems quite peculiar to Kalasha culture. This is the celebration of the midwinter festival of Chaomos (*čaomōs*), occupying almost the entire month of December, which is many respects the core observance of Kalasha religion.[5] The festival welcomes the annual visitation of a sovereign deity, Balimain, arriving on horseback from the mythical homeland of Tsiam at the winter solstice, whence he brings blessings of fertility. Balimain is known as the 'shameless god' (*bešārm dēwa*), who particularly enjoys the mutual slander and excited sexual feelings created between agonistically opposed parties of men and women. During the week prior to the solstice – when a ban (*diṣ*) on heterosexual contact is imposed, the men separated in their goat stables, while women take over the villages – the shameless god is said to 'tie a knot (of restraint) in peoples entrails' so as to feed on their heightened emotions created through agonistic sexual obscenity.

The rhythmic chanting of 'shameful songs' (*lač gřhũ*) or 'bad/rude songs' (*khāča gřhũ*) between the sexes is indeed a leitmotif of the whole festival.

Even weeks before its rites begin, groups of opposed youths and girls assemble on village rooftops to chant obscenities at one another, their songs often simply vulgar allusions to the genitals of the opposite sex (e.g. 'Itching, itching – beneath your skirts/Thrusting, rising – beneath your trousers'). But as the festival progresses, and older people begin to take part, the shaming verses become far more rudely inventive. Every despicable metaphor is used to personify the genitals of opponents, typically imagined as disgusting animals groaning and squealing with lust. The songs also become more pointed in attack, naming individuals with uninhibited reference to recent scandals, e.g.

Women   Bibi [a generic female, lit. 'queen'] sits proudly upon a golden throne/Making it creep and swell inside your trousers
Men   Bibi may take her pleasure on a golden throne/[But] the *pīnji* [vulva] must 'fast' inside your dress
Women   Violating your own step-mother, K's little mother's brother! ...
Men   Oh mother of M! From the old woman's smelly vagina a flying-fox emerged/With a 'bang, bang!' it opened up your buttocks like a broken drum

Such taunting songs are also chanted between rival 'up-valley' and 'down-valley' clan-moieties of men against men, and of women against women, boasting of known adulteries or revealing scandals whose public exposure can sometimes lead to outbreaks of fighting during the festival:

Up-Valley Man   I copulated with the mother of G, below D/Seeing my bare bottom, the balls of the father of G shrivelled up!
Down-Valley Man   You became a brushwood broom, my B.B./Sweeping up (the buttocks of) my J.K!

Despite a folk theory of quasi-catharsis or literal 'cleansing' through such exposed animosities, shaming songs perhaps more often provoke antagonisms that might better have remained dormant. Ritual hymns addressed to Balimain and other deities also continue this theme of aggressive obscenity: Balimain's magical horse is thus addressed as the 'hornless ram' (*khõṇḍa meṣalāk*), a 'deep-red blunt-headed ram', whose phallic imagery is rendered explicit in verses alluding to its 'striking' and 'thrusting' actions.

Such ritually licensed obscenity has evident parallels in saturnalian new year festivals documented elsewhere in south Asia, and indeed throughout Eurasia (and see Skinner, Chapter 11 in this volume). Leach's (1961) analysis of saturnalia in terms of van Gennep's threshold schema, entailing a liminal-sacred reversal of normal hierarchies at the turn of the year, applies quite well

to the ritual programme of Chaomos, as does Bloch's (1992) further development of this schema as an ideological drama of 'rebounding violence'
reinforcing traditional authority. For after women have taken over Kalasha
villages as their exclusive domain, when men are alternatively secluded in
their goat stables, the festival culminates with women's 'symbolic encompassment' or reappropriation by men. All adult males then line up into a
conga-like chain (*hui ṣāṭik*) in order of political influence, with senior ranking
leaders at the front, chanting hymns to the 'hornless ram' and grunting the
refrain *uahahahhā!* – mythically representing Balimain's whipping of his
magical horse, but also overtly enacting copulation – as they thrice encircle
the seated women.

Adequate symbolic analysis of such sexual obscenity would require further
consideration of Kalasha ritual dichotomies concerning sexual purity and
pollution (Parkes 1987), as well as contrastive representations of sexual
complementarity in other seasonal festivals. But it seems significant that sexual
antagonism and bodily rudeness should be so prominently highlighted in this
particular festival, which Kalasha consider emblematic of their cultural and
religious identity. Accounts of equivalent midwinter festivals among the pre-
Islamic Kafirs of Afghanistan indicate otherwise comparable rites,
accompanied by a licensed mocking of authority or hierarchical reversals of
age and status grades, but with rather little evidence of such extreme agonistic
sexuality (Jettmar 1975: 142f.). Within the Kalasha enclave, however, the
difference of sex is perhaps all that is available for an inverted symbolic constitution of ritual hierarchy, upon which other 'proto-hierarchies' of eldership
and political authority may be grounded (Parkes 1987; cf. Cacopardo and
Cacopardo 1989). Hence rude sexuality – already inherent in wife-elopement
disputes, in contrast to the sexual chastity emblematic of honour ranking in
surrounding Islamic cultures – must itself be chaotically exaggerated: as a
bacchanalian mirror of Kalasha identity, over-representing its anarchic egalitarian rivalries, upon which a minimal authority of arbitrating male elders
ultimately finds a precarious ritual justification (cf. Bloch 1985: 37–40).

Conclusions: wrapping up rudeness

This essay has briefly explored several senses of a polyvalent and complex
notion: rudeness as simplicity, as vulgarity, as abuse, and as obscenity. All of
these various senses of the impolite are also conveyed in Kalasha self-depic-
tion of their culture as 'wild' or literally rude in contrast to the 'civilised'
mores of Khó Chitrali culture. As James Boon argued, echoing Bakhtin as
much as Lévi-Strauss, it is not only anthropologists who exaggerate cultural
differences in terms of contrastive oppositions:

> [All] cultures, perfectly commonsensical from within, nevertheless flirt
> with their own 'alternities', gain critical self-distance, formulate complex

(rather than simply reactionary) perspectives on others, embrace negativi-
tites, confront (even admire) what they themselves are *not*.

(Boon 1982: 19)

Or as Michael Moerman put it more simply, echoing Edmund Leach on
the Kachin and other southeast Asian 'tribal' enclaves:

[M]embership in the set called 'tribal' can be described, defined, and
analyzed only in terms of that society's contrast to a civilized society
which it may fight, serve, mimic, or even become – but which it can
never ignore.

(Moerman 1974: 54)

I have suggested that the Kalasha, as an enclaved egalitarian minority, represent their culture in several respects as a 'rude reversal' or denial of Khó
Chitrali status hierarchy. Yet this is evidently *not* an absolute inversion of hierarchical status etiquette; nor does it entail a literal 'unwrapping' of social
decorum, except within defined ritual circumstances. Kalasha have long been
integrated within Chitrali culture, also being bilingual in the Khowar
language, and they have thus perforce mastered its *ta'árof*-like idioms of status
flattery in social interaction with outsiders. Kalasha have also not entirely
banished Chitrali hierarchy from their own internal culture. They expressly
incorporate Khó titles of nobility, for example, associated with feudal services
at the Mehtar's court, in panegyric oratory and praise songs (Parkes 1994;
1996b). We have also noted the adoption of festal symbols of rank from the
more hierarchically stratified Afghan Kafirs, as well as aspects of Pakhtun
honour rivalries and feuding institutions in Kalasha wife-elopement disputes.
Such 'heteroglossic' borrowings of alternative ideologies – indexed by adopted
loanwords or phrases, and sometimes full code-switching across several
languages – seem to be characteristic of peripheral enclaves, as Leach's Kachin
ethnography originally indicated. So perhaps is the demarcation of insulated
arenas of ceremonial performance in which 'ideal' symbolic hierarchies may
be temporarily manifested without overtly intruding into quotidian egalitarian morality (Leach 1954: 15–16). Such *plural* social etiquettes are arguably
more complex than well instituted hierarchies (Khó, Shan, Persian or Indic)
that rely on a simple mandala-like replication of ideal structures of tributary
authority – from family microcosm to state macrocosm – congruently stratified with openly acknowledged and emblematised diacritica of transitive rank
(cf. Tambiah 1985).[6]

Far from having a literally 'unwrapped' sociality – even if they may represent their supposedly rude-and-ready customs as such – egalitarian enclaves
thus arguably have more situationally sensitive 'dialogic' etiquettes of social
interaction than those of the dominant (monologic or homologic) hierarchical cultures in which they are encapsulated. Juxtaposing several different

registers of appropriate politeness and rudeness, drawing upon alternative ideological models or caricatures of social structure from dominant neighbours, and representing these in several performatively hedged ceremonial arenas, enclaved communities may even have more evocative implicational resources for oblique irony, indirection and dissimulation. Some of the most detailed ethnographies of status etiquette and gamesmanship significantly concern such egalitarian enclaves – agonistically competing to remain equal – rather than the ceremonial 'theatre states' of more politely instituted hierarchies.[7] Deceit or indirection in social interaction is also certainly not a prerogative of civilised state formation, even if hierarchically stratified cultures may be more reflexively concerned with the hidden lies and intentions that necessarily underwrite express politeness (Gilsenan 1976; Hughes-Freeland, Chapter 9 in this volume), while egalitarian enclaves may alternatively (mis)represent themselves as rudely transparent or 'simple' (cf. Moerman 1974: 63–5).

Several of these points were raised in Strecker's (1988: 154–69) critical modifications of politeness theory, pointing to a similarly *plural* or combinatory switching of categories of politeness characteristic of such enclaves as the Hamar of Ethiopia, where relations of social power are indeterminate and hence symbolically negotiable. But I am reluctant to replace a 'formal' model of politeness, elegantly outlined by Brown and Levinson, with a clumsier 'substantivist' typology of egalitarian rudeness(es). Politeness theory, allowing for multiply reflexive negations of its Gricean premises, including cooperative maxims of tit-for-tat opacity and slander, in fact applies quite well – even perhaps all too well – to such disparate discursive domains as praise oratory, dispute mediation, and obscene verbal duelling in Kalasha culture. Yet we should recognise that these *are* plural performative domains, with plural ideologies, that resist easy conflation into any simple societal 'type' of politeness or rudeness. In thus arguing that the situationally complex 'rudeness' of egalitarian enclaves may be more elaborately 'wrapped' in micro-performative arenas than the more uniformly staged 'politeness' of hierarchical cultures, I also suggest that our own conventional metaphors and cultural scripts of politeness and rudeness – of wrapped and unwrapped intentions, of polished and rough manners, or of indirect diplomacy and direct abuse – require further comparative ethnographic unravelling (Hendry 1993; cf. Janney and Arndt 1993).

Acknowledgements

I am grateful to Mary Douglas for longstanding correspondence on applying her notion of 'enclave' to Kalasha ethnography. This essay also benefited from the helpful comments of Jeremy MacClancy, Rodney Needham and Bill Watson. Research on Kalasha language and performance was supported by a grant from the Leverhulme Trust at the Queen's University of Belfast,

1988–90; while field research in 1989 was funded by the ESRC (R000 22 1087).

Notes

1 On Chitrali stratification, cf. Biddulph (1880: 61–8), Schomberg (1938: 211–18), Staley (1982: 188–95) and Eggert (1990); on milk-kinship (*chir-muži*), see Biddulph (1880: 82–3), Schomberg (1938: 225–6), and Parkes (2001).
2 Greeting between cross-sex bilateral kin entails three successive kisses on either male cheek (*ispaḍēk*) initiated by the female, who then initiates reciprocal hand-kissing (*hāstan sawāz hik*), similar to a reciprocal kissing of hair-braids (*čṻři sawāz hik*) among female kin; while distant female kin show respect to men with an initial curtsey accompanied by a sudden swivel upwards of their lowered hands (*hast khalēk*). Male greeting entails a simultaneous clasping of right and then left hands to each other's chest (*khūṭi dek*), followed by a reciprocal salute (*ispāte dek*).
3 E.g. brother *bāya*, sister *bāba*, father *dāda*, mother *āya*; grandparents *m. wāwa, f. āwa*, distinct from regular Old Indian derivations in the kinship lexica of all surrounding languages.
4 Such elopements are prominent among Kalasha, where over 70 per cent of betrothals and first marriages are dissolved through run-away wives (Parkes 1983: ch. 10; 1997: 49–50; forthcoming).
5 Cf. Jettmar (1975: 379–87), Wutt (1983), Loude and Lièvre (1984), Cacopardo and Cacopardo (1989).
6 This is not to deny that such hierarchies often have their own ceremonially circumscribed 'enclaved moments' of Bakhtinian carnival or Dumontian status reversal, typically self-enacted by enclaved social fractions (e.g. Boon 1982: 197ff., on Balinese clowning).
7 E.g. Bailey (1971) and Herzfeld (1985) on Mediterranean mountain enclaves; Parkin (1976; 1980) and Strecker (1988) on east African enclaves.

References

Abu al Fazl (1927) *The Ain-i-Akbari*, 2nd edn, trans. H. Blochmann, ed. D. C. Phillpot, Calcutta: Asiatic Society of Bengal.

Ahmed, A. (1980) *Pakhtun Economy and Society*, London: Routledge and Kegan Paul.

Aseer, S. W. K. (1996) 'The marriage of daughters in Chitral', in E. Bashir and Israr-ud-Din (eds) *Proceedings of the Second International Hindu Kush Cultural Conference*, Karachi: Oxford University Press, pp. 201–8.

Bahri, Hardev (1960) *Persian Influence on Hindi*, Allahabad: Bharati Press Publications.

Bailey, F. G. (ed.) (1971) *Gifts and Poison: The Politics of Reputation*, Oxford: Blackwell.

Barber, K. (1991) *I Could Speak until Tomorrow: Oriki, Women, and the Past in a Yoruba Town*, Edinburgh: Edinburgh University Press.

Barth, F. (1956) *Indus and Swat Kohistan: An Ethnographic Survey*, Oslo: Forenede Trykkerier.

Beeman, W. (1976) 'Status, style and strategy in Iranian interaction', *Anthropological Linguistics*, 18: 305–22.

——(1986) *Language, Status and Power in Iran*, Bloomington: Indiana University Press.

Biddulph, J. (1880) *Tribes of the Hindoo Koosh*, Calcutta: Office of the Superintendent of Government Printing.

Black-Michaud, J. (1975) *Cohesive Force/Feuding Societies*, Oxford: Blackwell.

Bloch, M. (1974) 'Symbols, songs, dance and features of articulation: is religion an extreme form of traditional authority?', *Archives Européennes Sociologiques*, 15: 55–181.

——(1985) 'From cognition to ideology', in R. Fardon (ed.) *Power and Knowledge*, Edinburgh: Scottish Academic Press, pp. 21–48.

——(1992) *Prey into Hunter: the Politics of Religious Experience*, Cambridge: Cambridge University Press.

Boon, J. (1982) *Other Tribes, Other Scribes: Symbolic Anthropology in the Comparative Study of Cultures, Histories, Religions and Texts*, Cambridge: Cambridge University Press.

Bourdieu, P. (1977) *Outline of a Theory of Practice*, trans. R. Nice, Cambridge: Cambridge University Press.

Brown, P. and Levinson, S. (1987) *Politeness: Some Universals in Language Use*, Cambridge: Cambridge University Press.

Cacopardo, A. M. and Cacopardo, A. S. (1989) 'The Kalasha (Pakistan) winter solstice festival', *Ethnology*, 28(4): 317–29.

Canfield, R. L. (ed.) (1991) *Turko-Persia in Historical Perspective*, Cambridge: Cambridge University Press.

Cohn, B. S. (1983) 'Representing authority in Victorian India', in *An Anthropologist Among The Historians and Other Essays*, Delhi: Oxford University Press, pp. 632–82.

Darling, E. G. (1979) 'Merit feasting among the Kalash Kafirs of northwest Pakistan', M.A. thesis, University of British Columbia.

Douglas, M. (1987) *How Institutions Think*, London: Routledge and Kegan Paul.

——(1993) *In The Wilderness: The Doctrine of Defilement in the Book of Numbers*, Sheffield: Sheffield University Press.

——(1996) Introduction to the 1996 edition, *Natural Symbols: Explorations in Cosmology*, London and New York: Routledge, pp. xi–xxx.

Eggert, P. (1990) *Die Frühere Sozialordnung Moolkhos und Turkhos (Chitral)*, Stuttgart: Franz Steiner (Beiträge zur Südasienforschung, Heidelberg 134).

Elias, N. (1978) [1939] *The Civilizing Process: Volume 1. The History of Manners*, Oxford: Blackwell.

Flanagan, J. G. (1989) 'Hierarchy in simple "egalitarian" societies', *Annual Review of Anthropology*, 18: 245–66.

Flanagan, J. G. and Rayner, S. (eds) (1988) *Rules, Decisions and Inequality in Egalitarian Societies*, Farnborough: Gower Press.

Ghulam Murtaza, M. (1962) *Nai Tarikh-i Chitral (New History of Chitral)* in Urdu; translated and compiled from the Persian Ms. *Tarikh-i Chitral* of Mirza Muhammad Ghufran, Peshawar: Ghulam Murtaza (Public Art Press).

Gilsenan, M. (1976) 'Lying, honour and contradiction', in B. Kapferer (ed.) *Transaction and Meaning*, Philadelphia: ISHI, pp. 192–219.

Goody, E. N. (1972) ' "Greeting", "begging" and the presentation of respect', in J. S. La Fontaine (ed.) *The Interpretation of Ritual*, London: Tavistock, pp. 39–71.

Grima, B. (1992) *The Performance of Emotion among Paxtun Women*, Karachi: Oxford University Press.

Hendry, J. (1993) *Wrapping Culture: Politeness, Presentation and Power in Japan and Other Societies*, Oxford: Clarendon Press.

Herzfeld, M. (1985) *The Poetics of Manhood: Contest and Identity in a Cretan Mountain Village*, Princeton: Princeton University Press.

Hussam-ul-Mulk, Shahzada (n.d.) 'The traditional culture of Chitral', Ms. edited and annotated by Karl Jettmar, typescript, 115 pp.

Hussam-ul-Mulk, Shahzada and Staley, J. (1968) 'Houses in Chitral: traditional design and function', *Folklore*, 79: 92–110.

Illi, D. W. (1991) *Das Hindukusch-Haus: zum symbolischen Prinzip der Sonderstellung von Raummitte und Raumhintergrund*, Stuttgart: Franz Steiner Verlag.

Irvine, J. T. (1974) 'Strategies of status manipulation in Wolof greeting', in R. Bauman and J. Sherzer (eds) *Explorations in the Ethnography of Speaking*, Cambridge: Cambridge University Press, pp. 167–91.

——(1979) 'Formality and informality in communicative events', *American Anthropologist*, 81: 773–90.

Janney, R. and Arndt, H. (1993) 'Universality and relativity in cross-cultural politeness research: a historical perspective', *Multilingua*, 12(1): 13–50.

Jettmar, K. (1975) *Die Religionen des Hindukusch*, Stuttgart, Berlin, etc.: W. Kohlhammer.

Katriel, T. (1986) *Talking Straight: Dugri Speech in Israeli Sabra Culture*, Cambridge: Cambridge University Press.

Leach, E. R. (1954) *Political Systems of Highland Burma: A Study of Kachin Social Structure*, London: Athlone Press.

——(1961) 'Time and false noses', in *Rethinking Anthropology*, London: Athlone Press, pp. 132–6.

Loude, J.-Y. and Lièvre, V. (1984) *Solstice päien: fêtes d'hiver chez les Kalash du Nord Pakistan*, Paris: Presse de la Renaissance.

Maggi, W. (1998) 'Our women are free: an ethnotheory of Kalasha women's agency', Ph.D. dissertation, Emory State University.

Moerman, M. (1974) 'Accomplishing ethnicity', in R. Turner (ed.) *Ethnomethodology*, Harmondsworth: Penguin, pp. 54–68.

Parkes, P. (1983) 'Alliance and elopement: economy, social order and sexual antagonism among the Kalasha (Kalash Kafirs) of Chitral', D.Phil. thesis, Oxford University.

——(1987) 'Livestock symbolism and pastoral ideology among the Kafirs of the Hindu Kush', *Man* (n.s.) 22: 637–70.

——(1992) 'Reciprocity and redistribution in Kalasha prestige feasts', *Anthropozoologica (L'Homme et L'Animal)*, 16: 35–44.

——(1994) 'Personal and collective identity in Kalasha song performance: the significance of music-making in a minority enclave', in M. Stokes (ed.) *Ethnicity, Identity and Music*, Oxford: Berg, pp. 157–85.

——(1996a) 'Kalasha oral literature and praise songs', in E. Bashir and Israr-ud-Din (eds) *Proceedings of the Second International Hindu Kush Cultural Conference*, Karachi: Oxford University Press, pp. 315–28.

——(1996b) 'Indigenous polo and the politics of regional identity in northern Pakistan', in J. MacClancy (ed.) *Sport, Identity and Ethnicity*, Oxford: Berg, pp. 43–67.

——(1997) 'Kalasha domestic society: practice, ceremony and domain', in H. Donnan and F. Selier (eds) *Family and Gender in Pakistan: Domestic Organization in a Muslim Society*, New Delhi: Hindustan Publishing Corporation, pp. 25–63.

——(2000a) 'Enclaved knowledge: indigent and indignant representations of environmental management and development among the Kalasha of Pakistan', in R. Ellen,

P. Parkes and A. Bicker (eds) *Indigenous Knowledge and Its Transformations: Critical Anthropological Perspectives*, New York: Harwood Academic, pp. 253–91.

——(2000b) 'Kinship as anger: relations of resentment in Kalasha divination', in A. Rao and M. Böck (eds) *Culture, Creation and Procreation in South Asia*, Oxford: Berghahn, pp. 271–96.

——(2001) 'Alternative social structures and foster relations in the Hindu Kush: milk kinship allegiance in former mountain kingdoms of northern Pakistan', in *Comparative Studies in Society and History*, 43(1): 4–36.

——(n.d.) 'A minority perspective on the history of Chitral: the Katore Dynasty in Kalasha oral tradition', forthcoming in Israr-ud-Din (ed.) *Proceedings of the 3rd International Hindu Kush Cultural Conference*, Karachi: Oxford University Press.

——(forthcoming) *Kalasha Community: Configurations of Enclavement in the Hindu Kush*, Oxford: Clarendon Press.

Parkin, D. (1976) 'Exchanging words', in B. Kapferer (ed.) *Transaction and Meaning*, Philadelphia: ISHI, pp. 163–90.

——(1980) 'The creativity of abuse', *Man* (n.s.) 15(1): 45–65.

Rayner, S. (1988) 'The rules that keep us equal: complexity and costs of egalitarian organization', in J. G. Flanagan and S. Rayner (eds) *Rules, Decisions and Inequality in Egalitarian Societies*, Farnborough: Gower Press.

Robertson, G. S. (1896) *The Káfirs of the Hind-Kush*, London: Lawrence & Bullen.

Schomberg, R. C. F. (1938) *Kafirs and Glaciers: Travels in Chitral*, London: Hopkinson.

Staley, J. (1982) *Words For my Brother: Travels between the Hindu Kush and the Himalayas*, Karachi: Oxford University Press.

Strand, R. F. (1974) 'A note on rank, political leadership and government among the pre-Islamic Kom', in K. Jettmar and L. Edelberg (eds) *Cultures of the Hindukush: Selected Papers from the Hindu-Kush Cultural Conference Held at Moesgård 1970*, Wiesbaden: Franz Steiner, pp. 57–63.

Strecker, I. (1988) *The Social Practice of Symbolization*, London: Athlone Press.

Tahir Ali (1981) 'Ceremonial and social structure among the Burusho of Hunza', in C. von Fürer-Haimendorf (ed.) *Asian Highland Societies in Anthropological Perspective*, Delhi: Sterling Publishers.

Tambiah, S. (1985) 'The galactic polity in Southeast Asia', in *Culture, Thought and Social Action: An Anthropological Perspective*, Cambridge MA: Harvard University Press, pp. 252–86.

Wutt (1983) 'Chaumus, "Vier mal Fleisch": Notizen zum winterlichen Festkalender der Kalash von Bumboret, Chitral', *Archiv für Völkerkunde*, 37: 107–48.

Part V

English – with diplomacy

Chapter 15

Ambiguity and verbal disguise within diplomatic culture

Annabel Black

This paper examines some of the ways in which ambiguity is used as a vehicle of indirect communication in diplomatic culture. It also looks at the importance of sometimes using indirect tactics to secure advantage or to eschew the overt meanings contained in words or gestures within diplomacy. Following some general observations and a discussion of the British Foreign Service, I shall relate the points raised to the experiences of those who marry officers within the profession. The question of spouses was the original focus of my research, and raises a set of interesting questions in itself. Diplomacy, more than many other walks of life, still tends to involve a high degree of behavioural and structural incorporation of spouses into the institutions within which their partners work. Yet, for all the effort that they often put in, spouses are of course in the main excluded from the central operations of diplomacy. Their relationship to foreign ministries and their hierarchies is obviously contingent, and this is reflected in the fact that their attitudes towards their position are often laden with ambiguity and the resort to indirect communication.

General observations

The manipulation of ambiguity, and indirectness within communication, lie at the heart of the diplomatic profession. The ambiguity built into language and the translation of language is a key tool in the process of diplomatic negotiation and compromise, and it is no accident that diplomacy has been dubbed (by a journalist) as the art of gentle obfuscation. An example of the use of ambiguity is found in the writing of the United Nations Security Council Resolution 242 in November 1967, following the Six Day War in the Middle East. Here a studied ambiguity in both the English and French texts was used to avoid specifying how much of the newly occupied territory should be required to be given up by Israel. In the case of the English text this involved the omission of either a definite or indefinite article: 'withdrawal of Israeli armed forces from territories occupied in the recent conflict'. In the

French text, the inbuilt ambiguity of *des* within the French language was used: 'retrait des forces armées des territoires occupés lors du récent conflit'.

There is also Sir Henry Wotton's[1] pun, which diplomats like to quote from time to time, defining an Ambassador as 'an honest man who is sent to lie abroad for the good of his country'.

A rather different example of tactics at another level of negotiation could be cited. Having observed the habits of an adversary during a rather long series of negotiations, an exasperated diplomat resorted to indirect measures: he sneaked into the conference room a few minutes before one of the sessions and vigorously shook the fizzy mineral water bottle sitting in front of his colleague's seat. Sure enough, five minutes into the session, the victim of this tactic sought some refreshment, instead to find himself doused in a shower and suffering, at least briefly, a considerable loss of face and possibly a couple of points in the ongoing argument.

The language of treaties, and pranks and skulduggery apart, we also need to consider the ambiguities and subtleties built into social relationships between diplomats. Talk to any diplomat and they will tell you that the outcome of many a negotiation has hung upon colleagues being mutually tuned into (or otherwise) personal preferences and quirks of character, and exercising some finesse when using this knowledge to complete a negotiation. Also, unlike other civil servants, diplomats have to strike an uneasy balance between presenting and representing the interests of their country abroad (or rather those of whichever government happens to be in power) at the same time as getting along well with foreign colleagues, or at least appearing to do so. This can involve a sharp testing of personal integrity as well as sometimes some pretty strenuous mental gymnastics.

Alongside this odd mixture of highly personalised relationships and the suppression of personal opinions, there is also the fact that the whole business of representation, at all levels, involves a good share of the infiltration of public life into the private and intimate spheres. In all missions, including the big multilateral ones in Brussels or New York, it is still true that informal contacts, whether in corridors, restaurants or around private dinner tables, inevitably play a major role in negotiating and decision-making. In spite of endless financial reviews, the role played by entertaining within representation is still seen as central. As a result of this, whilst living at post, those in representational grades are duty bound to give time, space and energy to entertaining in their homes, and are provided with living spaces appropriate for this. This is particularly true of Ambassadorial Residences, and it is often pointed out that inviting colleagues the Residence will often carry more clout than simply going to a restaurant, or putting up guests in hotels.

This emphasis on using 'private' places for public functions was a point taken up by Callan (1984: 10) when discussing the factors influencing wives' incorporation into men's work. Developing Ardener's (1981: 14) observation that 'the notion of "private" as opposed to "public" might be seen as a criterion for "mapping" metaphysical space … *regardless* of the fact that some "private places" can really be walked into', Callan observed that 'incorporation seems to belong to a class of situations where the "metaphysical map" *first* identifies a public and private sphere, *then* picks up the first and inserts it "into" the second'. The ways in which representational homes in diplomatic life are used, and above all the Residence itself, provide very obvious examples of this. It is significant that the official guide to running Head of Mission Residences states that they should be run like small hotels but *feel* like country houses around the world, thus quite literally involving the picking up of the public sphere and inserting it into the private. As we shall see later, this ambiguous prescription for spatial usage can generate its own pattern of indirect communication.

The example of the Foreign Office itself can also be cited. On the one hand it is an extremely public and grand place. Yet in a bizarre way there is an atmosphere whereby the private has somehow been inserted into the public: some of the offices emanate a country house atmosphere, complete with well upholstered three-piece suites in pleasing fabrics, and even the grand public spaces have a clubiness and surprising intimacy about them.[2]

Representation and wrapping

Given the above factors, it is hardly surprising that a number of mechanisms operate which serve to mediate the social intercourse of those involved. In an environment where appearances and public face matter so much, certain devices are needed both to mask off the public role of the individual from his or her private persona and to mediate encounters between colleagues. Indeed, it is the practised use of such mechanisms which gives rise to the image of diplomacy as consisting of a bunch of smooth and suave talking mandarins.

It follows that diplomacy pays the respect due to the fact that, quite apart from the content within any written or verbal communication or negotiation, its orchestration, form and the symbolic meanings conveyed also carry a substantive weight in their own right. Of interest here is Hendry's (1993) concept of 'wrapping'. In her discussion of Japanese culture she concentrates very explicitly on the variety of ways in which wrapping itself can provide fundamental insights into cultural meaning and communication. There are a number of ways in which the concept applies in this context. These include, as indicated above, the wrapping of space in general, but also the wrapping of the intimate space of the person. Clothes and dressing up feature a great deal in diplomatic life, and the wrapping of the person is used in ways which not only explicitly affirm the official position of the individual (as in the donning of diplomatic uniforms) but which also communicate various representational messages. When she was the Head of Mission spouse in Paris, Sylvia Jay became well known and was featured in magazines, not least for the stylish way in which she wore the clothes of leading British fashion designers.

Diplomatic parties sometimes feature fancy-dress themes, including ones involving everybody quite literally wrapping themselves up in representational cloth – the instructions being for everyone to turn up dressed in creatively tailored versions of their national flags.

Also important is the wrapping of language; diplomatic communication in general sometimes seems to be a perverse mixture of linguistic precision and ambiguity. It is a truism to say that civil servants are trained to express themselves in unambiguous language *except* where ambiguity is of the very essence. The British Foreign Office appears to carry this a little further, and still insists on the beauty and elegance of the language communicated within the sea of paper and electronic mail generated every day. The importance given to elegant drafting is undoubtedly one of the weapons within the art of diplomacy and, for all the insistence on clarity, it can also lead to a lack of transparency. For instance, certainly young officers find that the traditional tendency to pepper drafts with Latin phrases and classical or historical references, along with a long-standing addiction to the use of metaphor, can lead to obfuscation rather than clarification, with style winning out over content.

Further examples are found when it comes to food, social intercourse and time; and surrounding all these layers, there is the 'outer wrapping' provided by protocol.

Protocol ...

... or, as Moorhouse (1977: 235) has put it 'what grammar is to language and what theology is to religion'. Although less formally structured than in the past, protocol acts as a key mechanism for organising who does (or wears) what, when and how in diplomatic relationships. It also involves the orchestration of all the forms of understanding between governments about how their representatives conduct business and behave formally towards one another. As such, protocol is a good example of both direct and indirect communication: as a direct form it makes things happen; it also structures the way in which things happen; and it can be used as a medium to signal more general relationships and alignments between states. Thus there is a great deal more to protocol than *placement*[3], whether to bow or curtsey to a royal person, and how to pay calls and 'play' cards.

Within protocol, as with any system of classification, there is room for manipulation. Goldstein (1998: 54) has pointed out how gestures involving a breach of protocol, such as the refusal of a proffered handshake, can be used to convey independent messages, as in the example of Prince Charles pointedly ignoring Idi Amin's proffered hand at Jomo Kenyatta's funeral in 1978.

Goldstein also points out that the diplomatic insult can be 'a carefully crafted instrument of statecraft used as a way of communicating extreme displeasure when all other efforts of communication have failed' (*ibid.*), a tactic for which the French have a particular predilection. An example cited by Goldstein in this context involves the French expression of displeasure with a number of American policies during 1996 – notably over the UN secretary-generalship and the command of the NATO southern command. At the proposal of a toast at the US Secretary of State Warren Christopher's last NATO dinner, the French Foreign Minister abruptly left the room. To make the gesture clear, the French Ambassador to NATO took the minister's place ... and ostentatiously turned his back on the room while the toast was conducted.

Structure, ideology and communication within the British Foreign Service

In the case of the British Diplomatic Service a key source of ambiguity and indirectness in communication flows from the way in which an ideology of egalitarianism within the service has, since the 1940s, strained to temper the strict hierarchy and the overall elitist image of the Foreign Office as a whole. A strong theme within this ideology is the notion of the service as being 'family friendly' or even 'a family service', and as one operating according to a culture of dedication, duty and public service. Naturally, claims to 'culture' within institutions are themselves ideological, and need to be analysed as such, in order to examine how such claims are borne out in practice and to point to the contradictions involved.

Within the Foreign Office the notion of family friendliness is not at all new, although the meanings contained in the phrase have altered radically over the years. The origins of the family friendly image of the Foreign Office can be traced back to the postwar period of optimism and reform, which involved the liberalisation and democratisation of recruitment into the Service. During this period it was declared permissible for women to be recruited for diplomatic posts[4] and the two overall aims set down in the White Paper (Cmnd. 6420) upon which these reforms were based were to widen the sphere of the Foreign Office's activities and to make it more flexible in its recruitment and career development patterns. The idea was that the Foreign Office be opened to men and women from all walks of life, whether or not they had private means.

Certainly, in terms of trying to direct the policies governing the allowances system, the Foreign and Commonwealth Office (FCO) has served its members well. While as a way of life diplomacy is far from 'family friendly', over the years the Service has been able to negotiate conditions of service which go some way towards mitigating this. And it is the existence of an allowances system, and in particular one ensuring continuing education for children, which is often cited as a reason why officers remain in the Service having once joined it (within the armed forces a similar allowances system is referred to as 'the golden hand-cuffs').

Also important is the notion of loyalty and public duty. It should be remembered that officers are still given no written contract of employment and serve at Her Majesty's pleasure: they can be dismissed at any point, although resort to this is very rare.

To some extent and in some situations the common sense of shared loyalty and duty do lead to an egalitarianism within internal dealings and relationships in the Service. This is reflected in the fact the clear structural hierarchy is frequently tempered by an observance of egalitarianism in day-to-day dealings. Also, to date, there has been a certain egalitarianism built into the tradition of 'generalism' within the Foreign Office, whereby its policy has been to move people around both geographically and in their areas of specialisation.

One aspect of experience which reinforces a sense of common mission and egalitarianism is in cases where diplomats find themselves in challenging or dangerous situations, in circumstances which totally contradict the public image of the diplomat's life as being one of luxury, as when the missions are in so-called hardship posts.

But all missions at certain times exhibit and live up to the idea that all must work together for a common good, and that working together 'as a family' should take precedence over observance of the hierarchy. These are most obviously expressed in the mission get-togethers which punctuate the political year – for instance in the Christmas party. The Christmas party, and the pantomime or revue which usually accompanies it, has a special role to play in mission life. In a way which has often been used to describe carnivals, it is an occasion not only for collectively letting off steam, but one where the normal rules of courtesy and deference governing rank can be suspended for an evening. Officers at whom one would never dare poke fun in normal life are allowed to appear as funny and undignified in the guise of their 'dramatic' personalities. Also, diplomatic situations and negotiations normally associated with tension and tattered nerves can be sent up and, for an evening at least, be put in their place.

Yet, the fact remains that the FCO is not only extremely hierarchical, but is also an institution which, in common with foreign services throughout the world, has a reputation for elitism. The most telling examples of indirect communication, or at least a lack of transparency in communication, arise at those points where the realities of the hierarchy rub against the notion of team spirit; and when the issue of elitism comes up against the ideal that the Service should be open to men and women from all walks of life.

Until very recently, one of the most blatant facets of the overall structure undermining team spirit and any pretence of egalitarianism was the existence of a hierarchy within a hierarchy, insofar as there were two parallel grading streams: the 'fast' or 'A' stream and the 'main' or 'E' stream: fast streamers could expect promotion much faster and to higher levels than those in the main stream, and the existence of the two streams was reflected in the division of labour. Although not alluded to in day-to-day dealings, the existence of these two streams could lead to indirect put-downs and/or expressions of resentment between colleagues, and the system has now been abandoned.

Also important is the way in which the blend of egalitarianism and hierarchy has led both to a paternalistic style of management within the Foreign Office, and a lack of transparency when it comes to implementing personnel policies. It is one thing to be on first-name terms with a line manager, quite another to know that your fate may be in their hands when it comes to allocating your box 'ratings' in your annual report. Since the introduction of performance pay, it has become official that such ratings are crucial indices governing future pay and promotion, and in reality they always have been. Yet until recently officers were not allowed access to their annual reports, which record in small detail their line managers' views on both their own strengths and weaknesses and, until the late 1980s, the suitability of their spouses. When inevitable personality clashes and misunderstandings arise, there are cases when these might be arbitrarily reflected in an officer's box ratings, thus placing a blight on their future career. This is an important illustration of the fact that the constraints of the system can sometimes imply an inbuilt indirectness, obliqueness and lack of transparency.

Also, despite several attempts to reform the boarding system (i.e. the process through which officers are allocated new postings and tours of duty), there is always a lingering sense that undisclosed information and 'back room' deals play their part in determining who goes where and when. Provided an individual's career progresses well, this lack of transparency presents no problem, and it is commonplace to hear officers who have found themselves in prestigious posts occupying key positions attributing their progress to the 'good luck' that they have. However, those who suffer through the system can often end up feeling excluded, not allowed to take a hand in determining their own future, and sometimes paranoid. Some find that bids for jobs under the current boarding system are repeatedly rejected, occasionally resulting in extended periods of 'gardening leave'. To be shovelled mid-career into a metaphorical herbaceous border can be undermining, and lead to the feeling of being trapped in a system, yet excluded from the operations of power which direct it.

When problems arise, rank also intervenes in the way that they are dealt with. Part of this is due to what Jolly (1992) has referred to, in the case of the military, as the 'heavy hand of paternalism'. Although officers and their families in the Diplomatic Service are by no means subject to the same levels of obsession with standardisation and order as are those in the military, a parallel can be drawn. In the case of the Diplomatic Service, paternalism can have the effect of engendering a culture of dependency which may not always be welcomed by those those at the receiving end, but one which might simply serve to reinforce the power and authority of those bestowing 'help' upon the 'lower ranks'. Although it is amongst junior officers and their families that these experiences of rank take their most naked form, I believe that this culture of dependency is more general throughout service culture, even though often experienced in more covert forms: as someone put it, 'we are forever trying to urge spouses to be independent, but when they are at posts they are not even encouraged to change their own light bulbs!'.

Diplomatic spouses: an ambiguous category?

On the face of it the term 'diplomatic spouse' sounds like an anachronism, and the original aim of my research was to examine the ways in which identification with this category has declined over time. Although the research has borne this out to some extent, the reality is more complicated. It is true that spouses are often cagey, indeed far from direct, when it comes to revealing their own feelings, and sometimes comment that 'there is really no such thing as a diplomatic spouse' on the grounds that, given that so many individuals are involved, it is impossible to make any generalisations about how diplomats or indeed their spouses conduct and view their lives. A few actively reject such a category, and remain determined to pursue their own careers and/or family lives without being affected by the career of their officer spouses. However, for many, the category of 'diplomatic spouse' remains as a hook upon which to hang identity, for all that it is no longer either a safe or sometimes even welcome one. At the very least, marriage to a diplomat usually involves a degree of movement from place to place (although a few, particularly male, spouses do not always accompany their spouses to post), and life at post inevitably involves intimate contact with other diplomatic families and some participation within diplomatic culture.

Closely connected with the 'family friendly' ideology of the FCO, spouses are on the whole encouraged to participate in representational and mission life. In some cases they have very little choice but to participate – this is true of the majority of Heads of Mission spouses, who frequently become intimately clued up on the inner workings of diplomacy and called upon to put their intelligence, knowledge and charm, and not least their time and labour, to good use. Yet however incorporated spouses might be, or feel themselves to be, into the institution and profession, they have always been only indirectly connected to the institution, and often unclearly placed when it comes to the way that both its demands and its rights and privileges flow across the conjugal link. However, the situation has shifted over time.

In the years following World War II, with the introduction of an allowances system, the expectation was that wives would accompany their husbands to post, and once there they were viewed very much as a resource. They were not abroad simply to keep company with their spouses, but to put in their own share of work towards representing their country, and also to act as a kind of staff to the wife of the Ambassador. Of course, the idea of wives representing a resource was in itself nothing new. There are many examples of eighteenth- and nineteenth-century *grandes dames* excelling in representational duties in their capacities as Ambassadors' wives.[5] Most ambassadresses came from the same upper ranks of society as their husbands: they were used to managing large households, managing staff, and to the principle of *noblesse oblige*. Often distinguished and highly accomplished women in their own right, they played an essential role in developing contacts abroad.

Postwar reforms put the whole situation on a new footing. A large increase in intake meant that officers and their wives who were not necessarily used either to managing troops of servants or to the niceties of upper class manners were recruited into the service, and left in no doubt that once abroad they would be 'on duty'. Those who remember the postwar years recall that, however ridiculous it might seem now, people simply obeyed and saw the performance of representational duties as a natural extension of their role as wives. The incorporation of wives into the institution was very much on the lines of inclusion within a 'family organisation'. At post, 'junior wives' were expected to turn to their seniors for maternal advice, and were given appropriate tips in the various courses organised to prepare them before going. For instance, in her talk given to a going abroad course, Lady Henderson reassured 'new' wives that

> going abroad is not like going to another planet, abroad is very much like home. An Embassy is a family, in some ways rather an old-fashioned family. But you will find that if and when you need help, as in a family, you will always find someone who will help you.

The fact that the recruitment of this new informal part of the representational workforce took place through the idiom and the channel of the family, and that women were thus performing their duties by virtue of their status as wives, had an important effect upon how women perceived their role and sense of duty. Repeatedly, women have told me that the bottom line was that they loved their husbands, considered marriage to be a partnership, and that if this spilled over into performing roles which served public ends, this was to be accepted.

This equation of love/duty to husband = (if accidentally) duty to the Service itself might seem quaint and outdated now, but we should remember that many of the people who were recruited into the system thirty odd years ago are now married to officers of senior ranks within the Service. There are those who still retain some of the beliefs about their roles and the structure within which they live and work, attitudes which were developed and nurtured early on in their experiences. Others, whilst remembering their early days, would bend over backwards to avoid imposing similar experiences upon their youngers. Thus this theme of dedication is still of relevance when looking at the relationship of spouses to the Service. However, it seems that no sooner had wives been conditioned to the whole premise of dedication involved in incorporation, than the tables turned.

Writing in 1976, Callan introduced the concept of a premiss of dedication as operating as a kind of psychological means which served to resolve, or at least to fudge, the paradoxical issue that wives took on work which had a conspicuous number of non-salary-like features. It is significant that Callan was writing at a time of tremendous flux in attitudes, and it is possible that the mechanism she discussed reflected the uncertainty of that decade. It was a period in which, crucially, there was a shift in the overall ideology of the role from the firm territory of duty and obligation to the far more shifting one of choice.

As a result of debate and pressure from the Diplomatic Service Wives Association (later renamed the British Diplomatic Spouses Association and now called the Diplomatic Service Families Association) there was a gradual change in the stance of the Office towards the view that spouses were not expected to do anything in support of the officer but that anything the spouse did on a voluntary basis would be greatly appreciated by the Service. This quintessentially ambiguous position remains the stance to this day, and is now one of the arguments used by the Office against the idea that spouses (other than those of Heads of Mission) should be paid for the work they contribute. In spite of changes, several debates which began in the 1970s remain unresolved, and there are ways in which the constraints of diplomacy and of the Foreign Office itself continue to flow across the conjugal link.

Hierarchy and spouses

One of the questions which still causes disagreement and resentment is that of the extent to which the experiences of the spouse mirror the rank and position of their partner, and the degree to which rank and competition remain an issue amongst spouses. In talking to people about their experiences, these questions arise more frequently than practically any other and give rise to contradictory and uncertain responses.

There is a contradiction involved: spouses are often seen as the guardians of the maintenance of democracy yet it is sometimes amongst them that hierarchy is experienced in its most naked form. The dilemmas associated with the vicarious experience of rank and the ambiguities to which they can give rise are experienced at all levels. However, relative rank is perhaps most clearly brought out and experienced at the extreme ends of the scale: by those married to the most junior and to the most senior officers. One of the main problems that can be encountered by those married to junior officers is the experience of straightforward snobbery, and it is by these spouses that the vicarious experience of rank can be experienced in its most naked form. One example of this is the possibly apocryphal story of how a Deputy Head of mission was told that the wife of a Security Officer was studying for a high-powered university qualification and responded by saying 'who on earth does *she* think *she* is?'. There are also examples of Security Officers' wives who have offered to join the DSWA/BDSA Committee at post, only to be rejected on the quite vague grounds of 'not being quite suitable' or even very explicitly because of their vicarious rank. It is amongst the above groups of families that stresses and welfare problems most commonly arise.

There is a great difference in views as to how to negotiate the existence of a vicarious hierarchy and as to where the source of it lies. Some still feel that it is unrealistic and even dangerous to ignore its existence; others believe that if all the talk of choice means anything then this should very much involve the freedom to ignore the ranking system amongst officers' spouses. Some (not necessarily those married to senior officers) feel that it 'comes from below', others (not necessarily those married to junior officers) that 'it comes from above'. Evidence can be found for all these points of view; no wonder that there is a sense in which the question of rank seems to be everywhere and nowhere.

Role and representation

Putting on or giving a good show is integral to the representative side of diplomatic life, and is obviously an aspect of the institutional project which most encompasses spouses.

Most female spouses continue to 'opt in' in the sense that they accept, with varying degrees of relish, that living at post entails involvement in representing their country. At the very least this may involve organising supervision for childcare, phoning around for *traiteurs*,[6] and preparing the house for the occasional dinner or reception. More often, many labour hours end up expended in finding ingredients, either organising the cooking or doing it oneself, and clearing up afterwards when entertaining. Entertaining and being entertained can, in some posts, be exhausting, time-consuming and stressful, and spouses differ very much as to where they draw the line and how they do their accounting, both in terms of labour put in to organising entertainment and of time spent being entertained.

One example of a wife resorting to indirect means to limit the time spent being entertained, in the morning at least, is cited by Hickman (1999: 123). Harriet Granville, exasperated and bored by the custom of paying relentless morning visits within the Parisian society of *élégantes* (the principal society hostesses) in 1825, slyly commented that 'I seldom, now that I know their dear little habits and outings, find anybody at home'.

Many have stories to tell of the terrors of *placement*: Moorhouse (1977: 235) rather dismissively describes *placement* as being 'merely the crumbs under the table of protocol'. But tables and how to arrange people around them can give much pause for thought. When preparing for a party, many a spouse will bear in mind the apocryphal tale of the French guest who, insulted by the position he was given, turned his plate over and refused to be served food throughout the meal. Somebody who had been posted to Saudi Arabia described the havoc often caused by the fact that guests would often offer assurances that they were going to come with their wives, only to turn up at the last minute with a male cousin or brother as a substitute. As with all protocol, *placement* is open to some manipulation, but things do not always go according to plan: one self-important diplomat, entertaining some very important guests for dinner, managed to manipulate the *placement* in order to place himself directly opposite the most senior person present, only to find his plan thwarted by the presences of an unusually tall flower arrangement which severely hampered any dignified contact and conversation.

Heads of Mission spouses

The more senior the officer becomes, the less leeway the spouse has to with-draw once they go to post. In the vast majority of cases, spouses of Heads and Deputy Heads of Mission have realistically got no choice whatsoever but to involve themselves in the representational package. Indeed, the official attitude towards the role of the Head of Mission spouse provides a rather good example of indirectness and intention. For, in line with the rest of its policy on spouses, the administration still likes to stress that there is freedom of choice involved. The guide to running a mission goes so far as to say that 'London imposes no more restrictions on her as Head of Mission's spouse than they did when she was the wife of the First Secretary Commercial'. As many could testify, there is a certain disingenuousness in this remark. In reality there is little escaping that the role remains one which carries its own partic-ular set of responsibilities and privileges. It therefore deserves a brief discussion in its own right.

Earlier I mentioned that the aim of embassy entertainment is to give guests the impression that they are coming to a private house, and not to a hotel operated by a paid staff.[7] As well as providing a base for visitors and acting as the home for the Ambassador and his or her family, a Residence should also represent a showcase for all things British. Great care, time and money (within carefully controlled limits) need to be spent over selecting pictures, furniture and fittings (and in a few cases it is up to the spouse to find the Residence itself). Moreover, it is important to place a personal stamp upon the sometimes grand, but possibly rather impersonal, surroundings. The overall orchestration of all the above functions falls, in the vast majority of cases, to the wife of the Ambassador.

Apart from the managerial role of running a Residence, there is the ques-tion of the loss of privacy, and the ambiguity involved in maintaining the idea that visitors are 'visiting a private house'. Several wives of Ambassadors have mentioned that running a hotel would be easy in comparison – managers are not expected to entertain and remember all the names of their guests, let alone take breakfast with them.[8] The need to cater for the individual needs and tastes of guests can present its own set of difficulties, and it seems that ministers and MPs can be a pretty quirky lot. It is not unknown for government ministers to take the metaphor of Residence as a small hotel at face value. Hickman (1994) cites the example of shoes being left outside the door for cleaning. It is also said that it is important to know the individual quirks of members of the royal family, and preparing for royal visits can involve weeks of preparation and planning.

Also, although the FCO sometimes plays down the grandness of its Residences, the fact is that in many posts the whole point of having a Residence for the Head of Mission is to represent British interests and culture in the most effective way possible.[9] In those Residences which are historically notable buildings, the separation between public and private 'family' space can in some ways be very marked. For instance, at the Residence in Brussels, the accommodation occupied by the Ambassador and his family is tucked away at the top of the house, well separated from the grand reception rooms below. In other residences, this separation is not so obvious, but representation always lies at the core of Residence life: Ambassadors and their spouses are encouraged to make the fullest use possible of their homes to promote 'UK Ltd'.

Many of the ambiguities associated with the collision between public and private life experienced by diplomats and their families as a whole become far more pronounced when the officer is a Head of Mission. There are many ways in which Head of Mission spouses are inevitably caught up within a series of public roles in which the rank of their partner spills over to their own position and status, most importantly in terms of how they are seen by others. There is no other role occupied by a spouse which equates with it, if only for the simple reason that if and when it is taken on it very literally extends to the person involved. Whilst the public status might flow from being the partner of the Head of Mission, a wide range of roles are adopted by virtue of the individual's independent status as a public figure.

Relationships between Head of Mission spouses and other spouses

In spite of changes over the last two decades, the dilemmas associated with rank and ambiguity are most clearly brought out when it comes to considering the position of the Ambassador's spouse in relation to mission life as a whole. Although many Ambassadors' spouses insist on being addressed on first-name terms and try hard not to be stiff and formal with other mission wives, there is inevitably an air of secrecy and mystery surrounding them. They may be friendly, but can seem rather sphinx-like. One obvious reason for this is that they are often privy to information inaccessible to others. Also, however much it is a case of 'don't mention the hierarchy', a certain degree of *mana* is always carried by the person occupying the position, even though they might sometimes wish it were otherwise. One Head of Mission wife told me how, no sooner had she eventually persuaded people in the mission to speak to her on first-name terms, than, during their posting, her husband was awarded a KCMG and she became a 'Lady'. She was immediately robbed of her first name and addressed, against her own will, by her new title.

Another factor is that while, these days, many Ambassadors' wives shy away from presuming upon the labour and time of other mission spouses, this can have the unintended effect of making them appear more distant and inaccessible. Indeed, some occupying this position do feel that in terms of their relationships with the mission there is more distance than in the past.

Partially responsible for the continuing ambiguity built into the relationship between the spouse of the Head of Mission and other spouses is that old mythologies die hard. Important amongst these is the idea that the husband's standing and career will be prejudiced by signs of weakness in his wife. There is still the feeling that any shortcomings revealed to the spouse of the HoM will somehow filter back and cause damage to the officer, and under these circumstances informal and easy relationships become very difficult to establish.

Given all the above factors, the position of Ambassador's wife can require a sense of sacrificing her own identity in order to fulfil a role which is more encompassing and time-consuming than that played out by other spouses in the mission. Yet, like other spouses, the Ambassador's wife has no official position herself; she might be shown deference, but she is without official authority to make demands or to threaten formal sanctions. It can be an isolating role, and it is no wonder that some Ambassadors' wives have been known to crack up under the strain. Others learn to manage the role by re-defining their *mana* and resolving that 'it's only a game'; all the pomp, ceremony and deference are neither permanent or accruing to the person, but go with the job. One person I spoke to said how useful it was to see the performance of the duties involved quite literally as 'playing a role', in a theatrical sense. She found that remembering lessons from theatrical experience both gave her the stamina to carry out the role and a means through which to shrug off what might otherwise have felt like the occasional, inevitable, disaster: a device which may well be seen as applicable to the diplomatic profession more generally.

Conclusions

In this paper I have explored four main themes. First, the way in which diplomatic culture in general generates indirect patterns of communication owing to the need to employ subtle tactics in settling important matters of state. Second, the way in which individuals involved in diplomatic activity become involved in a set of relationships which contain elements which are highly personalised but which also involve both the suppression of personal opinions and the collision of private and public spaces. Third, in exploring the case of the British Foreign Service, I have looked at how contradictions inherent within the institution itself, between hierarchy and egalitarianism, generate their own patterns of indirect communication. Finally, I have tried to show how some of the sources of indirect communication discussed infiltrate the experiences of spouses, themselves only indirectly entangled with the inner workings of the art.

The practised use of ambiguity, verbal disguise and veiled intention remain central to diplomacy. Diplomats, and their partners, sometimes bemoan the fact that they are often under attack for being surrounded by secrecy and mythology, but it may be precisely these characteristics that help to mark out the distinctness of experience within this profession.

Notes

1 Sir Henry Wotton was King James I's envoy.
2 In designing the building, George Gilbert Scott had the vision of creating a 'kind of national palace, or drawing room for the nation'.
3 The rules governing whom to place where around a dinner table.
4 Women had already been admitted on a permanent basis as clerical and executive officers in 1921. It was not until 1971 that the rule was lifted requiring women to resign on marriage.
5 Hickman (1999) provides an excellent account of their experiences.
6 Catering establishments, producing ready made dishes which can often be bought both on the premises and for delivery to one's home.
7 In most Residences, guests are given written guidance in their rooms as to how much and whom to tip amongst the staff.
8 Although Hickman (1994) mentions how her mother was once enraged by one of her house guests, an MP, who informed her that breakfast the next day would be a working one, and that her presence was not required.
9 About a hundred of the buildings within the Overseas Estate are particularly notable, either for their historical connections, architectural importance or location. Some, like the Embassy in Tokyo or the Consulate-General in Istanbul, came to the UK on condition that they be used only for diplomatic or consular purposes.

References

Books and articles

Ammundsen, A. (1996) *From Pillar to Post*, London: Minerva Press.
Applebaum, A. (1994) 'Fall guys for a fallen state', *Spectator*, 2 April.
Ardener, S. (ed.) (1981) *Woman and Space: Ground Rules and Social Maps*, London: Croom Helm.
Callan, H. (1975) 'The premiss of dedication: notes towards an ethnography of diplomats' wives', in S. Ardener (ed.) *Perceiving Women*, London: Dent & Sons, pp. 87–104.
——(1984) 'Introduction', in H. Callan and S. Ardener (eds) *The Incorporated Wife*, London: Croom Helm.
Finch, J. (1983) *Married to the Job: Wives' Incorporation in Men's Work*, London: George Allen & Unwin.

Goldstein, E. (1998) 'Developments in protocol' in J. Kurbalija (ed.) *Modern Diplomacy*, Mediterranean Academy of Diplomatic Studies, University of Malta: Malta, pp. 49–56.

Hendry, J. (1993) *Wrapping Culture: Politeness, Presentation and Power in Japan and Other Societies*, Oxford: Clarendon Press.

Hickman, K. (1994) 'The dutiful and the damned', *Sunday Telegraph Review*, 9 October.

——(1999) *Daughters of Britannia: The Life and Times of Diplomatic Wives*, London: HarperCollins.

James, S. (1995) *Diplomatic Moves: Life in the Foreign Service*, London and New York: The Radcliffe Press.

Jenkins, S. and Sloman, A. (1985) *With Respect, Ambassador*, London: BBC Books.

Jolly, R. (1992) *Military Man, Family Man, Crown Property?*, London: Brassey's.

Moorhouse, G. (1977) *The Diplomats: The Foreign Office Today*, London: Jonathan Cape.

Murphy, G. (1996) 'The sad and lonely', unpublished paper.

Parris, M. (1998) 'Our man in resignation: the triumph of formality over content, or why I departed the Foreign Office', *The Times*, 3 January.

Paterson, H. (1989) ' "Incorporated wives" and the British Diplomatic Service: family, work and welfare', unpublished thesis for BSc. Social Policy and Administration, London School of Economics and Political Science.

Primary sources

Foreign and Commonwealth Office Including Overseas Development Administration (1996) *1996 Departmental Report: The Government's Expenditure Plans 1996–97 to 1998–99*, Cm. 3203, London: HMSO.

Hornby, Sir D. (1996) *Review of Overseas Allowances: Foreign and Commonwealth Office*.

Proposals for the Reform of the Foreign Service, Miscellaneous no. 2 (1943), Cmnd. 6420, London: HMSO.

Report on the Committee on Representational Services Overseas appointed by the Prime Minister under the Chairmanship of Lord Plowden 1962–3. Presented to Parliament by command of Her Majesty, February 1964. Miscellaneous no. 5 (1964), Cmnd. 2276, London: HMSO.

Resolutions and Decisions of Security Council, 1967, Security Council Official Records: 22nd year, p. 8.

The Civil Service: Taking Forward Continuity and Change (1995) Cm. 2748, London: HMSO.

Chapter 16

Delay and deception in Thai–British diplomatic encounters of the early nineteenth century

Andrew Turton

> See you now;
> Your bait of falsehood takes this carp of truth;
> And thus do we of wisdom and of reach,
> With windlasses, and with assays of bias,
> By indirections find directions out
>
> William Shakespeare, *Hamlet*, II, 1, lines 62–6[1]

Ethnography of diplomatic communication

Records of diplomatic encounters between Siamese (Thai) and British in the early nineteenth century are a rich field for anthropological examination of forms of indirect communication, and the notion of indirect communication itself. The British embassy to Siam in 1821 was the first European mission to that country for nearly 150 years. It signalled a new relation starting from a low point of mutual ignorance and mistrust. The period of diplomatic activity began with (indirect) accusations of spying and planning invasion on the one hand, and attributions of barbarism, despotism and 'national vanity' on the other. It culminated, between 1855–7, with an exchange of embassies, the signing of a treaty, and the reception of the English-speaking Siamese Ambassador at Windsor by Queen Victoria.[2]

Seen in hindsight as a linked, cumulative process, it was at first an encounter between two expansive empires. Despite vast differences between the two sides, Siam was a highly literate society, a strongly established monarchy,[3] a territorially aggrandising empire; it had a large commercial fleet of junks, and Bangkok and its environs was a commercial region within an increasingly commoditised economy. Nonetheless, British power increased exponentially during the period – most visibly to the Thai on visits to India and *vis-à-vis* Burma and China – and this was well understood by the Thai, whose readiness to learn and selectively adopt a range of modern practices contributed to their ability to retain autonomy of action and avoid direct colonial status.

The records can be read as ethnography of forms of communication in at least three senses: as attempts to characterise the culture or behaviour of the other side in terms of ethnicity, class, office, personality, etc.; as records and analyses of the particular events and the progress of the mission; and as a less witting ethnography of the assumptions, norms and prejudices of the authors. The records include largely published – and some unpublished or not fully published – accounts by the principal actors, but also commentaries by their superiors, and by members of the other sovereign state. They include subsequently published official papers (some declassified from 'secret'). They include accounts of the same or similar events by people of different nationalities, status and markedly different temperaments. And they include frequent comparisons and intertextual reference (by both sides) to previous accounts, including those of earlier centuries. There is much at stake: a degree of mutual interest, a desire to learn, a desire to be known (as well as a desire to manage this knowledge strategically), a desire to reach best possible outcomes, and some acceptance of a need to compromise, or at least to stay in communication. Thus the diplomacy, the forms of communication, more or less 'direct' or 'indirect', are continued in the texts themselves, with the timing of their publication, their editings and omissions, hyperboles and ironies, the extent to which they address the other side – whether more or less honorifically, more or less in terms that could have been expressed directly – and so on. In this chapter I make use particularly of the earlier missions, especially by Crawfurd and Richardson, which represent more challenging and difficult encounters.

Ingenuity and servility

I have elsewhere identified a number of tropes, or exaggerated and repetitive rhetorical figures that occur in the writings of the two sides; here I touch on several, though I do not have space to develop each (Turton 1997). To give examples: they include on the Thai side accusations of invasion and spying, and by the *Farang* (Europeans), of delaying tactics, practices of dress (to the point of 'nakedness'), 'grovelling' obeisance, and generally being too ceremonious. The latter set are most often elements in the meta-tropes of 'barbarism', 'despotism' and lack of 'civilisation', which are rather loosely and often contradictorily applied.

All these rhetorical figures could be subsumed under the rubric of forms of direct and indirect communication. Crawfurd's assertiveness and haughtiness, and the British team's keenness to observe and record – despite guidelines in their briefing not to give offence – were perceived to err on the side of over-directness. Thai behaviour was experienced as intolerably devious and obstructive, compounded by 'vanity' (namely, assumption of superior or at least equal status). One question, which I shall return to in conclusion, is whether, or to what extent, this was a matter of 'cultural misunderstanding' (one side's indirectness being the other's 'indelicacy' and rude calculation, e.g. the assessment of gifts) or whether the game was largely understood by both sides.

I use the material to challenge the dichotomising performed by the tropes 'direct' and 'indirect' and the tendency to attribute different modes to different sides. And I question the way this pushes the alternatives towards the extremes and ignores the extent to which 'indirect' tactics can be exercised within a broad middle pathway that is nonetheless direct, and certainly highly directed.

At this point we need to reflect on some of the terms in use. Part of my excuse here for a little decontextualised etymologising and semantic analysis, is that we are dealing – on one side – with an English language that is almost as close chronologically to that of Shakespeare as to contemporary English usage. We recognise words, but are less than usually certain of their valency (consider 'barbarism', 'vanity', etc.). This is to say that all language, while pretending a kind of directness, tends to indirectness, and that we may try to find out, or come nearer to, the one by means of the other. Physical behaviour perhaps tends in the other direction, to unambiguous signs of deference for example, which is a reason why bowing is so often a sticking point with ambassadors. Is it more difficult to perform an ironic bow (and cross-cultur-ally see Geertz 1973 on 'thick description') than to utter an ironic epithet? Those familiar with the English theatrical genre known as Restoration comedy (late seventeenth to early eighteenth century) will have seen each in support of the other.

In addition to the predominant sense in this volume of lacking circumlo-cution or ambiguity, one other sense of 'direct' has already been touched upon, namely the lack of intervening agency or mediation. Another is of rudeness contrasting with polished, polite and urbane behaviour. Of greater interest for my argument is the sense of straight, or upright and downright, or regular, which can easily move over into the moral value of rectitude and its opposites such as deviance, erring; downrightness of manner being a sign of moral uprightness. Two important near synonyms of 'direct' in several of its senses, are 'ingenuous' and 'frank'. All share the senses of open, candid, uncon-cealed, unreserved, without guile, art or dissimulation. 'Ingenuous' is not much used currently; less I would say than its often mis-used negative 'disingenuous' (insincere, naive or culpably lacking in frankness). I was curious to see an OED definition of ingenuity as 'free-born condition' (i.e. not servile in status or manner), and then to be able to make the connection with 'frank' (which normally connotes ingenuous, unreserved, *out*spoken in manner) in its older sense of 'free', 'freeman' and so to complete the circle with the Thai language term *Farang* for European (cf. *Franc*; see Yule and Burnell 1994: 352–4, under *Firinghee*; cf. the interchangeability of the French language terms *franc* and *libre*

[Bloch 1965: I, 255]). Ironically the term *Thai* has an analogous history of meaning both a non-servile social status and an 'ethnic' status or identity (cf. Turton 1999b).

The texts include a commentary on directness in a fairly non-figurative style. Crawfurd, for example uses the terms 'disingenuous', 'frank', 'artifice', 'falsehood', and the language of intention and motives, in characterising the Siamese and their diplomatic forms and actual practices. 'Judging from those with whom we held intercourse, I make no hesitation in confirming what has been often asserted of the Siamese by European writers, that they are servile, rapacious, slothful, disingenuous, pusillanimous, and extravagantly vain' (Crawfurd 1828: 342). Note that though unflattering (my own English under-statement?) these are not perhaps the most awful (ditto) epithets he might have chosen. And the reserving of adverbial and final place emphasis for the fault of vanity (i.e. pride, unsubmissiveness, not knowing their inferior place) hardly constitutes a crescendo of opprobrium.

Though indulging in stereotyping,[4] even Crawfurd is aware that the further from court, and among lesser, tributary chiefs, and in the company of monks (other authors would add women and perhaps children), greater degrees of 'directness', 'honesty', etc. may be found. He reports a visit from a 'Lao Chief' whom he finds 'frank and intelligent' and 'well-informed'.[5] And of an old abbot he writes 'In point of intelligence, he was greatly superior to any other Siamese with whom I had conversed, and he was always ready to communicate his knowledge without reserve or ostentation' (125–6); though several pages later we have 'but on matters of a temporal nature he refused to speak, showing above all a strong reluctance to touch on anything that was in the remotest degree of a political character' (147). The Thai side too were likely to have stereotyped prejudices of the Farang, hitherto derived from such direct contact as they had experience of, largely from visiting ships' captains and their crews, and the mainly low-class 'native Christians' (the *farang derm* or indigenous Farang, of Portuguese descent).

A passage in the account of the United States envoy Edmund Roberts (embassy 1833, return visit 1836; published account 1837) suggests a theme of mutual learning and adjustment of diplomatic perceptions and performances. 'Their [the Siamese] intercourse with the English and Americans is gradually bringing about a more honest, manly and open mode of expressing them-selves, both in speaking and writing' (Roberts 1837: 285). This was only twelve or fifteen years after the Crawfurd embassy, and moreover from an American who writes that in their prostrations towards his men, the servants in the Portuguese guest house adopted 'a more humble manner than suits our republican notions', while towards the Siamese they '[crouch] in brute-like attitude' (237), 'crawling like a dog on all fours' (246), 'crawling backwards "à la crab" or "à la lobster" '(258). There is nonetheless a perception and approval of a linear change in diplomatic style. There is evidence elsewhere too of a degree of learning and adaptation on the part of the Farang. On the other hand it is possible that some of the change can be put down to a pragmatic oscillation in specific diplomatic performances, a point to which I return at the end. Twenty-five years later, the Thai ambassadors at Windsor adopt the same 'peculiar mode enjoined by Siamese etiquette in approaching Majesty ... in between crouching and crawling' (*Annual Register*, 19 November 1857) or 'in a stooping position ... [the] suite follow [the Chief Ambassador] on their hands and knees, and as they approach the throne made a series of the most reverent obeisances' (*Illustrated Times*, 28 November 1857) – 'profound salaams' (*Hampshire Telegraph*, 5 December 1857, citing the *Dublin Freeman*). Reactions to this behaviour varied from amusement ('the royal gravity was sorely tried' – *Hampshire Telegraph*) to appreciation that the same mode of respect was being offered to the British sovereign as to the Thai king by Thai subjects (Thailand 1927).

The connotation of 'manliness', the gendering of directness, is of particular interest. Richardson observed that the comportment of the retinues of the northern Thai princes is 'more manly' than that in Bangkok. Several commentaries might be offered. The notion that an upright manner, posture and style of language are emblematic of honesty and trustworthiness, rectitude and respectfulness certainly contrasts with many Thai practices. But neither are to be generalised too far. Within 'Europe' – and more especially in pre-modern diplomatic culture – we would have to make strong distinctions between, say, Russia and western Europe, or between northern and Mediterranean Europe.[6] And within these we would have to make further distinctions between gendered versions, and within masculine cultures between military and civilian. We should bear in mind that most of the British diplomats under review were or had been military men, even if mostly serving in medical or administrative posts, and none were aristocrats.

The impossibility of direct communication

The highest – one could say the most direct – form of Siamese diplomatic communication, at least with a state of equal or higher status, was an exchange of royal letters, signed by the monarchs. The practice is attested from the sixteenth to nineteenth centuries with little apparent change, excepting that the practice of writing on gold leaf or plate was discontinued. The letter from the Thai side is treated as if it were the monarch himself, worthy of the same respect and not just another object worthy of great respect. The same respect is accorded to the monarch from the other side. The royal letter (Thai *rajasan*) is of a different order from any other diplomatic letter (Thai *ekkasan*). Thus there is frequent difficulty over the fact that some British embassies came from the Governor-General of India and not directly from the King or Queen of England; or in the seventeenth century that a mere East India Company official should address a letter direct to the king instead of to his senior minister; or that a letter might not have been delivered by an ambassador who had himself received it – and its wrappings – directly from the hands of the monarch. The latter shortcoming was invoked in the case of the American envoy Balestier in 1849, though there were other things wrong with that mission (Thailand 1936). The fact that Bowring could assert that he stood before King Mongkut dressed exactly as he had recently stood before Queen Victoria, was a strong argument in favour of tolerating some of Bowring's definition of diplomatic etiquette.

The royal letter had to be correctly composed and transmitted in a number of key respects, among which notably: the language used, the physical aspects of its construction and presentation, the mode of transport, and the mode of its final handing over and reading.

The royal letter to Queen Victoria in 1857 was presented in Thai (read by the first ambassador) and English (read by a Foreign Office official). Previous exchanges had made use of several other intermediary written and spoken languages: Persian in the seventeenth century, Malay in Crawfurd's mission, (mandarin) Chinese *and* Teochiu (the principal Chinese dialect of Bangkok) at Bowring's visit. The 'Burney Treaty' of 1826 was drawn up in Thai, Malay, Portuguese and English, since neither side had sufficient competence in the other's language, though after a stay of several months Burney had sufficient confidence to compose and deliver a brief speech of leave-taking in the Thai language.

There are instances of diplomatic letters being edited or simply not being passed on. For example, the Portuguese Governor of Macao expressed the wish to kiss the hand of the King of Siam; the phrase was erased before presentation. Crawfurd was told by an interpreter that to refer to the Burmese in the phrase 'the friends and neighbours of the British nation' was improper. On the Crawfurd mission – the nadir of Siamese-British relations – only the Thai translation was read in the presence of the king. With reference to the list of gifts, Crawfurd writes:

> I make no doubt they were represented as tribute or offerings, although of this it was impossible to obtain proof. The letter of the Governor-General was neither read nor exhibited, notwithstanding the distinct pledge which had been given to that effect.

Royal letters were carried on their own in a separate boat, placed on a throne as for a royal person. Pictorial records show such boats, and also a palanquin carried at Versailles in 1686. The letter had to be 'handed' not directly but on a gold tray on a stand (of fairly constant Thai design). The engraving of the French Ambassador at Ayuthaya in 1685 shows the king's minister (a Farang in the Siamese service) urging him to raise the tray higher, above his head, to reach the king, who is in a raised room with a window onto the audience hall (see Van der Cruysse 1991).

The proper diplomatic event, to be complete, had of course to be an exchange of letters with receipt confirmed. The first British royal embassy was conceived in 1608, departed London 1611, granted royal audience in Ayuthaya on 17 September 1612, and delivered a letter from James I (such dates are sure to be recorded). A reply from King Songtham was sent in 1617, but by late March 1622 King Songtham prevents an English ship leaving because he has still not received a reply from 'his brother, the King of England'. In 1857 King Mongkut travels to Samut Phrakarn at the mouth of the Chao Phraya, in a steamboat with the new British Consul at Bangkok (1857–64) Sir Robert Schomburgk, in order to receive Queen Victoria's letter which was accompanied by the returning Siamese embassy.

Ambassadors and intermediaries

Harold Nicholson, reviewing more than two millennia of 'diplomacy', makes it clear that both in the European and Asian spheres there have been historical changes of emphasis, or a continuing historical dialectic one might say, between the roles of the diplomatic, inter-state envoy as respectively messenger, orator, negotiator and 'trained observer'. Nicholson suggests that the choice of the Greek god Hermes as the patron deity of heralds and other diplomats is not entirely felicitous – i.e. it is embarrassing to diplomats – since Hermes embodied 'the qualities of charm, trickery and cunning' and he was also the patron of 'travellers, merchants and thieves'. 'It was he who endowed Pandora, the first woman [in Hellenistic theology], with the gift of flattery and deception [cf. 'lies, flattery and treachery' (Kerényi 1958: 192)] ... He came to be regarded as the intermediary between the upper and the lower worlds'. (Nicholson 1950: 19) The skills required of anyone who is to be a successful intermediary between social worlds may well in practice need something of all these characteristics. Hermes, one might say is an archetypal messenger and go-between, a director of indirection.

In theory, I suppose, a full 'royal embassy' involves the two principals (the monarchs, or from 1833 on also a more frequently changing US president) and the ambassador of the visiting side and 'minister for foreign affairs' of the home side. In theory, while relations between the countries change as the result of the mission, these parties remain unchanged in the process, like catalysts. In one sense formality can assist in this. In practice however, the parties may become involved, transformed and won over in varying degree. It must be borne in mind that we are writing of a time when the roles of diplomat, colonial administrator, spy, Asianist scholar (e.g. ethnographer) and so on were not distinct, formalised and professionalised. Arguably this could make them all the more susceptible to personal involvement with the other side. This line of enquiry could be pursued in a number of ways for which this paper has not the space; for example, the extent to which the British (male) 'diplomats' – and other intermediaries – married Asian women, became fluent linguists, reconciled themselves with other religions, and otherwise became knowledgeable in a scholarly way about the regions they worked in. David Richardson was most likely already married to a Thai (Shan) wife when he was received in audience by the King; he never returned to Britain – or even India – from his new home in Tenasserim. At another end of the scale, Crawfurd had already returned to London when his account of the 1821 mission was published – tactfully just after the follow-up mission by Burney in 1826 – and he did not ever return to Asia, as far as I know.

It is perhaps a commonplace that in hierarchical systems the degree of elaboration of codes increases the nearer the top. The closer the ambassador approaches the royal person, the more the encounter is set about with formality. The *raison d'être* of the audience requires, indeed by definition: proximity, sight and audience – and permits dialogue – but denies direct physical contact and too much other directness. The letter, if it is to be 'handed' over, must be on a tray, preferably wrapped in several layers of fine materials and enclosed in one or more boxes, and passed from lower to higher elevation. The king himself, though constrained by many rules, is in some respects not bound by them in the way his subjects are. He after all does not use royal language when speaking. Thus the king, when opening the conversation, offers 'the three gracious royal questions' (*song phraraja phatisanthan sam khrang*). These are usually along the lines of: How is your king? Is there peace and prosperity in your country? How long have you travelled? Small talk but strictly formulaic. This is followed by conversation between king and ambassador. In the early encounters this was through the chief minister, then another official, and thirdly an interpreter before reaching the ambassador; later King Mongkut was to converse directly in English. The length of this conversation is recorded in most accounts, apparently with care to count the minutes. Richardson in 1839 notes that the king conversed with him for one hour and twenty minutes, an exceptionally long time for a royal conversation.[7] Also noted is whether an audience of leave-taking is granted, and more exceptionally, whether a 'private' audience has taken place.

Interestingly the word 'private' passes quite early on into Thai official language of the nineteenth century (along with others like to fire a gun 'salute', *ying salut*, another carefully managed piece of diplomatic communication) during this period as *fao priwet* (to attend the king in private) which is an indication, I think, of the growing personalisation of such contacts, especially by King Mongkut, who was so curious for information and exchange of ideas. Bowring is, I am sure, aware of the quite exceptional etiquette involved when the king lights Bowring's cigar for him.

So there are varying sequences of more and less formal and direct speech and posture – together with food, stimulants, dress, and so on – within a single encounter or ritual element within an event, and even more so as between different moments of the embassy as a whole until its departure. But the ambassador, and certainly his retinue of assistants – whom I do not have space to treat adequately – engage as intermediaries with many other intermediaries and interlocutors. Further chords are struck in this progression of themes and variations which are partly scored and partly improvised. These present opportunities for both sides to sound each other out, to learn about personalities and intentions, and to gather routine or incidental, if not strategic intelligence. These other contacts or intermediaries are variously sought out by the visitors, or seek them out (political factions, political exiles, Farang residents, informers and pleaders), or are part of the formal structure of diplomatic reception. They can be a means both of indirect enquiry and of a more direct approach which would be unacceptable in more formal audiences. Crawfurd, for example, notes that ministers asked him in a very direct manner such questions as 'If your country is at peace, as you say [in 1821], why do you need such a large navy?'.

Crawfurd is quite proud of his own evasiveness in the cause of resisting the overt questioning of his hosts. 'We evaded giving any answer, except in very general terms, but we were cross-questioned with dexterity'. 'We put an end to all this importunity'. Similarly, when, immediately after the royal audience itself, he and his retinue are obliged to walk round the royal palace in wet socks 'to admire the splendour and magnificence of the Court – such being nearly the words made use of by the interpreter [e.g. the temple, the white elephant, the large cannon]', he writes: 'It would have been impolitic to have evinced ill-humour, or attempted remonstrance; and therefore we feigned a cheerful compliance with this inconvenient usage' (Crawfurd 1967: 96). There is also some selective appreciation or at least acceptance of Siamese etiquette – of the sort which, like so many things, rings true immediately to a late twentieth-century Thai speaking reader. For example, the following instance of a very direct, but polite, indirectness! 'We were not indeed forbidden to go about [the city], but it was stated to us, that to do so, before a public audience had placed us under the immediate protection of the court, might expose us to be treated with rudeness by the populace' (ibid.: 83).

Notorious among the official intermediaries is the Governor of Paknam (lit. mouth of the river), who is literally the gatekeeper to the kingdom for those – the great majority – who arrive by sea. His boats meet the ships when they are at the 'bar' of Siam at the mouth of the Chao Phraya, which may take several days to 'warp' across. He provides fresh food, counts the visitors, records the number of firearms on board for own use and as gifts, and examines the presents. An example of the latter is inspecting a horse for inauspicious markings (whorls of hair especially). This is a quite standard Thai practice (also for cattle) which gives offence to Europeans on more than one occasion, for whom it is an example, one might say, of the impoliteness of 'looking a gift horse in the mouth', i.e. to tell its age, or here on the coat. He sends letters to Bangkok, starting a veritable shuttle of written messages and movement of often quite high-ranking messengers which continues throughout the mission. He and his retinue are competent in all the major cultural modalities they have to deal with. He shakes the Farang by the hand.

For Farang visitors the Portuguese Christian servants/officials (descendants of a three-hundred-year-old resident community) interpret, advise and cook; they are required to watch over and take care of the visitors. In the governor's house there are tables and chairs, knives and forks and wineglasses, bottles of Dutch gin and so on, that, at least in the early years, may not be found or offered further upstream. Alas for goodwill and transparency, some of this friendly openness is often interpreted as 'indelicacy' and 'rapaciousness', whereas it may be intended as a discreet attempt to avoid embarrassment or confrontation later, for example the repeated questioning about the quantity and value of gifts. The behaviour of the Portuguese, who to the visiting Farang are embarrassingly indigenised and seem to mimic or travesty the European original, is seen as devious and untrustworthy; they are suspected of being among those who spy on the embassy.

Indirections and delay

With the exception of the Richardson and McLeod embassies (1829–39), European missions were sea-borne and could be protracted in the extreme. The first Thai embassy to Holland in 1608 seems not to have returned until at least four years later. The *Globe* sailed from London on 5 February 1611 for Ayuthaya with a letter from King James I. After various stopovers, notably three months in Pattani, they had a royal audience in Ayuthaya on 17 September 1612, some eighteen months later. Several Englishmen went up to Chiang Mai; the fate of two of them not being known for another five years, in 1617. In the meantime some Englishmen had returned with a royal Thai letter, but in 1622 some were still held virtual hostages while King Songtham waited for confirmation of the exchange. The strongly motivated exchanges between France and Siam between 1683–8 show what could be done to accelerate the pace of diplomatic exchange. Within a period of about four and a half years there had been two completed exchanges in five voyages on French ships, with approximately eighteen months spent on land and three years at sea, each voyage lasting then, as for the next 150 years, about six or seven months. The joint Thai and French journeys permitted intensive, and mutual diplomatic briefing and training to take place.

The nineteenth-century British missions were all from forward positions in Asia, Bowring doubling back from Hong Kong. Even so they took their time, or others took it for them. Crawfurd sailed from Calcutta in 1821 and took about four months (124 days) outward to Bangkok; returning via Vietnam; a total journey time of about thirteen months. Burney sailed from Penang and took about two months (fifty-seven days) outward; a total journey time of just under a year. Richardson took almost as long (fifty-two days) to walk to Bangkok from Moulmein, but he was repeatedly delayed and re-routed. He returned via Chiang Mai; a total journey time of about eight months.

Whether the arrival of the embassy was by land or sea, there were requests to wait at the frontier or some point away from the city until things were ready. On the river up to Ayuthaya there were eight scheduled stops and stages. Then there was admission to just outside the city gate. Then there was access to the audience to be negotiated. Then all the microspaces of the royal palace had to be negotiated; in Bangkok there were as many as four court-yards, and then several zones within the royal audience hall. At any stage there could be opportunities for variation in degrees of exclusion, tolerance and formality, whether of retinue, dress code, the bearing of arms, language, posture, and so on.

Following the audience there were other 'visits of ceremony', before the visitors were free to walk around the city and meet ordinary people. Cao Fa Noi, at that time considered by some to be the heir apparent, comes to see Richardson at night on a visiting 'whale ship' on the Chao Phraya river, apparently by some agreement ('I knew he wished to see me, but did not wish openly to come here until after the audience') the day before his royal audience, remarking, humorously it seems, that he should not be there before Richardson has seen the King. Richardson connived at this, recording, with light irony, that he had said 'this meeting was of course quite accidental'.

Sometimes delays and re-routings were substantial. I have not found examples of European embassies being turned back, as the Chinese sometimes did (and Thai [Khon Müang] vassal states turned away the Burmese). But McLeod was not allowed to continue beyond Chengrung to Puerh (the first major Chinese town beyond the Thai state of Sipsongpanna). Indeed he was told he should have gone via Canton. On Richardson's first embassy, he was refused permission to go on from Lamphun to Chiang Mai (a journey of half a day at most). Crawfurd was not allowed to go beyond Bangkok.

'Re-routing' is a spatial version of 'delay' in the sense of waiting. Richardson was aware his routes could take twice as long as ones known to Thai. The intermediary role of the Karen people who were tributary to Chiang Mai was crucial in this, since their tribute services included cutting and keeping roads open, as well as providing food, shelter and guides. Interestingly, a Persian embassy of 1685–6 is recorded as having been officially conducted from Mergui to Ayuthaya 'by a very roundabout route' precisely 'In order to be shown the extent of the kingdom, how the land and merchants flourish and *especially the defenses*' which would foil any attack or cause the enemy to lose his way in the wilderness' (Muhammad 1970: 48–9, emphasis added).

Richardson is in no doubt as to the concrete value of being able to travel freely – the free market in direct access and knowledge as well as goods. He remarks in 1839 on the opportunity presented by his – much delayed – journey to northern Thailand from Bangkok,

by which journey I hope I shall be able to throw some light on the geog-raphy of 5 degrees of latitude in this country, hitherto never visited by a

European; and *the very act of traversing the country*, when done without violence to any of their prejudices, will tend to break down the hitherto insurmountable objection to any intercourse with the interior of the kingdom.

(Richardson 1839–40: 243–4, emphasis added)

Given the overall time-scale of these missions, which were mobile but not brief as we have seen, it may be surprising that they complained about small delays. There were of course some serious practical considerations – for example the return monsoon for the sea-borne mission, and the onset of the rainy season, which was on occasion disastrous for the health of missions by land. Yet even the seemingly most practical necessities could be turned into opportunities for manipulation or charges of manipulation.

Here are some instances from the Richardson journals (all actual spelling and punctuation; within square brackets are my comments).

Richardson's first mission to Lamphun (Richardson 1836)

15 January 1830

A letter has been dispatched to the people here to-day, telling them who I am, and ordering them to supply me with every thing I want; and the messenger begged I would remain here two or three days, till the road was made smooth and every thing ready for my reception at the capital. There is no way of avoiding their ridiculous delays. [Blundell, Commissioner for Tenasserim Provinces, comments] Dr. R. was delayed here a few days [five] on the plea of preparing his reception, and ascertaining from the astrologers a lucky day for his visit.

8 February 1830

I have at length prepared to start in the morning by the shortest and best route to Maulamyne. The only reason for not starting to-day is its being a *black* one, [original italics] and it would be disrespectful to me, as well as dangerous to themselves, to begin a journey to-day …

… On taking leave of CHOW HOUA [Cao Ho Na ('Prince of front "palace"'), the 'Vice-Roy' of Lamphun] he gave me a rhinoceros horn, on which he seemed to set a great value, as a charm against every evil; and as I had expressed some impatience at their delays and suspicion, he begged I would not suspect them of any want of friendship in so long withholding permission to purchase bullocks and trade with their people; that our character was perfectly new to them; that they were like an elephant crossing the river; – they must feel before they proceeded; that their difficulty was now got over, they were aware of our intentions being good; and that we should now come there on the same terms as subjects of *Siam*.

Richardson's fourth mission to the Karen, Müang Ngai and Ava (Richardson 1869)

1 January 1837

The Governor of Mein-lun-ghee [Mae Sarieng, at that time a frontier town of Chiang Mai] … put some questions regarding the object and destination of my mission, stating that he was placed at one of the frontier stations to see that no suspicious or objectionable person passed the frontier, but said he supposed I would not stop if he wished me. I told him at once that I was going to Monay [Müang Ngai] with a letter to the Tsobua [ruler of the small state], and thence to Ava, but I would certainly stop if he obliged me. It was, however, for him to consider whether I was a suspicious person, or one likely to bring any sort of harm on his country, after he had known me for seven years as the instrument of the British Government in promoting friendship with their neighbours. I reminded him of the assistance I received from him about two years ago, under orders from the Zimmay [Chiang Mai] chiefs, when on my way to the Karean-nee [Karen] country, and threatened him with the displeasure of the Tsobua [ruler of Chiang Mai] and the King of Bankok [*sic*]. It was settled I should proceed; and before he left me *he told me privately (all the people present hearing him)* that he only wished to screen himself in case of any fault being found with him hereafter [emphasis added].

Time for manoeuvre

Some Farang (mis-)interpretations of delay were due to lack of local knowledge: for example not appreciating the time needed in order to mobilise (chiefly by requisitioning [Thai *ken*]) resources not only to build temporary accommodation and accumulate food supplies, but also to assemble the soldiers and police, the boatmen and chairmen, cooks and lamplighters, musicians and actors, grooms and valets, the layers of mats and carpets, the bearers of umbrellas, betel sets, and other insignia.

In the north, there is always a time of one or several days of 'preparation' (N. Thai *wan daa*) for any major event, for a village or household ceremony, let alone a major state event. Richardson's reference, above, to a 'black' or inauspicious day suggests that he must have been aware of the importance of astrological forecasts even for the most material of tasks. Departures on dangerous journeys through forest and potentially hostile territory, on uncertain trading missions, would have certainly occasioned anxious discussion of 'auspicious' timing of days certainly, and perhaps of hours. Arrivals and departures from cities on state business would be no less subject to these procedures.

In my own fieldwork experience in this region, most planning at the village level started with formal consultations to ascertain auspicious days (*haa wan dii wan monkhon*), and for some events a time of day (*yaam*), together with auspicious directions for alignments and routes, etc. In some lunar months there is a minority of safe days, let alone really good ones. There are practical needs to assemble quantities of rice; to allow people to plan or postpone their trips to the forest or their fields and swiddens, to assemble and assign the labour and then the materials (e.g. bamboo and rattan from the forest), to build temporary shelters which are a feature of almost any special event, and numerous other tasks. These needs dictate a pattern of timing, which includes in the first place mobilising the people required to initiate, take decisions and supervise the operation.

So it is not just pragmatic and practical considerations, but also intimate cultural and political-economic insight and knowledge that was lacking. Moreover, the Farang did not fully appreciate the style of political consultation: for example, the needs of (the related and allied) rulers of Lamphun, Lampang, and Chiang Mai to consult each other; the need for Chengtung and Chengrung to consult the local Burmese or Chinese commissioner or to send messages to their overlords in Ava and Puerh respectively; the desire perhaps for the Palace in Bangkok to listen to several sources of information and counsel. Likewise for any social event of any scale, it is a particularly marked part of regional Thai etiquette to invite people, or let people know well in advance (*bok luang naa*) or give them notice (*bok wai kon*), rather as, on the day itself, all sorts of 'non-human' agencies will be invited to 'witness' (*pen sakit payan*) and bless the proceedings. Visiting, witnessing and blessing have their own deep-seated rhythms at all social levels.

The 'delay' factor is largely a political perception on the part of the Farang diplomats. It is not to be explained in terms of any so-called 'lack of industrial time sense'. The organisation of diplomatic ceremony, conceivably one of the biggest non-military mobilisations of resources the state undertook, was conducted with (in my subjective judgement) impressive efficiency. Messages moved quickly; days were packed with to-ing and fro-ing; and once appointments were made people were seldom kept waiting.

'Channelling along a centering path'

Until the mid-nineteenth century, Siam and its neighbours (omitting here the Spanish Philippines and Dutch East Indies) were within the political and diplomatic sphere of influence of China. The last Thai 'tribute mission' to

China was in 1851; tribute obligations being renounced in 1882. Anthony Reid (1993: 190) adduces evidence that for centuries 'South East Asian' states (my anachronism) to a large extent replicated the Chinese tribute system and its diplomatic ritual (*bin li*, translated by Hevia [1995] as 'guest ritual'). Records show that Thai envoys had been visiting China since the thirteenth century, seldom less frequently than every four years, and at times annually (Sarasin 1977; Wills 1984). We know that at least two of the Thai ambassadors sent to Europe in the seventeenth century had been on missions to China. Burney had translated accounts by Burmese ambassadors to Beijing, some of whom are reported as being there at the same time as Macartney in 1793. So Chinese practices would be known at first hand, would be influential, and would have provided a diplomatic code within the region. Some elements seem almost liturgically replicated, such as the practice of the Chinese emperor offering 'soothing words' to open the audience (Hevia 1995: 176, see above). Or, for example, the practices surrounding provisioning of visiting embassies, which were geared to the purposes and perceived progress of the mission in the Chinese side's interest.

A central theme in Hevia's analysis of imperial Chinese 'guest ritual', or organisation of diplomatic missions, is the importance of the strategy of 'centering' (*fengjian shi zhong*), 'channelling along a centering path', 'negotiating a mean between overabundance and scarcity', in relations with foreigners. The notion of 'channelling along a centering path' requires us to think of temporal movements not only in terms of simultaneities and forward progression, as in music, but of steps to the side and back as in the paces of a dance, even though in a 'historical' sense these steps are irreversible. It also seems a fairly basic Buddhist idea: right timing, right positioning, with a resultant net movement along a middle path of indeterminate breadth.

'Direction' and 'indirection' are terms that tend to connote activity. But we have begun to see the importance of stasis and silence, of enforced stay, absence of messages, stand-offs, non-engagement (which could be thought of as another Buddhist value), of being prevented from speaking to the king, and of being kept virtually *incommunicado* (a contemporary piece of diplomatic jargon). All of these connote degrees of non-action or passivity. On the other hand, one of my concerns has been to identify and attribute agency to each side as fully as the material allows. The theme of delay, as a material and political form of indirection, is just one which permits this. 'Delays' are 'intervals' in the rhythm of the performance, and as Bourdieu nicely puts it 'to abolish the interval is to abolish strategy' (Bourdieu 1977: 6). Epithets such as 'ridiculous' and 'petty' seem to imply that the delayer is somehow being idle, frivolous, inattentive to what really matters, at best inefficient, and generally inactive. Whereas my reading suggests, to the contrary, that if one side has to be patient, it is precisely because the other is being active, taking the initiative (or actively avoiding taking the initiative) and creating the time for manoeuvre.

As in the Chinese case, 'delays' and other indirections were opportunities for probing for information, testing capacity and intention, controlling the process of negotiation, correcting for oversteer, and bringing the engagement to a relatively calm and friendly conclusion, even when not particularly successful. In Polonius' now archaic sounding terms they were 'windlasses' and 'assays of bias', indirections deployed in order to 'find directions out' (see note 1). The robust metaphor of the deputy ruler of Lamphun after his first diplomatic encounter with a Farang in 1830 (quoted in full above) is a nicely localised, particularised version of this, and at the end of the day, most explicit:

> he begged me I [Richardson] would not suspect them of any want of friendship in so long withholding permission … that our character was perfectly new to them; that they were *like an elephant crossing the river; they must feel before they proceeded*; that their difficulty was now got over, they were aware of our intentions being good.
>
> (emphasis added)

Hevia's many anthropological references do not include Bourdieu's *Outline of a Theory of Practice*, which seems to be pertinent here, especially the early discussion on the temporal structure – or better, *tempi* – of gift exchanges (in the section 'From the mechanics of the model to the dialectic of strategies'). Here he defines practices as 'defined by the fact that their temporal structure, direction, and rhythm are *constitutive* of their meaning' (Bourdieu 1977: 9). And he speaks of the unlimited scope, in the case of most kinds of action, even the more 'heavily ritualised',

> for strategies exploiting the possibilities offered by the manipulation of the tempo of the action – holding back or putting off, maintaining suspense or expectation, or on the other hand, hurrying, hustling, surprising, and stealing a march, not to mention the art of ostentatiously giving time … or withholding it.
>
> (Bourdieu 1977: 7)

We have seen something of the complexity of changing pace and timing, opening and closure, facilitation and obstruction, requirement and easement within various encounters, and in longer-term relationships between individuals and states. The study of diplomatic ceremony leads us to repudiate strong distinctions between 'ritual time' and 'practical time' as well as between 'direction' and 'indirection'. Richardson can speak of 'ridiculous delays' – and his editorialising superior underlines this – but he comes to speak of 'customary' requests to stay for four or five days, and refers understandingly to the Khon Müang New Year (an event lasting several days that I have participated in on several occasions) as the 'holidays at this joyous season'. In this light I would prefer to see the Thai–British diplomatic engagements – as Hevia does the

Qing-Macartney affair – more as potentially manageable encounters between two 'expansive empires' than instances of 'cross-cultural misunderstanding'.

Notes

1 Polonius (Lord Chamberlain to the King of Denmark) is instructing Reynaldo, his gentleman servant, to go to Paris to enquire indirectly about his son Laertes' behaviour:

> ... and finding
> By this encompassment and drift of question
> That they do know my son, come you more nearer
> Than your particular demands will touch it:
> Take you as 'twere, some distant knowledge of him;
>   ... and there put on him
> What forgeries you please; marry, none so rank
> As may dishonour him; take heed of that;
>   ... but breathe his faults so quaintly
> That they may seem the taints of liberty,
> ...
> See you now;
> Your bait of falsehood takes this carp of truth;
> And thus do we of wisdom and of reach,
> With windlasses, and with assays of bias
> By indirections find directions out:
> So by my former lecture and advice
> Shall you my son ...
>   William Shakespeare, *Hamlet*, Act II, Scene 1, lines 9–13, 19–21, 31–2, 62–8.

  Note: 'Windlass', OED (second entry, homophone but distinct etymology from windlass as winding device): '1. A circuit made to intercept the game in hunting; ... 2. fig. A circuitous course of action; a crafty device'; as a verb 'to decoy or ensnare'.

2 From a British perspective these tend to be known as the Crawfurd (1821–2) [Bangkok], Burney (1825–6) [Bangkok], Richardson (1829–30) [Lamphun], 1834 [Lamphun, Chiang Mai], 1834–5 [Lamphun, Chiang Mai, Karen], 1836–7 [Mone, Mokmai, Karen], 1838–9 [Bangkok], McLeod (1836–7) [Chiang Mai, Chengtung, Chenghung], Brooke (1850) [Bangkok], and Bowring (1855) [Bangkok] missions, and the return visit by the Thai to London (1857–8).

3 The same Chakri dynasty, founded in 1782, as is still regnant.

4 This is consonant with the philosophical or 'scientific' racialising theories he expounds elsewhere in his non-diplomatic writings. Crawfurd was later to become President of the Ethnological Society of London, which was founded in 1843.

5 It seems generally accepted that this was the ruler of the Lao kingdom of Vientiane, Cao Anou (see Mayoury and Pheuiphanh 1998: 111).

6 See, for example, Bremmer and Roodenburg (1993), especially 'Introduction' by Keith Thomas and 'Gesture, ritual and social order in sixteenth to eighteenth-century Poland' by Maria Bogucka.

7 Elsewhere unbroken conversations of four hours or so with princes and officials are mentioned. Peter Skalník (Charles University, Prague) in his paper for the 1998 ASA conference mentioned that his audience with the President of the Republic of Lebanon in 1992, when he was Czechoslovak ambassador to Lebanon, lasted a 'good half hour', implying satisfaction at this (Skalník 1998).

References

Bloch, Marc (1965) [1939–40] *Feudal Society*, 2 vols, London: Routledge and Kegan Paul.

Bourdieu, Pierre (1977) *Outline of a Theory of Practice*, Cambridge: Cambridge University Press.

Bowring, Sir John (1857) *The Kingdom and People of Siam, with a Narrative of the Mission to that Country in 1855*, 2 vols, London: John W. Parker and Son.

Bremmer, Jan and Roodenburg, Herman (eds) (1993) *A Cultural History of Gesture from Antiquity to the Present Day*, Cambridge: Polity Press.

Burney, Henry (1910–14) *The Burney Papers*, 5 vols, Bangkok: Vajirañana National Library.

Crawfurd, John (1915) *The Crawfurd Papers: A Collection of Official Records Relating to the Mission of Dr John Crawfurd Sent to Siam by the Government of India in the Year 1821*, Bangkok: Vajirañana National Library (reprinted 1971, London: Gregg International).

——(1967) [1828] *Journal of an Embassy to the Courts of Siam and Cochin China*, Kuala Lumpur: Oxford University Press (Oxford in Asia Historical Reprints) (first published 1828, London: H. Colburn).

Geertz, Clifford (1973) *The Interpretation of Cultures*, New York: Basic Books.

Hevia, James L. (1995) *Cherishing Men from Afar: Qing Guest Ritual and the Macartney Embassy of 1793*, Durham NC and London: Duke University Press.

Hutchinson, E. W. (1940) *Adventurers in Siam in the Seventeenth Century*, London: Royal Asiatic Society (RAS Prize Publication 18).

Kerényi, Carl (1958) *The Gods of the Greeks*, Harmondsworth: Penguin.

McLeod, W. C. (1869) 'Captain McLeod's Journal, in East India (McLeod and Richardson's Journeys). Copy of papers relating to the route of Captain *W. C. McLeod* from *Moulmein* to the frontiers of *China*, and to the route of Dr *Richardson* on his fourth mission to the *Shan* Provinces of *Burmah*, or Extracts from the same', in *India Papers 1864–1871*, London: India Office, Political Dept, 13–104 (see also *ibid*., map and introductory matter, pp. 1–13).

Mayoury Ngaosyvathn and Pheuiphanh Ngaosyvathn (1998) *Paths to Conflagration: Fifty Years of Diplomacy and Warfare in Laos, Thailand, and Vietnam, 1778–1828*, Ithaca NY: Cornell University, Southeast Asia Program Publications.

Muhammad Rabi ibn Muhammad Ibrahim (1970) *The Ship of Sulaiman*, trans. John O'Kane (Persian Heritage Series 11) London: Routledge and Kegan Paul.

Nicholson, Harold (1950) *Diplomacy*, 2nd edn, London: Oxford University Press.

Reid, Anthony (1993) *Southeast Asia in the Age of Commerce, 1450–1680: Vol. 2, Expansion and Crisis*, New Haven: Yale University Press.

Richardson, David (1836) 'An account of some of the petty states lying to the north of the Tenasserim Provinces, drawn up from the journals and reports of D. Richardson Esq., Surgeon to the Commissioner of the Tenasserim Provinces, compiled by E. A. Blundell, Commissioner', *Journal of the Asiatic Society of Bengal*, 5(58): October, 601–25; (59): November, 688–96; (59): 696–707.

——(1839–40) 'Journal of a mission from the Supreme Government of India to the court of Siam', *Journal of the Asiatic Society of Bengal*, 8(96): December 1839, 1016–6; 9(97): 1–3; 9(99): 219–50.

——(1869) 'Dr. Richardson's Journal Of a Fourth Mission to the Interior of the New Settlements in the Tenasserim Provinces, Being to the Chief of the Red Karens, to the Tso-Boa of

Monay, and thence to Ava, in East India [McLeod and Richardson's Journeys]. Copy of papers relating to the route of Captain *W. C. McLeod* from *Moulmein* to the frontiers of *China*, and to the route of Dr. *Richardson* on his fourth mission to the *Shan* Provinces of *Burmah*, or extracts from the same', in *India Papers 1864–1871*, London, India Office, Political Dept, 104–47 (see also *ibid.*, map and introductory matter, 1–13).

Roberts, Edmund (1837) *Embassy to the Eastern Courts of Cochin-China, Siam, and Muscat*, New York: Harper and Brothers.

Sarasin Viraphol (1977) *Tribute and Profit: Sino-Siamese Trade 1652–1853* (Harvard East Asian Monographs 76) Cambridge MA and London: Harvard University Press.

Shakespeare, William (1905, reprinted 1954) *The Complete Works of William Shakespeare*, ed. W. J. Craig, London: Oxford University Press.

Skalník, Peter (1998) 'Diplomatic culture in real diplomacy (a social anthropologist as Czech ambassador in Lebanon)', unpublished paper presented to the ASA conference on Indirection, Intention and Diplomacy, University of Kent, April 1998.

Thailand (1927) *Ruam Cotmaihet Ruang Thut Thai Pai Prathet Angkrit Phuttasakarat 2400* (Prachum pongsawadan 45) (Records of the Siamese embassy to England in AD 1857–58, including poem: *Nirat London*. Also English press comments on the Siamese embassy selected and edited by G. Coedès, with foreword and introduction on Siamese embassies to Europe by Prince Damrong Rajanubhab, translated into English by L. J. Robbins) Bangkok.

——(1936) *Thut Farang Samai Rathanakosin* (Prachum pongsawadan 62) (Foreign embassies in the Bangkok period) Bangkok.

Turton, Andrew (1997) 'Ethnography of Embassy: anthropological readings of records of diplomatic encounters between Britain and Thai states in the early nineteenth century', *South East Asia Research*, 5(2): 175–205.

——(ed.) (1999a) *Civility and Savagery: Social Identity in Thai States*, London: Curzon.

——(1999b) 'Inter-ethnic relations in Thai political domains', in Andrew Turton (ed.) *Civility and Savagery: Social Identity in Thai States*, London: Curzon.

Van der Cruysse, Dirk (1991) *Louis XIV et le Siam*, Paris: Fayard.

Wills, John E. Jnr (1984) *Embassies and Illusions: Dutch and Portuguese Envoys to K'anghsi, 1666–1687*, Cambridge MA and London: Harvard University Press.

Yule, Henry and Burnell, A. C. (1994) [1886] *Hobson-Jobson: A Glossary of Colloquial Anglo-Indian Words and Phrases, and of Kindred Terms, Etymological, Historical, Geographical and Discursive*, Sittingbourne: Linguasia.

Chapter 17

Diplomacy and indirection, constraint and authority

James G. Carrier

Indirection, diplomacy and intention frame a vast area that can be approached from a number of different directions. The approach I use here begins with the obvious point that indirection and diplomacy are means of communicating one's intentions to others in a relatively persuasive way. Such communication requires a language, which is to say, a social product that forms the bridge between speakers and their intentions on the one hand, and on the other, listeners and their responses. If you will, my approach to languages of indirection and diplomacy stresses the general term, that they are languages, rather than the specific, that they are indirect and diplomatic. One of the things that will concern me especially is the ways that this social bridge, this language, is not socially neutral, but can be a medium through which authority and, ultimately, power are claimed and exercised. Again, if you will, while language certainly can be seen in cultural terms as a system or way of conveying meaning, my approach is relatively social, concerned with the ways that language can structure communication, and so be a device of power and constraint. Such a social approach leaves much out, but it has the virtue of taking us beyond a perspective that sees the language of indirection and diplomacy as merely an 'ensemble of texts' (Geertz 1973: 5, 452) or the webs of meaning on which we stand, for it helps remind us that some are better able than others to spin those webs, just as some are more likely than others to become ensnared in them.

'Indirection' and 'diplomacy' conjure up the mannerly, treating people diplomatically, putting one's position indirectly. An important element of this image is the wrapping that Joy Hendry (1993) has described as a marked aspect of Japanese life. Wrapping does many things. Most obviously, it hides. The indirect or diplomatic request is not only mannerly, it also obscures the full intention of the person making the request; the wrapped present is obscured, to be revealed only on Christmas morning around the tree. As Hendry is at pains to point out, however, this diplomatic indirection, this wrapping, need not be intended to deceive. Rather, the hiding may entail two other aspects of wrapping, symbolisation and embellishment. And as Hendry observes, we should not fall into the trap of thinking that these are merely added on to what is wrapped. Rather, they can interact with it, and so change it. The wrapping takes the commodity acquired in Christmas shopping, embellishes it with the symbolism of Christmas and transforms it into a gift (Carrier 1993).

Underlying what I have said thus far is the fact that indirection and diplomacy are communicative. The diplomatic request and the wrapped gift convey meaning. One kind of meaning revolves around the performance of the communication. To produce the properly phrased request or the properly wrapped gift at the proper time is to convey that one is a competent member of the group in which these things are important. This sort of meaning can be significant, a point to which I return later on. Here, however, I am interested in a more straightforward kind of meaning, the meaning that the person intends to convey. The properly diplomatic request is an expression of the intentions of the person who utters it; the properly wrapped gift is an expression of the intentions of the person who gives it.

This is not, of course, straightforward expression. It is not straightforward because, more clearly than in many forms of communication, languages of indirection and diplomacy socialise the intentions that they express, though this socialisation is a feature of all forms of communication. These languages are the device by which desires that may be relatively private, incapable of full articulation or even inchoate, are expressed in a social form, a form that others can understand, and hence a form that may persuade. Over seventy years ago, Emily Post, an arbiter of etiquette in the United States, described the way that gifts could express intentions in a recognisable and potentially persuasive way. She did so when she decreed that the bride-to-be could accept from her affianced

> anything he chooses to select, except wearing apparel or a motor car or a house and furniture – anything that can be classified as 'maintenance'. ... [For] it would be starting life on a false basis, and putting herself in a category with women of another class, to be clothed by any man, whether he is soon to be her husband or not.
>
> (Post 1927: 311)

Much more recently, Russell Belk and Gregory Coon (1993) considered this same communicative aspect when they described how people who are courting give one another gifts of a sort and in a manner that communicates their intentions about their relationship, and that can persuade the recipient to accept that intention. I mention Belk and Coon's discussion partly because it makes clear what Post treats as fairly unproblematic, the way that this form of communication is more than simple expression. These courting couples did not always know clearly what their intentions about their relationships actually were. Thus, when they communicated through their giving, these couples did not just socialise their intentions, but also refined them. The decisions to give this item rather than another, to give on this occasion rather than another, certainly rendered their intentions more articulate, but did so in a consequential way. Having used the code of available gifts and occasions, the giver could communicate only certain messages, those permitted by the code.

My invocation of Belk and Coon's work points to another aspect of languages of indirection and diplomacy. While they are, as I have stressed, languages, they are not ordinary languages, but are special, precisely because they are not the quotidian languages of those who use them. Rather, they are a means of communication used in special circumstances, those in which one wants to communicate across the sort of social gap that makes the use of everyday language seem problematic or unwise. In his mind, our courting swain may be thinking 'I want you'; but because his relationship with the object of his affections is uncertain, he is likely to think also that this direct expression of desire is not likely to have the effect he seeks. So, he expresses his intentions in a special, indirect language. He says it, however inadequately, with flowers. There are, of course, other kinds of social gaps than those that separate courting couples. The gaps that particularly concern me here are those that occur in relationships of inequality, especially where that inequality needs to be rendered palatable by being rendered legitimate. As in courting relationships, compliance in the sort of relationships that concern me is especially uncertain, so that superior and inferior need a common, diplomatic language to address and persuade each other.

I have sketched an approach to indirection and diplomacy that makes these categories broader than they might appear at first glance. They remain special ways of communicating one's intentions, but what is special about them is that they are public languages, in that they are used not to communicate among those with whom everyday speech is appropriate, but to communicate publicly, in the sense of communication across a significant social gap. Treating them as public languages loses some of the nuances of 'indirection' and 'diplomacy'. In return for this loss, however, this approach may make it easier to draw connections between forms of communication that otherwise may seem to have little in common. Doing so may, in turn, make it easier than it would have been otherwise to discern some of the processes and relationships in which indirection and diplomacy are implicated.

Market talk

A form of talk that illustrates some of the points I have made is the language of the Market. This became especially important in Britain and the United States late in the 1970s, and achieved its greatest visibility under the administrations of Margaret Thatcher and Ronald Reagan. It became a public language in two important ways, which I mention here and will illustrate later in this section. First, it became common in public debate and came to predominate certain areas of that debate, especially some of those dealing with the proper functions of government. Second, it became the preferred language of certain powerful institutions.

One reason that I consider Market talk, the language of the Market, here is that it illustrates especially clearly an important aspect of public languages, including languages of indirection or diplomacy. It was not only a vocabulary and style of speaking, but also contained a view of the world. Market talk was a language that saw large parts of life in terms of the free market, and broadly reflected a simplified rendering of key elements of neo-classical economics (see Carrier 1997). This meant that it tended to see people as relatively rational and self-seeking autonomous individuals governed by a materialist orientation. As a part of this, Market talk stressed the value of free enterprise and a diminished role for the state. As a practical consequence, this meant that, in many areas of life, people were portrayed as rational entrepreneurs, with goals and plans, a concern with adding value and the like.

Market talk not only defined and constructed a world, in addition it did so in an authoritative way. This authority could be imposed as a political act, as I illustrate below. Equally, however, Market talk was taken to have authority in a more absolute sense. Thus those who supported Market talk did not see it as merely an embellishment, a pretty way of wrapping, or even hiding, the real. Rather, they saw it, and its underlying view of the world, as allowing the expression of important truths about the world, expression that they thought would allow important decisions to be made and actions to be taken. Supporters hoped that it would displace other forms of talk, which missed those truths and made it difficult for people to speak and think about them. This attraction is expressed nicely in the words of John O'Sullivan, a British advocate, who said that what I have described as Market talk 'provides clear, consistent and above all, simple solutions to the problems thrown up by society and the economy' (quoted in Cockett 1994: 194).

I said that Market talk was an important public language. In the opinion of Fredric Jameson (1991: 263, emphasis added), it had become the only acceptable public language:

> Everyone is now willing to mumble, as though it were an inconsequential concession in passing to public opinion and current received wisdom (*or shared communication presuppositions*) that no society can function effectively without the market and that planning is obviously impossible.

As part of this, people's lives at work were re-cast in the appropriate terms. They were no longer doing a job in the context of occupational and institutional relationships with others. Instead, they were producing a product, and those with whom they dealt were re-cast as customers. Railway guards, university lecturers, physicians and nurses no longer dealt with passengers, taught students or treated patients; they all were serving customers, consumers of their product. Moreover, as this was an important language, when railway guards, lecturers and the rest wanted to communicate with their superiors, they were constrained to present themselves and articulate their intentions in the appropriate way. This was particularly so on more ceremonious occasions, when people were obliged to present themselves formally to significant people within their organisation, such as when they sought promotion or, more generally, when they were required to explain and justify themselves and their activities.

In making this point I illustrate the way that a diplomatic language is not simply a neutral means of communication. Rather, to the degree that the language is authoritative, it shapes what can be said, what points can be raised, what arguments can be made. In writing this, I echo a point made by Kenneth Burke (1973), that language does not consist of neutral labels that attach unproblematically to different objects in the world. In addition, any language implicitly or explicitly evaluates them and motivates people to think about and act towards them in certain ways rather than others. Put this way, an authoritative language like Market talk is what Steven Lukes (1974) describes as the most subtle form of power, for it shapes what can be debated and how it can be debated. It provides the vocabulary and conceptual equipment that make it relatively easy to define certain sorts of things as problems and relatively hard to define other sorts of things that way. Just as it influences the sorts of problems that can be discerned, so it influences what is likely to appear as an acceptable, plausible solution. Jameson (1991: 263) points to this way that Market talk is a form of power, when he says that 'the rhetoric of the market has been a fundamental and central component of ... [the] struggle for the legitimation of left discourse'.

An illustration of Market talk as a form of power is the way that the public came to be defined as consumers, a variant of referring to them as customers. This is illustrated by the chairman of Unilever, who stated: 'The old, rigid barriers are disappearing – class and rank; blue collar and white collar; council tenant and home owner; employee and housewife. More and more we are simply consumers' (Perry 1994: 4, quoted in Gabriel and Lang 1995: 36). By defining people in this way, Market talk made it easier to discern some common interests than others, and so made it easier to define some interests as more worthy than others. More specifically, the easy portrayal of the public as a body of consumers makes it easy, in turn, to render illegitimate any who might threaten what Market talk construes as their common interest, the public interest. Those who might threaten that interest include workers, who might want changes in employment conditions that would raise the cost of what they produce, and so would confront consumers with more expensive products. Those who might threaten that interest include the state, which might want to spend more money, and hence would want to raise taxes and so would decrease the amount that consumers had to spend.

Authority and public language

Thus far I have illustrated how Market talk can shape the ways that people can represent themselves to the world and the world to themselves. I have done so to make the point that when we consider languages of indirection and diplomacy, we need to remember that, however indirect or diplomatic they may be, they are also languages, which means that they have practical political consequences. In pointing to the power of a public language like Market talk, I do not, however, mean that the power arises in some mysterious way from the talk itself. To repeat an earlier point, some people are more assiduous and successful at spinning webs of meaning; the rest are more likely to be ensnared by them (with regard to Market talk, the differences between the spiders and the flies is discussed at length in Cockett 1994). The social bases of the power of a language of indirection become particularly apparent when that language becomes authoritative because it becomes institutionalised.

I will illustrate this with a particular institutionalisation of Market talk, the use of cost-benefit analysis in the United States government, particularly with regard to regulatory agencies concerned with health and safety (this account relies on MacLennan 1997). Prior to the 1970s, government regulatory agencies were expected to pursue the goals defined for them in a relatively straightforward way. For instance, the National Highway Traffic Safety Administration was expected to propose regulations for the design of automobiles that would reduce accidents, injuries and fatalities. However, with the growing authority of Market talk in the 1970s and 1980s, there were changes in the way these agencies had to carry out their activities. The institutional force behind these changes was the growing involvement in the regulatory process of a part of the executive branch, the Office of Management and the Budget, the very name of which is redolent of Market talk. While the story of that growing involvement is an interesting one, my concern here is with its consequences.

In essence, regulatory agencies became obliged to submit their proposals to the Office for approval, an act of communication across a social gap of significant magnitude. With this change, what had persuaded previously no longer did so, for a new, authoritative language had been imposed by the executive branch. In particular, agencies increasingly were obliged to address the Office of Management and the Budget in the language of cost-benefit analysis. This meant that they had to analyse the costs of the proposed regulation and its benefits, and show that the latter exceeded the former. This was an important change, because hitherto agencies were supposed to justify their proposed regulations in terms of efficacy: they had not been obliged to consider costs in any rigorous way. Even if this was an important change, on its face it appears unexceptionable, given the temper of the times. However, the language in which costs and benefits were to be expressed was monetary, and like all languages, this one makes it relatively easy to describe certain aspects of the world and relatively difficult to describe others. It is in this relative ease and difficulty of description that we can see how this authoritative public language was a vehicle for the exercise of power.

Expressing costs in monetary terms is fairly easy. Consider the case of pollution regulations. The costs of such regulations overwhelmingly fall on companies, the main generators of pollution. As they were used to thinking of and accounting for their operations in monetary terms, in terms of Market talk, the cost of proposed regulations could be cast in terms of cost-benefit analysis relatively unproblematically. The situation regarding benefits is very different. Some benefits can be expressed in monetary terms without too much trouble, for instance, anticipated changes in land prices following the reduction in pollution. However, it is harder to express other benefits in this monetary language. How are we to assign a price to the fact that those who travel across the river no longer are bothered by the smell, that they see a river that is more pleasing to look at or even that they see a river that they know is cleaner than it used to be?

If forced to do so, one could speak of these benefits in the authoritative language of cost-benefit analysis, but doing so is much more difficult than speaking of the costs of reducing pollution. Partly this is because people do not normally speak of those benefits in terms of price, but in terms of other languages and other values, which may very well be contradicted by reduction to price and so, in effect, may not be translatable (consider, for example, the sort of contradiction entailed in pricing automobile fatalities). Speaking of these benefits in terms of price is difficult also for technical reasons. Particularly when cost-benefit techniques are new, there are few agreed ways of pricing many benefits, of translating benefits that are expressible in other forms of talk into the terms of Market talk. This absence of agreed monetary measures means that pricing the benefits itself costs regulatory agencies time and money, a cost that makes it less likely that the agency will be able to carry out an analysis of benefits, and less likely that the analysis will survive challenge by those who scrutinise it. In this situation, it is difficult to produce a cost-benefit analysis that would persuade the relevant audience to agree to the agency's intentions. Consequently, the likelihood of proposals for new regulations would decline, which was one of the purposes behind the introduction of Market talk in the United States government.

This discussion of the growing importance of cost-benefit analysis in government health and safety regulation in the United States is intended to illustrate one important point that I have made about languages of indirection or diplomacy. Those sorts of languages are, like all languages, not simply means of communication. They are also devices that constrain people to speak in certain ways, devices that can make it more difficult to express some things rather than others. As such, diplomatic languages are vehicles by which power can be exercised, webs that can be woven to ensnare, as those who imposed the language of cost-benefit analysis knew quite well.

People do not, however, automatically accept the constraints of authoritative language, any more than they automatically accept the definitions of the world and of their own intentions that the language implies. Rather, often they attempt to circumvent those constraints and redefinitions. Sometimes this circumventing is fairly straightforward. I will illustrate this in terms of authoritative forms of talk within businesses, specialist terminologies and related world-views that are associated with different approaches to the management of organisations (aspects of these are described in Thrift 1998; more generally, see Ouroussoff 1993). Conformity to such talk is important as a way to communicate indirectly the claim that one is suited to be a member of the organisation. Christina Wasson (n.d.) describes a heightened instance of this, a corporate meeting organised to present and disseminate the form of business talk that Wasson calls the 'entrepreneurial' model, a fairly straightforward form of Market talk that sees individuals and groups within the organisation as entrepreneurs providing products to customers elsewhere within the organisation.

The employees Wasson describes were presenting the activities of their group within the firm to senior managers and others as one of the 'success stories' of the application of the entrepreneurial approach. A key element of the talk to which they had to conform was the idea of 'empowerment', which, among other things, indicates that employees have the independence and initiative to decide for themselves how to operate their firm within the firm, to think of themselves as entrepreneurs. This form of talk, particularly in the formal situation Wasson describes, makes it relatively difficult for a group of employees to describe themselves as being constrained by the bureaucratic structure of the firm. Even so, however, the employees making the presentation did depart from the constraints of the authorised language, when they described how the actions of their superiors within the firm placed limits on the group's ability to behave in the approved way.

There is another way that people can circumvent the constraints and redefinitions of authoritative language. They can try to exploit the potentials of the language in a way that allows them to present their intentions in terms of it, even though this is likely to lead people to redefine their intentions to some degree. Thus the public language itself can become a device that people use to reject or weaken the authority of those who impose that language, through thwarting the constraints the language is intended to impose. One can see the potential for this in the case Wasson describes. Recall that a key element of the entrepreneurial model is the notion of empowerment. When, in their presentation, the employees mentioned the constraints imposed upon them by their superiors, they were arguing, at least implicitly, that they were not adequately empowered. That is, they were using the terms of the authoritative language to reject or weaken the authority of the corporate officers who imposed it.

One could expect a similar process to occur with cost-benefit analysis. As regulatory agencies became more familiar with it, they would be better able to state their intentions persuasively in terms of it, and so circumvent the intentions of those who imposed it. Thus, as it became more familiar with cost-benefit analysis, the National Highway Traffic Safety Administration worked harder at identifying the benefits of proposed regulations, which meant the costs of not having those regulations. 'It became imperative to leave no stone unturned in figuring out other costs [of traffic accidents] that had not yet been taken into consideration' (MacLennan pers. comm.). This meant a range of procedural changes within the agency. For instance, it was clear that national data collection was in poor shape, yet was critical to accuracy of figures about how many injuries, what types, of what ages, etc. This meant that the agency had to put more and more resources into developing better data, hiring more economists.

(MacLennan pers. comm.)

As a result, the agency became better able to persuade the Office of Management and the Budget to approve proposals for regulations.

This does not, of course, destroy the force of the language, for the presenting employees still speak in terms of the entrepreneurial model, just as agencies propose regulations in terms of costs and benefits. It does, however, suggest that the authoritative language can be a resource in conflicts with superiors, rather than just being a constraint upon inferiors.

Although the potential for this type of circumvention exists in all authoritative diplomatic languages, it is likely that the ability to exploit the potential increases with time, as people become familiar with them. This means in turn that the constraining power of such languages will decrease with time. Part of the power of these languages is, as I have noted repeatedly, that they oblige people to socialise their intentions in certain ways. Equally, however, part of their power lies in the fact that, initially, those on whom they are imposed are relatively unfamiliar with them. Regulatory agencies confronted with an unfamiliar language of policy justification are going to be especially constrained by it; employees confronted with an unfamiliar corporate language are going to be especially constrained by it. At this early stage, then, the authoritative language is like a ritual, the steps of which may be defined, but the bases and purposes of which are secret. Those constrained to use the language know it has power, but the bases of that power are unknown or only poorly known, alien and opaque. Logically, if not empirically, it is possible to keep the bases and purposes secret but still authoritative. In this imaginary case, the language could constrain for a relatively long time. However, the authoritative variants of Market talk that I have described here were legitimate in part because their bases were seen to be public and accessible to all who make the effort to learn them. If, then, they were secrets in their early stages, they were more like open secrets, the sort of thing that people know exists and that they think they could figure out if they took the trouble. However, as actors become more familiar with them, those languages will lose their secrecy and people will be more able to use them to present their intentions in persuasive ways.

This gradual decay in the constraining power of authoritative languages in turn has consequences for those who impose them. Because a language constrains less well the older it gets, the older the language the more those people are likely to be receptive to the attractions of a replacement language. In other words, one would expect there to be a succession of such languages, as those in dominant positions adopt and impose a new language as the old one becomes decreasingly useful for doing one of the things that it is intended to do, oblige people to act in certain ways. This succession of public languages appears in the history of attempts in the United States government to constrain regulatory agencies. From the 1970s onwards new authoritative languages were introduced: the Planning-Programing-Budget System, Management by Objectives, Zero-Based Budgeting, Inflation Impact Statements (see MacLennan 1997). From the point of view of those who imposed them, each had its own distinct disadvantages, stressed when a new one was being advocated. However, I am suggesting that all of them shared a common disadvantage: people became familiar with them and so became better able to circumvent some of the constraints that the languages were intended to impose.

This history of succession is even more apparent in the sorts of languages that are popular in the corporate world, like the language of empowerment. The fads of management style are too well known to require description here (see Thrift 1998). One of the reasons for this succession is commercial. There is a great deal of money to be made by writing the next trend-setting book and by setting up the consultancy firm that specialises in the trend. Similarly, employees of the larger consultancy firms constantly generate information about how different companies operate, and so are in a position to uncover new ways of organising corporate life. Consultancy firms can make a great deal of money by producing descriptions of the more interesting of these ways and advising other firms on how to implement them. However, the sheer passage of time is also a factor. As the power of the language to constrain employees decays, a new language becomes more attractive.

Conclusion

In arriving at changing fashions in managerial models and regulatory regimes, I have wandered some distance from diplomacy, indirection and intention, at least as they are commonly construed. This wandering is not meant to deny their importance. The ways that people couch their intentions in their communications with others raise a host of significant theoretical issues. In addition, making sense of indirection and diplomacy, the patterns of etiquette and the significance of the seemingly tangential, is not only difficult, but can produce a great deal of legitimate pleasure.

My wanderings can, however, be taken as a caution. We need to be careful not to become beguiled by the cultural intricacies and the empirical difficulties and delights of discerning and mapping out those intricacies. We need to remember that these intensely cultural forms can carry important social and political significance. Put in different words, we should be careful not to become so intrigued by the diplomacy and the indirection that we forget that these are channels of communication, means by which people seek not only to express themselves or enact cultural forms, but can also seek to induce their fellows to think and act in certain ways, to the benefit of some rather than others.

To make these points I have described forms of talk that hardly resemble the sorts of things one would normally consider to be languages of indirection and diplomacy. I have, after all, described forms of talk that exist in relationships characterised by degrees of inequality and dissent that are pronounced, forms of talk that often are imposed consciously, either politically or administratively, rather than evolving in a more spontaneous way through practice. However, these unusual languages and the unusual relationships in which they exist, the languages of Market talk, of cost-benefit analysis and of the entrepreneurial employee, are worthy of consideration. In their very abnormality, they make especially visible some important attributes that they share with all means of communication, including languages of indirection and diplomacy. If I have succeeded in making these attributes visible in a persuasive way, then I have been able to show not only the relevance of what I have said here for the languages that are the theme of this volume, but, conversely, also the ways that what we learn of the languages of indirection and diplomacy can illuminate other forms of talk.

References

Belk, Russell W. and Coon, Gregory S. (1993) 'Gift-giving as agapic love: an alternative to the exchange paradigm based on dating experiences', *Journal of Consumer Research*, 20(3): 393–417.

Burke, Kenneth (1973) [1941] *The Philosophy of Literary Form*, Berkeley: University of California Press.

Carrier, James G. (1993) 'The rituals of Christmas giving', in Daniel Miller (ed.) *Unwrapping Christmas*, Oxford: Oxford University Press, pp. 55–74.

——(1997) Introduction, in James G. Carrier (ed.) *Meanings of the Market: The Free Market in Western Culture*, Oxford: Berg, pp. 1–67.

Cockett, Richard (1994) *Thinking the Unthinkable: Think-Tanks and the Economic Counter-Revolution, 1931–83*, London: HarperCollins.

Gabriel, Yiannis and Lang, Tim (1995) *The Unmanageable Consumer: Contemporary Consumption and its Fragmentation*, London: Sage.

Geertz, Clifford (1973) *The Interpretation of Cultures*, New York: Basic Books.

Hendry, Joy (1993) *Wrapping Culture: Politeness, Presentation and Power in Japan and Other Societies*, Oxford: Clarendon Press.

Jameson, Fredric (1991) *Postmodernism, or the Cultural Logic of Late Capitalism*, Durham NC: Duke University Press.

Lukes, Steven (1974) *Power: A Radical View*, London: Macmillan.

MacLennan, Carol A. (1997) 'Democracy under the influence: cost-benefit analysis in the United States', in James G. Carrier (ed.) *Meanings of the Market: The Free Market in Western Culture*, Oxford: Berg, pp. 195–224.

Ouroussoff, Alexandra (1993) 'Illusions of rationality: false premises of the liberal tradition', *Man*, 28: 281–98.

Perry, Michael (1994) 'The brand vehicle for value in a changing marketplace', Advertising Association, President's Lecture, 7 July, London.

Post, Emily (1927) *Etiquette in Society, in Business, in Politics and at Home*, 17th edn, New York: Funk and Wagnalls.

Thrift, Nigel (1998) 'Virtual capitalism: the globalisation of reflexive business knowledge', in James G. Carrier and Daniel Miller (eds) *Virtualism: A New Political Economy*, Oxford: Berg, pp. 161–86

Wasson, Christina (n.d.) '"We took ownership": voicing agency in corporate America', MS.

Index